Translating Cultures

Translating Cultures

Perspectives on Translation and Anthropology

Edited by
Paula G. Rubel and Abraham Rosman

BERG

Oxford • New York

First published in 2003 by
Berg
Editorial offices:
1st Floor, Angel Court, 81 St Clements Street, Oxford, OX4 1AW, UK
838 Broadway, Third Floor, New York, NY 10003-4812, USA

Berg is an imprint of Oxford International Publishers Ltd.

Library of Congress Cataloging-in-Publication Data
Translating cultures : perspectives on translation and anthropology /
edited by Paula G. Rubel and Abraham Rosman.
    p. cm.
Includes bibliographical references and index.
    ISBN 1-85973-740-4 – ISBN 1-85973-745-5 (pbk.)
  1. Communication in ethnology. 2. Ethnology–Authorship. 3.
Translating and interpreting. 4. Intercultural communication. I.
Rubel, Paula G. II. Rosman, Abraham.

GN307.5.T73 2003
306—dc21

2003000652

British Library Cataloguing-in-Publication Data
A catalogue record for this book is available from the British Library.

ISBN 1 85973 740 4 (Cloth)
      1 85973 745 5 (Paper)

Typeset by JS Typesetting Ltd, Wellingborough, Northants.
Printed in the United Kingdom by Biddles Ltd, Guildford and King's Lynn.

Contents

Contents

Acknowledgments

The chapters of this volume were first presented as papers and discussed at a conference, Translation and Anthropology, held at Barnard College, Columbia University, 10–12 November 1998. We are very grateful to the Wenner Gren Foundation which sponsored the conference, and especially to Sydel Silverman, President of the Foundation at that time for her support. Barnard College provided the venue for the conference. We want to thank President Judith Shapiro and Provost Elizabeth Boylin who were particularly helpful. Jean McCurry and her staff made all the necessary arrangements, which made the conference a memorable event. We wish to thank Michael Silverstein, Michael Herzfeld, and Alan Segal for their input in helping us to organize the conference.

The participants at the conference included those whose papers comprise the chapters of this volume, and in addition Suzanne Blier, Serge Gavronsky, Arnold Krupat, Simon Ortiz, and Douglas Robinson. All the papers were circulated before the conference took place. We would like to thank all of the participants for their particularly illuminating and lively discussion during our meeting. Some of the points made during those discussions are included in the Introduction to this volume (referenced by name). As we talked and discussed the papers around a large table, the problem confronting another's ideas, interpreting them, grasping what the interlocutor was getting at, brought back to each of us the basic issue of translating a different and sometimes strange culture into our language and our culture.

Kathryn Earle of Berg press has been particularly helpful in organizing the publication of this volume. We also wish to thank Mansour Kamaletdinov for all his assistance in preparation of the manuscript and for particular attention to detail.

We hope that this volume fulfills the expectations of all those who helped to bring it about.

Paula Rubel
Abraham Rosman
New York City

Notes on Contributors

Michael Herzfeld is Professor of Anthropology at Harvard University. He is the author of eight books, the more recent being *Portrait of a Greek Imagination* and *Anthropology: Theoretical Practice In Culture and Society*. He is the winner of the J. B. Donne Prize on the Anthropology of Art and has been awarded the Rivers Memorial Medal (Royal Anthropological Institute). He has had fellowships and grants from the John Simon Guggenheim Foundation, the National Science Foundation, the National Endowment for the Humanities and the Social Science Research Council.

Todd Jones is Associate Professor of Philosophy at the University of Nevada, Las Vegas. He is the author of numerous articles in both philosophy and social science journals and is currently working on a volume about reductionism and belief in the Social Sciences.

Deborah Kapchan is Associate Professor of Anthropology at the University of Texas at Austin. She is the author of *Gender on the Market: Moroccan Women and the Revoicing of Tradition* (1996) and is currently completing a manuscript on music, narrative and trance in the context of the Moroccan Gnawa performance. She writes about performance, poetics, music and aesthetics. In 2001, she was the recipient of a John Simon Guggenheim Fellowship to translate Moroccan poetry in dialect into English.

Webb Keane is a Professor in the Department of Anthropology at the University of Michigan, Ann Arbor. He is the author of *Signs of Recognition: Powers and Hazards of Representation in an Indonesian Society* (1997), as well as many articles on missionaries and modernity, religious language, semiotics, etc. He has received fellowships from the John Simon Guggenheim Foundation, the Institute for Advanced Study, the Center for the Advanced Study of the Behavior Sciences and the National Endowment for the Humanities.

Wyatt MacGaffey is John R. Coleman Professor of Social Sciences Emeritus at Haverford College. He has published extensively on social scructures, politics, history and art of Central Africa and his most recent work is *Kongo Political Culture: the Conceptual Challenge of the Particular* (2000). He was a Ford Foundation Fellow and the recipient of a Guggenheim Fellowship.

Brinkley Messick is Professor of Anthropology at Columbia University. He is the author of *The Calligraphic State* and is completing a new work on *shari'a*, a regime of an Islamic State. His research has been funded by the Social Science Research Council, the John Simon Guggenheim Foundation and the Fulbright Program.

Abraham Rosman is Professor Emeritus of the Department of Anthropology at Barnard College, Columbia University. He has done anthropological research with Professor Paula Rubel for many years and they have jointly published many articles and books, including *Feasting with Mine Enemy: Rank and Exchange among Northwest Coast Societies, Second Edition*. They have done research in Iran, Afghanistan and Papua New Guinea and most recently have been doing research on the collecting of objects, most particularly ethnographic artifacts in America. Their book *The Tapestry of Culture* is going into its eighth edition. He has received a John Simon Guggenheim Fellowship as well as grants from the National Science Foundation, the Ford Foundation and the Social Science Research Council.

Paula G. Rubel is Professor Emerita of the Department of Anthropology at Barnard College, Columbia University. She has jointly done research with Professor Abraham Rosman for many years in Iran, Afghanistan and Papua New Guinea. They have published many articles and books, including *Feasting with Mine Enemy: Rank and Exchange among Northwest Coast Societies, Second Edition*. Their book *The Tapestry of Culture* is currently going into its eighth edition. Currently, they are doing research on collecting artifacts, particularly ethnographic objects, Disneyana and Black American, in the United States. She has been the recipient of a John Simon Guggenheim Fellowship, and grants from the National Institutes of Mental Health, the Social Science Research Council and the National Endowment for the Humanities.

Benson Saler is Professor Emeritus of Anthropology at Brandeis University. He is the author of *Conceptualizing Religion* (paperback edition 2000) and co-author of *UFO Crash at Roswell: The Genesis of a Modern Myth* (1997). Professor Saler has held grants and fellowships from the National Science Foundation, the National Endowment of the Arts and Humanities and the Wenner Gren Foundation.

Alan F. Segal is Professor of Religion and the Ingeborg Rennert Professor of Jewish Studies at Barnard College, Columbia University. He is the author of *Rebecca's Children: Judaism and Christianity in the Roman World, Paul the Convert* and *Charting the Hereafter: The Afterlife in Western Culture*. He was a Woodrow Wilson Fellow, and has received grants from the John Simon Guggenheim Foundation, the Annenberg Foundation, the Melton Foundation and the National Endowment for the Humanities.

Notes on Contributors

Michael Silverstein is Charles F. Grey Distinguished Service Professor in the Departments of Anthropology, of Linguistics and of Psychology at the University of Chicago. He has recently edited *Natural Histories of Discourse* with Greg Urban and has contributed to *Regimes of Language* edited by Paul Kroskrity. He has received grants from the Society of Fellows, Harvard University, the National Science Foundation, the National Endowment for the Humanities, the Max-Planck-Gesellschaft and the John Simon Guggenheim Foundation. He was also awarded a fellowship by the John D. and Catherine T. MacArthur Foundation.

Aram A. Yengoyan is Professor of Anthropology at the University of California, Davis. His recent publications include *Religion, Morality, and Prophetic Traditions: Conversion among the Pitjantjatjara of Central Australia; Origin, Hierarchy, and Egalitarianism among the Mandays of Southeast Mindanao, Philippines;* and *No Exit: Aboriginal Australians and the Historicizing of Interpretation and Theory.* He was the recipient of a John Simon Guggenheim Fellowship, and was a member of the Center for Advanced Study in the Behavioral Sciences and received grants from the Ford and Rockefeller Foundations.

Introduction: Translation
and Anthropology

Paula Rubel and *Abraham Rosman*

The central aim of the anthropological enterprise has always been to understand and comprehend a culture or cultures other than one's own. This inevitably involves either the translation of words, ideas and meanings from one culture to another, or the translation to a set of analytical concepts. Translation is central to "writing about culture". However, curiously, the role that translation has played in anthropology has not been systematically addressed by practitioners, even though translation has been so central to data-gathering procedures, and to the search for meanings and understandings, which is the goal of anthropology. One of the reasons for this has been the ongoing internal dialogue about the nature of the discipline. There are those who feel that anthropology is a social science, with the emphasis on science, whose methodology, which usually involves analytical concepts, sampling and quantification, must be spelled out in detail. On the other side are those who emphasize the humanistic face of the field, and who feel that the way to do fieldwork cannot be taught. Still others, who focus on achieving understanding of another culture, think it can only be achieved by "total immersion" and empathy.

Since its inception as a discipline and even in the "prehistory" of anthropology, translation has played a singularly important role. In its broadest sense, translation means cross-cultural understanding. The European explorers and travelers to Asia and later the New World were always being confronted with the problem of understanding the people whom they were encountering. Gesture and sign language, used in the first instance, were soon replaced by lingua francas and pidgins, and individuals who learned these lingua francas and pidgins became the translators and interpreters. These pioneers in cross-cultural communication not only brought back the words of the newly encountered people but also became the translators and communicators of all kinds of information about these people, and the interpreters of their very differing ways of life, for European intellectuals, and the European public at large. They were also the individuals who were the basis for the conceptions which the Others had of Europeans.

With the development of anthropology as a formal academic discipline in the mid-nineteenth century, and later as a social science, translation of course continued to play a significant role. At this point in time, anthropologists such as Edward Tylor, Lewis Henry Morgan and Johann Bachofen remained in their offices and libraries at home, while they theorized about the development of human society and the evolution of culture. But their theories depended upon ethnographic information collected by missionaries, travelers, traders and colonial government officials. These were the individuals who were in first-hand contact with the "primitive peoples", who were very different from themselves. Their descriptions of the ways of life of the people they were encountering were being published in the various professional journals and monographs, which were established during this period. At this point in time, the sources of this data were not questioned, nor was there concern with, or any evaluation of this information in terms of how it was collected, whether it was based on actual observations or casual conversations, which languages were used, who was doing the translations and what were the methods used. The degree of expertise of these Europeans in the local languages or whether they used interpreters, and who these interpreters were, was also not considered. Translation was the *modus vivendi*; however, the anthropologists of the time were not concerned with questions of translation but only with the information itself, and the ways in which it could be used to buttress the evolutionary schemas and theories which they were hypothesizing.

Even when anthropologists themselves began to do fieldwork and gather ethnographic data at the end of the nineteenth and beginning of the twentieth century, field methodology and the role translation would play in the data-gathering enterprise were not really addressed. Though Boas, the founding father of professional anthropology in the United States, emphasized the importance of linguistics and the central role that language played in culture, he did not deal with the question of translation. In the training of his students he emphasized the necessity of learning the native language. The students were to collect information about the various aspects of a culture by recording texts in the native language. He himself published the results of his research with the Kwakiutl in the form of texts as, for example, in the two-volume *Ethnology of the Kwakiutl*, with the Kwakiutl version of the text transcribed in phonetics on the bottom half of the page and the English translation on the top half. There was a brief note about transcription at the beginning of the work entitled *Explanation of Alphabet Used in Rendering Indian Sounds* (Boas 1921: 47). He sent his Columbia University students to various American Indian tribes, whose languages were in danger of disappearing because of the shift to the use of English. This was to record valuable linguistic information about these languages, using phonetic transcription, before knowledge of them was lost. Though he did not deal with translation in general, Boas recognized that the languages of the New World were organized in a totally different manner than European languages and Latin. Such differences in grammatical categories are central to problems of translation. The fact that grammatically, a speaker of the

Kwakiutl language indicates how he knows about an action a particular individual is performing, whether he saw the action himself, or heard about it from someone else, while the speaker of English does not, surely plays a role in the translation of Kwakiutl to English or English to Kwakiutl.

Malinowski, in his Introduction to *Argonauts of the Western Pacific*, was the first anthropologist to systematically address the topic of the procedures which one should use to conduct fieldwork. Acquiring the local language was essential since it was to be used as the "instrument of inquiry". Malinowski noted the necessity of drawing a line between, ". . . on the one hand, the results of direct observation and of native statements and interpretations, and on the other hand the insights of the author . . ." (1961 [1922]: 3). He noted that "pidgin English" was a very imperfect instrument for gaining information. He recognized the importance of acquiring a knowledge of the native language to use it as an instrument of inquiry. He talked about the way in which he himself shifted from taking notes in trans-lation which, as he noted, ". . . robbed the text of all its significant characteristics – rubbed off all its points . . . at last I found myself writing exclusively in that language [Kiriwinian], rapidly taking note, word for word of each statement" (Malinowski 1961 [1922]: 23–4). By and large, though, anthropologists trained during the period of the ascendancy of British social anthropology and the func-tionalist paradigm – such as Radcliffe-Brown, Evans-Pritchard, Fortes, Leach, Shapera, et al. – always considered it important to learn the language or languages being used in the areas in which they worked. They did long periods of intensive fieldwork during which translation was constantly involved, but they did not formally consider translation's impact on their work or their theorizing. They recognized that it was important to use the languages spoken locally and not pidgins, lingua francas, interpreters or the languages in use by the hegemonic colonial governments, in order to understand the nature of the local culture and its meanings. More recently, the authors of *Ethnographic Research: A Guide to General Conduct*, a text devoted to an explication of research methods written for British social anthropologists, note that fieldwork ". . . requires some systematic understanding of it [the local language] and an accurate transcription. In the absence of a local writing system (which, in any case would have to be learned) one must make one's own phonemic one, using a recognized system like the International Phonetic Alphabet" (Tonkin in Ellen 1984: 181). In addition, learn-ing the lingua franca of the wider area, be it a pidgin or Creole, is also deemed essential.

During the postwar period in America and Britain – despite the turn in interest toward symbolic and later interpretive anthropology with its primary focus on cultural understandings – translation, such a central part of the search for meaning, was never a subject of discussion and seems to have been of minimal importance. The same point can be made with respect to structuralism. Cultural meanings and understandings were significant for the structuralist enterprise, which was also important in the postwar era, since the data being analyzed were the products of translation, yet translation issues were never directly confronted by structuralists. Postmodernism has been the subject of continuing debate and controversy among American cultural anthropologists. James Clifford and other postmodernists have forced us to reconsider the anthropological enterprise, from fieldwork and data gathering to the production of the ethnographic text. Since cultural understanding is based on the premise that translation is possible, translation and all its aspects should be a primary focus in this discussion, but this has not been the case. Clifford in a recent work finally confronts the issue of translation. He supports the idea embodied in the crucial term *traduttore traditore*, that is "The translator is a traitor". He notes further that one should have an appreciation of the reality of what is missed and what is distorted in the very act of understanding, appreciating and describing another culture (Clifford 1997).

In the United States, cultural anthropology is still going through a period of assessment and the rethinking of its goals, procedures and *raison d'être*. Thus, this is an excellent time to consider a series of issues arising from the fact that for anthropology, translation is and must be a central concern. Is translation from one culture to another possible and if so under what conditions? Can an anthropological researcher control another language adequately enough to carry out a translation? How should a researcher deal with the presence of class dialects, multilingualism and special-outsider language use? What constitutes an acceptable translation, one which contains more of the original or source language or one which focuses on the target language and the reader's understanding? What is the relationship between translation and the conceptual framework of anthropology?

At the outset we should explore where translation fits in terms of what anthropologists do during fieldwork, the analysis of the data and the writing of the ethnographic text. Anthropologists, going to do fieldwork in a culture foreign to their own, usually try to ascertain which language or languages are spoken in the area of their interest and to begin to learn these before they leave their home base or immediately upon arriving at the field site. Field assistants or interpreters may need to be used at first, and it is their translations upon which the anthropologist relies. Data that the fieldworker records, what people recount to him or her, words associated with rituals or conversations and observations may initially be written in the native language to be translated into their own language – English, German, etc. – soon after or in a procedure which combines both, which Malinowski used, as his field notes reveal. The phonetic recording of the material in the native language is essential, but often this is not the procedure used.

We might call this translation in the first instance. How does one approximate as closely as possible the original words and ideas of the culture being studied in the translation? Glossing and contextualizing is one of the methods used, which we will discuss later in greater detail. Clifford has made us very aware of the constructed nature of the ethnographic text and the various messages such texts convey. The ethnographic texts, which anthropologists publish today, never consist of the data exactly as collected in the field. Only Boas frequently did publish texts in the same form as they were received from his primary field assistant, George Hunt. Taking the postmodern message of subjectivity to heart, some postmodernist anthropologists publish their ethnographic material in very self-reflexive accounts, which describe what happened to them in the field, and the understandings of the other society which they themselves gained. They usually do not deal with the question of translation. This emphasizes the humanistic, hermeneutic focus on how the self constructs understandings of the Other. Other anthropologists, after doing their translations from the source language, chose to examine their data in terms of reoccurring patterns of behavior and ideas and present their understandings of the culture in a series of generalizations. At this level, the translation is in terms of the analytical concepts developed in anthropology, which permit the possibility of considering cross-cultural similarities if such are relevant. The question of the fit between the cultural understandings of one group and the level of analytical constructs is a very important issue. The development of analytical concepts in anthropology was based upon the premise of cross-cultural similarities at a higher analytical level than the generalizations formed about a single culture. At this level of generalization, some of the individuality and specificity of cultural phenomena which translation has revealed "falls by the wayside". This last step is one which some younger American anthropologists today do not wish to take, precisely because they feel that analytical concepts do not cognitively resonate sufficiently with the meanings of the particular culture they have studied. More importantly, some see these analytical concepts as emanating from the hegemonic West to be imposed upon the Third World Others compromising the specificity of their cultural concepts.

Though translation in anthropology clearly involves a more complex procedure than literary translation, Translation Studies, which has recently emerged in the United States as a distinct discipline dealing not only with the historical and cultural context of translation, but also with the problems associated with translating texts, may offer some assistance to anthropologists confronting similar problems in their own work. The work of translation specialists has revealed that at different historic periods in the Western world, there were different translation paradigms. These varied in terms of the degree to which translations were oriented toward the target language or to the source language. What kind of connection should there be between the original text and the translation? Is the role of the translator, as it is imprinted on the translation, parallel to the role of the anthropologist as the interpreter of a culture not his own (though some anthropologists today study their own cultures).

Translation theory rests on two different assumptions about language use. The instrumental concept of language, which sees it as a mode of communication of objective information, expressive of thought and meanings where meanings refer to an empirical reality or encompass a pragmatic situation. The hermeneutic concept of language emphasizes interpretation, consisting of thought and meanings, where the latter shape reality and the interpretation of creative values is privileged (Venuti 2000: 5).

Competing models of translation have also developed. There are those who see translation as a natural act, being the basis for the intercultural communication which has always characterized human existence. This approach emphasizes the commonality and universality of human experience and the similarities in what appear, at first, to be disparate languages and cultures. In contrast, there is the view that translation, seen as the uprooting and transplanting of the fragile meanings of the source language, is unnatural. Translating is seen as a "traitorous act". Cultural differences are emphasized and translation is seen as coming to terms with "Otherness" by "resistive" or "foreignizing" translations which emphasize the difference and the foreignness of the text. The foreignized translation is one that engages ". . . readers in domestic terms that have been defamiliarized to some extent" (Venuti 1998: 5) These models clearly reveal the ideological implications of translation, one of the features which translation-studies specialists have strongly emphasized. As Basnett notes, "All rewritings, whatever their intention reflect a certain ideology and a poetics and as such manipulate literature to function in a society in a given way. Rewriting is manipulation, undertaken in the service of power and in its positive aspect can help in the evolution of a literature and a society" (Basnett in Venuti 1995: vii). Hierarchy, hegemony and cultural dominance are often said to be reflected in translations, especially those which were done during the colonial period. These features are also said to be present in translations, which are being done now in the postcolonial period. The translation of foreign texts may also reflect the ideological and political agendas of the target culture. As Cronin notes, "Translation relationships between minority and majority languages are rarely divorced from issues of power and identity, that in turn destabilize universalist theoretical prescriptions on the translation process" (Cronin 1996: 4). The values of the culture of the source language may be different from those of the target language and this difference must be dealt with in any kind of translation. It is clear that the translations done by anthropologists cannot help but have ideological implications. How does one preserve the cultural values of the source language in the translation into the target language, which is usually the aim of the translation. The values of the local culture are a central aspect of most of the cultural phenomena which anthropologists try to describe, and these may differ from and be in conflict with the values of the target culture. How to make that difference comprehensible to audiences is the major question at issue.

What constitutes "fidelity" to the original text? Walter Benjamin, in his famous essay entitled "The Task of the Translator", notes that "The task of the translator consists of finding that intended effect [intention] into which he is translating, which produces in it the echo of the original" (Benjamin 1923 in Venuti 2000). To him, a translation constituted the continued life of the original. Benjamin is seen by translation specialists as espousing what is referred to as "foreignizing translation". Benjamin sees the basic *error* of the translator as preserving the state ". . . in which his own language happens to be, instead of allowing his language to be powerfully affected by the foreign tongue. He must expand and deepen his language by means of the foreign language. It is not generally realized to what extent this is possible, to what extent any language may be transformed" (Benjamin in Venuti 2000: 22).

The nineteenth-century German theorist Schleiermacher, who wrote "On the Different Methods of Translating" in 1813, thought that a translation could move in either of two directions: either the author is brought to the language of the reader or the reader is carried to the language of the author. In the latter case, when the reader is forced from his linguistic habits and obligations to move within those of the author, there is actual translation (Venuti 2000: 60). Foreignizing a text means that one must disrupt the cultural codes of the target language in the course of the translation. This method seeks to ". . . restrain the ethnocentric violence of translation and is an intervention . . . pitted against hegemonic English language nations and the unequal cultural exchanges in which they engage their global others" (Venuti 1995: 20). This approach would seem to be compatible with the goals of anthropology.

Moving in the direction of the reader is referred to as the domestication of translation. The position of Venuti, and others, is that in this way translation has served the global purposes of the Western modernized industrial nations, at the expense of the subaltern nations and peoples around the world. Foreignizing translation is a way of rectifying the power imbalance by allowing the voice of these latter nations to be heard in their own terms. Minoritizing translation which relies on discursive heterogeneity contrasts with fluency which is assimilationist, according to Venuti (1998: 12)

In the 1970s in the United States, notions of cultural and linguistic relativity began to come to the fore. This direction, in anthropology, led to the postmodernist position, discussed above, that all cultures are unique and different and that cultural translation is a difficult if not impossible task but that cultural translation into a Western language should be attempted since cross-cultural understanding is an important goal. However, there are also some who support the position that at some level of generalization there are universals of language and culture. Given this perspective, foreign texts are seen as entities with invariants, capable of reduction to precisely defined units, levels and categories of language and textuality.

Jakobson, whose research has had significance for both linguists and anthropologists, takes his perspective from Pierce, the semiotician, and points out that ". . . the meaning of a linguistic sign is its translation into some further alternative sign, especially one which is more fully developed "(Jakobson 1959 in Venuti 2000). Jakobson distinguishes between intra-lingual translation – the rewording or interpretation of verbal signs by other signs of the same language; inter-lingual translation – translation proper, the interpretation of verbal signs by means of some other language; and inter-semiotic translation – the interpretation of verbal signs by signs of a non-verbal sign system. He recognized, as did Boas before him, that the grammatical pattern of a language determines those aspects of experience which must be expressed and that translations often require supplementary information since languages are different in what they must convey, and in what they may convey (Jakobson 1959 in Venuti 2000: 114). He cites an excellent example of the kind of supplementary information, which must be provided, in his discussion of inanimate nouns which are personified by gender. In Russian, the word death is feminine, represented as a woman, while in German, the word is masculine and therefore represented as a man (Jakobson 1959 in Venuti 2000: 117). Clearly, distinctions of this sort are significant when one does any type of translation. The cultural context of the translation must always be presented.

How close can any translation come to the original text or statement? Nida notes that "Since no two languages are identical either in meanings given to corresponding symbols, or in ways in which such symbols are arranged in phrases and sentences, it stands to reason that there can be no absolute correspondence between languages . . . no fully exact translation . . . the impact may be reasonably close to the original but no identity in detail" (Nida 1964 in Venuti 2000: 126). Therefore, the process of translation must involve a certain degree of interpretation on the part of the translator. As Nida describes it, the message in the receptor language should match as closely as possible the different elements of the source language; constant comparison of the two is necessary to determine accuracy and correspondence. Phillips' method of back translation in which equivalencies are constantly checked is one way to achieve as exact a correspondence as possible. One must reproduce as literally and meaningfully the form and content of the original, and make as close an approximation as possible. One should identify with the person in the source language, understand his or her customs, manner of thought, and means of expression. A good translation should fulfil the same purpose in the new language as the original did in the source language. It should have the feel of the original. This would seem to be a prescription which most anthropologists should follow in their own fieldwork. But Nida also attends to the needs of the reader, noting that the translation should be characterized by "naturalness of expression" in the translation and that it should relate to the culture of the "receptor". For this reason, he is seen as being in the camp of those who advocate the "domestication" of translation. In Nida's eyes, the translation must make sense and convey the spirit and manner of the original, being sensitive to the style of the original, and should have the same effect upon the receiving audience as the original had on its audience (Nida in Venuti 2000: 134). The solution, as he sees it, is some sort of dynamic equivalence that balances both concerns. Though the equivalence should be source-oriented, at the same time it must conform to and be comprehensible in the receptor language and culture. Nida goes into details in his volume, *The Science of Translation*, regarding the methods the translator should use to get the closest approximation of the source language, including using footnotes to illuminate cultural differences when close approximations cannot be found. This is what has been referred to above as glossing. He also talks about problems of translating the emotional content of the original, and the need to convey the sarcasm, irony, whimsy, and emotive elements of meaning of the original (Nida in Venuti 2000: 139–40). Nida's theories are based on a transcendental concept of humanity as an essence unchanged by time and space, since "that which unites mankind is greater than that which divides, hence even in cases of very disparate languages and cultures there is a basis for communication" (Nida in Venuti 2000: 24). However, one must keep in mind that Nida's work, in general, is informed by missionary values since he developed his science of translation with the express purpose of being used by missionaries in their task of translating biblical and religious texts for use by people speaking languages in remote parts of the world.

Venuti sees people like Nida as emphasizing semantic unity while those who emphasize foreignization stress discontinuities and the diversity of cultural and linguistic formations, translation being seen as the ". . . violent rewriting of the foreign text" (Venuti 1995: 24). The differences of the foreign text are to be stressed. A foreignized translation is one which reflects and emphasizes the cultural differences between source and target languages. In anthropology, the goal is to present the different aspects of the culture or society being examined in a "translation" which is as true to the original as possible. No concessions should be made to make the description more acceptable and palatable to the target audience except for intelligibility.

Venuti also talks about "the illusion of transparency", meaning that the translation must be characterized by easy readability, making the translator and the conditions under which the translation was made invisible. Different societies have different traditions regarding translation. Fluency is the dominant idea for the English. This means that there is a preference for the use of current English usage in translation, rather than colloquial and archaic language though the translator may see the latter as more suitable in conveying the meanings and genre of the original. The importance of immediate intelligibility is associated with the purely instrumental use of language and the emphasis on facts (Venuti 1995: 1–5). Since domesticating the text is said to exclude and conceal the cultural and social conditions of the original text to provide the illusion of transparency and immediate intelligibility, this is referred to as "the ethnocentric violence of translation". The "canonization of fluency in English language translations", developed during the early modern period, dominated and limited the translator's options (Venuti 1995: 810). Other translation specialists talk about the need to seek functional equivalence even if one must make explicit in the target language what is implicit in the source language (Levy in Venuti 2000: 167). One must realize in the target language the textual relations of the source language with no breach of the target language's basic linguistic system. However, incompatibilities will always be present which must be dealt with by additional discussion and contextualization, what we called glossing above. Clearly, anthropologists need to deal with these different aspects of translation and to concern themselves with which kind of balance should be achieved in the work that they do.

An important point raised, which relates more directly to translations by anthropologists, is that the foreign text depends upon its own culture for intelligibility. It is therefore usually necessary to supply supplementary information, annotations and the like to anthropological translations. This is what is referred to as glossing. This is especially necessary when the source language and its culture have no exact linguistic and cultural equivalent in the target language. Quine suggests that one ". . . steep oneself in the language disdainful of English parallels to speak it like a native, eventually becoming like a bilingual (Quine 1959 in Venuti 2000: 108).

The turn toward thinking, which emphasizes cultural relativity, revived ". . . the theme of untranslatability in translation theory" (Venuti 2000: 218). Irreducible differences in language and culture, the inherent indeterminacy of language, as well as the unavoidable instability of the signifying process, are seen as problems which must be overcome if one is to do a translation. The polysemy of languages and the heterogeneous and diverse nature of linguistic and cultural materials which " destabilize signification" and make meaning plural and divided, are now seen as complicating factors in translation (Venuti 2000: 219).

Translation is doomed to inadequacy because of irreducible differences not only between languages and cultures, but within them as well. The view that language itself is indeterminate and the signifying process unstable would seem to preclude the possibility of any kind of adequate translation. Interestingly, Venuti sees the foreign text itself as the site of "many different semantic possibilities" which any one translation only fixes in a provisional sense. Meaning itself is seen as a ". . . plural and contingent relation, not an unchanging unified essence" (Venuti 1995: 18). When a text is retranslated at a latter period in time, it frequently differs from the first translation because of the changes in the historical and cultural context.

However, many subscribe to the counter-argument, holding that translation is possible if it ". . . seeks to match [the] polyvalences or plurivocatives or [the] expressive stress of the original . . ., [resisting the] constraints of the translating language and interrogates the structure of the foreign text" (Lewis in Venuti 2000: 218). Translation is a re-codification, a transfer of codes. Synonymy is not necessarily possible, but a form of translation can still take place. As Frawley notes, "Translation when it occurs has to move whatever meanings it captures from the original into a framework that tends to impose a different set of discursive relations and a different construction of reality" (Frawley in Venuti 2000: 268). The inadequacies of the translation must be dealt with in an accompanying commentary. The transformations, which a translation embodies, should take place on the semantic, syntactic and discursive levels.

As Venuti notes, "Translation is a process that involves looking for similarities between language and culture – particularly similar messages and formal techniques – but it does this because it is constantly confronting dissimilarities. It can never and should never aim to remove these dissimilarities entirely. A translated text should be the site at which a different culture emerges, where a reader gets a glimpse of a cultural other and resistency. A translation strategy based on an aesthetic of discontinuity can best preserve that difference, that otherness, by reminding the reader of the gains and losses in the translation process and the unbridgeable gaps between cultures" (Venuti 1995: 305).

To Venuti, translation has become a battleground between the hegemonic forces – the target culture and language, and the formerly subjugated non-Western world. The nature of translation must be shifted to emphasize the resistance of the latter to the domination of the former. Where does translation in anthropology stand in this ongoing dialogue in Translation Studies? Certainly, anthropology tries to preserve as much as possible of the source culture and language (the object of investigation) in the "translation" or ethnography. This begins in the field, in the recording of information, and continues in the analysis of data and in decisions as to the nature of the ethnographic text which will be produced. In this respect, Venuti's remarks parallel the position of most anthropologists. On the other hand, the text must be comprehensible to the readership of that text, professional or non-professional. In some ways, writing a popular version of one's ethnographic text is itself a translation from the ethnographic text, which is oriented toward the professional anthropologist. In the final analysis, it is a matter of the balance or trade-off between the need to be comprehensible to the particular readership of the text and the need to convey as much of the original as is possible. The question at issue is how to achieve this balance. Translations should, in the final analysis, negotiate the linguistic and cultural differences between the source language and culture and that of the target audience for the translation.

The concerns of anthropologists regarding translation are similar to many of the concerns of translation specialists, whose ideas we have detailed above. However, there are many features of translation in anthropology which are unique. Translation within the context of fieldwork, the subsequent analysis of the field material to gain understanding of the meanings and behaviors of a people other than one's own, and the writing of the ethnographic text parallel only in part the translation of literary texts. In addition to the ethnography as the translation of a culture in order to understand it, meaning its translation into some Western language, there is another kind of translation which ethnographers perform as we have noted above. The ethnographer, who sees societies as having similarities as well as differences, will "translate" what has been found on the local level into a series of analytical concepts which will then enable comparison with other societies. The development of analytical concepts presumes that there is a limited number of natural possibilities when it comes to cultural categories like kinship, social organization, etc. which we have noted above. One might call these "natural normativities", that is the features of human existence, which are universal, and those of which there are only a finite number of possible permutations (Silverstein in Chapter 3). The development of analytical categories has been based upon this important premise of a finite number of possibilities. The translation of kinship terminology as it relates to the finite number of variations in the sphere of kinship is explored by Rosman and Rubel in Chapter 11. The translation of the "meanings" of a culture into analytical concepts for the purpose of cross-cultural comparison has no equivalent in literary translation. Translation relates the local and particular to the universal or semi-universal by relating the local or the source culture to a set of analytical concepts.

Linguistic theories regarding the nature and characteristics of language, still an important concern for many anthropologists today, are very relevant to the issue of translation. What has been referred to as the Sapir-Whorf hypothesis ". . . asserts that human beings speaking different languages do not live in the same 'real' world with different labels attached: they live in different worlds – language itself acts as a filter on reality, moulding our perceptions of the universe around us" (Werner and Campbell 1970: 398). This principle, which combines linguistic determinism with linguistic relativity, is in clear opposition to Chomsky's ideas of the universality of mental structures pertaining to language. The fact that translations are possible would seem to negate the Sapir–Whorf hypothesis and support the theory of Chomskian universals. Unfortunately, however, most linguists have not been concerned with the relationship and implications of their theoretical ideas to the translation of culture.

Werner and Campbell talk about symmetrical or decentered translation which aims at both ". . . loyalty of meaning and equal familiarity and colloquialness in each language which [to them] contrasts with asymmetrical or unicentered translation, in which loyalty to one language, usually the source language dominates (Werner and Campbell 1970: 398–9). Symmetrical or decentered translation would seem to be similar to Nida's idea of dynamic equivalence, discussed above. In contrast, focus on the source language characterizes many literary translations. The lexical fields provide the contexts within which one searches for equivalencies. In decentered translation, a set of equivalent or near-equivalent sentences of the source language is seen as corresponding to a similar set of sentences in the target language, making the source and target languages coordinate (Werner and Campbell 1970: 402). Behind this is the assumption that there is more similarity and less difference (in contrast to the Sapir-Whorf hypothesis which assumes the opposite). Underlying this conceptualization of symmetrical equivalence is Chomsky's transformational theory which, as we noted above, sees all languages as formally similar in their deep structures. Finding coordinates does not mean exact translation, which is impossible, but rather searching for the best approximation.

What people say or write, which may subsequently be translated, always involves intentionality. The translation should capture what the words were intended to mean, the thinking of the individual. Sometimes the translation of the words themselves may not immediately reveal intention, nor what the speaker is thinking when he or she speaks. Intention may be intuited from external factors, which may sometimes not be included or indicated in the translation. Yet should this not be part of the translation? In the context of anthropological fieldwork, when people say or write something, the intention may not be immediately comprehensible. When the fieldworker records information from informants, factors such as affect may reveal intentions which may be different from the words themselves. This data is important for the translation itself. In oral presentation, affect may be visible and reveal intention. Affect and intentionality are culturally specific. The way in which these operate and are conceptualized in particular societies, clearly relate to translation and to the understanding of the intent of the words which are being translated. When we translate words and their meanings, we are ascribing intention to a speaker. But we must pay attention to how we translate the thinking and intent of the speaker of those words. Even intra-culturally, as Herzfeld notes in Chapter 4, Greeks don't know what is in another's head, yet they attribute intentionality to individuals. The translator must try to do this inter-culturally as well as intra-culturally.

The translation of affect and psychological states, in general, is another issue which must be considered. Some raise the question of whether translation can deal with psychological states and issues of affect. Affect and emotions, which are based on cultural conventions, constitute the setting or context of the material, and must be translated. Hence, it is essential for the translator to pay attention to the setting of the translation. In the translation of oral material associated with ritual, the performance aspect is also relevant to the translation, since it is part of the message being conveyed.

The translator not only crosses, but can be said to violate boundaries and the intimacy of the cultural setting within which he or she is working. Cultural intimacy is what is goes on "inside" a cultural group, as opposed to what is external. It is here that dialects may operate in contrast to the "official" or national language. This distinction must be considered in any translation. Though translation crosses boundaries, on the other hand, it can be said to create boundaries. Translation can also be seen as a betrayal since it can be said to violate the cultural intimacy of the "inside" (Herzfeld in Chapter 4). Translations are negotiations between that local experience and the target language – the kind of dynamic equivalence referred to above. Translation can also be said to constitute a bridge to the target audience.

When there are a diversity of "translations" the question arises regarding which of several translations should be "the" translation. Differing translations at different points in time reflect different style and ideas about translation, as we have noted above, and this difference must be considered. Political factors may be involved in the decision about which translation is "*the* translation". Need one translation be promoted over others or is a diversity of translations desirable?

The anthropologist, in particular, recognizes that there are always local or folk theories and ideas about translation. These clearly relate to local or folk theories about meanings or what some refer to as folk psychology. Ideas about meaning are different from one culture to another and one must understand them in their own terms. We may raise the question of whether the notions of translation of the translator, anthropologist or not, may contrast with or even violate the folk theories of the source language and culture. Messick, in Chapter 7, gives an example of Islamic jurists and their theories of translation. It is intention not words that count to them. The words that are used are not representative of intention, which is divined in other ways. There is another point of view which says that words *do* tell intentions, and that one can analyze words though they lack certainty. How do local processes of translation deal with foreign "things" and "domesticate" or translate them? What does it mean to translate locally (Keane in Chapter 6)? How do local people incorporate ideas and material objects which come from the outside? This is also a kind of translation. In this time of "globalization", this is a significant process which needs to be investigated. How does translation relate to "stealing words"? Stealing words has significant meanings in some cultural settings, but not in others. It depends on the meanings of information and know-ledge and the local notion of possession (Keane in Chapter 6). According to Herzfeld, stealing words is the sign of the true Cretan man. Does translation constitute "stealing words"?

What does the actual process of translation involve? According to views expres-sed at the conference by Silverstein, one subjects the words and the expressions of language A in a text to grammatical analysis and one then finds in language B a grammatical analysis which conforms to the grammar in language A. This linguistics project is based on a universal grammar and specific grammatical structures, that is, categories of language which are inter-translatable. This involves structural equivalence. Comparative grammar anchors the translation. A text has a context, a shared or implicitly shared set of cultural beliefs, which are systems or categories of differentiation, "stereotypic knowledge", and are sociocentric – that is, part of a social organization and structure of authority (Silverstein). Translation is a matter of comparing systems of contextualization of one language and culture with systems of contextualization of another. The presence of a range of differences is what makes translation a matter of judgment or guess. One must also distinguish between translation which is word for word, in which comparative grammar or structural equivalents anchor the translation, and translation which is transduction. The latter, transduction, is translation where sense-for-sense or category equivalents are sought (Silverstein).

Silverstein makes the point that the problem of translation is cultural not individual. The individual mind operates in a cultural context. Therefore when we translate, it is not simply propositional knowledge ascribed to the individual mind which is involved, but translation is the communication of cultural knowledge. Every act of translation is a social act, involving social relationships, transforming as well as crossing boundaries (Silverstein).

The translator or interpreter himself or herself may be said to constitute a boundary or border (Robinson). Translation also separates what is self and what is other. However, by and large, as we noted above, translation bridges boundaries and enables understanding across boundaries. Translation breaks down genre. Genre relates to intentionality, affect, and motivation which we have discussed above. How to translate genre forms and preserve the various aspects of genre which are so significant to form is an important question.

Can belief systems, with all that they encompass, including their counter-intuitive aspects and inconsistencies, be translated? Saler, in Chapter 8 of this volume, considers the way in which the Spanish tried to translate ideas about the Trinity and the difficulties encountered. Translating the idea of the virgin birth is the same sort of problem. As we noted above, understanding is a requisite for good translation. Jones, in Chapter 2, sees belief as a relational entity. What does a belief do, how does it function in cognitive and social settings? According to Jones, one should use the native term and show how it works in their conceptual economy. "What does the native term do" (Jones)? This approach has been a standard anthropological technique, used not only for belief systems. Alternatively, one could translate the native term into an abstract syntactic primitive relating to the kind of universal syntactic cognitive structure we have discussed above, and deal with its "doxastic" surround (Jones). This universal cognitive structure would require a kind of natural meta-language. There are areas of grammar where this can be done (Silverstein). (Does the development of pidgins relate to this?) Clearly this relates to the discussion above regarding use of analytical concepts at successively higher levels of abstraction.

In the situations in which the anthropologist usually works, the role, status and identity of the translator is also an issue. In colonial situations, those local people who were able to learn the language of the colonial power themselves came to be in powerful positions as a consequence of their being middlemen, mediators or bridges in the colonial situation. The position of the translator in a particular culture needs to be ascertained historically. The translator is in a sense a trickster: he or she can clarify or obfuscate. To which side does her or she hold allegiance? He or she may be a person of greater or lesser authority (Kapchan). There are different norms in regard to the position of the translator in different societies. The translator is a mediator between the local society and the outside world.

Anthropologists are listeners who are "translating" the local culture, creating a picture of it for the outside world, but they are also seen as outsiders or marginals. What he or she produces is an ethnographic text, a descriptive ethnography, which must involve glossing and contextualizing local concepts, which may not have equivalents in the target language. As is the case for all texts, the anthropologist's text is conditional in nature, paralleling the storyteller's performance of a classical Arabic text, with all its "imperfections", which Kapchan in Chapter 5 describes as "conditional in its authority". As the anthropologist gains in knowledge and understanding, the "translation" of the culture will be progressively more accurate. Some say that the closure of knowledge is bad (Kapchan). However, the anthropologist must present "some reading of the culture", and there must be some closure, some product, or anthropologists will not be taken seriously or listened to (Jones at the conference). We may say that this is the best we can do at this time, the best account or "translation of the culture" for this time (Yengoyan at the conference). However, we all recognize that newer thinking and developments in the field may require us to revisit that reading and improve it in the light of new developments at some future date. For example, newer translations or Church texts such as the Bible have been done over time and this belies the idea that there is a fixity of religious beliefs (Blier). To what extent can the public accept the provisionality of the anthropologist's account? Some say they can (Herzfeld at the conference). Others see this provisionality as undercutting anthropology as a discipline (Jones at the conference). There is a difference regarding this point if we are talking about the anthropological public or the general public. The public needs to be educated about the provisional nature of anthropological categories, and the way in which anthropologists "translate" native categories. This is necessary in order to refute the Native American critique that we are not translating "their categories" but imposing our own categories, with their distortions, upon them and other native peoples, a powerful critique, as noted earlier in this introduction (Ortiz).

It seems unlikely that a translation can be perfect, that is, that it catches all the meanings and nuances of the original. A perfect translation is a utopian dream

(Jones). We know this empirically. Even intra-lingual communication itself is not perfect. The speaker's intention may be not to be understood, but rather to deceive.

In many societies such as Haiti, diglossia is operative, often related to class and upward mobility. The poorer classes speak Haitian Creole, while the upper classes speak French. But with growing nationalism, there has been a movement to make Creole, the minor language, into the major language and the signifier of Haitian nationalism and independence. Such asymmetrical stratification of languages is universal. Anthropologists doing fieldwork in diglossic situations have to make decisions regarding which language they will use in their fieldwork. In Papua New Guinea, Neomelanesian or, as it was known earlier, Pidgin English or Police Motu were lingua francas used by people speaking many different frequently non-intelligible local languages. Multilingualism was a significant feature of Papua New Guinea society. In many societies, use of the localized language alone was often seen as hindering an upwardly mobile individual, while learning the standard language was seen as liberating. In field situations such as these, one should acquire facility in the languages being used and the nature of the code switching being done and the significance of the language shifting present. Translation in such a situation becomes a problem of translating the multilingual "mix" people are using and the significance of language shifting as it occurs.

In earlier times, some anthropologists would do their research in Pidgin or a local lingua franca, learning the native language only to a minimal degree. The degree of facility in, or knowledge of the local language on the part of the anthropologist can often be ascertained from the ethnography. Examining ethnographies will reveal that though anthropologists frequently present exact quotes which are translations, they must use the method of glossing and contextualizing words in order to fully understand what those quotes mean (Messick). The anthropologist must also be concerned with the way in which quotations appear in the ethnographic text itself. Should they, for example, be set up in block form separate from the ongoing text or is some other method more clearly a "translation" of the quote?

When anthropologists began to deal with written texts, transliteration and transcription became issues of concern. As noted earlier, Boas himself was concerned with the transcription of oral texts and the use of phonetics to accomplish that task. Transcription creates an artifact from an oral event, and this can only be done by phonological transcription (Silverstein). In anthropology, in particular, the transcription and subsequent translation, the writing down of native oral literature was an important task. Translated native literature often becomes a commodity. The power dimension and power differentials were clearly operative throughout this process. It is of significance not only when one works with a local group with only an oral tradition. Working with African-Americans, one has the same problem in representing Black English.

Oral, written and printed texts are different modes of representation and need to be distinguished. How does translation deal with these different forms (Yengoyan)? One could say further that print culture reworks the notion of knowledge and discourse (Yengoyan). Visual conventions certainly will affect the way in which the reader responds to a translated text. The translator's preface and notes must discuss the decisions which have been made regarding the modes of representation which the translator has chosen to use.

The performativity aspect of a translation are also of some importance. In Kapchan's discussion of local translators who interpret classical Arabic texts in oral performances, in Chapter 5, the performance aspect of the translation is a significant factor in determining receptor response. Anthropologists doing translations of oral performances must attend not only to the words of the ritual. The action or performance aspect is equally important in providing meanings which are to be translated.

As noted above, translation always has political implications. In the colonial context, within which many anthropologists worked, the power differential was always an important factor in the nature of the translation. The conquest by the Western industrialized countries of much of the rest of the world, and its subsequent control and domination, importantly involved the process of translation, as Saler points out in his Chapter 8 in this volume. Niranjana notes, ". . . the practices of subjection implicit in the colonial enterprise operate not merely through the coercive machinery of the state, but through discourses of philosophy, history, anthropology, philology, linguistics and literary interpretation, the colonial 'subject' – constructed through technologies or practice of power/knowledge – is brought into being within multiple discourses and on multiple sites. One such site is translation" (Niranjana 1992: 1–2). The colonized population had to be represented in a particular manner so as to justify colonial domination. Translation, using certain modes of representation of the Other, reinforced "hegemonic" versions of the colonized in which they acquired the status of representations or objects without history, as Said has noted. These became facts which governed events in the colonies (Niranjana 1992: 3)

To whom are we answerable when we do a translation? This is a matter of ethics as well as power differentials, and is a much discussed topic. The first question posed is whether we translate at all. There are things which are "dangerous" to translate, since they are considered "untranslatable" locally. There is a difference between what translation means locally and our ideas about what we should translate. Often sacred rituals and spells must be kept secret, and untranslated in the eyes of a particular group, for if the material is translated, it might have deleterious effects. If we do translate in such situations, it can be considered an act of betrayal. An ethical position requires that the effects of a translation on local populations always be considered. The anthropologist must determine in particular situations which cultural materials it is not ethical to translate. Some years ago an anthropologist doing fieldwork with the Cherokee in Oklahoma wrote an article in *Current Anthropology*, detailing the reasons why he did not publish the results of his research. He felt it was unethical to describe rituals which the Cherokee had revealed to him but considered to be sacred and not to be revealed to the outside world. Since what "they" mean by translation and what "we" mean by it may not be the same, translation may sometimes have difficult and unforeseen consequences. The ethical issue involves us in rethinking our own assumptions about our enterprise. We must consider what we do and why we do it and our assumption of our role as "translators" of the cultures and ways of life of others. We are mediators between two worlds, metaphorically like priests with the anthropologist having the sacerdotal authority of priests (Saler at the conference).

Though translation always starts with a prescriptive approach to equivalence, the social context, the politics, whom the translation is being done for, why and how, as well as the translator's relationship to those in the source and those in the target cultures, often determine the nature of the translation. Some Native Americans may resist translation, feeling that anthropologists "don't translate but they impose" (Ortiz). Anthropologists are seen as interfering "(fucking around)" with people's souls and with reality (Ortiz). One Native American expressed the feeling that even Native American anthropologists themselves are "torn apart" in the context of their anthropological research with their own people, in terms of what they do or do not reveal and translate. As anthropologists, we use particular concepts and words which are seen by non-anthropologists as jargon. The use of these concepts is seen as imposing categories upon the culture and way of life of the people, acting as a counter to the uniqueness of their culture, and serving to distort the encounter between the anthropologist and the native person. Some Native Americans in the Southwest have reached the point of refusing anthropologists permission to do research in their communities, even to the point of putting up signs that say "White man Keep Out". In a curious way, although translation crosses boundaries it also creates barriers and antagonism.

As we noted above, mistranslation is sometimes intentional, and falsification and mistranslation for political purposes sometimes occur. For example, Blier (at the conference) noted the fact the Freud, in his work on Michelangelo's statue of Moses, did not discuss the horns on Moses' head. These horns represent a deliberate and intentional mistranslation of "rays of light" from the Bible into horns, and was a way of demonizing Jews, in line with the general anti-Semitic attitude of the Catholic Church at that time. Obfuscation versus faithfulness is the issue here. Translation clearly involves dangers and difficulties for all who translate including anthropologists (Saler). One might pose the question, is faithfulness of translation always important? Are there situations where this axiom is not or should not be held to?

In what ways may translations be critiqued? Some say that only translators themselves can critique translations. One could also say that only an ethnographer who has done fieldwork in the same society can criticize an anthropological translation. For literary translations, it is the translation itself into the target language which has priority. The style and poetics exhibited in the translation are usually the basis for critical judgments. In anthropology, those who translate oral ritual and mythic materials have debated whether prose or poetic form better reflects the essence of this material, but this is clearly not a major aspect of translation in anthropology. Making decisions about the acceptance of an ethnographic text as a good translation relate to the ethnographer's knowledge of the language as well as to various other factors such as the anthropologist's grasp of the internal logic of the system and its meaning.

The categorizations and classifications found in particular cultures, as we have noted above, are significant and this is true of the concept of translation itself. Only recently has the term "translation" been reduced in the scope of its meaning in the Western World to refer only to the translation from one language to another. Earlier, during the Renaissance, for example, it had many more meanings, and a much fuller semiotic range. Included in that range of meanings was the use of the word to refer to the movement or translation of souls or the body to heaven and the movement of something from one place to another (Segal in Chapter 9). Architecture is also seen as a form of translation. This is understandable if one sees architecture and language as homologous structures (Blier). However, one must recognize that many subject matters which we now see as distinct and separate categories had not been recognized as separate domains earlier. For example, in the West, the category, "art", crystallized in the seventeenth century as did that of "religion" (Saler). As we can see, we in the West have our own categories which have changed through time. We must always be aware that indigenous categories may frequently differ from our own and we should not simply impose our categories in our translations. In the field situation we must be aware of the possibility of this difference. For example, Navajo sand painting has now come to be considered art by the Western world. Among the Navajo, the sand painting and its method of construction is part of the curing ritual. It is a transitory phenomenon whose existence is not prolonged after the ritual is concluded.

A comparison of our discussion of translation studies and that concerning translation and anthropology reveals that translation is conceived of differently disciplinarily. Many of the issues with which literary translation and the literary critiques of translation are concerned do not parallel issues of concern to anthropologists in their translations (Yengoyan). We mentioned above the discussion relating to whether Native American cultural materials should be translated into prose or poetic forms. The aesthetic form of the translation is one factor with which literary translators concern themselves more than anthropologists do in their translations. Though the particular genres which are used in anthropological translations, the style and voice, the losses and gains, as well as the nature of the transliteration if that is involved, all constitute problems with which anthropologists must deal (Keane, Yengoyan).

In our discussion of the various contributions of Translation Studies, concern for and emphasis upon the "consumer" of the translation and his or her comprehension was seen as an important issue. In a way, it is not only translators but also consumers who produce meaning (Herzfeld at the conference). They bring their own background and sensibility to the comprehension of the translation, though the translator still has the primary role of constructing the meaning of the translation. It is he or she who, in the final analysis, controls what is put out to the consumer. The cultural biases, conscious or unconscious, are operative unless the translator controls for these in the production of the translation. The anthropologist, in the "translation" of the local culture, sometimes conveys a particular message, as for example Malinowski, whose "translation" of the Trobriand Islanders was intended to convey the message of the "prelogical savage" (Yengoyan). Other anthropologists like Mead had their own sense of translation. In some of her ethnologies, the translation presented was consumer-oriented, that is, intended for the general public. One might further argue that the particular theoretical framework, which the anthropologist brings to the field situation, including the meta-theory of anthropology, has an effect on the "translation" of the local culture which is being made. It determines what is held back, what is pushed, in terms of what the translator thinks the receiver should receive (Yengoyan).

In an interesting way, during this postmodern period, James Clifford and others have become "translators" for the discipline of anthropology, examining and deconstructing what we do for non-anthropologists and academics at large. Literary critics act as translators in the same manner, "translating" for those who read their critiques. Clifford's translations have brought about a rethinking and a fundamental reexamination of how we do anthropology. The Translation and Anthropology Conference brought together individuals from different disciplines. Besides anthropology, art history, translation studies, Native American literature, religion and French were represented. Being from different disciplines meant that the participants brought their different disciplinary dispositions and presuppositions, making us recognize a very basic aspect of translation since the participants sometimes had to do some "translation" across disciplinary lines during the course of the discussions.

References

Boas, Franz. *Ethnology of the Kwakiutl. Thirty-fifth Annual Report of the Bureau Of American Ethnology for the Years 1913–1914*. Washington, D.C. Smithsonian Institution, 1921.

Clifford, James. *Routes: Travel and Translation in the late Twentieth Century*. Cambridge: Harvard University Press, 1997.

Cronin, M. *Translating Ireland: Translation, Languages and Cultures*. Cork: Cork University Press, 1996.

Ellen, R. F. *Ethnographic Research: A Guide to General Conduct*. New York: Academic Press, 1984,

Malinowski, Bronislaw. *Argonauts of the Western Pacific*. New York: E.P. Dutton, 1961 [1922].

Niranjana, Tejaswini. *Siting Translation: History, Post-Structuralism and the Colonial Contest*. Berkeley: University of California Press, 1992.

Venuti, Lawrence. *The Translator's Invisibibility: A History of Translation*. London and New York: Routledge, 1995.

—— *The Scandals of Translation: Towards and Ethics of Difference*. London and New York: Routledge, 1998.

Venuti, Lawrence (ed.). *The Translation Studies Reader*. London and New York: Routledge, 2000.

Werner, Oswald and Donald T. Campbell. "Translating, Working Through Interpreters, and the Problem of Decentering." in *A Handbook of Method in Cultural Anthropology*. Naroll, Raoul and Ronald Cohen (eds). New York: Columbia University Press, 1970.

Part I
General Problems of Translation

−1−

Lyotard and Wittgenstein and the Question of Translation

Aram A. Yengoyan

Translations and the tensions in translation have always plagued anthropology, be it in its scientific version or humanistic side, with the persistent question of how cultural translations can be made without destroying the very subjects which we are attempting to convey. From Boas onward, anthropological theory regarding translation has been caught up in various conceptual developments, in our attempts toward comparison and what that meant, as well as in our efforts to generalize or forge a systematic study of human societies as Radcliffe-Brown demanded.

Yet, cultural translation (even linguistic translation) has seldom been directly addressed as an issue. Aside from some similarities, cultural translations and linguistic translations differ in a number of ways. Usually cultural translations have been done through a frame which either stresses differences or serves as a means in which the "other" is portrayed in categories which are understandable to a Western audience. Although traditional anthropological categories (such as kinship, lineage, family, etc.) have been used as glosses, cultural translations are less exacting and also less scientific. On this matter, not only do linguistic translations bring forth the language of the investigator, but also linguistics – as a discipline which covers phonological, morphological, and grammatical categories and distinctions – is usually more exacting in terms of rigor. Furthermore, what linguists mean by semantics is hardly comparable to anthropological usage. The distinction between cultural and linguistic translation is blurred, but in general, a more dominating framework on how translations are done can be imposed by linguistic methods and means of inquiry which are absent in more vague cultural translation attempts.

I

The first part of this chapter attempts to demarcate some of the intellectual concerns which stimulated various types of translation but also may have neglected other potential expressions of translation. Under Boas and his students, American historical anthropology stressed particularism which was closely connected to theories of relativism. The Americanists insisted that comparison and generalization were the ultimate goals which could only be achieved after the particular and the local were analyzed and understood.

The Boasians, however, moved in many different directions regarding these matters. Boas, Lowie in *Primitive Society* (1920), Radin (1923, 1933) and even Kroeber in his own way, all accepted an anti-nominalistic position, basically arguing against categories of analysis. They also stressed that the laws, comparisons and generalizations of the evolutionists and the founders of British social anthropology (Malinowski and Radcliffe-Brown) were only "law-like" because of the way phenomena were defined apart from an empirical existence. For example, Lowie's *Primitive Society* (1920) reads from one chapter to another like an attack on the creation and use of categories such as economy, politics, kinship and social organization. Thus, Lowie leaves the reader with the impression that kinship or polity in various societies embrace a series of institutions and behaviors which are highly variable, with limited or no connection to anything else. The reason they are called 'kinship' is simply the result of our definition of kinship as a category but, in fact, the empirical content therein is so diverse as to make the label meaningless. However, Kroeber (1952: 175–81) also differed in part from the Boasian anti-nominalist position. As early as 1909 Kroeber proposed categories of kinship analysis which later became analytic categories for componential analysis in the 1960s and 1970s. In particular, Kroeber insisted that kinship terms were primarily linguistic rather than sociological.

Radin's (1923) ethnography of the Winnebago goes further in denying all categories and generalizations. If Radin is simply the passive scribe of the tribe, enumerating cultural things the way people gave them to him, then one is left to read 500 pages of text with virtually no conclusions. Radin, whose only theoretical position was historical, translated Winnebago ethnography by simply giving the "facts" to the reader in the way the Winnebago gave the "facts" to him. From my reading of this ethnography, I would conclude that Radin's account is the best and only example we have of a postmodern treatise which has eluded any contemporary notice of postmodern description.

Written in the early 1930s, Radin's *Method and Theory in Ethnology* (1933) is not only an attack on British anthropology but a devastating critique of Boas, Kroeber and Benedict in their insistence that generalizations, even weak comparisons, and cultural portraits (via Benedict) must be one of anthropology's aims, even one with minimal priority. Radin's heavy intellectual and moral commitment to localism, particularism and relativism might have been an embarrassment to Boas and some of the Boasians, but the ideas did resonate well with Lowie and with some of Sapir's non-linguistic writings.

Kroeber's position on particularism and relativism is somewhat more obtuse. In his historical writings on Western civilization as expressed in *The Configurations of Cultural Growth* (1944) and other works and essays from the 1930s on, Kroeber moves toward a form of generalization, comparison and interpretation which culminates in *Anthropology* (1948). Most of these developments were attacked by Boas in the 1930s, and they were heavily criticized by Radin throughout his writings. But Kroeber has another side in which the argument regarding generalization and facile theory is accepted with marked caution and even contempt. In *Anthropology* (1948), Kroeber discusses "odd customs," such as the couvade, and reviews theories which may explain the practice. His critique is a heavy attack on Malinowski's hypotheses which explain couvade and other "exotic" behaviors. Kroeber argues that these explanations are trite and even worthless; he also makes it clear that some customs/practices should only be described and that is the best we can do. In support of this position, Kroeber stresses that we should always be concerned with the potential violation of the nature of the object which may succumb to vapid and banal explanations; he further warns that analysis may cause the phenomena to dissolve into something else with no reality. There have been few, if any, past or contemporary writers who would argue such a position – only in the heyday of theoretical triteness.

Furthermore, textbooks noted that what anthropology conveyed was the range of socio-cultural differences and similarities expressed within the arc of human variation. While the Americans stressed differences over similarities, early British anthropology took the reverse position. For Malinowski, there were only surface differences in culture which were directed toward the universality of our biological constitution as well as what human nature meant. Radcliffe-Brown stressed that societal differences could be related to a finite number of social structural types and/or subtypes. Kroeber, however, was simply warning that the "heavy greasy hand" of the anthropologist in regard to explanation and interpretation must always be scrutinized, since it violates the very subject it treats.

II

The emphasis on the particular and the enhancing and deepening of the idea of difference, which has been part of our intellectual genealogy, has a critical and marked impact on our concerns for translation. While such is an issue (if not a problem) in anthropology, we might extend our inquiries to how problems of translation have been comprehended by Wittgenstein and Lyotard. Although their approaches differ somewhat, both writers have started their inquiries with marked particularism and relativism.

In *Philosophical Investigations* (1958), Wittgenstein makes it clear that "obeying a rule," which has been one of the markers of grammatical analysis, can only capture one facet of how the game of language is played. In this sense obeying a rule can only be done by one individual and only once, since the context in which rules are played changes and those changes have an impact on what the rule is and how it is expressed. Rules are caught up in customs, which for Wittgenstein means uses and institutions, and the context, which establishes how the performance of rules occur. As an avid chess player, Wittgenstein knows the rules of chess but also notes that the stamping of feet or yelling during the match might be part of the context of the game. Do the rules of chess exclude such behaviors or customs?

From this postulate Wittgenstein (1958: para. 199) states "To understand a sentence means to understand a language. To understand a language means to be master of a technique." The technique is far beyond the rules *per se* and would embrace the whole context of language, or what Becker (1995) has called "languaging." This type of specificity would never be limited to a rule which is privately conceived, since the private aspect of language would have to collapse and combine the act of thinking about a rule as isomorphic to obeying a rule. Although Wittgenstein has a relatively negative view of the privatization of language, his major challenge to the issue is how language is evoked by memory and memory-reaction. Some writers have wrongly concluded that many aspects of Wittgenstein's thoughts on language are a form of behaviorism, but it is fairly clear that when Wittgenstein enunciates the word "pain," and although "pain" is expressive of behavioral parameters, "pain" is still first and foremost a mental term which is not reducible.

Throughout his discussion of language and any possibility of translation, Wittgenstein's position is nearly always linked to the contrast between the argument and the counterargument or, in more recent contemporary thinking, as the contrast between the factual and the counterfactual. Both sets of contrasts I consider as parallel. The implications of these contrasts sharpen Wittgenstein's conception of language and language games, but of more importance to me is that the idea of difference becomes the barometer of accepting statements which we can call truth. As long as difference(s) become the bottom line, which one might never fully contemplate or even arrive at, it becomes virtually impossible to invoke any form of translation.

For Wittgenstein, the issue of difference and specificity is only one facet of particularism; it must be understood as the essence of language. From Wittgenstein to the recent work by Becker, language is a form of life or a frame which embeds all of what we consider as grammar. But grammar *per se* does not and will not capture the essence of language games. Language as image creates the varying propositions which we use and state and express to ourselves throughout our language experiences. Thus language is an organizer of experience as well as the framing of contexts which bear on the speaker and also evoke memories which speakers bring forth to explain experience. As Wittgenstein (1958, para. 114) states "One thinks that one is tracing the outline of the thing's nature over and over again, and one is merely tracing round the frame through which we look at it."

Following from Wittgenstein's approach, Becker (1995: 288) concludes that the specificity of language is primarily orientational (as opposed to denotational);

consequently language, and what Becker calls languaging, shapes and attunes speakers to context and in turn defines how context bears on speakers. Yet in dealing with distantly related languages, these problems are not only difficult but virtually insurmountable. Contexts are radically and differently shaped, and they also require both memory retrieval and new memories combined with possibly radical prior texts which an outsider might be unable to master or even approximate. Becker's (1995) appeal for a return to philology, what he labels Modern Philology, is premised on the approach that the primary task of the modern version of philology is describing and interpreting these different frames. In Becker's analysis, frames involve a range of contexts which include the physical world, social factors, prior texts, the parts to the whole, and how silence is constituted.

In both Wittgenstein and Becker, the problem remains: namely, what are we translating, and, even if we know what that is, can any form of translation be adequately accomplished? The conclusion from my reading is that it cannot be done. I suspect that, for the anthropologist, translation is the writing of cultural portraits or language portraits as texts, prior texts and frames which embed and create action, either as cultural behavior or as speech. Each of these portraits, a tradition which goes from Benedict to Geertz in cultural anthropology, must be comprehended as portraits and readings which are basically non-comparable.

Lyotard's *The Differend: Phrases in Dispute* (1988) represents an even more acute and radical move in the direction of particularism and difference. Although Lyotard is concerned about the political aspects of differend, his conviction is that only a sense of difference and heterodoxy can minimize political domination based on global theory and homogeneity which sweeps away and obliterates all voices based on the local and the particular.

But the political agenda has far-reaching effects in regards to language and any possibility of translation. Lyotard's concern is to move toward the most minimal "thing" which creates and maintains difference, that being the phrase. The overall idea is that the differend cannot or should not be collapsed into another in which one phrase regimen is dissolved into the other, or both sides of the phrase regimen are dissolved into something else. In a series of examples, Lyotard develops the idea that the phrase is the most minimal unit of analysis which embeds and combines the context in which language occurs. Lyotard takes the phrase from Stendhal "Be a popular hero of virtù like Bonaparte" as an assignment of prescriptive value to the name/label Bonaparte. On this basis, Lyotard (1988: 48) states: "A phrase which attaches a life-ideal to a man's name and which turns that name into a *watchword* is a potentiality of instructions, an ethics and a strategy. This name is an Ideal of practical or political reason in the Kantian sense."

In this vein, Lyotard (1988: 48) emphatically argues that phrases are governed by different regimens which cannot be translated into each other. Any translation from one language to another assumes that the phrase of the departing language is recoverable in the phrase of the receiving language. Translations assume that the regimen and its corresponding genre are analogous to another language or one set of regimen/genre in language "A" has a counterpart in language "B." Furthermore, translations from one language to another are one type of translation; other forms are not directly translated from language A to B and back, but also in what Lyotard calls pertinences which are "transversal." Here Lyotard sees translation as a triangulation in which both languages resonate with one another through a third meta-structure which produces or generates similar analogies with each other. This is what linguists have done with the procedures of parsing and glossing which have been accepted as a normal methodology. Lyotard, who does not address the problems of parsing and glossing, still concludes "How then can phrases belonging to different regimes and/or genres (whether within the same language or between two languages) be translated from one into the other?" (Lyotard 1988: 49).

The process of glossing from one language to another is seldom if ever a neutral act. As Becker (1995) emphatically notes, the claims of universality through translation is a political expression in which the language of the powerful becomes the measure or barometer in which universality is forged. Lyotard would probably support this position, but his critique is that translation in any form is virtually impossible, since the phrase regimen is highly specific within each language and not only is that phrase regimen a qualitative variable between languages, but each language through its history must work from different regimens which are temporally specific. In this sense languages can only be described within their own historical contexts, just as Stendhal used the Bonaparte imagery.

In *Postmodern Fables* (1997), Lyotard casts translation as partly a cultural matter. In reading his essay "Directions to Servants" (based on Jonathan Swift's essay on how one talks to servants), Lyotard is more open to the possibility of translation, but the barriers are still as marked as in his 1988 position. One's thought is translatable as much as the speaker's, due to the fact that languages by definition are translatable (Lyotard; 1997: 153). But the final problem still exists in that we might extrapolate one's language or even phrase regimens, yet we can never get into how one/the speaker inhabits the language or the culture, thus one is never at home in another's home.

Any adequate translation for Lyotard is not only a matter of respecting thought, it must also approximate the "manners" of thought. Again we return to the problem which Wittgenstein noted and which Becker calls languaging. Lyotard recognizes the possibility and also correctly argues that translation is not only an infinite task with no closure, but that every translation begets another one. Even if translation is attempted in language (a position which was unacceptable in *The Differend*), the baggage of culture from near texts to distant texts in time and space cannot be surmounted. At best we can only get glimpses of the past and the distant as bits of this and that: either the bits impose on our thought, or we can impose our thought on the bits, once again by glossing the particular and possibly unique into our thought with all of the political facets of domination which our thought might embrace.

Furthermore, Lyotard is also keenly aware of the impact of noise (and possibly silence though not directly addressed) on thought. Thought for Lyotard is linked to the noise of language either through discourse or through writing, which is another form of discourse. One cannot address one's thought, one can only listen to noise which generates thought. Though I would argue against this position, it returns to Wittgenstein's caution regarding private language games.

Translation is a combination and exchange of representation and self-effacement, one where difference is paramount and the contradictions can only be noted but not resolved, since there is no resolution in translation. Yet, translation between languages is still somewhat more feasible in comparison to translation between phrase regimes which cannot be translated. In his attack on grand theory, Lyotard also moves the discussion from discourse to contextualization, situational analysis, and a phenomenological commitment in which figure reigns over discourse, where figure presupposes reference and is configured in difference.

Returning to language, we could conclude that in Lyotard's philosophy of language (like Wittgenstein's) the grammatical mode of the sentence is primary, but the sentence cannot rest on grammar *per se*. The model logic of each sentence (or phrase) is primarily comprehended by the different logics which impinge on the sentence. Many writers view Lyotard as the most dominant voice in postmodernism, but my reading is that his postmodernism is an intellectual and political appeal for the situational and the particular. For anthropologists, situational and particular events/data would include observations which we think might be incomparable. Translation is thus a form of house-cleaning which might be tidy, but the real beauty of housecleaning as translation is to keep disorder and partial chaos as part of the process.

III

Apart from the cautionary strictures regarding translation as set forth by Wittgenstein, Lyotard and Becker, the problems of any "adequate and approximate" translation might be insurmountable. Becker (1995) readily notes that grammar is limiting in what we can or cannot say, but each life style of speech is filled with silences which might escape any translation. Citing Ortega y Gasset (1957, 1959), "Two apparently contradictory laws are involved in all uttering." One says, "Every utterance is deficient" – it says less than it wishes to say. The other law, the opposite, declares, "Every utterance is exuberant" – it conveys more than it plans and includes not a few things we would wish left silent. The exuberances and deficiencies either say more than we know or less than what we intend.

All translations face this problem, but we can also learn something about the procedural basis of translation. Both conditions (deficiencies and exuberances) rest in the language of the translator, and they would also exist in the metalanguage of the translation process, in the process of parsing and glossing. This is not the only issue, however, since what is of more interest is to demarcate what is deficient and exuberant in the home language of the translator and also to note what the near or distant text, be it spoken or written, does with deficient and exuberant markers. Again, in comparing the language of the translator to the language of the distant speaker, does one find certain features which fall into one or the other category? Translation is not neutral, but one could speculate that certain aspects of language and languaging might have a cross-cultural basis from which one aspect of languaging across languages falls more in one direction as opposed to its counterpart.

If we return to our common thinking about traditional grammars, we might recast the problem in another way. Most grammars deal with rules, but they do not tell us how to say things. As Pawley (1991) notes, grammars of the type we have read are seldom done in an idiomatic mode which is useful for the speakers of the language as well as for the translator. Pawley (1991: 434) stresses the point that "Translation is something that *language users do with particular ideas expressed by particular texts*." The job of the translator can be defined roughly as taking the message or idea that someone has expressed in language A and rendering the message in language B in a way that speakers of B will understand readily. Working with Kalam, a language in the central highlands of Papua New Guinea, Pawley correctly notes that the problem in translation is to find adequate equivalents between English and Kalam, but this might reflect that the speakers of the two languages do not share conceptual categories in common and their ways of talking about the world might not resonate with one another.

Even a "simple" label like hunting might have no good equivalent in both languages, and thus the speakers live in partially different conceptual schemes (Pawley 1991: 442). In a literal rendering which maintains the conceptual scheme of the original language, often speakers of the receiving language might be unable to comprehend the categories. Pawley, following Bulmer, attempts a looser translation which might lose some of the subtleness of information but the meaning will be conveyed. In his appeal for pragmatic translation, the matter of glossing is still an issue, but the difficult strictures which make glossing an impossibility are minimized. Even though hunting in Kalam is not the same as hunting in English, nevertheless, hunting in Kalam can be grasped. In this sense, translation involves explicating their conceptual scheme even if it does not completely "resonate" with ours. Glossing of this type would be easier (and probably safer) between languages which are related. However, glossing between distant languages is and has always been a problem. Boas faced this issue in working on Kwakiutl texts and English, and the same problem occurs in moving from German to Aranda, which will be elaborated on in more detail in the discussion. If a subject matter which vaguely resonates with speakers of two different languages can be created, it might be easier to devise some semi-conventional modes of thinking and articulation between both languages and their speakers.

IV

In order to devise a method for cultural translation, I propose a basic distinction between culture as a potential set of categories of thought, and culture as consciousness. The former refers to the mental ability to categorize and abstract, not only in the mind's dealings with reality in any specific situation, but also in its overall potential for abstraction, its capacity to operate in situations not specifically given in a particular culture context. Culture consciousness designates that part of the total mental capacity which is actualized or realized by or 'in' a particular culture. Universal forms of thought occur not only in terms of categories of thought, but also as intersecting structures of categories. In either case, the universal refers to the ability and potential of the mind to abstract, conceptualize and categorize in terms of various combinations of thought which are not determined by the content of thought. Most important is the assumption that this universal set of thought is a mental process characteristic of and shared equally by all human cultures.

The quest for universals requires an analytic distinction between innate and experiential universals. Innate universals are probably genetically programmed and they may include certain specific categories such as features of shape (flat, round, long, etc.). Such universals are roughly equivalent to Chomskian universals or categories of thought/structural categories in the Lévi-Straussian sense. Experiential universals are those of experience, but more important they are 'inductive' and 'empirical'. When Freud or Turner (1967: 88) state that red symbolizes blood they are claiming that this is a universal inductive generalization from a universal human experience.

From this range of possible forms, each particular society takes a segment as 'its' culture (cf. Lévi-Strauss 1963). What sets off one culture from another, and what each culture emphasizes, either consciously or unconsciously, is a set of realized categories or structures. Culture is composed of those categories, actual and conscious, which provide lifestyles and meaning to a particular society. It should be noted that the contrast between actualized categories and unconscious categories has some connections with the Boasian and Lévi-Straussian distinction between surface structures and underlying structures. Where I would differ from the latter contrast is that actualized categories need not be completely at the level of the unconscious. They come into play when consciousness is expanded and when different (and possibly new) categories and groupings emerge to explain the growth of consciousness. From actualized categories only a portion ever fall into the realm of consciousness to the participants. Categories, abstractions and conceptualizations as well as certain processes which are not verbalized or cannot be linguistically labeled will be unconscious, but this does not mean that such mental processes are absent. In fact, the creativity of the mind is precisely in those areas of thought and ideas which are not readily transmittable through verbal discourse. This point is critical since I am assuming that more ideas and thought exist than words or linguistic forms to express these ideas. The assumption is basically similar to what the philosopher Michael Polanyi (1966) designates as tacit knowledge. Thus the existence of metaphor and rhetoric and their differential utilization in various cultures brings forth the unique human ability to create and transmit ideas through the manipulation of language.

Although some aspects of a culture are unconscious to its members, much of culture is conscious and is manifest through behavior and verbalized rules and patterns to explain what the behavior means and why it exists. The expression of rules pertaining to marriage, ritualized behavior, myth and cosmology are conscious to individual participants. In reality each individual is aware of his cultural context; thus what is needed is the determination of how consciousness can be evoked for other areas of thought which are both/either subconscious and/or unconscious.

Universal sets of categorization and structures of thought are contrasted to particular manifestations which occurs as "a culture." The two are quite different due to a number of distortions which occur through the process of history and change. Structures change over time, and history is the critical link between the universal and 'a' culture. Diachronic processes gradually modify and channel what is universal, and in many cases the overt expression of cultural forms cannot be related to antecedent conditions. We should not assume that history and change have destroyed the existence of the universal, since the universal as a concept might not appear in every case or its appearance may be modified. Culture rests in both actual and conscious categories, and it is at this level where history manipulates and, at times, mutilates structure.

The distinction between implicit categories of culture and the conscious categories of a culture is also distorted by anthropological inquiry. Normally anthropologists assume that what people are conscious of is isomorphic with the totality of potential knowledge. Not only does the anthropological inquiry collapse consciousness of actual and potential categories into a single level of analysis, but it also compounds the problem when the anthropologist imposes his consciousness or his models on the culture. This type of activity violates the nature of the phenomena and it also displaces our inquiry further from the realm of their knowledge. Imposition of etic consciousness on the consciousness of the people results in conclusions and theory which are doubly removed from what culture encompasses or from the total potential which the mind is capable of comprehending. It is imperative that for analytical and theoretical purposes we must not fail to distinguish between each form of consciousness, thus consciousness only deals with a fragment of cultural systems, and furthermore recognizes a portion of the total potential. Thus we can never assume that what people say or do represents the totality of what they know.

The mind can devise and create all sorts of categories and relationships: it can abstract in infinite ways, yet language expresses a small segment of this vast assortment of thought, only some of which is "logical" as Western science and humanities know it. An illustration of this variation is found in a work on numeral classification systems among certain languages in south-east Asia and other Austronesian languages (Adams and Conklin 1973). In the analysis of numeral classifiers, most parameters of classification are based on animateness, shape and function. In the distinction between human/non-human there is more than one class for humans. Humans are grouped according to social rank or according to kinship but not both. In some languages such as Vietnamese, age is the primary distinction, occupation is secondary while sex is tertiary; thus, a woman is classified by the occupation she holds and not by gender. In most languages, humans are not categorized on the basis of gender alone. The criterion of gender appears in all of the kinship-based classifier systems, but only as a secondary differentiation among members of a specific generation. Gender often occurs in status-based systems but again only as a secondary or tertiary categorization. However, the mind may classify by gender alone and the fact that certain Malayo-Polynesian languages do not verbalize it should not be accepted as an indicator that the mental ability to categorize by gender is absent.

What appears of interest in numeral classifications is the almost total dependence on the visual feature of form. There are few metaphors based on sound, feel, taste or smell. Underlying this particular linguistic function is the sense of sight while the sense of smell is ignored. Regardless of the yield which eyes or smell present, the mind's ability to classify in many ways, most of which are not linguistic, is vast and in all probability infinite. Thus returning to my original assumption, the ability of the mind for abstraction, conceptualization and categorization is greater than language as well as being prior to the evolution of language. But more important is the ability of the mind to be more inclusive for thought while only a fragment of its potential emerges on the behavioral and linguistic level of discourse.

The second critical issue relates to the problem of methodology. In the analysis of culture, fieldworkers are primarily concerned with the relationship of their conceptual models to those known and accepted for the groups one is studying. Thus in East Africa one expects to find lineages, age grades, and segmentary societies, since previous accounts note their existence, while in insular Southeast

Asia cognatic societies are prevalent and from this knowledge the fieldworker can generate specific ethnographic models which fit a broader picture. Fieldwork in a particular culture usually reifies one's conceptual scheme, and it may add more "credence" to the existing knowledge of a particular cultural area or cultural type. This form of standard anthropological investigation is adequate, but such inquiry *does not evoke consciousness* among cultural participants.

Seeking jural rules provides one mode of access to ethnographic order, but it does this at the expense of real insight into the structures underlying emic interpretations and behavior. Of more importance and interest is to take rules as the starting point and determine how far rules and order can be manipulated in different ways and varying directions, yet maintain meaning to cultural participants. The linguist starts from order in grammar and gradually re-alters order and meaning in different ways with the objective of determining if different utterances still maintain meaning to consultants. What commonly results is that a person can relate to this variation and manipulation of order in that it transmits meaning though the particular utterance is far from 'correct'. The tolerance for understanding speech is truly vast; however, a point is eventually reached when a consultant states that an utterance is nonsense; it is simply wrong and he or she does not recognize what is transmitted. At this point it could be said that the consultant's acceptance of expressive possibility has reached its limit, and the meaning for consciousness of a particular form is absent.

In cultural translation, anthropologists should redirect research to an understanding of how consciousness on the implicit cultural level may be evoked. By starting from cultural categories and conscious codes, we can determine how informants recognize patterns or rules, and by conscious manipulation of rules we might detect how informants relate to variations and modifications without complete loss of meaning. Traditional anthropological translations have simply not recognized the problem of how consciousness may be evoked. Such attempts in cultural translation would focus on how qualitatively different cultural forms are translatable into other cultural systems which on the overt level possess no common similarities. It is in the realm of evoking consciousness that mental processes can be detected, that how these processes are connected to other activities can be observed, and that the extent to which one's conscious abilities permit comprehension of other cultural forms can be determined. Traditional social inquiry has focused on the opposite direction. Rules are regarded as paramount, but once we accept this we are in a dilemma of dealing with cultural differences on the one hand and structural similarities on the other hand. However, the structures that result from these inquiries are the result of our own anthropological etic. Translation of culture through the evoking of consciousness in consultants minimizes the influence of these etic interpretations, since the final product of the translation is a mental exercise in the minds of cultural participants, and not solely within the terms of the anthropological etic (Yengoyan 1978, 1979). In this scenario, the consultant participates actively in producing the cultural translation.

The distinction between different spheres of knowledge, either as conscious categories or as the potential of thought, is critical in developing the relationship between the universal and the particular. The universal is a concept and the particular manifestation of the universal might be absent in certain cases of cultural analysis. This involves the issue of embeddedness in which the presence of a feature is subsumed under another category or set of features. Initially, the distinction has been discussed by Kenneth Hale (1975) who brilliantly demonstrates that counting is a universal, but that among the Walbiri it does not exist as part of the cultural context. However, with the introduction of money along with the English counting system, the whole idea of counting was mastered with virtually no problem. The kinds of gaps which exist in particular languages or grammars may also provide parallel gaps in "Cultures." It is illusory to argue that gaps in particular cultural systems are a denial of the universal. In the case of potential categories as a universal set of concepts or forms, the particular conscious manifestation takes numerous forms; in some cases it is absent while in other cultures certain universal features are distorted or are embedded in other forms, thus masking their appearance. The problem of embeddedness of one form or concept in another is critical and widespread, and anthropologists and linguists must devise means for analyzing how this process operates. Linguists are aware of embeddedness and its implications in understanding universals, however, anthropologists have assumed the position that, if a cultural form is not apparent, it is nonexistent, as opposed to assuming that the universal exists as a concept and attempting to realize how the process of embeddedness operates in masking and altering appearances.

Discussion

As previously noted, the art and act of translation is never neutral. In tracing the processes regarding neutrality in translation, it also appears that in some cases, the first or earliest translations might be closer to "neutrality" as opposed to succeeding translations of the same language. A case in support of this is found in the work of the German Lutheran missionary, Carl Strehlow who lived among the Aranda of Central Australia from about 1894 to 1922. During this period, Strehlow translated various parts of the Bible into Aranda, a language which has a highly complex set of tenses (and/or aspect) which are used in remarkable ways in regard to the matters of sacredness as opposed to mundane activities, as well as how matters of time link the most ancient past to the near past to the recent past and to the present. In attempting to capture the nuances of how time and sacredness co-vary, Strehlow realized that the use of the past tense in German distorted how Aranda myths based in the most distant past were propelled into the present (and possibly the most distant future). In Aranda, this movement through time without finalization is done through the use of the imperfective, which is the nearest equivalent in German (and English) to what is found in Aranda.

But the imperfective is relatively "awkward," especially in English. Strehlow, understanding that Aranda was to be the standard from which other translations flowed, correctly realized that the problem was not in Aranda, but in the limitations of German. Since his work, translations of these biblical texts have been done in English in which the translators have gradually moved away from the imperfective to the past tense, which is problematic and in most cases has hardly any reflex in Aranda.

This small case is instructive on a number of grounds. First, I am arguing that the study of languages became more and more "scientific" as linguistics emerged as an empirical and theoretical endeavour so that the study of language was undertaken in order to verify or dispute certain facets of theoretical linguistics. Thus, it appears that early translations by individuals who were not professional linguists probably were a closer approximation of these languages and also how a translation could be done without a gross violation of the language under observation. Again, Strehlow, who possessed a fine knowledge of Aranda without having the baggage of an intellectual discipline on his shoulders, could capture the nuances of how biblical texts could be translated into Aranda and how Aranda texts on myth could be brought into German. Yet, there is always loss in translation, but surely the loss in his case is far less than what happens when the subject matter of disciplines becomes oversystemized and -formalized. The Strehlow case is hardly unique. In the analysis of Burmese, the grammar and dictionary by Adoniram Judson, written in the early 1850s, is still considered one of the best grammars on Burmese. Again, one finds Burmese flowing in and through his analysis which in turn is almost vacuous of what the science of language had to offer at that time.

Second, if neutrality is a vague ideal which might be approximated, the problem is compounded by what Asad (1993: 189) calls "unequal languages." Languages of some equality, meaning some semblance of economic and political uniformity and dominance – such as English and French in which translation and critique evolve as a dialectic expression – have the virtue of rendering access and creativity in each language as a positive critique of itself and the other. Yet, even among "equal" languages such as English and French, the current global cultural wars between Anglophone and Francophone worlds of influence and domination is approaching a state of semi-inequality. Asad (1993: 189) warns us that a critique must be based on a good translation, assuming that a good translation is in part based on two languages which are more or less equal according to the strictures of power, although even in such a case one might not find this possible. Again, returning to Ortega y Gasset (1937, reprinted in Schulte et al. 1992), even translations from Spanish to French and from French to Spanish are chaotic in terms of what is lost let alone misunderstood.

The impact of loss in translation is even greater in languages which are not only distant, but also characterized by a marked and radical differentiation in inequality; namely the power relationships of the dominant socio-political context is such that the languages of the third- or fourth-world speakers receive no voice. The problem of power differences is the basis of linguistic imperialism as expressed in our attempts at translation. Asad (1993) explores the various facets in which the translation process becomes a forcible transformation, yielding a situation in which the language of the colonized is framed and re-framed into the language of the colonizer.

This expression of inequality was noted by Walter Benjamin (1969 [1923]) in his reference to and citation of Pannwitz:

> Our translations, even the best ones, proceed from a wrong premise. They want to turn Hindi, Greek, English into German instead of turning German into Hindi, Greek, English. Our translators have a far greater reverence for the usage of their own language than for the spirit of the foreign works.
>
> . . . The basic error of the translator is that he preserves the state in which his own language happens to be instead of allowing his language to be powerfully affected by the foreign tongue. Particularly when translating from a language very remote from his own he must go back to the primal elements of language itself and penetrate to the point where work, image, and tone converge. He must expand and deepen his language by means of the foreign language. It is not generally realized to what extent this is possible, to what extent any language can be transformed, how language differs from language almost the way dialect differs from dialect; however, this last is true only if one takes language seriously enough, not if one takes it lightly.

The contemporary far-reaching effects of globalization and the transnational movements of a global culture have a lineal connection to what Benjamin might have predicted. If anthropologists like Asad and myself and linguists like Becker lament how the language and power of the colonizer have formed relations of inequality which are irreversible, it goes without saying that current concerns about language extinction and cultural genocide are the parts of a process which started and unfolded in the nineteenth century. In part this process was not only a matter of world imperialism; it is also connected to the intellectual hegemony of Western academia as it spread globally. Professionalization combined with desires to create uniformity in method and theory throughout the social sciences always work against the idea of difference.

Perspectives

The essential challenge for anthropology lies in the process of translation – both linguistic and cultural translation. Works by Wittgenstein and Lyotard address the implications and complexities involved in this process. By stressing the importance of difference as an intellectual concern and as a political agenda, both Wittgenstein and more so Lyotard keenly understood the dangers of uniformity in its various expressions. For Wittgenstein, language creates the varying propositions which we use in daily expressions, and while one imagines that the nature of something has been stated, really only the frame through which we see the thing is traced in expression. Wittgenstein invokes the sentence as the final expression where difference lies whereas Lyotard moves even closer toward difference and particularism, invoking the phrase regime as the ultimate level where difference exists.

Difference as the start and the end of the translation endeavour is always there. The roots of this position return us to the Ancient Greeks captured in Heraclitus' insight that one can never step in the same river again. Contexts and events change, frames are altered and at most we again return to Wittgenstein's previously cited warning that we are perpetually tracing the frame. Does this mean that the frame and framing is the only venture which we can accomplish? Is there any possibility of entering into the whole from one frame, from one picture which only yields one image or one portrait? We can never enter the same river twice but what, if anything, can we say about the river?

Entering the frame must always be a task of translation, a task undertaken with the utmost caution. For Heidegger (*Being and Time*, 1962), the problem is aptly summarized by his concern that "What is decisive is not to get out of the circle but to come into it the right way." For anthropologists and less so for linguists, there might be no "right way" but the task is still before us, especially in dealing with distant texts and languages.

These differences in philosophical approaches again bring us back to two fundamental points of departure. One is the ongoing critical discussion in Marxist aesthetics between form and content. Introducing the contrast between form and content to the problem of translation might allow us to clarify in what directions previous attempts in translation theory have moved and to what extent we can go beyond them. Wittgenstein and Becker, both of whom are fully aware of how content is as critical as form, echo the ongoing debate between form and content. Although these developments are hardly Marxist, they direct our focus on how forms as frames are delimited and perpetually changing. At most, we can describe frames and form, but this also brings forth the issues of content and dialectics, and the possible manifestation of chaos, which results from the nuanced interrelations between form and content in any given context, be it translation, language, or even a class-driven social system.

To cast the issue in another way with more implications for anthropology is to raise again the age-old problem of accounts/descriptions which move from the inside to the outside, and those which start on the outside and move to the inside. If Heidegger saw the problem as one of moving from the external to the internal, it was Benjamin's attempts at translation which invoked the inside position, a framework which questioned the assumption that form is primary to content. For Benjamin, the words in a language were simply not signifiers, which is the classic Saussurean assumption, but an inward direction to the idea of what words mean. In a recent piece, the novelist and literary critic J. M. Coetzee (2001) clarifies this matter in Benjamin's writing by stressing that words are not simply binary trans-actions, but that they also reflect a directiveness which resonates with the Idea which is Benjamin's critical concern for language as a form of mimesis. As Coetzee (2001: 30) notes, the idea of mimesis in language is out of step with current linguistic science. But in the history of language, the Benjamin position goes back to the sixteenth- and seventeenth-century concepts that language was essentially a ternary linkage, which is quite different from binary theories of language that culminate in the nineteenth century and eventually in the works of Saussure.

But Benjamin was always leery of theorizing, since it imposed an external constraint on the very phenomena which he was attempting to interpret from the inside. Coetzee (2001) clearly demonstrates that Benjamin's atheoretical approach to the Arcades Project reveals the limitations of this perspective, stimulating negative responses from Adorno and Brecht. The parallel to the Arcades project is apparent in Benjamin's approach to translation which was also committed to an internal approach linking words and meanings towards the Idea. Apart from the inside/outside contrast, the perpetual conflict between translation of form and translation of content and how these can be combined theoretically is a continual dilemma in either a Marxist or a non-Marxist approach.

Anthropology as a cultural translation might appear peripheral to these geneal-ogies of intellectual history. Our language and meta-language regarding translation differs from other intellectual traditions, but the problems encountered by Benjamin remain our problems. Most of our translations can be characterized as develop-ments in form over content and possibly the dominance of the outside over the inside. But if anthropology, or some segments of anthropology, argue that to know and convey a culture is to know its *geist*, then that can only be understood and interpreted as a matter of content which provides the uniqueness which local cultures and languages express, create and manifest.

The challenge for translation is that it must convey simultaneously both differ-ence and similarity of meaning. Thus translations, cultural or linguistic, might be full of misery and fraught with problems which are almost insurmountable, but we must realize that translations are performed so that difference is always presented as part of our quest for understanding the variability in the human condition. Translation is an impossibility, and our attempts are *only* approximations which *only* the speakers of a language can critique. It is only the "inside" and the "content" which is the final jury on closure. And the jury is the speakers of a language, and the actors of a culture.

Acknowledgments

I wish to thank Victor Golla and Kendall House for their acute and perceptive reading of the first version of this chapter; their efforts saved me from some critical mistakes.

References

Adams, K. L. and N. F. Conklin. "Toward a Theory of Natural Classification." In *Papers from the Ninth Regional Meeting: Chicago Linguistic Society.* Corum, C. T., C. Smith-Stark, and A. Weisler (eds.), pp. 1–10. Chicago: Chicago Linguistic Society, 1973.

Asad, Talal. *Genealogies of Religion: Discipline and Reasons of Power in Christianity and Islam.* Baltimore: Johns Hopkins University Press, 1993.

Becker, A. L. *Beyond Translation: Essays Toward a Modern Philology.* Ann Arbor: University of Michigan Press, 1995.

Benjamin, Walter. *Illuminations.* New York: Schocken, 1969[1923].

Coetzee, J. M. "The Marvels of Walter Benjamin." *New York Review of Books* 48, January 11, 2001, pp. 28–33.

Hale, K. L. "Gaps in Grammars and Cultures." In *Linguistics and Anthropology: In Honor of C. F. Voegelin.* Kinkade, M. D., K. L. Hale and O. Werner (eds.), pp. 295–315. Lisse: Peter de Ridder Press, 1975.

Heidegger, Martin. *Being and Time.* New York: Harper, 1962.

Kroeber, A. L. *Configurations of Culture Growth.* Berkeley: University of California Press, 1944.

—— *Anthropology.* New York: Harcourt, Brace and World, 1948.

—— *The Nature of Culture.* Chicago: University of Chicago Press, 1952.

Lévi-Strauss, Claude. *Structural Anthropology.* New York: Basic, 1963.

Lowie, Robert. *Primitive Society.* New York: Horace Liveright Publishing Corp, 1920.

Lyotard, Jean-François. *The Differend: Phrases in Dispute.* Minneapolis: University of Minnesota Press, 1988.

—— *Postmodern Fables.* Minneapolis: University of Minnesota Press, 1997.

Ortega y Gasset, José. "The Misery and Splendor of Translation," In *Theories of Translation: An Anthology of Essays from Dryden to Derrida.* Schulte, Rainer and John Biguenet (eds.), pp. 93–112. Chicago: University of Chicago Press, 1937/1992.

—— *Man and People.* New York: W. W. Norton, 1957.

—— "The Difficulty of Reading." *Diogenes*, No. 28, Winter, 1959.

Pawley, Andrew. "Saying Things in Kalam: Reflections on Language and Translation." In *Man and a Half: Essays in Pacific Anthropology and Ethnobiology in Honor of Ralph Bulmer.* Pawley, Andrew (ed.). Auckland: The Polynesian Society. 1991.

Polanyi, Michael. *The Tacit Dimension.* New York: Doubleday, 1966.

Radin, Paul. *The Winnebago Tribe.* Washington: Bureau of American Ethnology, Smithsonian Institution, 1923.

—— *The Method and Theory of Ethnology: An Essay in Criticism.* New York: Basic, 1933. Reissued 1965.

Turner, V. W. *The Forest of Symbols: Aspects of Ndembu Ritual.* Ithaca: Cornell University Press, 1967.

Wittgenstein, Ludwig. *Philosophical Investigations.* New York: Macmillan, 3rd ed., 1958.

Yengoyan, A. A. "Culture, Consciousness, and Problems of Translation: The Kariera System in Cross-Cultural Perspective." In *Australian Aboriginal Concepts*, Hiatt, L. R. (ed.), pp. 146–155. Canberra: Australian Institute of Aboriginal Studies, 1978.

—— "Cultural Forms and a Theory of Constraints." In *The Imagination of Reality: Essays in Southeast Asian Coherence Systems.* Becker, Alton L. and Aram A. Yengoyan (eds.), pp. 325–330. New Jersey: Ablex, 1979.

–2–

Translation and Belief Ascription: Fundamental Barriers
Todd Jones

Introduction

Translation is hard. Anyone who's ever tried to converse beyond asking for directions in a language other than one's own is well aware of this. Many scholars have
written about how much is lost in the process of translating one language to
another. Venuti has even described this process as being like "terrorism," in its
ability to "reconstitute and cheapen foreign texts" (1991). In this chapter, I will
attempt to systematically explain the fundamental reasons *why* translation is such
a difficult endeavor. I will argue that the root causes of the difficulties with
translation have to do with problems intrinsic to *intentional* characterization.[1]
Ascribing beliefs to someone, I will argue, is a much more difficult epistemological
task than is commonly appreciated, and is especially difficult in the sorts of
situations that translators are in. I will also argue that, even if one were to successfully figure out what alien peoples believe at a particular time, trying to restate
those beliefs using the intentional terminology of the translator's home language
involves self-reference in a way that often inevitably distorts things. If translation
is construed as figuring out what others believe when they utter or write certain
words, then fundamental difficulties in *alien belief ascription* will create many of
the fundamental difficulties for *translation* that writers have frequently spoken
about. The latter parts of the chapter consist of a discussion of some suggestions
for how translators and belief ascribers can get around these fundamental problems.

Translation and Belief Ascription

In the academic world there are numerous theories of what translation is all about.
The view that continues to be dominant in philosophy (and cognitive science) is
one that views translation – interpreting the sentences of an alien speaker – as a
species of the problem of ascribing beliefs to an agent. The basic idea is the quite

simple one that the task of understanding the assertions someone makes in an unknown tongue centers around figuring out what the speaker believes and wants others to believe when he or she makes those utterances. Writes philosopher and cognitive scientist Stephen Stich:

> In light of the strong parallelism between the project of translating a speaker's sincere assertions and the project of interpreting or intentionally characterizing his mental sentences [his beliefs] it should come as no surprise that the principles governing and constraining translation will be mirrored by principles governing and constraining intentional interpretation. (1990: 34)

In what follows I will not argue the merits of this conceptualization of translation. What I will argue is that *if* this is explicitly or implicitly the theory of translation that one is working with (and I believe it often is), then the difficulties inherent in both *figuring out* what people believe and in *saying* what they believe are going to cause many of the fundamental difficulties in translation that so many commentators have noted.

Epistemological Barriers in Uncovering Beliefs

Let me begin by saying why the task of uncovering beliefs is often an inherently difficult one. (I will discuss why the task of uncovering *alien* beliefs during translation is *especially* difficult in due course.) In discussing belief ascription, one needs to start by recognizing that the task of describing unobservable states of mind in others is just one instance of the very common and general problem of trying to uncover information about entities we can't directly observe. For some time, there have been several methods for justifying claims about the unobservable. One of the main ways is to try to *infer* what an unseen entity must be like by deriving information about it from our current theories of what the world is like under certain conditions, and using knowledge of those conditions. There are two general methods of gathering evidence and using theories to make this sort of inference. One method might be termed "the environmental strategy." Here one starts by observing external conditions that are thought to cause certain unseen states of affairs to result, according to certain general regular patterns or laws. In the case of belief ascription, the environmental strategy begins with the idea that certain beliefs *result from* exposure to certain perceptual/environmental situations. Showing that a person was exposed to a certain natural or social environment is taken as evidence of his or her having the typical resulting belief. (So, someone using the environmental strategy will view the presence of an attacking dog as evidence that the person being attacked *believes* him- or herself to be under attack by a dog.) The other method, which might be termed "the behavioral strategy," starts with the assumption that only certain sorts of things can *cause* certain resulting actions, according to our theories. So when those resulting behaviors are observed, that's taken to be good evidence that those purported hidden causes are in fact there. In the cases we are discussing, observing certain resulting behaviors (including verbal utterances) is taken to be evidence that certain internal beliefs must be there, causing such behaviors to occur. (So, seeing a man run, while continuing to look behind him with a frightened expression on his face, is taken as evidence that the man believes something is chasing him.) Whether they ever explicitly discuss it or not, people-watchers of various stripes, like most scholars examining unseen entities, use a combination of environmental and behavioral strategies, along with various sorts of theories about the given domain, to help come to the conclusions that they do.

Behavioral Strategies: The Problem of Alternative Hypotheses

Ascribing beliefs based on behavioral evidence begins with the idea that having certain beliefs tends to *cause* certain behaviors. In our everyday lives, because we think that choosing vanilla over chocolate is caused by believing that vanilla is tastier, we would typically infer that a friend believes that vanilla ice cream is tastier than chocolate when he or she chooses vanilla at the ice-cream stand. One of the main ways in which a person learning to translate an unfamiliar tongue proceeds is to assume that certain verbal outbursts and certain accompanying behavior would only be produced if certain sets of beliefs and desires were in place. Thus, an anthropologist might reasonably assume that a Nepali shouting "jhar suru garchu," looking upward and scrambling for shelter or a makeshift umbrella believed that it was about to rain. This inferred-from-behavior belief ascription is the basis for the initial hypothesis that "jhar suru garchu" should be translated as something like "rain's coming."

It is a point of elementary logic, however, that merely showing that one can confirm a prediction entailed by a hypothesis isn't enough to show that hypothesis is true. If there are plenty of viable alternative hypotheses that could generate the observed prediction, then observing that prediction doesn't give you *any* evidence that the hypothesis in question, rather than its equally well-predicting rivals, is true. If different beliefs and desires could have led to the same behavior, then observing that behavior provides no evidence for the existence of any particular beliefs or desires.

One of the root difficulties of belief ascription is that, unlike the sparse fund-amental building blocks of some other sciences, there exists not merely a few dozen or even a few thousand different possible beliefs and desires – but an infinite number of them. We must begin, then, by selecting from an unlimited number of potential belief posits. The beliefs we can reasonably ascribe using a behavioral strategy are, of course, only those that could possibly cause the behavior we observe. This, however, is a fairly weak restriction. We can think of beliefs as something like maps used for getting around the world. A central problem is that many different sorts of maps could usefully lead you to the same destination. Any given behavior is, thus, consistent with positing numerous different core beliefs and desires. When the Trobrianders initially pointed to an outrigger canoe, for example, and said "Kewo'u," Malinowski (1922) initially had no firm way of telling whether they were thinking "there's a boat," "there's a group of undetached boat parts," or "there's a stage in a boat's existence."[2]

The fact that an inordinate number of different sets of beliefs and desires can all generate the same behavior is the central reason for the precariousness of belief ascription using the behavioral strategy alone. Margaret Mead (1928) once attributed to a particular Samoan chief the belief that his beautiful lover Manita was far too haughty and aggressive to be a proper wife. She thought that this belief accounted for his lack of betrothal to Manita and his traveling to other villages to pursue other women. This chief's desire for a less proud and arrogant wife than Manita might indeed have led him to other villages. It is also possible, however, that he sought women in other villages:

1. Because he believed Manita had become attracted to another man and he wanted revenge.
2. Because he had become attracted to a woman in the next village.
3. Because he desired stronger ties with friends and relatives in the next village.
4. Because he desired children and believed Manita couldn't have any.
5. Because he believed Manita would show more interest in marrying *him,* if he showed he could not be taken for granted.
6. Because he believed that he was not really good enough for Manita.
7. Because he believed that the women in the next village would find him more exotic and interesting than Manita would . . . etc.

Finding that the chief actually ended up taking a more docile lover in the next village would confirm *each* of these other hypotheses just as much as it confirms Mead's "left in search of a more docile wife" ascription. The number of different belief and desire sets that can be alternatively responsible for the same behaviors, then, makes strategies of inferring beliefs on the basis of such observations inherently risky. Not knowing which of a number of different possible beliefs underlies the production of certain gestures and verbal utterances makes translation risky as well.

While those engaged in qualitative research seldom explicitly acknowledge the problems discussed above, most researchers are keenly aware that claims they make about people's internal states are more problematic than claims they make about directly observable behavior. Many techniques, then, are employed by practicing ethnographers who use behavioral strategies in their work, in hopes of increasing the likelihood that the beliefs they ascribe are more than idle speculation. One can, for example, take on many different roles and observe people in numerous different settings in order to see behavior in a wide realm of situations (Agar 1980, Carpenter et al. 1980, Cahill 1987). What most of such methods boil down to, however, is an attempt to enhance behavioral strategies by increasing the number of behavioral observations made. Increasing the amount of observed behaviors of various sorts is certainly something to be applauded and, no doubt, greatly increases the accuracy of our belief ascriptions by enabling us to eliminate conjectures that are inconsistent with these further observations. It must be noted, however, that such attempts do not enable one to get around the fundamental epistemological limitations of the behavioral strategy. Whether one is talking about one observed behavior or ten, and despite the variety of behaviors observed, the same problems of plausible alternatives will still be present.[3]

Environmental Strategies

The basic idea behind environmental strategies is that exposure to certain natural and social environments tends to *cause* people to form certain beliefs. When we use such strategies, we use the information that people have been exposed to certain environments to infer that they now hold certain beliefs. A translator is similarly aided in his ascription of the belief that rain is coming to the native who utters, "jhar suru garchu," and his consequent translation of this as "rain's coming" by seeing that the native is looking at storm clouds.

But it is easy to see how environmental strategies can be bedeviled by problems of knowing about the presence and absence of surrounding beliefs. Just as determining which beliefs cause a behavior depends on making assumptions about which other auxiliary beliefs are present, helping to cause the behavior, it is the case that which beliefs will *be formed* in a given environment also depends on which *other* beliefs someone holds at the time. During his study of police patrols, for example, Pepinsky (1980) claimed that the officers he was working with once singled out a car to pull over because they believed that the driver was an American Indian. Pepinsky was certainly in a position to see what the officers saw, and they may well have had this belief. But the officers could form this belief only if they also knew what an American Indian was and which features were Indian rather than Chicano or Chinese. They would only come to such a belief if they *didn't* also have the belief that other locals were fond of dressing up as Indians or if they were too nearsighted to take in ethnic identities at a glance.

To be able to ascribe a belief to a person on the basis of his environment, we need to know what other surrounding auxiliary beliefs are also present. To know what these other beliefs are, we must assume the presence of still other particular auxiliary beliefs that help to form the auxiliaries in question. The worry is that one can either regress infinitely, proposing auxiliaries without any real evidential support, or one can circularly recruit some of the original proposed beliefs that these other auxiliaries were themselves supposed to help justify. With such assumptions about which auxiliary beliefs are present lacking firm support, our inferences about what beliefs must result from environmental circumstances will correspondingly lack firm support. Trying to translate alien *speech* by looking to the surrounding environment to enable you to discover which beliefs lie behind the verbal utterances has the same problems.

The "Makeshift" Solution – Using One's Self

Ascribing beliefs to others on the basis of their behavior or environmental exposure is fraught with fundamental epistemological difficulties. These difficulties are especially notable when we are dealing with alien cultures; but all the same problems exist for ascribing beliefs within a culture. At the same time, however, belief ascription is one of our most ubiquitous human activities. When we walk down a city street on a busy afternoon, we typically ascribe dozens of beliefs and desires to the people around us. Surely we must be successful in our endeavors a good deal of the time, or we would never be able to coordinate our activities with others. How are we able to have so much success in navigating the social world, given the fundamental limits we've been discussing? And if there are steps we take in our everyday lives to achieve this success, surely translators could also use such methods to make successful ascriptions to their subjects.

There is a "makeshift" solution that people-watchers can use to try to overcome the problems described above. If we start out knowing that a certain set of beliefs and desires must be there, then there is a much smaller possibility space of what other beliefs must be present to produce some set of behaviors, or as the result of certain environmental conditions. We need, in other words, to start out assuming that a "bridgehead" of beliefs is there, which prevents us from positing various and sundry logically possible belief-desire combinations (see Hollis 1982). If we can safely assume the existence of this bridgehead of neighboring beliefs, then we know some of the particular conditions existing which interact with general patterns of belief formation and behavior production, and we can begin to infer what the unknown beliefs in question must be. In our everyday lives there do seem to be some ways of getting an initial bridgehead of beliefs whose existence we can be confident about, providing a "makeshift" solution to the problems described above.

The behavioral and environmental strategy are ways of trying to infer the existence of unobservable factors using some (at least rough) *theories* of belief formation and behavioral production and lots of observations. (Our lack of knowledge about the *particular conditions* – other beliefs – that we need to conjoin with these theories, to tell us what primary beliefs are there, gets us into trouble.) But an additional way that scientists and lay people alike typically try to understand the nature of unobserved factors, besides knowing theories and conditions, is through the use of *analogy*. We may not be able to see inside other people's heads – but we actually can see inside the heads of people who seem to be very much like them: ourselves. If we can assume that others, both inside and outside our culture, think a lot like we do, then even without knowing much about perceptual mechanisms or about others' surrounding beliefs, we know what they are likely to believe and desire in particular circumstances. They believe the same things *we* would be believing in those circumstances. What they are trying to communicate when they speak is likely to be the same things we believe and would try to communicate.

We could infer what others' beliefs and desires are like by using analogy in several ways. One proposal found in the belief-ascription literature is that we attribute beliefs by performing a kind of *simulation*. Ascribing beliefs in this way requires very little prior *knowledge* about how people's minds work, or about the various primary and surrounding beliefs and desires they hold. All one has to do to see what they believe is to physically put oneself in their position – or imagine oneself in the other's position – and then check to see what beliefs and desires pop into one's own mind. If others' minds indeed work like ours do, and the simulation is a realistic one, this provides a pretty good indication that these thoughts are what appear in their minds in such situations (see Gordon 1986, Goldman 1989, Davies and Stone 1995).

Other philosophers and psychologists have proposed that in ascribing beliefs to others we do make use of vague *theories* about how minds work, and about the types of beliefs and desires people tend to have. When using such theories to ascribe beliefs to others, however, instead of using our observations of others to try to justify the positing of auxiliary beliefs one by one, we tend to make a blanket default assumption that the relevant surrounding interacting beliefs held by others in a given situation are similar to those that we have – unless there are specific reasons to believe otherwise. Which beliefs others will form on the basis of certain environmental exposure and certain previously held beliefs, then, are generally assumed to be the same ones that we would form in these circumstances (see Stich and Nichols 1997).

Whatever the details of how we go about actually ascribing beliefs to others, it is clear that if others really are like us, we can use ourselves as models both of what prior beliefs exist and which beliefs get formed in certain circumstances. We do not need to establish all of these with the intensive unending empirical investigations required by the behavioral and environmental strategies. It is likely that one of the main reasons we are as successful as we are at belief ascription is that we do use ourselves as models, and that others are often indeed a lot like us.

Problems for Using the "Makeshift" Solution in Exotic Translation Cases

A central problem for the kind of belief ascription a translator needs to do, however, is that often the people whose language we want to translate hold beliefs that are quite different from our own. We can't assume we can uncover the beliefs of exotic people just by imagining what we would believe were we in their shoes. None of Captain Cook's men, for example, were in any position to know by introspection that the Hawaiian natives saw their ship as carrying a forest, or that Captain Cook was believed to be the god Lono. Similarly, an anthropologist could not tell how Western airplanes were perceived by Melanesian "cargo cultists" just by looking up at the planes and introspecting. In exotic cases, a vast knowledge of the native belief system is often needed to know what natives believe, even in what seems like very straightforward perceptual situations. Self-knowledge and simulation are not enough.

People interested in ascribing beliefs to exotic peoples and translating their utterances can also be thrown off the track by a lack of familiarity with the local conventions about when it is permissible to make assertions using non-literal metaphorical language. In everyday English, for example, it is quite permissible for us to talk using words that seem to imply we believe that luck is a person determining the outcome of games of chance (Keesing 1985) or that we make decisions with our stomachs (see also Lakoff and Johnson 1980). Our familiarity with this convention means that none of our compatriots takes this verbal behavior to signal an underlying belief that chance or decision-making works this way. A worry for translators, however, is that less familiarity with the linguistic conventions and the surrounding beliefs gives them more difficulty with inferring what the underlying beliefs really are when they hear such possibly metaphorical phrases. "We have no reason to assume either that other peoples' schemes of conventional metaphor are more deeply expressive of cosmological schemes than our own or that their 'cultural models' are more uniform than ours," writes anthropologist Roger Keesing. "The danger of our constructing nonexistent metaphysical schemes that seem to be implied by conventional metaphors but would be meaningless or absurd to native speakers if they could read what we write about them raises ethnographic nightmares for me." Such nightmarish inaccurate attributions do not seem to be uncommon. The linguist Heine for example restudied the Ik, a tribe now well known to the world through the ethnographic writings of Colin Turnbull. Heine writes,

We are told . . . that there is *gor*, the soul, which "flies past the moon that is good and the sun that is bad, and on to the stars where the abang have their eternal existence" (Turnbull 1974: 161). We are further informed that "A soul is round and red but it has no arms or legs. It rests somewhere in the vicinity of the stomach . . ." (Turnbull 1974: 161). This is hardly surprising since *gor* (more precisely *gur*) is the Ik word for heart which is occasionally used to mean "spirit," "soul." That gor is able to fly to the stars where the abang live is, however, a strange idea to the Ik. The word abang means "my father" and in no way refers to "ancestors" or "ancestral spirits," as Turnbull (1974: 153, 167) claims. (Heine 1985).

Self-introspection, while making it easier to ascribe beliefs in one's own culture, then, is often far less helpful for uncovering beliefs in alien cultures. The exacerbation of the belief-ascription problems stemming from the unfamiliarity of other cultures can certainly be lessened the more experience one has with the exotic culture. More observation, and more participation in the exotic culture, will certainly enhance knowledge of linguistic-behavior conventions and perhaps allow one to "think more like a native" oneself. But no matter how fully nativized an ethnographer may become through participant observation, he or she is likely to always make errors due to interference from old ingrained western ideas about the significance of some external item, or the likely source of behavior. And even if the ethnographer somehow manages to become *completely* nativized, and thinks and talks just like the natives do, he or she has only elevated him- or herself to the same unsure ground that people are on in ascribing beliefs to people in one's own culture.

Problems in Communicating Exotic Beliefs

Difficult as it is to correctly ascribe beliefs to exotic peoples, a potential translator's troubles would not be over, even if he or she could somehow overcome these problems. Once the beliefs underlying a speaker's utterances have been understood, a translator also has the task of *communicating* what these speech-generating beliefs are. This task of trying to communicate by giving intentional characterizations of the native beliefs also leads to fundamental problems. On the communication end, the problems are less epistemological than metaphysical. Most contemporary philosophers assume a "functional role" theory of what gives a belief (at least part of) its content. What makes a particular mental state the belief that p, is the way in which that belief interacts with the rest of a person's beliefs and with perception and behavior. Stephen Stich argues that a consequence of this view is that when the surrounding network of beliefs that a mental state interacts with is very different from that of the mental state we typically call "the belief that p," then, because these relationships define the belief, such a belief *does not count* as the belief that p. Similarly, if what makes some mental state the belief that p is partly a function of *how* a belief interacts with other beliefs in the process of inference, then a belief existing in a cognitive economy that produced very different *inferences* than our beliefs would should also be unable to be characterized as "the belief that p." The central problem for describing the beliefs of exotic people is that if they have beliefs surrounded by networks of other beliefs that are very different from ours, or if their beliefs dynamically interact with each other in ways different than our beliefs do, then these differences make alien mental states, essentially, different sorts of belief states than ones we'd characterize with the English phrase "the belief that p." Indeed, no English characterization will suffice, for any English charact-erization implicitly claims that the belief characterized this way is linked to a particular set of other beliefs in the ways that these beliefs are typically linked in our culture – linkages that may well not be there in the alien culture.

Consider the case of someone whose beliefs in a given realm interact with each other differently and cause different inferences than the mental states we usually term "the belief that p" and "the belief that q" do in our culture. Stich argues that if a person's beliefs interact with each other and with external stimuli in ways different from the ways our beliefs interact with each other, we cannot clearly say what those beliefs are. If we want to have an intentional characterization of a subject's mental states, writes Stich,

> . . . we must be able to identify certain of his beliefs as conditionals and others as disjunctions; we must be able to say that certain of his beliefs are (or are not) about elephants; we must be able to determine whether eating chocolate ice cream is the object of one of his desires. None of this is possible, however, unless the subject's beliefs and desires, and the pattern of causal interactions with each other and with stimuli are reasonably similar to our own . . . If a subject's mental state does not interact with other mental states in a pattern which approximates the pattern exhibited by our own con-ditional beliefs, *it does not count as a conditional belief.* Similarly, if a subject's mental state is not caused by stimuli similar to the ones which lead me to believe there is an elephant in front of me, and if it does not interact with other mental states in a way similar to the way mine would, then *it does not count as a belief that there is an elephant in front of him.* (1990: 47)

Our intuitions that the contents of a truly alien belief state cannot be character-ized by an English sentence are particularly strong when we consider other types of case in which the network of beliefs that a particular mental state interacts with (what Stich calls the doxastic surround) is different from the network of beliefs surrounding our mental states. Stich asks us to consider the case of John who is told he has latent homosexual tendencies and who accepts this diagnosis. When we ask about John's beliefs about sexuality, however, we find that they are quite bizarre, for he claims that the quite normally endowed male and female couple, John and Mary are homosexuals, asserting:

What sex a person is is not a function of anatomy. Maleness and femaleness are basic irreducible properties of people. These properties are often correlated with anatomical differences, but sometimes they are not . . . I know John and Mary quite well and I am convinced that, despite their anatomy, they are both female. Of course, homosexual acts never result in pregnancy, so no children will result from their sexual relations.

What is it that John believes when he says "I have latent homosexual tendencies?" Writes Stich,

when the question is raised without some specific context in mind, there is simply no saying. The doxastic surround of [his] belief – his theory of sexuality – is sufficiently different from the doxastic surround of the belief that we might express with the same sentence, that it is just not clear whether or not his belief counts as the belief that he has latent homosexual tendencies. Nor is there any other content sentence available in our language which folk intuition would clearly find appropriate in this case. (1983: 138–9)

If Stich's claims about these cases are correct, there is clearly a problem for anthropologists and other translators when they try to make claims about the beliefs and utterances of exotic peoples with very different beliefs or thinking patterns from ours. How are we to characterize the precise contents of the beliefs of Azande tribesmen who make statements that we translate as saying that all the Azande are related, and that every relative of a witch is also a witch, but that some but not all Azande are witches (Evans-Prichard 1937: 24)? What do the Nuer believe when they make a claim that we try to translate as "twins are birds" (Evans-Prichard 1956)? What do the Bororo believe when they make a claim translated as "we are red Macaws" (Lévy-Bruhl 1926)? Surely, in these cases we are dealing with beliefs with a doxastic surround that is radically different from the doxastic environment of any of our beliefs. Even with a less exotic claim like "Cohen believed he was owed five times the value of the merchandise stolen from him by the robbers' tribe" (Geertz 1973: 8), we are surely dealing with ideas that have a doxastic surround that is unlike the network of assumptions surrounding our own beliefs. For the concept of "owing" and the related concept of "compensation" will be linked to beliefs in the alien culture that are different in our belief-networks. With a different doxastic surround, the mental states in question here is likely to function very differently than the mental state that we expect to be there on the basis of that English characterization. Yet if we tried to attribute a belief using any other of our content-sentences, we would still have the same problem. Any English sentences we'd use to attribute particular beliefs to them would lead our compatriots to think that the natives have mental states surrounded by the kind of belief networks that surround *our* mental states characterized by such sentences. When people use the belief labels associated with a particular doxastic surround in our culture to characterize the mental states of an alien person, they are prevented from accurately conceptualizing this native belief in terms of the doxastic surround typically assumed to be there by those in the native culture. If we don't really know how to characterize the beliefs of the person from our own culture with odd beliefs about sexuality, how can we hope to be able to say clearly what Tibetans believe about lamas having sex when they say that "all the details of the affair, including the sex act itself, are an illusion; phantom activities of a phantom body in which the true body is not involved" (Ekvall 1964: 70).

One Way of Resolving these Problems

Let us take stock. If translating the statements of exotic people involves uncovering and communicating their beliefs, we must be able to uncover and communicate their beliefs. I have argued that there are serious difficulties inherent in the ways we usually try to do both. The problems seem to stem from the same source. To understand others' beliefs, we seem to rely on a rough particularistic model/theory of what beliefs are there and how they function: they work pretty much like they do in our own cases. Translators typically try to uncover unknown beliefs by gathering information on behavior and environment, and figuring out what unknown "missing variable" beliefs must be there, using our minds as models. Translators communicate information about others' beliefs to a target audience by assuming that the members of this audience possess a certain model of which mental states do what (based on themselves), and assuming that they can describe the beliefs of others by identifying them with mental states from this familiar model. Relying on these models may work well enough when we are talking about people like ourselves whose minds really do work according to the way the model says they should. These theories/models *won't* work for uncovering or describing mental states when the states in question do *not* function like ours.

Functional Role Descriptions of Mental States

It is important to note that the problems described above should not be thought of as unique to anthropology or translation studies. There are many areas of study that are interested in uncovering and describing the mental states responsible for behavior. Many of these areas would suffer from the same problems described above if they tried to describe mental states using English-language belief-content sentences. Very few disciplines are concerned to uncover only generalizations about the mental lives of people like ourselves. Psychologists often investigate the mental lives of very young children, of psychotics, and of monkeys or rats. All of the same problems of belief ascription should surely pop up in these cases as well as among the Yanamamo. The same is true for artificial-intelligence researchers investigating how to get machines to think and understand. While the problems discussed above should manifest themselves most severely in certain types of cultural anthropology, they have the potential to cause havoc in various disciplines investigating the mind. Are there ways that such disciplines have managed to avoid these problems, ways that those interested in translation should pay attention to?

Let us look first at the issue of communicating and describing exotic mental states. It seems to me that contemporary cognitive psychology is a subdiscipline that has come to be structured in a manner that enables the kinds of problem described above to be bypassed. In much of cognitive psychology, mental states are individuated on the basis of how these states interact with surrounding mental states, with inputs and with outputs. When mental states are individuated in this manner, in terms of each state's role in a cognitive economy, one needn't rely on English language content characterizations to identify which mental states are which.

Much of contemporary cognitive psychology subscribes to what is known as the computational paradigm. The central assumption of the computational paradigm is that the mind is a kind of computer. A computer is a physical instantiation of a formal system. In a formal system there are syntactic rules specifying the ways in which some tokens can combine with other tokens to produce certain resulting "legal" token sequences. A physical computer is a machine configured in a way such that certain physical states are set up to combine with and produce other states in ways that mirror the specified relations and sequences in the abstract formal system it is instantiating. The computational paradigm assumes that the brain is one such physical machine that instantiates complex formal systems. Describing someone's thinking, in this approach, is analogous to describing the way a mechanical computer program interacts with and transforms various data structure items in response to inputs. The various "data structure items" or "tokens" that the brain computes with are neurological states. Knowing the exact physical makeup of the neurological states involved in the computation, however, is unimportant for describing how thinking works, so long as the neurological states involved interact with other neurological states in ways that mirror the syntactic rules of the formal system that the computing brain is supposed to be instantiating. In the view of philosophers like Stich, Ned Block (1980), Robert Cummins (1983), and Hartry Field (1977), the computational paradigm is committed to the view that what determines the nature of any particular mental state is the way that these states are positioned to interact with the other mental states within the cognitive system. Such states can thus be identified by the relations they have with the other states in the formal system that they instantiate.

In Stich's view, the great advantage of describing mental states using cognitive science's computational vocabulary is that this allows us to more efficiently describe peoples' thought processes by "eliminating the middleman." Stich, like

Quine (1960) believes that when we characterize a belief by giving it the label "the belief that p," we are saying that the person the belief is being attributed to is in a mental state similar to the one I would be in were I to sincerely assert p (Stich 1990: 48). What we think of as the content of a belief is determined, in part, by the way that this mental state interacts with other surrounding mental states. When we want to identify which belief we are talking about, however, we don't do it in a long-winded manner, specifying the numerous causal connections this mental state has to other states (and to input and behavior). Instead, we characterize such states in a relatively quick and dirty way by labeling them as being states that are similar to the internal states that lead *us* to sincerely assert p. Giving it this label enables us to tell what kind of state it is and what connections it has with other states in one fell swoop. It is that state that interacts with other states in the same way that the state which causes me to assert p interacts with its neighbors. While characterizing a mental state this way enables us to understand lots about its connections with other mental states quickly, this type of characterization, as we have seen, becomes very problematic when we use it to describe the thinking of people different from ourselves. The problem is that the mental states of exotic people may well not have the kind of doxastic surround that our beliefs which we label "the belief that p" have. They may also not interact with each other to produce the same inferences. Giving these alien mental states English characterizations, however, will lead people to think they do interact with surrounding states the way our beliefs do. But we can avoid giving people such misleading characterizations of alien mental states if we eliminate the "middleman move" in which we specify the connections by comparing these states to our own states and the connections they have. Instead, the computational paradigm lets us identify mental states by directly specifying these states' roles in the *native* cognitive economy (once we uncover what that is, using methods discussed below). With the computational paradigm, we can directly say things like "then Majid will go into mental state y" where y has been defined in terms of its actual doxastic surround and its role in inference producing. We can do this instead of having to say "Majid believes that p" which leads others to assume that Majid is in a mental state that really interacts with the particular surrounding belief network in the way that the hearer's "belief that p" does. With a computational description like this, Stich writes, we

> are able to characterize the cognitive state of a subject in terms appropriate to the subject rather than in terms that force a comparison between the subject and ourselves. And this eliminates the central problem of [intentional ascription], since there is no risk of generalizations being lost when subjects are so different from us that folk psychology is at a loss to describe them. (1983: 158)

A functional-role computational description, in other words, gives us a fine-grained and flexible way of describing the dynamics of other peoples' mental states, as opposed to the coarse-grained intentional descriptions, whose causal relations with other mental states are pre-specified as having the connections with the specific doxastic surrounding states of our cognitive economy.

The computational paradigm, then, is structured in a way that enables researchers to avoid the problems associated with characterizing mental states with ordinary intentional descriptions. By directly describing mental states in terms of their relations to perceptual inputs, behavioral outputs and other mental states, we can avoid using a vocabulary that forces all cognitive agents to be described as if they think like us or that is unable to describe their mental life at all.

Functional-Role Strategies in Anthropology

It seems to me that anthropologists often manage to avoid the types of intentional-ascription problem discussed by philosophers by using a strategy that is sub-stantively similar to cognitive psychology's functional-role approach. A good example of the similarity between anthropological approaches to belief ascription and the kind of functional-role approach used in cognitive psychology can be seen in Catherine Lutz's works on emotion terms used among the Ifaluk people of Micronesia.[4] Like many anthropologists, Lutz claims that Ifaluk thinking in a certain realm differs drastically from the way we think about this realm in the West and seeks to describe these differences. Numerous philosophers, however, would claim that if the Ifaluk really think quite differently from us, in that realm, there is no way we can characterize Ifaluk thinking by saying "the Ifaluk believe p." The holistic network of thoughts we assume to be there interacting with the type of mental state we label "the belief that p" will not be the network in Ifaluk minds. So what we might be tempted to term "the belief that p" among the Ifaluk isn't really the same kind of mental state as the one we call "belief that p" among ourselves at all. Nevertheless, Lutz appears to do a credible job telling us how the Ifaluk think about emotions. I believe that the way she is able to do this, despite intentional-ascription difficulties, is by avoiding "middleman" intentional ascriptions based on comparison to our own supposedly similar mental states and, instead, by character-izing Ifaluk mental states more directly through functional-role descriptions. This strategy, recall, seeks to directly identify a mental state in terms of how it interacts with perception, behavior, and other mental states. Lutz explicitly avoids using direct English translations to describe how the Ifaluk are thinking. Instead, she talks about Ifaluk thinking by beginning with the terms that the natives use for conceptualizing what is going on in a given realm. These native terms are then explicated by carefully describing the typical perceptual situations that lead to this state, the other mental states it tends to lead to, and the behaviors it tends to cause. Lutz, for example, tells us of an Ifaluk woman who doesn't want to look at the people she sees in a U.S. Navy film because of the *fago* she feels for them. She goes on to talk of fighting brothers being separated and asked why they aren't showing *fago* for each other. Drunk Ifaluk sometimes say they *fago* themselves. Ifaluk men are said to feel *fago* for their drunken compatriots. Lutz also reports on an Ifaluk man criticizing his brother's persistent drinking by saying "you do not *fago* my thoughts" (1985: 120). By giving us a series of rich contextualized examples, Lutz slowly and carefully makes clear just how the Ifaluk are concept-ualizing each others' emotions and behaviors when they speak of them using the term of *fago*. We slowly build up a sense of when Ifaluk people will and won't see someone as feeling *fago*, and how the *fago* concept interacts with other central Ifaluk ideas. When English terminology is introduced, it is not done as a translation of Ifaluk thinking but instead serves 1) to quickly get us into the general ball-park 'genus' functional role that this concept is playing, and 2) to name English-language terms that we should specifically *avoid* thinking of the Ifaluk concept (e.g. as when *fago* is described in terms of an amalgam of what we would call compassion, love, and sadness). Ifaluk thinking and terminology is instead expli-cated by describing how these ideas function in Ifaluk conceptualizations of their social worlds. Lutz discusses, for example, when an Ifaluk woman may think that another woman is *maluwelu*. A *maluwelu* person is one a Westerner might think of as calm. But calmness among the Ifaluk, Lutz tells us, is not really what we mean by "calmness" in the West. Calmness is not something that stems at all from inner confidence, but rather more from inner fearfulness. A calm *maluwelu* person is gentle, timid and shy, avoiding scaring or offending others. Indeed, the term *maluwelu* is closely related to the Ifaluk term *metagu* – which means something like afraid or anxious. However, we should not think of *metagu* as really being what we mean by fearful, Lutz tells us, for unlike our notion of timid or fearful, the *metagu* state is regarded by the Ifaluk as a highly desirable state that it is not bad to be in. The Ifaluk will regularly tell each other stories in which they freely and shamelessly admit how *metagu* they were in certain situations. Being *metagu* is seen as a state that prevents one from being offensive and boastful. What is a bad state to be in, however, is one that the Ifaluk call *ker*. A *ker* state is something like happiness or excitement. The Ifaluk do not think of this as we think of happiness, however, for they see it as invariably leading to raucous misbehavior. The notion of misbehavior, itself, however, is one that must be explicated carefully in terms of its place in the network of Ifaluk ideas and not just translated into a Western counterpart. Disobedience among children, for example, Lutz writes, "is both tolerated and even positively sanctioned if it derives from the timidity associated with being calm" (1987: 112). One must keep children in line, though, by prevent-ing them from becoming *ker*. One does this by showing them that you are *song* about their behavior. *Song*, Lutz tells us, is something like anger, but it includes an emphasis on moral condemnation directed at social taboo-breaking that is lacking in Western notions of anger.

Here, *maluwelu* and other Ifaluk notions are explicated by Lutz, in part, by showing how vast numbers of other Ifaluk notions are bound up in their use. The meaning of a term like *maluwelu* is further explicated by Lutz describing numerous types of perceptual situation in which someone would be labeled *maluwelu* or not labeled *maluwelu*. She also describes the types of behavior the Ifaluk would engage in toward someone that they thought of as *maluwelu*. Ifaluk thinking about *maluwelu* persons is described here by characterizing how it is that such thoughts interact with other thoughts (and behavior, etc.). This is just the way mental states are characterized in cognitive psychology. As in cognitive psychology, "middleman" intentional descriptions, in which a mental state is named according to its supposed similarity with one of our labeled mental states, are avoided. Lutz's anthropological approach, which directly characterizes mental states in terms of their place in a detailed holistic causal network, is essentially the functional-role strategy, avoiding the philosophical intentional-ascription problems in roughly the same manner. Her "translations" are not done by describing the ideas and mental states underlying Ifaluk utterances using English belief sentences. The ideas underlying Ifaluk utterances are thus described more accurately.

This "thick description" approach to translation, of course, has a long history in anthropology. As Rosman and Rubel point out in Chapter 11 of this volume, Malinowski himself wrote of words that can only be translated "not by giving their imaginary equivalent – a real one obviously cannot be found – but by explaining the meaning of each of them through an exact Ethnographic account of the sociology, culture, and tradition of that community " (1923: 300). (They also point out that Malinowski often did not practice what he preached). In his Chapter 3 contribution to this volume, Michael Silverstein describes how it is highly commonplace for anthropologists to deal with "untranslatable" by doing just what Lutz does – using the native term and giving long ethnographic descriptions of the context of use for this term. Benson Saler, in his Chapter 8 of this volume, imaginatively describes this process of making the native term clear where the point is not to substitute our familiar terms for native unfamiliar ones, but to teach us anew the polysemic senses of the native terms in a manner analogous to the way in which priests are expected to make sense of exotic doctrines to their flocks. I believe that this approach to translation is certainly superior to one that seeks to find English equivalents for native terms. Below, I describe another "functionalist" approach that I believe could work even better.

Making Anthropological Functional Role More Precise

In the last section I discussed the heretofore unnoticed similarities between certain approaches in anthropology and functional-role approaches in cognitive psychology.

However, one should not overlook the fact that, currently, there are numerous differences in the research foci of the two approaches as well. One of the chief differences is the level of precision sought in describing and modeling peoples' mental activities. Cognitive psychologists have long been very interested in the particular mechanisms by which certain mental states are formed and certain inferences made. In making a claim that a person will tend to go into a certain mental state in certain circumstances, cognitive psychologists usually specify fairly precise theories, often implementable as a computer program, about the kinds of mental structure that have to be in place in order to produce such inferences (see for example Anderson 1983, Wyer and Srull 1986).

By contrast, while some anthropologists are very interested in which kinds of inference and association are produced at what times as we have seen, most give little thought to the kinds of mechanism needed to enact these kinds of mental-state linkage. An anthropologist such as Geertz, for example, is interested in which ideas typically interact with what other items in the belief networks of members of a particular culture, but he shows little interest in examining the details of the kind of architecture needed to enable these mental states to interact with one another in particular ways. Such anthropologists seem content with the idea that these mental states have some sort of associative connection where some thoughts somehow "call up" other thoughts. I believe that "thick description" of this sort could be made more precise and more accurate if such anthropologists incorporated specific computational models into their functional-role descriptions of mental-state interconnections. This sort of work is already going on in what is sometimes called cognitive anthropology (see for example Hutchins 1980, Colby 1985). In my own work, I have looked at how universal cognitive constraints (as described by Anderson 1983) in the formation and retrieval of knowledge lead Tibetans, growing up in the environments they do, to recurrently recount the same religious explanations for certain types of event (Jones 1987). This provides an account for why certain ideas and actions stereotypically occur as they do in Tibetan culture.

By incorporating precise models of mental structures into their work, functional-role-oriented anthropologists would be able to greatly increase the plausibility of any claim that their subjects were likely to be in particular mental states at any given time. They would be able to make such claims, not only by using their knowledge of which particular kinds of thing have come to be mentally associated with each other in that culture, but also by using a knowledge of what general types of mentally associated item tend to be activated in a mental economy at what times. The benefits of moving in the direction of more detailed and precise models of the native thinking would not likely be all one-sided. If anthropologists find that models of native thinking, created by plugging particularistic information about native knowledge into general models of human cognition, don't work very well, they might easily suggest new models of *human cognition* that better explain the thinking of the people studied. These new proposed models could then be tested with other populations, and integrated with other new ideas about cognition. Cognitive psychology would then derive some benefits from anthropology as well.

What such a more precise functional-role-oriented anthropology would ultimately look like, of course, would depend on which models of the various proposed internal cognitive mechanisms would be used. What it would look like would depend even more heavily, however, on which of the various general formulations of cognitive functional-role theory was adopted. In my view, the most natural approach for anthropologists interested in describing the mental states of exotic people to use is one that Stich terms the "fat syntax" view of cognition.

The fat-syntax view of mental functioning, like many theories in cognitive science, holds that the defining criterion of being a particular mental state is based on the way in which that state interacts with other mental states, rather than by, say, neurological characteristics or phenomenal "feel." Unlike many cognitive theories, however, the fat-syntax view holds that no attention needs to be paid to the *semantic* evaluation of mental states. What's important in theories of cognition, on this view, is what mental states do, not what they are about. Stich describes the fat-syntax view this way:

> The basic idea . . . is that cognitive states whose interaction is (in part) responsible for behavior can be systematically mapped to abstract syntactic objects in such a way that causal interactions among cognitive states, as well as causal links with stimuli and behavioral events, can be described in terms of the syntactic properties and relations of the abstract objects to which the cognitive states are mapped. More briefly, the idea is that causal relations among cognitive states mirror formal relations among syntactic objects. If this is right, then it will be natural to view cognitive states as tokens of abstract syntactic objects. (1983: 149)

What characterizes a particular mental state, then, in this view, is not the semantic content of that state but the way it syntactically interacts with other syntactic relationally-defined states. What makes it a "fat" syntax is that the state's relations to stimuli and behavior are as essential to its characterization as its relation to other internal inference-producing states.

If functional-role-oriented anthropological approaches were to develop in more precise ways which made them more akin to functional-role theories in cognitive psychology, the fat-syntax view of cognition is the most natural approach to adopt. This claim may seem surprising. After all, Lutz's work seems to explain what tends to happen in the mental lives of her subjects by giving complex descriptions of the contents of their mental states. I believe this is illusory. On closer inspection, semantic content plays little role in explaining native thinking using anthropological functional-role approaches, even their current vague form. Indeed, I would claim that these anthropological descriptions of the mental are more easily seen as making use of a syntactic theory of the mind (albeit currently in a vague way) than are most other descriptions of mental functioning.

Because of a basis in the computational paradigm, it is clear that most functional-role theories of the mental (not just fat syntax) are largely centered around formal syntactic structuring. Indeed, even Jerry Fodor, the syntactic theory of mind's most vocal critic, once wrote that "What we're doing [in AI, linguistics, and cognitive psychology] is really a kind of logical syntax (only psychologized)" (1978: 223). The computational paradigm, recall, views the mind as a sort of computer. Computer programs are a physical instantiation of a system of formal syntactic rules specifying the ways in which some token entities can combine with other tokens in order to produce certain resulting "legal" token combinations. On most (non-connectionist) views of cognitive science, three central tasks of cognitive theories are: to describe a set of primitive symbols; to specify some formal rules stating the ways these primitives can be combined into more complex objects; and to specify state-to-state transition rules, stating which types of new resulting string sequence should be produced at which time (Fodor 1975, Stich 1983, Cummins 1983). Imagine, now, that anthropologists began using sophisticated cognitive theories to explain what their subjects are likely to be thinking at certain times. They would have to make use of ideas about the rules governing state-to-state transitions (the kinds of generalizations most cognitive psychologists spend most of their time trying to uncover). They also, however, have to be able to give some description of the particular sets of symbol strings that are causing other symbol strings to be produced in a rule-governed way. In everyday English, we refer to this sort of thing as "saying what beliefs a person has."

Now it is easy to see how someone could give a syntactic characterization of particular combinations of internal symbol strings. An anthropologist might describe how there is a mental state EFG, which Ifaluk persons commonly go into, which:

1) is often produced when children are seen laughing and chasing each other,
2) is sometime produced when drunken men are seen laughing and singing,
3) generally leads a typical Ifaluk to go into another internal state KLM, during which small sounds can startle them immensely and has numerous effects on other dispositions,
4) usually causes them to go into go another internal state, HIJ, which makes them unlikely to leave the area where the event they've been observing is happening,
5) will inferentially produce the mental state NOP, if the people observed are close to 50 years old or over (typical other causal antecedents, behavioral effects, and inferential effects for each of these other internal states can also be specified),
6) causes them to say "those people have become *ker*" when asked,
7) causes them to scold the *ker* people, if they have authority over them.

If mental states were described this way by anthropologists, you would have syntactic characterizations of such mental states. They would be described by specifying what they *do,* rather than by giving a "meaning" or "content" using a substitutable English-language phrase. While one might additionally give a description of the content of a mental state to quickly give readers a general heuristic ball-park picture of the mental states, the semantics would not really be playing any part in the explanation of the thinking and behavior of the peoples described.

While semantic-centered accounts of thinking seem to be unable to tell us how alien peoples are thinking in difficult cases, syntactic characterizations avoid these difficulties. Take a sentence that initially seems to translate as the assertion by Nuer people that "a twin is not a person *(ran),* he is a bird *(dit)*" (Evans-Prichard 1956: 129). A semantic evaluation of this sentence is problematic because there is no sentence we can imagine ourselves sincerely uttering that would have the kind of doxastic inferential links to other beliefs that our utterance of that sentence would require in our language. (Alternatively, it is problematic because it seems to be wildly untrue, when a conceptual constraint on something's counting as linguistic behavior at all is that most utterances are true (see Davidson 1984).) With a syntactic account we don't have to translate this state by giving some sort of equiv-alent sentence. We can characterize the mental state underlying the Nuer assertion by saying what kinds of input, output, and other mental state syntactically produce and are produced by this state. We can show how the state underlying the Nuer assertion is one that they enter when they say that twins are conceived in a special holy manner, making them *gaat kwoth,* (something like "children of god/spirit") – a term also used to describe the birds which freely fly through the sky/spirit realm. It is a mental state which can combine with a different state – one which we see has the function of prohibiting kin to harm other close kin – to produce an inferred mental state which underlies an assertion we translate as saying that twins should never eat birds' eggs. It is a state that, in combination with other states, leads the Nuer to place the bodies of dead twins on platforms, rather than burying them, so that their souls can depart into the air where they belong. Looking at it in terms of it's entire doxastic surround (which is far richer then merely calling it a "meta-phorical belief") we can also show that it is not a mental state which ever produces the inference that twins can fly – an inference that might be made, if we were to characterize that state merely by using the content sentence that seemed to fit it best.

Mental states that result in, or result from, non-standard inferences are also straightforwardly describable using a fat-syntax approach. We can't comfortably ascribe to the Azande the belief that all relatives of a witch are also witches, because this would contradict their claim that not all the Azande, who are all related to the witches among them, are witches. It is not clear which statements they hold true. It is not clear which content sentences are accurately ascribable to them, as no English pair of sentences corresponding to what seems to be the Azande belief pair could normally be sincerely asserted at the same time. With a syntactic theory, on the other hand, there is no problem in holding that the Azande do indeed have mental states we might roughly characterize in this way. We just have to show that there is a mental state (or mental states) that functions in the cognitive economy in a way that the belief that "not all the Azande are witches" would, while at the same time, a different mental state produces actions and inferences etc. in the way we would expect a state labeled "witches' relatives are also witches" would. The fact that such states can easily be labeled with semantic descriptions that contradict each other is no problem as long as their syntactic characterizations can account for what these people do. Moreover, there is nothing implausible about such states coexisting in a single mind, so long as there is no mechanism for detecting and eliminating what can be seen as contradictory beliefs – or if there is only a weak mechanism for doing so. Slightly more problematic is the explanation of joint perseverance of certain mental states after they have been pointed out as being contradictory in their semantic characterizations. Many cognitive psychologists, however, have carefully documented that belief perseverance in the face of various contrary evidence of this sort is a remarkably widespread phenomenon. They have proposed various mechanisms for explaining how such perseverance might work (see Nisbett and Ross 1980). As most of the mechanisms proposed are very general mechanisms that work, irrespective of what the persevering beliefs are about, there is little problem giving such mechanisms a completely syntactic characterization (see Stich 1983, chapter 6, for an example). This sort of mental functioning is consequently more easily described using syntactic rather than a semantic characterization.

If using functional-role theories is indeed the way anthropological descriptions can get around intentional-ascription worries, I suggest that, contrary to first impressions, a completely syntactic version of functional-role theory will be the most useful one to adopt. Syntactic characterizations of mental statements seem to show a great deal of promise at precisely the places content-sentence-based ascription fails most strikingly. However useful content-sentence-based or other semantic descriptions of mental states may be in some realms, syntactic descriptions do a far better job of characterizing the functioning of kinds of mental state anthropologists are interested in. Anthropologists using thick description could most easily extend and make more precise the sort of functional-role characterization they are already engaged in by formulating descriptions of specific mental mechanisms and mental states using the terminology of fat syntax. This is the best way to get at the exotic beliefs that really underlie the utterances we wish to translate.

Using Cognitive Theories in Uncovering Mental States

I've argued that using cognitive theories could allow belief ascribers and translators to describe and communicate about others' mental states more effectively than could be done by strategies which use ourselves as models. I think the same can be said about *uncovering* which beliefs or other mental states exotic people hold. If we use models centered around ourselves as our guides for uncovering belief, then observing others' behavior leads us to infer that the beliefs underlying that behavior must be the beliefs that would produce such behavior in ourselves. Such a strategy will not work to the extent that others' minds work differently than our own. We would be better at uncovering beliefs, then, by starting off with a more universalistic model of mind which specified the sorts of mental states that underlie human behavior *in general*, rather than a model that specifies the sorts of mental states that underlie *our own* behavior. We could then construct more specific models of particular minds, starting from this universal base. Instead of ascribing beliefs based on the environmental and behavioral strategies, constrained only by a rough self-based model, lots of constraints specifying what could be believed at a given time could come from constraints on the possible ways information can be *internally* organized. Presumably, all human beings are born equipped with 1) some innate belief-forming mechanisms and innate beliefs, and 2) some innate desires and desire-forming mechanisms. People also come with some innate mechanisms for putting innate beliefs and desires – and the new ones formed as a result of these mechanisms interacting with the environment – into use at particular times to create new behaviors and thoughts. The more information we have about these general-information-processing and -organizing mechanisms, the more restrictions we can put on which beliefs and desires are likely to result from the *specific* inputs people are receiving from certain environments. The more information we have on which general types of structure tend to produce certain behaviors, the more information we will have about which type of internal structure must be at work producing a particular behavior. If we know, for example, that people cannot perceive colors beyond a certain wavelength, we know they'll have no beliefs about such colors. If we know that almost all people desire to avoid sex with close kin, this is an auxiliary desire we can usually count on as being there. Models of associative memory could tell us about the relative importance of the frequency of seeing an example of a category (like dog) and its effects on the likelihood of recalling that particular example when the category is mentioned (as opposed to the effect of other factors like recency, tendency to abstract, etc.). And ethnographic research could tell us about the types of dog that natives are likely to most frequently encounter. We would then know more about what particular examples of dogs they are most likely thinking of when they seem to be speaking about dogs. Earlier I discussed how one can more adequately *describe* the mental states underling verbal and non-verbal behavior by showing how these states are the product of particular local ideas, interacting with each other in ways that are specified by general (universal) rules of mental interaction. One can similarly use ideas of what general underlying mental structures *must always be there* (often organizing more culturally idiosyncratic information) to more adequately *uncover* which resulting mental states are the ones likely to be generating behavior at a given time. By behavior, of course, I am not merely referring to large-scale physical activity. Uttering sounds is also behavior. The act of trying to translate an alien utterance, to figure out what beliefs lie behind an act of verbal behavior, will be done better by knowing something about the types of cognitive structure that guide and constrain belief-formation. These sorts of mental-state constraining model are being studied in the cognitive sciences every day, in fields ranging from neuroscience to ethology. We would be do well to monitor their findings.

Concluding Remarks

Many scholars have written about the difficulties of translation. In this chapter, I've tried to explain the root cause of these difficulties. The dominant philosophical theory of translation, and the implicit theory held by many practitioners, sees the act of translating someone's utterances or inscriptions as centering around uncovering and communicating the beliefs held by the speakers. I've argued that our usual ways of doing this – using models of ourselves to infer that certain mental states are present, and using intentional English-language characterizations to say what those are, are inherently fraught with epistemological and metaphysical difficulties. Some, like the postmodernists, have responded to these and other difficulties by nihilistically refusing to attempt to construct correct representations of the thoughts that really lie behind others' words. I believe there are better responses. I've argued that "thick description" which describes mental states in terms of their overall role in a cognitive economy, gives us a way to characterize mental states, even if a people's mental states are too different from our mental states to ascribe content sentences to them in the usual way. With thick description, successful mental-state description need not imply successful intentional ascription and similarity to ourselves. I've argued that a syntactic functional-role cognitive theory is even more able to adequately characterize mental states that are different from our own. Cognitive diversity beyond a certain point leaves us unable to label anything "the belief that p," as such a state would be so different from anything labeled the "belief that p" in our language and culture. A "fat-syntax" cognitive theory can enable us to describe mental states even if they are beyond these similarity-based limits of what's intentionally describable.

Such an approach also puts us in a better position to adequately uncover the mental states underlying verbal and non-verbal behavior. Cognitive psychology can play a role in helping specify the general architecture of human cognition and the ways in which mental states tend to interact with one another. Anthropology, along with disciplines like history, can specify how, in a given culture, a vast amount of specific information is used by this general cognitive architecture to enable people to perceive and think about the world in the ways that they do. Such approaches provide better strategies for uncovering behavior than raw behavioral and environmental strategies constrained only by self-based models.

The nature of belief is such that we may never be sure we know what others are thinking and saying. But understanding what others believe is certainly an important enough task to be worth exploring with more than our everyday tools. If translators would begin to more fully integrate their vast knowledge of other's lifeways, with other researchers' knowledge about the mind, we could come much closer to what Clifford Geertz describes as the fundamental goal of studying others. What we ultimately want from the peoples studied, writes Geertz, is "in the widened sense of the term in which it encompasses much more than talk, to converse with them" (1973: 13).

Notes

1. Philosophers use the term "intentional" to refer to descriptions of utterances and actions that involving meanings, beliefs, and desires. This use of "intentional" is different from its common usage as "on purpose."
2. This example is just a recasting of philosopher Willard Quine's (1960) famous example. The idea that behavioral evidence, by itself, can never really confirm a particular belief ascription is a central idea in his celebrated claim that whether an alien's cry of "Gavagai" in the presence of a rabbit really means "rabbit" or "undetached rabbit parts" is, in principle, indeterminate.
3. At this point, some may protest that the sorts of problem described above are certainly not unique to belief ascription. The failures of positivism has led many to be skeptical of finding firm epistemic foundations for any types of knowledge. Why, then, shouldn't other sciences be charged with regress or circularity? And scholars from Duhem to Quine to Kuhn have argued that all scientific posits rely on vast interconnected webs of knowledge. In other sciences, making certain types of alteration in the auxiliary premises can enable a different "core" theory to account for the same observations as the previous theory. These

possibilities do not make other sciences especially difficult or undoable. Why, then, should social-scientific belief attribution be thought to be particularly bedeviled by underdetermination and the holistic nature of justification?

There are several responses one might have to such worries. One is to agree that all sciences are plagued by these sorts of underdetermination worries. Many anti-realist philosophers and sociologists take this line (e.g. Collins and Pinch 1985, Bloor 1991). This response of course can only agree with my worries about belief ascription. It merely says other sciences have similar problems.

Another response is to say that the very holism that anti-foundationalists advocate is a feature that actually *inhibits* the possibility of having numerous alternative theoretical posits in some domains of science. A consequence of holism is that making changes in the assumptions needed for verifying posits in one domain would require us to alter many well-established views in realms far afield. For example, claims about the distance between Mercury and Venus have relied on the correctness of numerous auxiliary assumptions about the nature of telescopes. Many of these assumptions are well supported by direct observations of telescopes. Claims that we are wrong about this distance would require us to claim that our basic observations of telescopes or our beliefs about their powers are wrong. Claims that our beliefs about curved lenses were wrong might require us to say that we are wrong in our views about what microscopes show, and, consequently, about certain features of micro-organisms. It might force us to change our views on the propagation of light, which could force changes in our views of the powers of lasers. If our previous views about lasers or micro-organisms are well supported by still other data, then suggested changes in our premises regarding telescopes would be regarded as changes that come at an unreasonably high price. (See Laudan 1996 for a full articulation of the argument that while *logically* possible alterations are always available, *rationally possible* ones are not.) It may be that at a given point in time, only a single set of theoretical posits can satisfy all of the constraints that these mutually constraining theories impose on them.

This is not the situation we face when talking about belief claims. First, the auxiliaries used to make behavioral predictions here are never auxiliaries supported by direct observation – they are postulated auxiliary *beliefs and desires*. Beliefs and desires are not the sort of thing that can be directly observed. Second, making alterations in the auxiliaries and comparable alterations in the core theories in ways that produce alternative accounts for the same behavioral evidence can often be done without incurring the high costs one incurs in other sciences. In the telescope example, making numerous alterations in our assumptions about optics that balanced each other in a way that ensured our astronomical predictions remained the same would be very costly, because of the havoc such alterations would wreak *in other realms* that relied on our knowledge of optics. With belief ascription, on the other hand, making changes in the auxiliary and core beliefs in ways that keep the same observable predictions does not usually affect our knowledge of matters in other realms at all. Belief holism is a "within-theory" holism. The only costs that are incurred come from forcing us to make changes in *other postulated beliefs*. But there is nothing irrational about making these changes. Changing our postulations about what other beliefs are present does not force us to deny any direct observations, or deny any of the postulates that other well-supported sciences rely on. Here, unlike in many natural science cases, the logically possible alterations are rationally possible alterations as well.

4. Elsewhere (Jones 1997), I have termed Lutz's work a "thick description" approach to explicating the meaning of alien terms because of its affinities with Clifford Geertz's approach. In that work I also argued that, contrary to initial appearances, Geertz's work like Lutz's has much in common with functional-role cognitive approaches.

References

Agar, M. *The Professional Stranger.* London: Academic Press, 1980.

Anderson, J. *The Architecture of Cognition.* Cambridge, MA: Harvard University Press, 1983.

Block, N. "Introduction: What is Functionalism?" In *Readings in the Philosophy of Psychology, Vol. 1.* N. Block (ed.), Cambridge, MA: MIT Press, 1980.

Bloor, D. *Knowledge and Social Imagery.* Chicago: University of Chicago Press, 1991.

Cahill, S. "Children and Civility: Ceremonial Deviance and the Acquisition of Ritual Competence." *Social Psychology Quarterly* 50, 1987, pp. 312–321.

Carpenter, C., Glassner, B., Johnson, B. and Loughlin, B. J. *Kids, Drugs and Crime.* Lexington MA: Lexington, 1980.

Colby, B. "Toward an Encyclopedic Ethnography for Use in 'Intelligent' Computer Programs". In *New Directions in Cognitive Anthropology.* J. Keller (ed.), pp. 269–290. Urbana, IL: University of Illinois Press, 1985.

Collins, H. and Pinch, T. *Frames of Meaning: The Social Construction of Extraordinary Science.* London: Routledge and Kegan Paul, 1985.

Cummins, R. *The Nature of Psychological Explanation.* Cambridge, MA: MIT Press, 1983.

Davies, M. and Stone, T. *Mental Simulation: Evaluations and Applications.* Oxford: Blackwell, 1995.

Ekvall, R. *Religious Observances in Tibet.* Chicago: University of Chicago Press, 1964.

Evans-Prichard. E. *Witchcraft, Oracles, and Magic among the Azande.* Oxford: Oxford University Press, 1937.
—— *Nuer Religion.* Oxford: Clarendon, 1956.
Field, H. "Mental Representation." *Erkenntnis* 13(1), 1977, pp. 9–61.
Fodor, J. *The Language of Thought.* New York: Thomas Y. Crowell, 1975.
—— "Tom Swift and his Procedural Grandmother." *Cognition* 6, 1978.
Geertz, C. *The Interpretation of Cultures.* New York: Basic, 1973.
Goldman, A. "Interpretation Psychologized." *Mind and Language* 4, 1989, pp. 161–185.
Gordon, R. "Folk Psychology as Simulation." *Mind and Language* 1, 1986, pp. 158–171.
Heine, B. "The Mountain People: Some Notes on the Ik of Northeastern Uganda." *Africa* 55, 1985, pp. 3–16.
Hollis, M. "The Social Construction of Reality." In *Rationality and relativism.* Hollis, M. and S. Lukes (eds.), pp. 149–180. Cambridge, MA: MIT Press, 1982.
Hutchins, E. *Culture and Inference.* Cambridge, MA: Harvard University Press, 1980.
Jones, T. "When the Mind Makes the World: An Explanation of the Use of Constructivist Ideas In Tibet." MA thesis. University of Illinois, 1987.
—— "Thick Description, Fat Syntax, and Alternative Conceptual Schemes." *Pragmatics and Cognition* 5, 1997, pp. 131–162.
Keesing, R. "Conventional Metaphors and Anthropological Metaphysics: The Problem of Cultural Translation." *Journal of Anthropological Research* 31, 1985, pp. 201–217.
Lakoff, G. and Johnson, M. *Metaphors We Live By.* Chicago: University of Chicago Press, 1980.
Laudan, L. *Beyond Positivism and Relativism.* Boulder, CO: Westview, 1996.
Lévy-Bruhl, L. *How Natives Think,* New York: Alfred Knopf, 1926.
Lutz, C. *Unnatural Emotions.* Chicago: University of Chicago Press, 1988.
Malinowski, Bronislaw. *Argonauts of the Western Pacific.* New York: E. P. Dutton, 1961[1922].
—— Supplement to C. K. Ogden and I. A. Richards. *Meaning of Meaning.* New York: Harcourt Brace, 1923.
Mead, M. *Coming of Age in Samoa.* New York: Morrow, 1928.
Nisbett, R. and Ross, L. *Human Inference: Strategies and Shortcomings of Social Judgement.* Englewood Cliffs, NJ.: Prentice Hall, 1980.
Pepinsky, H. "A Sociologist on Police Patrol". In *Fieldwork Experience: Qualitative Aproaches to Social Research.* Schaffir, W., R. Stebbins and A.Turowetz (eds.). New York: St. Martin's, 1980.
Quine, W. *Word and Object.* Cambridge, MA: MIT Press, 1960.

Stich, S. *From Folk Psychology to Cognitive Science, the Case Against Belief.* Cambridge, MA: Bradford, 1983.

—— *The Fragmentation of Reason.* Cambridge, MA: Bradford, 1990.

Stich, S. and Nichols, S. "Cognitive Penetrability, Rationality, and Restricted Simulation." *Mind and Language* 12, 1997, pp. 297–326.

Turnbull, C. *The Forest People.* New York: Simon and Schuster, 1974.

Venuti, L. "Translation as a Social Process; or, The Violence of Translation." Paper presented at conference, Humanistic Dilemmas: Translation in the Humanities and Social Sciences, 26–28 September, 1991, at SUNY Binghamton, NY.

Wyer, R. and Srull, T. "Human Cognition in its Social Context." *Psychological Review 93*, 1986, pp. 322–359.

Translation, Transduction, Transformation: Skating "Glossando" on Thin Semiotic Ice
Michael Silverstein

In this chapter I engage the issue of how it is possible to "translate" materials of language, which must be seen as cultural matter at least as much as – perhaps much more than – strictly denotational expression. My argument, not surprisingly, turns on constructing kinds and degrees of possibility for various aspects of language material, and I conceptualize the gradations here in semiotic terms. For today we recognize that language is in some respects just like other cultural forms, that is, composed of analytically separable partials of semiosis and hence of kinds of "meaning," even though these interact in complex, layered ways. We must therefore recognize that those semiotic partials of language that are cultural in various complex ways indicate different susceptibilities of purported "translation."[1]

When and where language conforms most to traditional European ideological construals of it, I want to suggest, there is indeed a core of actually translatable semiosis in language, one that anchors the aspirations of bilingual dictionaries and so-called literal translations of expository prose documents. But as we move semiotically in increments away from that core, we increasingly are attempting to accomplish cross-linguistic/cross-cultural feats of qualitatively, let alone quant-itatively distinct conceptual sorts, that we might therefore label with distinct "t"-terms, which I propose here and hope to elucidate in this discussion.

The Narrowest Concept of "Translation"

There is a slippery surface, if not slope, across which one glissandos by attempting the feat of an intercultural 'gloss', or "**translation**." Translation is always a process that begins and ends with textual objects, whether word-sized fragments of denot-ational text (sometimes, as isolated, mistaken for grammatical forms!) or book-length verbal discourses, or even otherwise (en)textual(ized) objects in other media and modes. At least in our own European ethnometapragmatic tradition, so-called translation theory centers on the ideologically well-trod area of denotational language and its translatability into other such denotational languages. (This is, of course, what is principally meant by the natives when they claim for example that they are reading a "translation" of Saussure's [1916] *Cours de linguistique générale* "from French into English.") This ideological focus on **denotational textuality** – coherent language-as-used to represent states-of-affairs involving things-in-universes-of-reference – provides the benchmark as well as starting point for millennia of wishful as well as wistful theorizing about "translation" and its various (im)possibilities.[2] The current fashion seems to be rather uninformed lamentations over impossibilities and headaches of one or another disconstrualist[3] or identity-political sort (formulated, note, from well within the ideological focus on denotation, though aching to get out).

Even for "language" itself in this purely denotationalist imaginary, it should be noted, there are severe limits to how we can THEORETICALLY justify what we do as interlingual glossers. As Quine (1960: 28) would say, very close by to our starting point in the comfortable confines of perfectly semantically compositional expressions,[4] we are in the area of "radical translation," taking an intercultural stab-at-it by in principle unsystematizable commonsense shortcuts. Look at where this landed Dorothy on her way to Oz, who did not cleave to the Boasian yellow brick road, on which she would have been guided by structures of obligatory grammatical categories in each language concerned – "source" and "target" – as the building blocks of compositionality! Recall that Quine distinguishes the mere fact of doing a reasonable denotational translation across two arbitrary languages, which we do accomplish somehow, from systematic or theoretical justification of it. But we can clarify Quine's stricture by saying that if we could solve the problem of what Whorf (1956a [1940]: 214) called the "calibration" of linguistic systems, in effect constructing a framework of universal grammar in terms of denotational categories and their formal codings, then we could provide systematic or theoretical justification for translating an arbitrary expression from one language to another.

The following are involved, then, in justifying the "translation" we might propose of some particular expression-token (even in the form of a word or expression) we are concerned with in a text we encounter on some occasion of discourse, an 'entextualization-in-context' (see Silverstein and Urban 1996). The feat involves, first, projecting justifiable grammatical categories immanent in the expression-type in the determinable "source" denotational code. This means determining what are the implicit or immanent type-level formal distributional relations that map into structures of denotational differentiation, each such regularity of mapping being a grammatical category, and grammatical categories being combined in interesting structural ways in the (Saussurean) 'sense' of a word or expression. The second step, logically speaking, involves bringing another, "target" denotational code in by in essence proposing a comparison of denotational language-structure with denotational language-structure. Observe that constructing this bridge across languages can only be accomplished in grammatical-categorial space, and it is only success in this enterprise that permits us to locate approximate lexicalizations of languages in general one with respect to another.

So the third aspect of simple denotational translation is to complete a triangulation, comparing grammatically projectible expression-types in the source language with those in the target language so as to determine a fitting token expression in the target language suitable (on other semiotic grounds) to the translation-occasion. In respect of the properties of the source-language expression, the point is to find a word or expression in the target language [a] that is centered on or headed by the most categorially encompassing lexicalization possible (from the grammatical categorial point of view) at the same time as [b] it is the narrowest differential one denotationally corresponding to its would-be counterpart in the source language. Then there are further considerations of how to narrow the target expression's denotation (and total meaningfulness) to as precise a scope as can be managed.

Put this way, it all sounds exceedingly complicated to implement, even though, one would claim, this is exactly what is accomplished whenever we implicitly manage to overcome the Quinean impedimenta in an at least retrospectively principled way. So what, then, is it safe to assume about real translation? If the entire course of structural theorizing about the denotational use of language has validity – and my own (dare I assert?) professional scholarly opinion is that it does – then we **can** denotationally "translate" across languages to the extent that we follow these dictates: grammatically projectible words and expressions in denotational text in a source language can be given at least one closest-possible gloss in a target language modulo the grammatical-categorial systems (including lexical semantic categories with distributional correlates) of the two respective languages into which the words and expressions of the denotational texts (source and target) are resolved.

Why should this be so? Why, under these assumptions, can we so guarantee? Because, we can note, Saussurean 'sense'[5] is a component of the "meaning" of any word or expression only by virtue of the fact of grammar, which makes it an instance or token of an underlying or immanent lexical type. From this it follows that to the extent all languages are indeed Saussurean systems, such 'sense's of any word or expression in any source and target languages are expressible as structured complexes of categories of communicable difference-of-denotation. And in turn, such categories are justifiable only to the extent that those of any one particular language come out of the universe of grammatical-categorial types *in potentia* that underlie all languages.[6]

Hence, we can translate (note the directionality:) from one language (in)to another in various zones or regions of grammaticosemantic space, reference to the structural possibilities of which is essential in translating. For example, the English kinship terms, like those in any language, exemplify a specialized semantic subset of inherently interpersonally relational status terms. We can translate English (my) father with a term in another language, say Worora (northwestern Australia) (ngayu) iraaya. The Worora term, part of a quasi-"Omaha-type" lexical set, matches the English term in certain categorial stipulations of the denotatum's 'human'ness, 'anima[te]'cy, 'count'ness, 'male'ness, and 'k^{fa}(x$_i$,Y$_j$)',[7] among others; these can be shown to be categories at least compatible with the differential (Saussurean) coding structures of the two linguistic systems. And this, even though the actual Worora term is applied RECIPROCALLY by a man and his actual genitor, reciprocally also to any male's first – and 2n+1st – ascending/descending generation patriclan male, evincing a kind of alternating-adjacent-generation agnatic denotational solidarity. (Hence it can be noted, from our point of view, both that I refer to 'my father' as ngayu iraaya and that he so refers to me, whom we would expect to be referred to in English by the other person as my son; similarly 'my father's father's father' and my 'son's son's son'; etc.) And note that while a female also terms her actual or classificatory 'father' ngayu iraaya, both of my father's sister and my daughter as denoted for a male possessor are ngayu bamraanja, which is also the coding of the reciprocal relationship by which each of these two people in a 'fasi' – 'brodau' relationship would denote the other.

Note, then, that the respective English-language and Worora-language kinterminological "meanings" in their respective systems overlap in the 'f(,)' component by the difference of absolute vs. signed generational value between the denoted individuables, (□1□vs. □1: 'generational difference of one [between relata]' vs. 'ascending/descending generational difference of one [between relata]'), insofar as this constitutes part of the Saussurean 'sense', though clearly the denotational range of the English term is only a subset – though, to be sure, a structured subset – of the denotational range of the Worora one. Were one translating in the direction from Worora to English, though Worora ngayu iraaya codes an absolute generational value between its relata, we must introduce the specific sign, + or −, in order to get the "proper" translation into English, as my father or my son – not to speak of greater generational distances – even for a denotationally "male( )" possessor.[8]

And this overlap, though not identity, of Saussurean "sense" allows the identification, in the move of "translation" preserving as much as possible of "sense", of the initial English term with the target Worora term in that particular direction. Note, further, that were we translating English my son, only in the case where the "x$_i$", the grammatically construed possessor, indexes someone of whom "male( )" is true, does the Worora expression ngayu iraaya still serve. Otherwise, the situation puts the relationship in the denotational set of a distinctly lexicalized form. Observe then that the sex of each of the denotata, that associated with the possessive element, if present, as well as that of the actual head-noun stem, is apparently coded in the variations of the Worora noun-stem. In first- or second-person usage ('my/our', 'thy/your') or in vocative usage without explicit possessor, it is of course the individual in the role of speaker/sender of whom the sex is relevant to proper use of a noun stem – a "pragmatic" or indexical fact in the instance, and hence marginal to the ethnotheory of language with which we are thus far working.[9]

It is important to see the translation task in terms of language forms in two languages that in very different ways code pieces of the denotational differentiations we can recognize as common to the two systems of lexicogrammatical structure. English (<u>my</u>) <u>father</u> and (<u>my</u>) <u>son</u> comprise a lexical pair such that each codes a signed direction-of-relationship with respect to Worora (<u>ngayu</u>) <u>iraaya</u>, under particular further conditions. Those conditions are that both of the two relata – one needs to remember that kinship terms are inherently possessed, i.e., occur only in nominal coding constructions with explicit or semantically projectible possessor as well as head noun – are both 'male'. Outside of this condition, i.e., for 'female' possessor of '<u>father</u>', and for the reciprocal kinship relationship, that '<u>father</u>'s <u>daughter</u>', Worora uses a lexical PAIR that codes the comparable denotational range, (<u>ngayu</u>) <u>iraaya</u> / (<u>ngayu</u>) <u>bamraanja</u>. But the point is that in the directional task of translating in the denotational mode, one can in principle determine what is a semanticogrammatically justifiable translation in the target language by appeal to the fact that denotational meanings are anchored by paradigms of categorial mappings in and across particular languages.

The Saussurean 'sense' systems called grammars anchor words and expressions in a particular language in the universals of coding principles for all languages. Going back to our example of kinterm translation, for example, we know that in every language kinterms are a subset of status terms (certainly for denotata classifiable as 'human' and perhaps for other classes of 'being's as well). Such terms characterize the status of a particular denotatum in terms of a two-place relational property with respect to membership in a social dyad. This same relational property is most clearly seen in explicit natural language in such phenomena as the English predicating expressions of ascriptive status and "habitual agency," (<u>be</u>) <u>father</u> <u>to</u> [X], parallel to (<u>be</u>) <u>baker</u> <u>to</u> [X], which in fully nominalized form come out as [X]'<u>s</u> <u>father</u> / <u>father</u> <u>of</u> [X], [X]'<u>s</u> <u>baker</u> (/ <u>baker</u> <u>of</u> [X]).[10] Kinterms in any language will have much of the formal-distributional and associated sense properties of such Nouns of Agency ascribed to, or habitual for, someone with respect to a benefactee/recipient/addressee. They will also have some specialized properties as status-characterizing terms usable to denote and even to refer to particular individuals. For example, along with only a small set of such grammatically coded relationalities, such as 'part-whole' constructions, they iterate possessor coding so as to create complex relational expressions that characterize a denotatum through a nested chain of two-place linkages, whence the well-known "relative product" expressions such as <u>John</u>'<u>s</u> <u>father</u>'<u>s</u> <u>sister</u>'<u>s</u> <u>husband</u>'<u>s</u> <u>cousin</u>['<u>s</u> . . .]; i.e., <u>cousin</u> <u>to</u>

[John's father's sister's husband], i.e., cousin to [husband to [John's father's sister]], . . . that can be made in any language from its simplex kinterminological lexemes.

Now it appears that this infinitely extensible "kinship universe" as so coded – through the magic of iterative possessive-phrase grammar – has a certain conceptual integrity when viewed through the lens of universals of lexicalization. Put otherwise, this means that '(egocentrically focused) kinship' constitutes a DENOTATIONAL LEXICAL DOMAIN, sometimes also loosely called a "semantic field," in which there is a set of structural regularities of how certain classes of denotata within the theoretically infinite universe as so described can regularly be characterized by a single, noniteratively possessed simplex lexical form. This has constituted for sociocultural anthropologists the typology of kinship systems – Dakota, Dravidian, Hawaiian, etc. – which have been investigated through various "genealogical methods," "ethno-" and otherwise.[11] These regularities of a specifically **lexicosemantic** (as opposed to grammaticosemantic more broadly) sort within a denotational domain serve further to anchor translatability, in that they provide guides to coding a source-language kinship expression with a target-language phrase built around an appropriate head lexeme. The head will emerge from the closeness of fit of classes overlapping in denotational membership in the kinship universe in the respective languages. Thus, in our Worora-to-English translation example above, father- and son-, whether by themselves or with (iterated) possessives, are the appropriate heads of the translation-expressions, because of the overlap of two respective typological classes of lexicalization in Worora and English.

Yet another pair of factors in ease-of-justification of "translation" in the usual sense is constituted by the **lexicopragmatic** and **grammaticopragmatic** regularities of languages, that is, the way that lexemes on the one hand and morphological and syntactic forms on the other code pragmatic, or co(n)textual, information as denotational characterizations. These two forms of what is generally called the DEICTIC ("pointing") aspect of denotational language can be seen in English in such lexical pairings as today vs. yesterday for example, and such 'Tense'-paradigm members as ["present"] (it) goes vs. ["past"] (it) went. The first pair shows lexical coding of the pragmatic scheme of 'proximal' vs. 'distal-and-prior' overlaid on standard (conceptual) intervals of duration-reckoning (here, 'day'-intervals); the latter pair shows grammatical coding of the same pragmatic scheme to be applied by interlocutors to the locatability of validity-realms for predicated events. In both cases, note, the event of communication is the DEFAULT CENTERPOINT from which 'proximity' is conceptualizable; this centerpoint "shifts" as discursive event-realtime moves on.[12] In the first case, there is a lexical paradigm that codes a 'distal-subsequent' of this interval type as well (the lexical coding is tomorrow); there is, further, a phrasal construction day before [X] and day after [X] for each of the 'distal' terms that takes us to two days' remove from the 'proximal' day presupposed for the communicative context. In the second case, there is no morphological paradigm of the Tense category in English beyond the dichotomous "past" [= 'distal-prior'] vs. 'nonpast' [=> ('proximal')[13]]; for more specific intervals within the 'nonpast' such as to indicate futurity, we get along in English grammatical form with modalizations such as (it) will go and other vernacular-register approximations such as (it) is going to go.

On the comparative plane, deixis, too, shows various calibrational regularities when viewed in terms of lexical and morphosyntactic codings of form. There emerge certain typologies of categorial elaborateness of deictic systems like Tense or Person or Evidentiality, among numerous others. All of these, however, are based on certain common schematic and structured understandings of communicative events and situations that are made the basis of denotational characterization of what is being communicated about. From the point of view of language, these schemata are general and abstract, and constitute the baseline onto which culture-specific elaborations are laminated. So there seem to be certain recognizable DEICTIC DOMAINS where a certain overlap obtains across languages of what is indexically presupposed in-and-by the use of a token of a categorial form. Cross-linguistically, for example, we can identify the presupposition that someone is inhabiting the communicative role of 'sender' or (loosely) 'speaker', as opposed to 'receiver' or (loosely) 'hearer'/'addressee' as the focal notion – there are elaborations and extensions of it, to be sure – of the grammaticopragmatic category of First Person. A First Person form differentially characterizes some 'referent' as the individual inhabiting this relational role at the moment of use of the form (alone or with others), thus in effect using the schematic presumed to apply to the momentary communicative role-structure differentially to denote something. Similarly, by contrast, for other Person-category forms. And similarly across all languages, the Person systems of which allow of calibration, so that in our example above we can justify our translation of Worora ngayu by English I/me/my (note the contrast of grammatical Case in English, not at issue here).

Each one of these kinds of successful translation in the technical sense depends upon the way we can read text-in-co(n)text via systematic abstractions of structure that lie immanent in text-in-co(n)text insofar as anchored by the fact of grammar (and its dependent constitutive part, lexicon). Yet even the denotational value of words and expressions in co(n)text is a function of much more than grammar and lexicon. There are other kinds of meaning communicated by words and expressions in co(n)text, and therefore to the extent that these are systematic, there are distinct principles of meaningfulness that organize their systematicity. Here, we must leave the plane of grammar-and-lexicon – even in the hybrid mode it appears in deictic phenomena – in relation to text-in-co(n)text. We move to the plane of principles of cotextuality and contextuality for words and expressions only as they occur in discursive realtime, generally known as culture. This is how we capture the indexical and iconic modalities through which words and expressions are endowed with significances in their co(n)textual matrix.

Deictic forms, to recapitulate, denote by virtue of pointing to a context some aspect of the structure of which they presuppose; they characterize some aspect of what is denoted in terms of that presupposed structure. Indexical forms more generally simply point to their co(n)textual surround, meaning co(n)text both as the form's matrix of structuredness PRESUPPOSED and as its matrix of structuredness ENTAILED or CREATED – in effect, performatively (Austin 1975 [1962]) summoned into being – in-and-by the very event of use of the particular form.

We must recognize that the greater part of the meaningfulness of words and expressions comes first from various directly indexical modalities of semiosis and second from complex, dialectic, though indexically-based ones, above and beyond any Saussurean-anchored "translatable" concepts. Words and expressions have directly indexical RULES OF USE, whether by being elements of more abstract sociolinguistic REGISTERS or by themselves having a distinct indexical loading that points to a particular location in society as their normatively authorizing site of use (who/to-whom/where/when/with-what-meaning).[14] Words and expressions also are organized into textual structures, the significant emergent unitizations of which have internal cotextuality at hierarchically inclusive levels of structure as they unfold one with respect to another. The specific meanings of words-and-expressions as used are at least in part a function of this – as Jakobson (1981 [1960]: 18–21) termed it, from Aristotle – "poetic" order of organization of discourse. Both of these kinds of indexical system are essentially part of the text-in-co(n)text plane at which words and expressions are endowed with meaning; of course, therefore, they require some "translational" attention.

The most fundamental kind of iconism in language (sometimes loosely called "sound symbolism," focusing again on the denotational relation between a lexical form and some real-world object of denotation; see Hinton et al. 1994) is the diagrammatic characteristic of what Jakobson identified as the "poetic" – read: *cotextual* – organization of ritual discourse into textual form. By contrast, as Saussure long ago pointed out (in the *Cours*, §I.1.2 [1916: 101f.]), actual imitation, or imagistic iconicity of lexical signal form to denoted object is, universally, distinctly marginal to denotation as such: it is always at least partly convention-alized in terms of the language-culture nexus in which a denotational system of words and expressions exists, and it is antithetical to the formal, rule-governed structuredness of grammar in its preponderant totality (whence Saussurean sense emerges). But, through various culturally specific processes (and thereby possibly universal ones at a very different level of explanation), direct "iconic" values of certain formal aspects of the signals of language are frequently understood as part of what is communicated by words and expressions in co(n)text (see Jakobson and Waugh 1979: chapter 4; Silverstein 1994 for examples). The quasi- or sub-lexical "ideophones" or "morpheme partials" that seem to associate sound imagistically with concepts – English splat, splash, splutter and the like are classic chestnuts for the [spl-. . .] initial sound-image – are indeed important to understand and "translationally" to capture as components of source-material expressions. Qualities of alliteration, assonance, and other iconic tropes of classical poetics do seem to be realities of the meaningfulness of expressions for addressees in source languages that need attention in the translational process so that these realities are accommodated in the target-language textual equivalent.

These indexical and iconic values of words and expressions in co(n)textualized texts constitute a distinct area of problems we must consider for the would-be translator, because they rely on a different approach to "translation" than the clear-cut areas of Saussurean and deictic denotation, one that takes account of rather distinct semiotic properties.

"Translation" as Transduction

As folk of semiotic *Wissenschaften*, we anchor our understanding of the first kind of systematizable aspect of translation in the universal fact of (Saussurean) grammar and its consequences for semantico- and pragmaticogrammatical organization of words and expressions in their cotextual and contextual surround. Once we get beyond the systematizable in this Saussurean respect, as discussed above, we are, in essence, in what I would term a kind of semiotic **transduction**. By this I mean a process of reorganizing the source semiotic organization (here, in the original problem, denotationally meaningful words and expressions of a source language occurring in co[n]text) by target expressions-in-co(n)text of another language presented through perhaps semiotically diverse modalities differently organized. (And let us stipulate for the time being that both source and target are, in general outlines, multidimensionally "like.") As was noted above, this additional, non-Saussurean semiosis always manifests in fundamentally indexical and iconic meaning processes (in the Peircean sense). So the "translation"-relevant meaningfulness of words and expressions consists in the interaction of such modalities of semiosis together with the denotational modality anchored by Saussurean 'sense' and by deixis. Hence, how these other kinds of semiotic system can be said to correspond across source and target texts – paralleling the Whorfian concept of grammaticosemantic "calibration" – is the focus of *transductional* relationships of words and expressions across languages.

We should think seriously of the underlying metaphor of the energy transducer that I invoke, such as a hydroelectric generator. Here, one form of organized energy [e.g. the gravitationally aided downstream and downward linear rush of water against turbine blades] is asymmetrically converted into another kind of energy at an energetic transduction site [e.g. circular motion of a coil-in-a-magnetic-field gizmo around an axle with torque, connected thus to the energy of the flowing water on turbine blades], harnessing at least some of it across energetic frameworks. In this transducer, the two modes of mechanical energy are converted in a functionally regular way into another kind of energy altogether [e.g. Franklinian electric current of certain intensity (amperage), driven by a certain force (voltage) against the forces of its conductors (resistance/conductance)], of course with some slippage between the two systems of energy organization, due to "friction," "inefficiencies," "random contingent factors," and other tragedies of the laws of thermodynamics and of uncertainty.

The point is, much of what goes into connecting an actual source-language expression to a target-language one is like such a transduction of energy: for here we are dealing with the transduction of semiosis beyond what Saussurean sense-systematics informs us about. We are dealing with the non-Saussurean aspects of meaningfulness of words and expressions, a traditionally undertheorized waste-basket to which, nevertheless, we have been trying to bring some conceptual order through a philosophically acute linguistic anthropology fashioned in recent years. (See, for example, Lee 1997; Parmentier 1997.)[15] These non-Saussurean aspects of meaningfulness are bound up in discursive processes, interlocutors collaborating in multiple modalities to create text-structures-in-context over the course of realtime interaction. To achieve text-structures-in-context, interlocutors draw on all of the various modalities of meaningfulness coded in relatively stable ways in sign form so as to produce that fragile something. By contrast, the denotation-coding words and expressions into which the learnèd reconstruction of interlocution parses this complex semiotic activity turn out to be just a small, reflexively salient partial of what it precipitates. But inasmuch as theorizing "translation" has inordinately focused essentially upon this learnèd reconstruction, let us consider some of the effects of non-Saussurean semiotic partials of discursive activity starting from this usual starting point, how to "translate" words and expressions from source language into target.

Consider, for instance, the 'vocative' forms that correspond to the Worora expression (<u>ngayu</u>) <u>iraaya</u> '(my) father'. There is the regularly formed "bare stem" form of vocative, <u>ira</u>, that we might translate by any one of the denotationally appropriate English vocatives that correspond: <u>father</u>!, <u>dad</u>!, <u>dada</u>!, <u>daddy</u>!, <u>pop</u>!, <u>papa</u>!, etc. for the first-ascending-generation forms. But which of these? We must note that Worora has another vocative, <u>djidja</u> in a pragmatic paradigm of indexical meaningfulness, the latter considered to be something of a Baby Talk Register[16] word and thence a word ascribed to children's Worora usage. For example, people's accounts of their, or their child's, pre-fetal and active impregnation of their would-be father (social anthropological "genitor") as his about-to-be-conceived child, from which derives each normal person's "great name" (see Silverstein ms.a), all contain the formulaic utterance, *"Djidja, ngayueguwaligee!"* 'Daddy! It's (precisely) **me**!' – using the vocative in question. Thus, insofar as there is a distinction among the various English language forms, for Worora djidja it would be the more Baby Talk types, daddy, dada, perhaps papa, that are the correct **transductions** from one system of indexical contextualization to another. One tries to equate Worora and Anglo-American (at least) CULTURAL SYSTEMS OF VALUE that endow the register forms with indexical meaningfulness – capturing this way how both source expression and target expression point to appropriate contexts and create effective contexts in systems of use as verbally mediated social action. Grown men exchange the vocative *"ira!"* in Worora, transducible in my English-language pragmatics as "dad!" or "pop!" (not "son!") though, lacking any alternative forms in local Pidgin English, my grown Worora-speaking friends of the mid-1970s, in switching codes sometimes, would alternate the only translation-equivalent they knew, "daddy," which always caused me to remark its inappropriateness in the American English system of vocative register sets.

We might, then, conceptualize something like a ratio of LINGUISTIC-STRUCTURALLY JUSTIFIABLE OR SYSTEMATIC **'translation'** on the one hand to the various additional factors that go into giving an interlingual gloss, on the other. These other factors comprise, in the first instance, what underlies an intuitive **'transduction'** of the source expression in the first language into some (organization of) target expression(s) of the second.[17] We know that various classes of words and expressions have particular complexities – besides the semanticogrammatical (Saussurean 'sense') structures and pragmaticogrammatical ones – that to different degrees play roles in their complete "meanings" (cf. Lee 1997: 170–74; Lucy 1992a: 65–71, 1992b: 95–102; Silverstein 1987). So as a function of different classes of words and expressions in a source text, the ratio of "true" translation in our narrowed sense to at best systematic transduction will obviously vary.

Of course, the mere fact that there might be paraphrases in a source language where one form is a grammatically conforming and compositional expression while its "synonym" is a grammatically classifiable lexical simplex, already illustrates a difference of translation/transduction ratio. In any language, given a semanticogrammatical composite, e.g. a fully productive syntactic collocation, and its denotationally closest (termed "synonymous") correspondent expression in simplex lexical form, it is the simplex lexical form that inevitably has a "meaning" that adds multiple pragmatic (indexical) and metapragmatic factors – in short, cultural ones – to the compositional meaning of the seemingly isosemantic [= same-"sense"d; Whorf 1956c [1945]: 99] collocation. Hence, English [X] murder [Y] (with the simplex verb) means not merely the same as '[X] cause [Y] to die' (with the grammatically constructed phrasal collocation),[18] but share the semantic meaning of the latter **plus** some indexed presuppositions in the realms of normative cultural knowledge. These indexed presuppositions are associated with (rational) agency, (conscious) intentionality, and similar attributes of humans projected onto the denotatum of X, as well as unmediated qualities of 'caus[e]'al interaction by which X causes Y to die, etc. – all of interest, ultimately, to formalizers in legal institutions, which sociologically center or anchor "authorized" usage of the term <u>murder</u> in a larger cultural "division of linguistic labor" (Putnam 1975). Bakhtin (1981) long ago pointed out the essential dialogical or mimetic *renvoi* to such authorizing contexts that each (at least logically) "successive" usage of any word or expression so centered in (hence, indexical of) an institutionalized social structure bears as part of its meaningfulness – of course this is **every** term, as it turns out!

To the degree such complexes of presupposition contribute particularly to the performative efficacy of textual use of words and expressions as social action they constitute the very limits of normal, denotationally centered approaches to "translation." For in dealing with performative efficacy, we can dispute the very possibility of systematic expressibility of the targeted performative effect of indexicals in some pragmatic metalanguage.[19] And can such performable effects, notwithstanding being unexpressed in denotationally explicit code, be "translated," then, from an arbitrary source structure to some augmented, semanticogrammatically conforming textual structure of the target language?

Hence, in translation, the question is how, even were one able to "express," i.e., REPRESENT, such performative indexicalities, could we work them back into some target textual object in the – in principle – right way? This would be to preserve all of the properties of the original save for this transduction of semiosis. Hence, consider the textual appearance in an English source of, say, a word like <u>murder-</u>, use of a token of which constitutes a type of act that indexes judgments of a culturally rich sort. Is there a determinate way to use a corresponding word or expression in the target plus all the metapragmatic description that fills in the presupposed contextual invocations of the source word? Would this require a shadow apparatus of a cultural encyclopedia to answer such questions as, what kinds of text in what kinds of context is this source-language term or expression characteristically used in? How practical, after all, is all this?

The translation/transduction ratio – or, really, interval of ratios permissible as the translator's wiggle-room – is a function of such properties in both source and target languages. So the ratio is in fact doubly relative in this way. It is systematically relative to how transductional aspects of interlingual glossing depend on the pragmatic aspects of both languages, centrally those ways in which a language is part of 'culture' by virtue of the sociocultural contextualization – i.e., indexical presupposition and especially indexical entailment (performativity) – of the flow of language-in-use. That is to say, much of what goes for the "translation" even of simplex words in a text of a language actually constitutes transduction of indexical systems invoked by token usage of the words in the source text. Such source-text indexical values have to be reconstructed in indexical systems of another culture as these can be made relevant to shaping the target text to be doing effectively equivalent 'functional' work. (Or we need as transducer an elaborate, though pragmatically neutral, supplementary textual apparatus – like notes – in effect to "explain" the pragmatic particulars that make the original text work so that the target text can also work in "like" ways for those who wish to encounter it.)

To the extent to which there are, in fact, REGULARITIES across such (as we can term them) grammaticopragmatic systems – distinct from Saussurean grammar in analytic fact if not in the overt signal of words and expressions in text – we can understand that there is the possibility of a certain systematicity of transductions as well as of translations. Think of transducing obscenities, imprecations, curses, etc., in one pragmatic register of a source language into "equivalents" in a target language; the denotational literalness of the first generally play a small role in the choice of a proper or best "translation," i.e., transduction. Thus, Harry Hoijer (1933: 135) reports that the Tonkawa[20] curse *Hemayan!* 'ghost' is "a fairly mild oath," while *Hemayan gadau shilwan!* 'may you give birth to a wandering [*shilwan*] ghost' "is the very acme of profanity." Are these the equivalents of American English "Darn!" and "Eat me, you motherfucker!" or some such? Clearly, just translating the denotational content does not seem to suggest the difference of original indexical (here, performative) effect in Tonkawa.

Sometimes we are tempted to assimilate such systematic transductions to the narrower ethnometapragmatic "translation" concept that everything must fit into target-language denotational code. So we try, for example, to translate a word laden with lots of indexical rules of use (e.g., Worora <u>iraaya</u>, discussed above) with a whole denotational phrase (viz., <u>son of a man</u>; <u>man's son</u>) and be done with it. This move causes such conceptual confusion of the denoted and the indexed, of the semantic and the purely pragmatic, as well as of their meta-levels, as makes our Quines quiver.

We must resist this temptation, even if our forebears have not, because we better understand how even the simplest attempt at interlingual glossing is laden with 'culture' in a very specific way, as valuated conceptual distinctions indexically invoked in-and-by the use of words and expressions in inhabited social-actional context. Those contexts or those conceptual distinctions in a source usage are indexed in-and-by the use of certain words or expressions in particular events of communicative usage. We can understand these indexical values frequently in terms of describable social differentiations of kinds of actors who take various roles in sociocultural context, frequently coinciding with roles in communication itself, like speaker–addressee–overhearer (audience), etc.

In the nature of things, such *description* of context is metapragmatic, both as conceptualization and as discourse. So if the original source-language word or expression communicates such contextual information indexically, then to transduce it into a target-language word or expression is to find a way to index something comparable in the way the resultant target text communicates to its intended receivers. As can be easily seen now, the attempt is to build the erstwhile indexical meaningfulness of source-language words and expressions used with certain effect in context into the purported "translation meaning." By contrast, simply to use expressions that **describe** the context of use of a word or expression in the source language (rather than ones that index, *mutatis mutandis*, a comparable context in the target), mixes together many distinct semiotic levels and essentially transforms the source text-in-co(n)text, at least partially, into an object of contemplation and characterization.

But perhaps because it is so difficult to avoid the blunder, and because we do indeed have metapragmatic descriptive machinery for describing social context, we anthropologists seem easily to despair of the transductions necessary to deal ethnographically with key labels for cultural concepts. Finding no easy and "meaning"-exhausting translation in our narrower sense, and being wary of functionally distorting transduction, we are always tempted simply to reproduce a phonologically adapted form of a "native" term in an otherwise target-language ethnographic text. In essence, this makes the target-language ethnographic text the supervening 'context' (strictly speaking, the contextually exhausting 'cotext') for the now-borrowed term. Such co(n)text implicitly defines this now-borrowed foreign term or at least it provides *in toto* a chunk of something of a descriptive backing so the term can denote something for the reader who makes it to the end of the relevant prose.

In this way, note, the borrowed term is not so much translated as at best transduced modulo the very ethnographic text, now interposed between source-language users of the term and target-language users of it. The ethnographic text becomes its secondary indexical origo for a substitutive system of indexical meanings. Every subsequent usage of the term-labeling-the-concept is a textual reference or Bakhtinian *renvoi* to the ethnographic text. So, driven by our own ideology of sloppy "translational" failure, there emerges at best an effective transduction of each such term an ethnographic author refuses to "translate," its ineffable source-language indexicalities replaced by the target-language indexicalities located in the ethnographic text that co(n)textualizes it.[21]

It tends, further, to make of the author of such an ethnographic text the patron of the untranslated term/concept as his or her own, thus being indexically known by it and becoming a *topos* of disciplinary discourse, much as in the ideology of technical concept/term coinage rampant in scientific circles.[22] Authorial begging of indulgence to suspend translation on grounds of "ineffability" may thus also be a discursive move to guarantee to said author the authority of having "been there" (see Clifford 1983; Crapanzano 1986; Geertz 1988). We must note that only rarely has the "untranslated" term undergone a transformation into an actual technical term or even popular catchword in a generation or two (think of how laypersons speak of American society's "taboos," for example!). Rather, such a term has tended to remain an index of the particular ethnographer's authority over the way we think of the culture whose term remains untranslated but instead revalued so as to index some ethnographic interpretative text.

So there is no easy solution to the problem posed by textual words and expressions requiring transduction. When there is an easy transduction of an indexical system of meaning from one language-culture to another, substitution of the proper sort can be easily accomplished. But this is clearly only the case where the contextualizing indexical systems of how forms are used are more or less comparable across source and target – as in Whorf's "Standard Average European" (1956b [1941]: 138) languages. Here, all that is at issue in "translating" is finding the proper lexical equivalents at the denotational plane (translation in the narrow sense), modulo transducible indexical values. Hence, the "T/V" systems (Brown and Gilman 1960) of European languages transduce easily, German Sie (: du) easily translating into Italian Lei (: tu) or Russian vy (: ty). This ease of indexical transduction is the exceptional case, however. It rests on the fact that structurally comparable distinctions constitute the respective languages' indexical machinery, even though the denotational (semanticogrammatical) categories along with which these indexical distinctions are signaled differ from language to language. (Observe that, in strictly grammatical categorial terms, German uses a formally 'third person plural' denotational pronominal for "V"-ing someone; Italian a formally 'third person singular feminine'; and Russian a 'second person plural'.)

Much more common is the situation in which the transductional equivalents are not obvious: how does one capture the "tone," i.e., indexical penumbra, of a word or expression in a source text by one in a target language used in a highly distinct culture? Clearly, something on the order of a cultural analysis of both systems of usage is a prerequisite to finding a route of transduction, in analytic terms that reveal both the similarities and the differences, so as to be able to navigate a proper transduction from the source to the target.

Consider the famous "speech levels" of languages like Japanese, Javanese, Sundanese, Korean, Tibetan, etc.[23] Traditionally they have operated in societies in which systems of stratificational rank of interlocutors and denoted others constitute the basis for gradated indexical acts of deference from one person (as speaker/ sender) to another (as addressee and/or referent). Modulo this indexing of someone's deference entitlement with respect to a speaker, the systems manifest themselves in elaborate pragmatic paradigms of what native users think of as gradiently alternate ways of denoting "the same thing." The words and expressions cluster around a limited number of denotational domains – thus never the whole lexicon – as used in certain kinds of grammatically parsable collocations. In every one of these systems, moreover, a speaker's control of the higher reaches of the lexical alternants indexes someone as well of considerable deference entitlement and/or a formal, public occasion.

But of course the SAE "T/V" systems, though focused on pronominal usage, line up as somewhat comparable in their total usage (see Agha 1994; Morford 1997), though with fewer, hence less subtly entextualizable, forms in the pragmatic paradigm. American English (Brown and Ford 1964[1961]; Murphy 1988) does equivalent social indexing with paradigms of alternant personal names, even though it does not have a pronominally focused "T/V" system.[24]

Note, moreover, that there exist systems of stratified registers of language use like that of American English or any other SAE language in a diverse but standard-ized language community. In any of these language communities, the stratification of registers is reflected in context-appropriate and context-entailing "stylistic" adjustments that speakers make. Using various technical, euphemistic, and other highly valued functional alternants comprehended in standard (e.g. in English, Greco-Latin forms with complex morphological structure), all the while "saying the same thing" as one could in more prosaic register, indexes a range of contextual states of affairs. In one mode, it is the difference between relatively "formal" vs. "informal," and/or between relatively "impersonal/institutional" vs. "(inter)-personal/biographical" contexts of communication. It allows a speaker to recognize the deference entitlement of an addressee as a contributing factor to these. In another order of indexical effects, it points to relatively high self-positioning of the speaker as well within the schemata of stratification made relevant to the situation. Thus, speaking "well" is speaking with an indexical *renvoi* – signaled by use of higher register – to having inhabited or inhabiting superordinate positions in important contexts of social action.

The point here is that across these cultural systems there are comparabilities we can recognize in the discursive facts catalogued above. Notwithstanding some fundamental differences in how these indexical variations are understood in local cultural terms, there seem to be parallels across languages both of how people use the forms and of their contextualizing indexical values, even though all functions may not be associable with an equal diversity of comparable forms in moving from language-culture to language-culture. Hence, the registers created by the fact of standardization in SAE languages are at least partially implemented in ways parallel to the "speech-level" deference indexicals of the various Southeast Asian languages mentioned. The latter registers are at least partially comparable in func-tion to "T/V" systems of SAE languages, centering as they do on honorification and indexical gestures of deference.

Hence, one can transduce a high Javanese term by an elaborate latinate, rather than monosyllabic term in English, both giving off something of the same indexical effect modulo their systems of cultural interpretation of such. One can transduce a "T" or "V" form usage in an SAE language by one of the several different 'second person singular' personal deictics in the various Southeast Asian systems. And so forth. Finding comparabilities and overlaps in the way words and expressions do their culture-specific indexical work is a task eminently anthropological, inasmuch as it is comparison of cultural forms of social action. Doing so in the proper kind of framework of comparison allows us not to obliterate the very real differences in total cultural effect while recognizing parallelisms of how certain semiotic machinery – here, use of words and expressions – does abstractly similar communicative work. On the basis of such, a "translator" can attempt to induce in an addressee of the selected and deployed target-language form some understanding comparable to what an addressee of the source-language form would understand in the originary communication. So whether we see it pretheoretically as the problem of stylistically matching an original's "tone" with a translated one, or we see it more theoretically as dealing with the limits of comparability of cultural indexicalities keyed by particular words and expressions, transduction constitutes a distinct problem area for "translation." It is not to be confused with translation in our narrower usage.

The Transformation of Cultural Meaning

More than really translating material (in my narrowed sense), then, transducing material moves us between a source cultural system and a target one. In each system words and expressions are indexically anchored within entextualizations-in-context, and we attempt to move across these. But this leads us to consider that in transduction, operating as we do in the realm of culture more frankly, there is always the possibility of **transformation** of the [en]textual[ized] source material contextualized in specific ways into configurations of cultural semiosis of a sort substantially or completely different from those one has started with.

In one sense, transformation can be considered to result from a kind of misfire of intent with respect to translation and transduction. Recall the discussion above of "untranslated" cultural terms in ethnographies. Scientifically unsystematic practices of generations of anthropologists-as-ethnographic-"translators" have turned source-language/culture material willy-nilly into signs of the structures of power and influence of the professional and scholarly worlds in which the discourse of ethnography is carried on as a central social practice.[25] But in another sense, we can think of determinately intentional aesthetic genre transformation, one of many types of transformation of [en]text[ualization]s defined by the semiotic axes along which it happens. It is the stuff of ever-evolving performance institutions in our own society's cultural life, as for example William Shakespeare's *Romeo and Juliet* becoming – being "translated" into – Leonard Bernstein's *West Side Story*; Victor Hugo's novel *Les Misérables* "adapted" – "translated" – to the musical stage by Sir Andrew Lloyd Webber and associates. These are wholesale exercises in transformation in our sense of the term.

From the point of view of semiotic transformation now, consider again the case of nontranslation of ethnographic words and expressions. If the effect is, as noted, to give the ethnographic author a kind of "ownership" over the scholarly term from "one's people," immediately this ownership becomes indexically convertible with one's name, one's fame as it were: the professional descriptive backing associated with the use of the proper name of the author is, then, the untranslated but cotextually transduced material, the label for the ineffable concept. This fits into the general scientific-scholarly notions of precedence of attributed or at least ascribed coinage for technical terminology of a field's discourse – a sociocultural fact if ever there was one, complete with a durational interval of relevant half-life! But here the "coinages" are words from another language/culture. *Kula*? Bronislaw Malinowski. *Gumlao*? Edmund Leach. There is a kind of Hall of Fame principle organizing such a social system, in which the conceptual labels of other cultures, intendedly transduced so as to get their technical meaning from one's target-language ethnographic text, become the trophies displayed (the ethnographic text being the pedestal) for those elected.[26]

The point here is not to praise or condemn this other meaningfulness (that is, indexically manifested cultural value) that emerges for imported source-language terms in anthropological and wider discursive usages. The point is that the meaningfulness of the very terms that originate in some source language in source-culture usage has been transformed significantly in the target-language and especially target-cultural usage. For the **culture of** anthropologists renders us members of the academic and other professional institutional orders and endows originary technical terms – among them, exotic, "untranslated" words and expressions from ethnographic loci – with special kinds of meaningfulness. Part of this involves indexing identities and qualities of the terms' creators ("discoverers"), users (implicit "referencers" or explicit "citers"), etc., in their own stratified discursive regimes. So the overall co(n)textual meaning of such a term has been profoundly transformed.

Thus can practitioners of identity creation and management within disciplinary and more popular circles learn how to institutionalize such transformations of value in a highly deliberate manner. Because of the transformation of semiosis just described, carrying forward this style of "nontranslational practice" in ethnographic genres becomes centrally involved in social reproduction of a disciplinary line or category through the establishment of a canonical text site.

Sometimes there is no way sufficiently to systematize and limit the transduction of verbal material across functionally intersecting pragmatic systems. Even trying to play it as safe as we can with the textual stuff with which, by hypothesis, we start, semiotic transformation then occurs. Of course, then, to the degree that there is transduction beyond a translator's intended limits, there is always something of the transformational in every attempted translation! Usually, the very organization of pragmatic systems that are involved in the source situation of usage cannot be duplicated in the target situation, as noted above. Sometimes it is possible selectively to reshape an organization of them so that the target verbal material appears in texts of very different functional characteristics, as different, while remaining language, as musical "text" and painting-as-"text," as it were. Even when a token of a word appears printed on a page in an expository prose text and when a token of it appears printed on a page of concrete poetry, these are at least in part transformations one of the other. For verbal, as for other semiotic material, the condition of emergence of meaning is textuality-in-context. Hence, transformation of source material, rather than transduction or translation of it, seems to occur as a risk (or license!) of starting from source entextualizations far from home that require radical reshaping in the "translational" attempt to domesticate them. The "translations" that result must perforce be shaped as discourse genres that license the effectiveness of target verbal forms in sociocultural ways highly different from the originary ones.

At the same time, we must remind ourselves, transformed material, emerging out of an [en]text[ualization]-in-context, can be put in correspondence with source material as IT occurs in [en]text[ualization]-in-context, yielding a relationship of transformation of a certain localized, hence graspable "tropic" appearance. Transformation is, of course, the very condition of trope, and, to the degree to which the source and target elements constitute parts of diagrammatic forms of each other in their respective cotexts, a higher-order notion of "translation-prime" is in a sense suggested. Think for example of transforming a schema of moral values into a color code, and rendering a painting according to the scheme. Think of allegorical embodiment of moral values, as in so much of Renaissance painting. So to the extent to which there is a concept of "tropic meaning" attached to the respective elements of source and target texts, the effects of trope-generating transformation come to play a role in any further stability of actual translation in our narrow sense – starting the cycle all over again!

It is clear now, I hope, that translation and its more fluid – as opposed to gelid – extensions, such as transduction and transformation, occur in a kind of nested set of relationships that emerge in the process of explicit interlingual glossing. I expect that for semiotic systems unlike human language, which thus operate without a true grammaticosemantic system of the Saussurean type to anchor them, transduction and transformation play the unrecognized – or at least untheorized! – major role in what is sometimes loosely termed "translation." (And of course this is true as well for all those aspects of text-in-context itself that are not conformingly Saussurean.)

Perhaps, then, the translation metaphor in these other realms – for that is what it is – does more harm than good, since it misconstrues the vast gulf that exists between language and these other systems in the way of manifestation of semiotic capacities. As well, it misplaces its interest at levels of abstraction and organization that are far from what can be "translated." "Cultures" as such cannot be (in our narrower sense) "translated," for example, insofar as most of their manifestations are in fact nonlinguistic. And even within a cultural tradition, we hardly treat a ballet (entextualization of tableaux of bodily movement) set to music (entextualization of pitches and tonal intensities in metered combination-and-sequence) in the same way as [= as homology of] how we treat a denotationally-centered "bilingual edition" of, say, Wittgenstein or a Greek or Latin author in the *Loeb Classical Library*, perhaps revealing the ineptness or just looseness of the metaphors invoked.

For the critical and inevitable point about "translating cultures" is that at beginning and end of these processes we are dealing with **textual objects** experienceable and intelligible only within – or as the mathematicians would say, "under" – a culture, and hence if we are to understand the nature of the three T's, we have to understand something of the nature of such textual objects in culture. Not, note, **text-artifacts**, which exist, even perdure, in some physical form and, circulating, mediate the entextualization/contextualization process between two or more people.

As a form of social action, language use in entextualizing/contextualizing events is endowed with all the dialectically emergent creativity (technically, indexical entailments) of any such cultural semiosis; the precipitated record of this is a text, of varying degrees of coherence. We are speaking here of texts, then, as contingency-bound semiotic objects that arise as structures of informational or conceptual coherence in context. But it is with respect to texts that people mutually adjust one to another in realtime social interaction, only the explicit mediating "stuff" of which, things like linguistic forms and other traceable bodily signs, is available to us. (Even reading a – text-artifactual – book or looking at a – text-artifactual – painting are contingent acts that result, to the degree that something is communicated, in the generation of at least one text in this sense.)[27]

And let us recall yet further critical points for "translation" within the domain of phenomenal language itself. Much of what looks like 'language' in a superficial, ideologically driven view of the continuous signals of denotational textuality is actually semiotically complex cultural material. Such material is defined not by its Saussurean-centered "denotationality," but by its indexical characteristics and related modalities of meaningfulness that interweave with Saussurean-based denotational form. In this sense, culture penetrates into phenomenal language via indexicality and iconicity[28] so that transduction and transformation, rather than translation, are of the essence, for such parts of a text.

The very forms of abstract language structure, in fact, can be distinguished by the concentrated cultural lumpiness they embody as an important functional aspect of their categorial differentiation. Such parts of language already inherently require different kinds of "translational" treatment. The very act of "translating" according to the intents of the usual, denotationally focused ethnotheory – wherein at least one text must be construed – is a process that thus cannot but be INHERENTLY TRANSFORMING of any such cultural material in the source text that has indexically entailing potential realized in context.

Notes

1. Not in and of itself a startling or new point, of course. Sapir's ([1921] 1949: 221–31) discussion of "Language and Literature," for example, drawing on Benedetto Croce (1909; [2]1922), says that the latter is therefore perfectly right in saying that a work of literary art can never be translated. Nevertheless literature does get itself translated, sometimes with astonishing adequacy. This brings up the question of whether in the art of literature there are not intertwined two distinct kinds or levels of art – a generalized, non-linguistic art, which can be transferred without loss into an alien linguistic medium, and a specifically linguistic art that is not transferrable . . . Literature moves in language as a medium, but that medium comprises two layers, the latent content of language – our intuitive record of experience – and the particular conformation of a given language – the specific how of our record of experience. Literature that draws its sustenance mainly – never entirely – from the lower level, say a play of Shakespeare's, is translatable without too great a loss of character. If it moves in the upper rather than the lower level – a fair example is a lyric of Swinburne's – it is as good as untranslatable. Both types of literary expression may be great or mediocre.

   Here, my argument attempts to be more subtle both in respect of language form (Sapir's "particular conformation of a given language") and of cultural form (Sapir's "latent content"), since we now understand culture in fact to be semiotic form, and we now understand language to have a complex semiotic manifestation.

2. Thus, note the progression outward, as it were, from denotational textuality (and especially its lexicogrammatical underpinnings in language systems), as translation theory has attempted to take account of the sociocultural nature of language in all its contextualized varieties. One can follow this in the historical accounts of twentieth-century translation theories, e.g. Gentzler 1993, and in the admirable, chronologically organized anthology of Venuti (2000). The crisis

of finding the right semiotic aspect of language about which to anchor translational practice always seems to start from conflicts of "fidelity" that are, in European ethnolinguistic reflexivity, centered in the first instance on denotation, though we would now see them as proceeding from the semiotic complexity of textuality-in-context. Both Walter Benjamin (1923; cf. Venuti 2000: 15–25) and George Steiner (1975; ³1998), two pillars of translation studies, illustrate the anxiety. Recent writers in translation studies (Venuti 2000: 331–488; Bassnett and Trivedi 1999) are concerned with "identity" and "culture" in relation to translation, especially sensitive in postcolonial contexts, but do not seem to have realized that the semiotic re-partialling of language/textuality itself is necessary to theorizing these matters in a more productive and systematic way.

3. Note the re-lexicalization by translating [!] with a view to the originary attack to counter the deep-rooted French – and other – school practice of "construing" a text as to form and determinate "meaning," my English from the French déconstruire, déconstruction; cf. construire 'construe'. Alas, the [building-] demolition image seems to have caught the fancy of generations of writers feeling themselves to have been liberated in their aggressions.

4. A grammatically complex expression 'C' consisting of elements 'A' and 'B' is said to be semantically compositional if, given the meanings of A and B plus the rule of construction by which A and B are joined to form C, we can regularly compute the meaning of C. Thus, in English attributive constructions of modifying adjective preceding modified noun, there is generally compositionality, e.g. yellow- [=A, an adjective] plus bird- [=B, a noun] yields a nominal expression [=C] yellow bird-, the meaning of which *modulo the grammar* is a computable function of the meanings of the two simplex stems. Observe that denotationally speaking, English blue bird- is compositional, while bluebird- is not.

5. What I am terming 'Saussurean sense' is, of course, Saussure's "signified" (*signifié*), which is only synthetically or constructively associable with any given sign-type (Saussure's *signifiant*) after one has, in principle, done a complete grammaticosemantic analysis of the entire language system of which signifier and signified are correlative partials at the level of synchronic norm.

6. This is the Boasian or Whorfian idea of the "calibration" of languages one with respect to another *modulo* a universal grammar or space of possible categorial systems (Silverstein 2000: 86–94). It is also, of course, the logic of the Praguean revolution in the study of phonology, the functioning of sound systems in languages and in language, leading to the theory of '[distinctive] features'; cf. Silverstein 1993.

7. Capital letters in this rough-and-ready notation key the argument that becomes the apparent phrasal denotatum of the linguistic expression; subscripts key individuable entities as indexed; predicate-argument notation with a given

number of variables suggests a semantically n-place *relational* 'sense', here one with two arguments notated as 'x' and 'Y'.

8. Observe the proper relationship between Saussurean 'sense' and denotational range: the 'simpler' the Saussurean 'sense', the greater the denotational range; the more 'complex' the Saussurean 'sense,' the lesser or more specific the denotational range. The simplicity and complexity involve at least an intuitive, if not formalized, understanding of atomicness of 'sense' elements and a compositional algebra in terms of which simplex and complex 'senses' are relatively definable. All this follows from the Saussurean assumptions of modern linguistic semantics, and especially, in areas of lexical semantics, from models that involve Boolean and other kinds of combinatorics (configurational "syntax") of 'sense' elements themselves.

9. Anthropologists will recall the charming way that European native ideologies of reference pack all this into translations of the lexical heads of such grammatically complex expressions, such as "iraaya 'father; son of a man'," or ". . . 'father; son [man speaking]'," the first of the glosses, if taken literally, suggesting a newly discovered antipodean parthenogenesis among Australian Aboriginal men, the second confusing grammatically construable possessor (the first occurring NP as in [NP's NP]$_{NP}$) with the individual inhabiting the speaker role in a vocative or equivalent use (which would in any case be accomplished with a special vocative form of stem [in Worora ira; intimate register, djidja], marking the identity of *speaker* and possessor!).

10. Observe that when used with the underlying verb bake-, here used in the active intransitive implying a generic direct object [*sc.*, "things"], the X occurs as the 'benefactee,' coded in a phrase-type like [Y] bake- for [X]. This makes the denotatum of Y '[X]'s bake- + -(e)r' or 'bake- + -er to [X].' The kinterms do not have such completely verbal constructions in a language like English, where they are lexical nouns. Importantly, also, the denominative transitive verbs, such as [Y] (to) father- [X], [Y] (to) mother- [X] are *derivative* (denominal) forms meaning [Y] 'to be(come) father/mother to/of' [X]; cf. the forms in the text.

11. It is, of course, impossible for me to review here the long, somewhat sad, and now much abandoned field of "kinship and social organization" focused on lexical items that was once the mainstay of self-described "social" anthropology (comparative sociology of kin-based societies), as also one of the major fields of play for "ethnoscience"/ "cognitive anthropology" and especially its notions of "componential analysis." It is an object lesson in how bad theorizing emerges in anthropological work in realms of culture when language and other central, meaning-giving semiotic systems are neglected, poorly theorized, or theorized by bad analogies, or even altogether avoided in favor of identifying culture with a heap of simple word-and-"thing" mappings.

12. Note that there are ways of constructing secondary deictic origins by describing (in language) the context in which such a situation is to be conceptualized. In literary narrative, the combination of primary origin-point with partially transposed secondary one from a narrated character's point of view constitutes "indirect free style" of narration of "represented speech and thought," for which see especially Banfield 1993 [1978] and references there, and Lee 1997: 277–320. Complex (e.g. 'conditional') and relative (e.g. 'pluperfect'). Tense categories incorporate such secondary *origines* into their very morphological codings.

13. The symbolization here is with an arrow to indicate 'implicature' (Grice 1989 [1967]: 24ff.) and a parenthetical presentation of the specific semantic content implicated by the 'nonpast' value of the category. This captures the essential insight of Jakobson's (1971 [1939]: 211ff.) introduction of MARKEDNESS into lexicogrammatical analysis, the tendency of dichotomously opposed categorial values to be asymmetric, in that one categorial form specifically communicates a denotational value, the other fails so to communicate [the so-called neutral meaning], and in pragmatic discursive context is generally used so as to "implicate" – suggest unless countered – the negative, complementary, or polar-opposite denotational value. A related fact is that the neutral-negative **form** of obligatory grammatical categories is thus also used where no specific value is communicated, e.g. "timeless" truths expressed in English – where a Tense marking is obligatory on a finite clause verb – with a 'nonpast' [=> ('present')] inflectional form.

14. Bakhtin (see for example 1981: 270ff., 291ff.) termed this the fundamentally "heteroglossic" nature of a language and of its linguistic community, both in respect of thoroughgoing sociolinguistic differentiation such that the very use of certain pronunciations, words, expressions indexes (in literary gesture, constitutes a *renvoi* to) some site of normatively originary discursive production, or indeed of someone else's actually more originary production. Elaborate sociolinguistic processes bring this into being, and constantly maintain and renew this indexical value of words and expressions in (con)text; see Silverstein 1996.

15. This approach early on converged with the Kripke–Putnam understanding of a "causal theory" of reference (see Griffiths 1997: 171–201; Kripke 1972; Putnam 1975; Schwartz 1977), though it subsumes these narrower worryings of the problem of referring and renders them generalizable and useful to the anthropologist and other student of sociocultural conceptualization.

16. Baby Talk Register consists of forms that **adults** use in characterizing infants' or young children's usage, and/or that adults actually use in addressing an infant or young child. Since instruction in discursive interaction is frequently given in Baby Talk Register, children sometimes do acquire these terms,

locutions, pronunciations, etc. of the register as a secondary process; cf. Jakobson 1962 [1959]. The register's lexical forms and even its other formal aspects frequently become, delocutionarily, emblems of immaturity, endearment, etc. and can be found widely in contexts that, in pragmatic metaphor, indexically summon up the affective qualities of speaking with/to children, e.g. talk between lovers. See Casagrande (1964 [1948]) for one of the early recognitions and treatments of this phenomenon, and the classic papers of Ferguson that developed the topic in both universal-typological terms and in terms of functional relations to other "simplified registers" (1964; 1971; 1977; Ferguson and DeBose 1977); cf. also Dil 1971.

17. For the time being let us not worry about the fact that in order to translate/ transduce a given expression in a unitary text in a source language it may be necessary to formulate more than one type of expression in the target language in some complex textual organization of partials, like "main text" and "footnote," or "text" printed in many "typefaces" or similar diacritics, notwithstanding the unitary character of the original in its source language. See below on anthropological non-translation in these circumstances.

18. In these structural formulae, the 'X' and 'Y' represent Noun Phrases or their grammatical equivalents that can be substituted in the respective syntactic positions so as to project 'Agentive' readings for X and 'Patientive' readings for Y.

19. This constitutes Searle's (1969: 30–33) problem of how to formulate determinate "illocutionary force indicating devices" [IFIDs] for each and every performatively consequential act of using any natural human language – which he stipulatively resolves by creating a set of language- and culture-independent basic illocutionary act types fully parallel to the famous Berlin and Kay (1969) *Basic Color Terms*.

20. An indigenous American language spoken by "an important and warlike tribe living in central Texas during most of the 18th and 19th centuries" (Hoijer 1933: ix).

21. In several places Geertz (1983: 10; 157–58, 185) and those close to him in the trend called "symbolic" and especially "interpretive" anthropology celebrate this substitutive transduction as the hermeneutic glory of anthropological accounts of other cultures' concepts.

> [The anthropological concern] tends to focus on key terms that seem, when their meaning is unpacked, to light up a whole way of going at the world. (1983: 157)

It thus replaces the traditional comparative and philological goal of translation of culture in my revised, narrowed sense. It argues that what we can hope at best to achieve in ethnography is a goal of transduction specifically of "key terms" of a culture to reco(n)textualization within a target-language ethnographic text. The ethnographic text thus becomes interpolated (interpellated, too!) between at least the indexical value of the source-language word or expression and our ability to understand its conceptual value. Now much in the way of such "interpretive" ethnographic description consists of describing those very contexts in which the term occurs. So the ethnographic reader's sense of the "meaning" of such a term, via this Geertzian "unpacking," is at best (in the most elaborate and sensitive "unpackings") its rules of illocutionary use, not, in fact, its original denotational meaning or its indexical characteristics! (See here Searle [1969: 136–41] on "the speech act fallacy" about the 'meaning' of words and expressions.) Hence, it would seem, merely the "thickness" of the transductional co(n)text provides the basis for and measure of the success of this attempt in place of "translation" or even our more narrowly drawn translation-with-transduction. Geertz and others have very much stressed the locally "unpacking" mission of interpretative ethnography, eschewing translation of the local into cross-culturally generalizing metapragmatic descriptors on the one hand or into other local terms in a natural target language. This angers scientistic types like Dan Sperber (1996: 32–59), who would hold up to anthropology as a "science of the social" the necessity to determine the latter by the former (eschewing transduction and transformation in our senses).

22. An "untranslated" term incorporated into the comparative and theoretical discourse of anthropology turns any textual occurrence of the originary form in some source language into a mere ethnographic instance once more, labeled by the (borrowed) term in question ultimately only as the prototype instance [think of <u>taboo</u>?] of the theoretical concept in question. Here, the originary word or expression takes its place as part of a translational set along with all other instances of such-and-so phenomenon in one or another society. By making such a move one does, in fact, reintroduce the task of having to translate the original term in our sense, by growing it a theoretical semantic meaning as well as an ethnographic-descriptive one. But note that the borrowed term in such comparative and theoretical discourse has a meaning different from those of either the source original or any target translation in any other natural language.

23. There are immense literatures on each one of these languages and their systems of stratified lexical registers, which are similar to each other as indexical systems in many interesting ways. The most semiotically astute treatments in modern terms are Errington's (1988) of Javanese and Agha's (1993, 1998) of Tibetan. See also Agha 1994 for an overview of these systems in the larger area of "honorification," and Irvine 1995, 1998 for an analysis of the relation of cultural ideologies of honorification to the semiotics of how the indexical systems operate.

24. English essentially lost the inherited and comparable thou/ye system by the end of the seventeenth century; see Silverstein 1985: 242–51 and refs. there for the explanation of its final slide into desuetude.

25. A postmodernist "Translation Studies" would debunk *any* pretensions to systematic grounding of "translation" by showing how the enterprise always already involves necessary transformation, let alone transduction, not to mention that the transformations are in the direction of power over/through terms in the target regime of discourse. As one says *qua* scientist to "Science Studies," so what? The point is not that there is not a route to complete inter-cultural translation in my narrow sense such that anything goes; the point is that there is some interlinguistic translation, and that there are plausible transductions as well. And that we should be doing them.

26. And of course the wider the electorate, and the longer the time elapsed, the greater the chance that the term has come to be used outside of the technical-professional discourse, winding up as a layperson's word borrowed from language to language, like taboo – which then needs translation all over again when applied to understanding the culture of the place from which it came in the first place! (See n. 22 *supra*.)

27. One is reminded of the conceptual mischief done by Paul Ricoeur's (1971) "model of the text," unfortunately invoked by Clifford Geertz in very influential contexts, in its metaphorical misidentification of the textual object with acts of "inscription" of text-*artifacts*! While we do, in fact, create such text-artifacts, e.g. manuscript or printed transcripts of oral-aural discursive interactions, the better to be able to study them analytically, given the frailties even of our own human cognitive processing, these artifacts and the way we produce them cannot be taken as a good starting point for the notion of how coherent meaningfulness is achieved in the realtime social events of communicating.

28. A point nicely spelled out some years ago in the lengthy essay, "The Symbol and its Relative Non-arbitrariness," by Paul Friedrich (1979 [1975]); cf. also Friedrich 1986.

References

Agha, Asif. "Grammatical and Indexical Convention in Honorific Discourse." *Journal of Linguistic Anthropology* 3, 1993, 131–63.

—— "Honorification." *Annual Review of Anthropology* 23, 1994, 277–302.

—— "Stereotypes and Registers of Honorific Language." *Language in Society* 27, 1998, 151–93.

Austin, John L. *How To Do Things With Words* (2nd ed.). Urmson, J. O. and Marina Sbisà (eds.). Cambridge, MA: Harvard University Press. 1975 [1962].

Bakhtin, Mikhail M. *The Dialogic Imagination: Four Essays*. Trans. Caryl Emerson and Michael Holquist. Michael Holquist (ed.). Austin, TX: University of Texas Press, 1981.

Banfield, Ann. "Where Epistemology, Style, and Grammar Meet Literary History: The Development of Represented Speech and Thought." In *Reflexive Language: Reported Speech and Metapragmatics*. John A. Lucy (ed.), pp. 339–64. Cambridge: Cambridge University Press, 1993 [1978].

Bassnett, Susan and Trivedi, Harish (eds.). *Post-colonial Translation: Theory and Practice*. London and New York: Routledge, 1999.

Berlin, Brent and Kay, Paul. *Basic Color Terms:Their Universality and Evolution*. Berkeley and Los Angeles: University of California Press, 1969.

Brown, Roger and Ford, Marguerite. "Address in American English." In *Language in Culture and Society: A Reader in Linguistics and Anthropology*. Dell Hymes (ed.), pp. 234–44. New York: Harper and Row, 1964 [1961].

Brown, Roger and Gilman, Albert. "The Pronouns of Power and Solidarity." In *Style in Language*. Thomas A. Sebeok (ed.), pp. 253–76. Cambridge, MA: MIT Press, 1964 [1961].

Casagrande, Joseph B. "Comanche Baby Language." In *Language in Culture and Society: A Reader in Linguistics and Anthropology*. Dell Hymes (ed.), pp. 245–50. New York: Harper and Row, 1964 [1948].

Clifford, James. "On Ethnographic Authority." *Representations* 1(2): 1983, pp. 118–46.

Crapanzano, Vincent. "Hermes' Dilemma: The Masking of Subversion in Ethnographic Description." In *Writing Culture: The Poetics and Politics of Ethnography*. James Clifford and George E. Marcus (eds.), pp. 51–76. Berkeley and Los Angeles: University of California Press, 1986.

Croce, Benedetto. *Aesthetic As Science of Expression and General Linguistic*. Trans. Douglas Ainslie. London: Macmillan & Co. 1909; [2]1922.

Dil, Afia. "Bengali Baby Talk." *Word* 27, 1971, 11–27.

Errington, J. Joseph. *Structure and Style in Javanese: A Semiotic View of Linguistic Etiquette*. Philadelphia: University of Pennsylvania Press, 1988.

Ferguson, Charles A. "Baby Talk in Six Languages." *The Ethnography of Communication*. John J. Gumperz and Dell H. Hymes (eds.), pp. 103–14. *American Anthropologist* 66(6), part 2, 1964.

—— "Absence of Copula and the Notion of Simplicity: A Study of Normal Speech, Baby Talk, Foreigner Talk, and Pidgins." In *Pidginization and Creolization of Languages: Proceedings . . . 1968*. Dell Hymes (ed.0, pp. 141–50. Cambridge: Cambridge University Press, 1971.

—— "Baby Talk as a Simplified Register." In *Talking to Children: Language Input and Acquisition*. Catherine E. Snow and Charles A. Ferguson (eds.), pp. 209–35. Cambridge: Cambridge University Press, 1977.

Ferguson, Charles A. and DeBose, Charles E. "Simplified Registers, Broken Language, and Pidginization." In *Pidgin and Creole Linguistics*. Albert Valdman (ed.), pp. 99–125. Bloomington, IN: Indiana University Press, 1977.

Friedrich, Paul. "The Symbol and its Relative Non-arbitrariness." In *Language, Context, and the Imagination: Essays of Paul Friedrich*. Anwar S. Dil (ed.), pp. 1–61. Stanford, CA: Stanford University Press, 1979 [1975].

—— *The Language Parallax: Linguistic Relativism and Poetic Indeterminacy*. Austin, TX: University of Texas Press, 1986.

Geertz, Clifford. *Local Knowledge: Further Essays in Interpretive Anthropology*. New York: Basic, 1983.

—— *Works and Lives: The Anthropologist as Author*. Stanford, CA: Stanford University Press, 1988.

Gentzler, Edwin. *Contemporary Translation Theories*. London and New York: Routledge, 1993.

Grice, H. Paul. "Logic and Conversation." In *Studies in the Way of Words*, pp. 3–143. Cambridge, MA: Harvard University Press, 1989 [1967].

Griffiths, Paul E. *What Emotions **Really** Are: The Problem of Psychological Categories*. Chicago: University of Chicago Press, 1997.

Hinton, Leanne, Nichols, Johanna, and Ohala, John J. "Introduction: Sound-symbolic Processes." In *Sound Symbolism*, pp. 1–12. Cambridge: Cambridge University Press, 1994.

Hoijer, Harry. *Tonkawa, An Indian Language of Texas*. Extract from *Handbook of American Indian Languages*, vol. 3. Franz Boas (ed.). (Separately paginated.) New York: Columbia University Press, 1933.

Irvine, Judith T. "Honorification." In *Handbook of Pragmatics*. Jef Verschueren, Jan-Ola Östman, Jan Blommaert, and Chris Bulcaen (eds.). *S.v.* Separately paginated, pp. 1–22. Amsterdam: John Benjamins, 1995.

—— "Ideologies of Honorific Language." In *Language Ideologies: Practice and Theory*. Bambi B. Schieffelin, Kathryn A. Woolard, and Paul V. Kroskrity (eds.), pp. 51–67. New York: Oxford University Press, 1998.

Jakobson, Roman "Why "Mama" and "Papa"?" In *Selected Writings of Roman Jakobson*, vol. 1, *Phonological Studies*, pp. 538–45. The Hague: Mouton, 1962 [1960].

—— "Signe zéro." In *Selected Writings of Roman Jakobson*, vol. 2, *Word and Language*, pp. 211–19. The Hague: Mouton, 1971 [1939].

—— [Concluding statement:] "Linguistics and Poetics." In *Selected Writings of Roman Jakobson*, vol. 3, *Poetry of Grammar and Grammar of Poetry*. Stephen Rudy (ed.), pp. 18–51. The Hague: Mouton, 1981 [1960].

Jakobson, Roman and Waugh, Linda R. *The Sound Shape of Language*. Bloomington, IN: Indiana University Press, 1979.

Kripke, Saul A. "Naming and Necessity." In *Semantics of Natural Language*. Donald Davidson and Gilbert Harman (eds.), pp. 253–355. Dordrecht: D. Reidel Publishing Co., 1972.

Lee, Benjamin. *Talking Heads: Language, Metalanguage, and the Semiotics of Subjectivity*. Durham, NC: Duke University Press, 1997.

Lucy, John A. *Grammatical Categories and Cognition: A Case Study of the Linguistic Relativity Hypothesis*. Cambridge: Cambridge University Press. 1992a.

—— *Language Diversity and Thought: A Reformulation of the Linguistic Relativity Hypothesis*. Cambridge: Cambridge University Press, 1992b.

Morford, Janet H. "Social Indexicality in French Pronominal Address." *Journal of Linguistic Anthropology* 7, 1997, 3–37.

Murphy, Gregory L. "Personal Reference in English." *Language in Society* 17, 1988, 317–49.

Parmentier, Richard J. *The Pragmatic Semiotics of Cultures*. [Special Issue.] *Semiotica* 116(1), 1997.

Putnam, Hilary. "The Meaning of 'Meaning'." In *Philosophical Papers*, vol. 2, *Mind, Language, and Reality*, pp. 215–71. Cambridge: Cambridge University Press. 1975.

Quine, Willard V. *Word and Object*. Cambridge, MA: MIT Press, 1960.

Ricoeur, Paul V. "The Model of the Text: Meaningful Action Considered as a Text." In *Hermeneutics and the Human Sciences: Essays on Language, Action, and Interpretation*. John B. Thompson (trans. and ed.), pp. 197–221. Cambridge: Cambridge University Press and Paris: Editions de la Maison des Sciences de l'Homme, 1981 [1971].

Sapir, Edward. *Language: An Introduction to the Study of Speech*. New York: Harcourt, Brace & World, 1949 [1921].

Saussure, Ferdinand de. *Cours de linguistique générale*. Charles Bally and Albert Sèchehaye (eds.). Lausanne and Paris: Payot & Cie, 1916.

Schwartz, Stephen P. (ed.). *Naming, Necessity, and Natural Kinds*. Ithaca, NY: Cornell University Press, 1977.

Searle, John R. *Speech Acts: An Essay in the Philosophy of Language*. Cambridge: Cambridge University Press, 1969.

Silverstein, Michael. "Language and the Culture of Gender: At the Intersection of Structure, Usage, and Ideology." In *Semiotic Mediation: Sociocultural and Psychological Perspectives*. Elizabeth Mertz and Richard J. Parmentier (eds.), pp. 219–59. Orlando, FL: Academic Press, 1985.

—— "Cognitive Implications of a Referential Hierarchy." In *Social and Functional Approaches to Language and Thought*. Maya Hichman (ed.), pp. 125–64. Orlando, FL: Academic Press, 1987.

—— "Of Nominatives and Datives: Universal Grammar from the Bottom up." In *Advances in Role and Reference Grammar*. Robert D. Van Valin, Jr. (ed.), pp. 465–98. Amsterdam: John Benjamins, 1993.

—— "Relative Motivation in Denotational and Indexical Sound Symbolism of Wasco-Wishram Chinookan." In *Sound Symbolism*. Leanne Hinton, Johanna Nichols, and John J. Ohala (eds.), pp. 40–60. Cambridge: Cambridge University Press, 1994.

—— "Indexical Order and the Dialectics of Sociolinguistic Life." *Symposium About Language and Society – Austin [SALSA]* 3: 266–95. (*=Texas Linguistic Forum*, no. 36 [Austin, TX: University of Texas, Department of Linguistics]), 1996.

—— "Whorfianism and the Linguistic Imagination of Nationality." In *Regimes of Language: Ideologies, Polities, and Identities*. Paul V. Kroskrity (ed.), pp. 85–138. Santa Fe, NM: School of American Research Press, 2000.

—— "Naming Sets among the Worora." ms.a [1980].

Silverstein, Michael and Urban, Greg. "The Natural History of Discourse." In *Natural Histories of Discourse*. Michael Silverstein & Greg Urban (eds.), pp. 1–17. Chicago: University of Chicago Press, 1996.

Sperber, Dan. *Explaining Culture: A Naturalistic Approach*. Oxford: Blackwell Publishers, 1996.

Steiner, George. *After Babel: Aspects of Language and Translation*. London and New York: Oxford University Press, 1975. 3rd ed. 1998.

Venuti, Lawrence (ed.). *The Translation Studies Reader*. London and New York: Routledge, 2000.

Whorf, Benjamin Lee. "Science and Linguistics." In *Language, Thought, and Reality: Selected Writings of Benjamin Lee Whorf*. John B. Carroll (ed.), pp. 207–19. Cambridge, MA: MIT Press, 1956a [1940].

—— "The Relation of Habitual Thought and Behavior to Language." In *LTR*. pp. 134–59, 1956b [1941].

—— "Grammatical Categories." In *LTR*, pp. 87–101. 1956c [1945].

Part II
Specific Applications

–4–

The Unspeakable in Pursuit of the Ineffable: Representations of Untranslatability in Ethnographic Discourse
Michael Herzfeld

Problems of Translation

My title paraphrases Oscar Wilde's memorable description of an English gentle-man hunting a fox. For most ethnographers, translating local terms as though they had stable meanings is intellectually indigestible, yet we cannot dispense with it – any more than we could survive without reifying the categories of ordinary social life. Our descriptions, designed to illuminate how and for what the words are used, deprecatingly suggest that the language of the other is so different, so exotic, that we cannot really translate at all. We are all, in this sense, Whorfian extremists, if only by affectation.

But in fact this position, viewed pragmatically rather than referentially, is not an affectation at all. It is, rather, the simple fact that, as John Leavitt (1996) has observed, even those of us who believe that psychological inner states are neither attributable to whole populations nor even safely identifiable in individuals write our best ethnographic vignettes as though we could do both those things. The act of translating terms-in-context is a useful fiction because it suggests that we can identify the meanings that social actors intend. We all engage in this fiction, with-out which ethnographic description would be impossible.

And so the central paradox emerges: the plausibility of our accounts depends on a device that is itself predicated on an imaginative act of empathy with inform-ants. We write as though we deduced those intuitions from regularly occurring actions and contexts, just as we do in our own everyday lives. This is a common-sense approach – but it fails to ask whose common sense is being invoked. We translate by declaring the terms untranslatable; we make translation the key metaphor of our reporting; and yet we know that translation, like comparison in Evans-Pritchard's famous adage, is ultimately impossible. (Greek shepherds and peasants say much the same thing about knowing other people's intentions, and similarly keep guessing at them.) But what else can we do?

Here I shall argue that the difficulty disappears if we treat ethnographic translation and literary translation as two different, if closely related, enterprises. This has to do with the difference between ethnography and fiction at the most basic level. Following Gregory Bateson (1958: 1) and Michael Jackson (personal communication, cited in Herzfeld 1997b: 24), I subscribe to the view that the major difference between these two representational genres concerns their management of psychological explicitness: a novelist usually backgrounds all the formal cultural principles that the ethnographer would want to spell out, but does describe innermost thoughts (see Herzfeld 1997b: 23). In an ethnography, by contrast, everything is at the level of collective representation because even highly individualistic acts are usually mentioned for the light they shed on communal values or on the scope of deviation. The very choice of marginal communities – and sometimes of marginalized viewpoints within them (Steedly 1993: 31) – is often a strategic and methodological device with which to explore the very forces that decide what is marginal or central.

In this context, the translation of local terms is an attempt, however flawed, to specify cultural principles. Meanings are given as though they were largely constant and predictable, sometimes with contextual information that shows the extent and variety of observed variation. Instead of dealing with translations as devices of art for the purpose of releasing the text from its dependence on prior cultural knowledge, as a literary translator would do, ethnographic translations are attempts to explain the cultural knowledge that local actors bring to their interpretations of each other's actions. My old mentor, the late classicist Philip Vellacott, once wrote that the purpose of a translation from the (ancient) Greek was achieved when the reader threw it away and began to learn the language of the original (1954). In the case of ethnography, this charming conceit is at best an impracticable dream: imagine thousands of anthropologists all "set down" in the coral reefs of the Trobriands. And so the ethnographer, returned home and writing up, has to devise means of making the trip seem quite unnecessary – to be an authoritative guide to the reader.

There are those who view all anthropology as a form of translation. But whether they view ethnography as a practice of translation (Beidelman 1970; Crick 1976; Geertz 1973) or contest that characterization as expressing a hegemonic relationship with the world (Asad 1993), anthropologists are, willy-nilly, engaged in a project that requires some degree of understanding of what translation entails. Their access to key data is through languages of which they have variably competent understandings; their discourse is littered with attempts at contextualization of the kind that would drive any lexicographer to despair; and their choice of key terms veers between expressions of modest uncertainty about the validity of their translations and implicit but unmistakable claims to epistemological authority.

In this chapter, I propose to explore these issue by discussing the representation of "other meanings" in ethnographic description. I shall approach this from two angles, that of my reading of colleagues' and predecessors' attempts and that of my own difficulties as I moved among different genres. I shall try to deal especially with what I consider to be two central issues: first, the intractable problem of intentionality as this is related to etymological history; and second, the politics of translation (as well as transliteration). I shall especially take advantage of the fact that, as I have primarily worked in various forms of modern Greek to date, I am dealing with a language with a richly documented past.

Why Greece?

The ethnography of Greece is extremely suggestive for our present discussion. First, given the hegemonic construction of modern Greek identity under the shadow of foreign models of its ancient predecessors, it is something of a test case for Asad's gloomy dismissal of translation as the key to anthropological under-standing: is the power of the dominant models of Hellas so great as to render our attempts to decipher the modern culture irretrievably Sisyphean? Or might it be that a determined appeal to Greek frameworks that do *not* hew to the official line could destabilize precisely those after-effects of Enlightenment intellectual despotism?

Second, and in a related vein, the modern Greek language presents a particular set of epistemological issues for the critical ethnographer. If modern Greece holds up a looking-glass to the discipline that shares with it a history of elaborating the meaning of "the West" (Herzfeld 1987), its language enshrines many of the most piquant paradoxes of its dual role as incarnation of Hellas and orientalized land of unredeemable marginality. Indeed, it is never quite clear what "its" language really is. The "high register" of its diglossic pair, *katharevousa* (see Ferguson 1959), was officially abolished over two decades ago, yet it continues to appear as the dis-course of the unfashionable political Right and, much more significantly, as an ironic shadow for those who instead can still mimic its orotund pomposity.

A third point again concerns intentionality: if the Greeks themselves generally hold a skeptical view of the possibility of deciphering psychological inner states, how far does the very idea of translation violate their own culturally routinized skepticism? This is a particularly delicate issue because, in a country where one of the defenses against external hegemonies consists in arguing that the Greek language is impenetrable to foreigners, translation offers both the only logically available means of communicating Greek culture to outsiders and a guarantee that such communication will be severely limited. The problem becomes especially intractable when what is to be translated is itself the language of intentionality and inner knowledge. If, as Needham (1972) has argued, the term "belief" cannot serve as a gloss on the collective psychological inner states of other peoples, this is in part because the English-language term preserves, by etymological association, some elements of the classical and New Testament term *pistis,* with its further implications of a comprehensive, desexualized concept of "love" (cf. German *lieben*) (Needham 1972: 42). Just how important is this historical connection? On the one hand, as Austin (1971) demonstrated in respect of excuses, it is not necessary for a speaker to be consciously aware of language history for an excuse to be socially plausible: the aura of antiquity – what Austin called "trailing clouds of etymology" (1971: 99–100) – usually suffices, and indeed its effects might be dissipated by too analytic an examination of their implicit claims. On the other hand, however, the modern Greek version of New Testament "love" (MG *aghapi;* NT *agape),* conceived in a world where what defines a Christian is inherited sinfulness rather than socially innocent sanctity (Campbell 1964: 326; Herzfeld 1997a: 119), is the uncontrolled sexual attraction that undermines the moral restraints and social decorum of formally arranged marriages. Although Campbell translates *pistevoume* as "we believe" (1964: 323), moreover, it is clear that this is a social representation and begs no questions about actual credence. Indeed, it is inimical to questioning of any kind at all, since faith, here following doctrinal prescription, is taken to be incompatible with doubt (see Herzfeld 1997a: 123). Since this view of faith undergirds the socially sanctioned reluctance to challenge the honesty of fellow-villagers yet whom one may not trust, those socially recognized as faithful in a religious sense do not depend on actual belief for this reputation. They *may* believe, but neither can we literally know whether they do nor is it particularly relevant for normal social purposes.

What are we to make of the fact that Greek "belief" thus looks further removed from – and certainly more resolutely social than – its classical and religious moorings than do ordinary English usages? Or is this perception simply the effect of a hegemony that claims both the classical and the Christian heritage for a West unprepared to grant equality to its orientalized client state in today's Greece? These problems are compounded for us by the historical entailment of anthropology as a discipline in the Western project of world domination. Our recognition of this entailment is what makes anthropology today such a strong source of insight into the workings of cultural hegemony, and Greece is, precisely because of its own ambiguous entailment in those processes, an excellent vantage point for further exploration. Yet few anthropologists now working in Greece know classical tongue or New Testament Greek, and almost none of the younger ones have experienced *katharevousa* as the living fossil it was thirty years ago.

I may be the only non-Greek anthropologist to have endured a year of classes in strict *katharevousa.* This prepared me well for today's constant, politically charged language play, and helped me see that rhetoric, far from being socially epiphenomenal, could be constitutive of social relations. I came to believe that any description of social structure and cultural form would be incomplete without due recognition of this quality, one that many Greeks themselves explicitly described. Of the first two major English-speaking ethnographers of Greece, John Campbell also knew the classical language before he went into the field, while Ernestine Friedl was accompanied by her classicist husband, the late Harry Levy. Both writers, albeit in very different ways, provide us with rich details that – as in all good ethnography, I suggest – ultimately allow us to view the translation of purely linguistic elements from a relatively pragmatic and grounded perspective. Thus, these first ethnographies (Campbell 1964; Friedl 1962) constitute sites of ling-uistically well-informed analysis. But by that same token they also set a pattern that less well-informed successors came to accept uncritically in respect of the prevail-ing assumptions about meaning and translation, and here the problems become more serious, necessitating a re-examination of how they translated certain terms.

Many anthropologists provide glossaries of key terms or insert such terms with one-on-one translations in the main texts of their ethnographies. That this was not altogether wise perhaps first became apparent in kinship studies, when it was discovered that informants were disobligingly apt to use terms in ways that were not predicted by "the kinship terminology" (see especially Karp 1978). Analog-ously, too, the idea that economic categories would permit the conflation of local practices with national legal norms has obscured the long-standing resistance to the institution of the dowry in precisely those communities where this stereotypically "traditional Greek custom" has been most vividly present.

The purpose of providing original terms is a double one. On the one hand, it allows a kind of shorthand referentiality: the reader is first educated into the significance of the term by "seeing" it used in a set of diagnostic contexts, after which its appearance in the text is routinized and assumed to be semantically stable. On the other hand, the recurrence of foreign words serves to remind the reader that no translation is ever perfect, that the author is watching out for possible misinterpretations, and that the author can reliably interpret native speakers' intentions.

Rather than playing a deliberate game of deception, ethnographers have elab-orated a device derived from philology and history, where the semantic instability of brief encounters is rarely a serious issue. The consequences of this move conflict with one of anthropologists' commonest assumptions: that the personal intentions behind declarations of affect or motive are opaque, so that all the anthropologist can do is to record the representations of such inner states and observe people's reactions. This seems to be the basic assumption made by the editors of the three major collections of ethnographic approaches to sentiment and psychology (Lutz and Abu-Lughod 1990; Heelas and Lock 1981; Rosen 1995). It is consistent with the detailed logical critique advanced by Rodney Needham (1972; but cf. Cohen

1994; Leavitt 1996). But it potentially sidesteps an important issue. For if inner life can be represented, then at least social actors agree on the existence of something subjective, whether or not they agree about its significance. That subjectivity is always "about" something collectively presumed to exist (Jackson 1996: 29). And translation depends on a recognition of that commonality, fractured though its image must be through the uneven glass of our instruments of perception and reproduction: as Mary Steedly writes of her translations of her informants' narratives, in a lucid statement that captures the *pragmatic* necessities entailed in the task of translation, "readers should not mistake these representations of others' speech for the actual presence of other voices . . . any more than they should regard the stories themselves as unmediated and disinterested accounts of 'real' experience" (1993: 37). Ethnographers are social actors too, and one basis of their intersubjective relationship with their informants lies in the similarity of the translational tasks in which both are continually involved.

Meaning implies intention; when we ask what a word means, we should really be asking what the *speaker* "meant" – that is, intended – by it. Only the compiler of a socially decontextualized lexicography could entertain the possibility of meanings divorced from actors' intentions. We would do well to pay close attention to ordinary-language usage here, with its underlying "folk theory." Such a theory may not recognize or privilege intentionality at all, but knowing what it *does* entail should help us understand how the absence of any such recognition can coexist with actions that appear to presuppose intentions and motives – the attribution of venality by people who claim one can never read others' minds is a case in point.

To what extent should we isolate semantics from other kinds of meaning? There are those who would prefer to separate the two kinds of meaning (which I am presenting here as fundamentally of a single kind) in the same way that they object to the identification of a local theory of meaning that, from their perspective, conflates semantics ("this word means X") with social importance ("that action doesn't mean anything") (e.g. Just 1987). That position makes perfectly good sense in the context of an academic world that seeks forms of pure reference, and it is a fair reflection of many folk theories as well. But the separation of meaning from context is grounded in a cosmology that, in other cultural settings, makes very little sense. Thus, when I interpret Cretan shepherds as having a "theory of meaning," which they indicate by their discussions of the concept of *simasia*, I am not ignoring the fact that they "conflate" semantic and social meaning; I am, instead, trying to learn something from, and about, this striking difference from both our own referentialist assumptions and those of the Greek bureaucratic state (see Herzfeld 1985a, 1997a). I also remain unimpressed by the argument that these shepherds have taken the term *simasia* from formal (and partly *katharevousa*) discourse: their ability to use *simasia* for a very different understanding of meaning than that of the learned writers from whom they may indeed have indirectly borrowed the term itself supports their, and my, sense of the limits of referentiality. (These shepherds are adepts at turning the mechanisms of state against officialdom, as when they make police officers eat the meat the shepherds have just stolen and then inform their guests that the latter have just consumed the evidence!) Indeed, it is the apparent transparency of official-sounding words in everyday speech that makes ethnographic translation such an interesting issue.

But let me return briefly to intentionality here. A referential representation of meaning, even if contextualized, confuses performance with intent. One may declare that it is impossible to read another's mind; but one can also, at the same time, try to read it, or at least make attributions of motive that suggest that possibility. The stated theory may be at odds with actual practice, and the theory informing the practice may entail a rejection of the stated principles. Indeed, all this shows that *claims* about intentions are key elements of social performance even when *generalizations* about intentionality seem to preclude the very possibility.

This is where a referential view of language especially fails. For it suggests that if we know what a word or phrase means (as opposed to what So-and-so means *by* it), we can rely on the constancy of that meaning wherever it appears – and, by extension, on the referential meaning of "statements," as opposed to their performative force (whether intended or not) – an insight central to Austin's entire philosophy. The assumption of referentiality has particular resonances in the Greek context. Although few classicists today take a narrowly referential view of meaning, they deal with texts for which there is usually assumed to be an original version *(Urtext),* fixed in time as well as form. This harmonizes with the nationalist image of a classical culture that has undergone frequent distortions but that will be fully reconstituted today – a premise few Greeks seem to accept! The use of transliteration systems that recall the classical alphabet reinforces that referential illusion and lends ethnographic texts a spurious semantic stability.

Thus the use of standardized translations and a classical mode of transliteration obliterates the play of actors' perhaps quite divergent intentions in favor of structural unity and images of social stability and equilibrium. It occludes the possibility of intentions other than those sanctioned by the official semantics – or, indeed, the possibility of a total absence of conscious intention altogether. A word of caution is in order, however, as this might be taken to mean that the early ethnographers of Greece were guilty of the ahistoricism of which Evans-Pritchard has been accused (see Rosaldo 1986: 93; cf. Fabian 1983: 41). Even for Evans-Pritchard the charge is partial, as Fabian (1983) in particular acknowledges, since the British scholar addressed questions of historicity both within his ethnographic writing and, perhaps most notably, in a well-known essay on the relevance of history to anthropology (Evans-Pritchard 1962: 46–65). But Evans-Pritchard still frames his account as though the larger context of power were secondary, although his self-deprecation does at least enable us to extract a clear sense of how the unequal terms on which he confronted the Nuer affected both his methods and the results he obtained by them.

Perhaps in part because of the symbolic importance of Greece in the constellation of European history, however, both Campbell and Friedl were acutely aware from the start that they were operating in a cultural space where history was the object of an intense political struggle over the definition of the past. Campbell pays particular attention to the nationalist arguments over the origins of transhumant groups in the region (1964: 1–6) and documents shepherds' awareness of their antecedents in the War of Independence and the way they learn this awareness in their childhood (1964: 2–3, 307), while Friedl (1962: 106), more passively, notes that the inhabitants of the village where she worked had learned to invoke classical mythology as a keystone for their national identity. It would have made little sense to do fieldwork in even the most illiterate Greek community – and the Sarakatsani perhaps qualified for that title – without the regard that Campbell, a historian as well as an anthropologist, paid to their sense of the past and its relationship to encompassing geopolitical struggles that still continue.

Nonetheless, old habits die hard. Campbell opted for using the Greek alphabet, and rarely notes evidence that certain terms were almost certainly reintroductions via the standardized national language. Friedl (1962) adopts a modern phonemic transcription method – a device that was not followed by most subsequent writers on the ethnography of Greece for some twenty years or more thereafter. Campbell's approach was appropriate in a context when he could safely assume that many educated readers had enough ancient Greek to make the national alphabet the appropriate medium, and that those who lacked this knowledge would probably not care. But it may have overdetermined some subsequent readings of his work. Friedl's method was perhaps ideologically more neutral, and it suited her insistence that she did not want to deal with the classical past except, briefly (1962: 106), to mention the villagers' awareness of it – her book is significantly subtitled *A Village in Modern Greece* – but it meant sacrificing the etymological sensibility of Campbell's writings.

I have dwelt on the issue of transliteration at some length because the politics of transliteration often gets short shrift in discussions of ethnographic representation, and because in the Greek cases we have one of the ideologically most sensitive fields for considering the issue. Moreover, transliteration sets a key for knowledgeable readers' response to the translations that accompany it. Modern Greece was fundamentally a land created as a reincarnation of ancient Hellas, now made obedient to its modern descendants – the western Europeans – who had, in a paradox reminiscent of many origin myths (see Drummond 1981; Leach 1961), together given it birth and assured its survival under conditions of constant surveillance. For many Greeks the links with the ancient past, which foreigners saw as corrupted by Turkish and Slavic influence and as evidence that the Greek people belonged to the European past rather than the present, were their sole inalienable lien on modernity. Thus the politics of language choice – including questions of transliteration – was also a politics of temporality and cultural identity. Under these circumstances, the choices made by ethnographers could not but be ideologically fraught.

These early ethnographers were, in general terms, faithful to the philhellenic vision. Campbell found Romanian claims on the Sarakatsani and their territories absurd because they were based on bad philology and bad historical method; he did not have to deal with similar problems in Greek historiography as he probably would have been forced to do had he decided, as some of his successors chose, to deal instead with non-Greek-speaking minority groups in Greece. When he wrote, too, the "monotonic" reform of Greek, which removed one of its most visible but phonetically least justified resemblances with ancient Greek, had not yet occurred, and there was little discussion of issues that the rise of sociolinguistics in the same decade was to invest with central importance. It is all the more remarkable, under these conditions, that he provided the detailed assessment of shifting contexts that we encounter in his ethnography despite the lingering flavor of a classicizing philology. Friedl, whose ethnography was written for a less specialist audience in a country where a much smaller percentage of her readership could be expected to decipher the Greek alphabet, actually seems more innocent of the ideological issues, although she recognizes points of language that have subsequently become highly important in the confrontation between social anthropology and Greek nationalist historiography – notably, that women tended to use the Turkish names of local communities that had been given Greek names by the state authorities, apparently because their relative lack of engagement in the public sphere sheltered them to some extent from knowledge of official changes (1962: 7; cf. Karakasidou 1997).

I shall now examine some of the translations encountered in Campbell's and Friedl's work, turning thereafter in much the same vein to some more recent studies, and will conclude with some examples from my own attempts to grapple with these issues across a wide spectrum ranging from Cretan shepherds to a cosmopolitan if traditionalizing novelist – whose work poses special challenges for potential choices between "literary" and "literal" (or "ethnographic") translations.

Words at the Wedding: Sarakatsan Agonism

Campbell's description of wedding practices remains unmatched. When he did his fieldwork, the Sarakatsani still engaged in highly ritualized enactments of the mutual hostility that normatively governed relations between the two groups being affinally conjoined, and that was now supposed to dissolve – leaving only a suggestive residue – in the goodwill created by the new relationship.

There is a pattern of such transformations of negative into positive affect (or at least reciprocity) in Greek society generally. Campbell's description, which set the model for my own explorations of the ways in which reciprocal animal-theft led to alliances between shepherds, is methodical in its description of the ritualized stages of this process, and is embedded in a detailed account of the ideology whereby marriage provides the balance against the atomized, agonistic quality of most social relations in this society. By thus conjoining a description of ritual form with an explanation of Sarakatsan ideas about the quality of social relationships, Campbell offers us a way of making sense of a society in which aggressive overtures may be a prelude to violence but may also be a means of creating mutual respect and alliance.

In this description, he inserts relatively few Greek expressions. He notes the terms for the affinal relationship itself, the term for the five young men who ride ahead of the groom's party that goes to claim the bride from her parents, a formulaic expression in which the bride's male kin ritualistically object to the groom's kinsmen's first attempt to take the trousseau away with them, conventional greetings shared by the two groups of new affines, a ritual exchange object (the special loaf of bread known as the "bread of the bride"), a song in which the groom's kin declare their good intentions and their admiration for the hospitality they have received from the bride's natal family, the act of "return" (the bride's first visit to her natal home with her new husband and his close male kin), and the term for a married couple (1964: 132–138).

It is interesting, first of all, to note which of the terms Campbell chose to translate are given in Greek. He does not provide the original of the phrase "We shall wait for you," uttered in anticipation of the bride's "return" visit, and he gives the text of the song of praise in a footnote. All the other terms I have mentioned here are given in Greek. With the exception of the song, which uses generic Epirot dialect forms, all the other terms are in standard Greek, and some – notably *epistrofi,* "return" – may be relatively recent importations from official language.

This mixture of terms establishes early on the absurdity of treating local and official usage as hermetically discrete entities. In accordance with Ferguson's (1959) model, the decay of the diglossic structure of Greek – hastened by its association with the military regime of 1967–74 – resulted in a "mixed" idiom spoken more or less by all Greeks. It would not have required much literacy, even in the late 1950s, for a Sarakatsan shepherd to absorb formal phrases from the radio or even from someone with a smattering of grade-school education. Their obvious association with the learnèd elite enhanced their local prestige within the local community while bringing it more firmly within the state's cultural embrace.

Campbell, as a sensitive ethnographer, did not accept the idealized picture that accompanied such formalism – as we see in his detailed descriptions of social tension (for example, when a rainstorm breaks out, causing the bride's party to demand her immediate return home while the groom's party responded with a fusillade and the irate response that it would be unlucky for the bride even to look round at her parents' home). Such descriptions show that even the most formal norms and cosmological precepts are elements in a complex process of negotiation, and this ethnographic illumination thus effectively counterbalances the formality suggested by Campbell's choice of translated words and phrases as significant.

Campbell's awareness of the history of the Greek language and his own delicate sense of nuance allowed him to preserve in this, one of the most central segments of his book, a strong sense of the play of formality and adventurism that is so characteristic of these rather rebellious citizens of a bureaucratic state that in turn treats them with considerable disregard. Indeed, when Campbell describes the interactions between shepherds and educated Greeks, emphasizing both the unequal use of "pronouns of power and solidarity" (Brown and Gilman 1960) and the political and economic inequalities that these asymmetrical usages index, he allows us to see how the choice of linguistic forms actually helps to determine or perpetuate the quality of social relations.

But he does not spell this out; and a reader who knew no Greek would only get part of the picture. At the time when he was writing there had been very little sociolinguistic work of any sort on Greece, and its arrival on the scene created, as it did elsewhere, a division of labor that was ultimately harmful to the study of both society and language. For it entrenched the idea that language use was epiphenomenal – whether to social relations or to our knowledge of "the language" – and so obscured the role of linguistic politics and ideologies in the management of everyday relationships.

The one Greek phrase that Campbell reports from the less prepossessing side of social relations is the phrase for "the affines have got into a fight," which he simply paraphrases in English as "in-law trouble." Doubtless for the purposes of his ethnography this seemed sufficient, yet it often implies a degree of physical violence (or at least the potential for it) that is not revealed by the gloss. The phrase breaks the otherwise unruffled surface of formality on the one side and bucolic innocence (portrayed in the song) on the other. It can hardly be coincidental that this phrase, so redolent of what Campbell identifies as the fundamentally agonistic quality of Sarakatsan life, erupts into the text as one irrepressible local voice, apparently a commonly heard one, that marks dissent in a society that generally does not display to outsiders anything that might redound to its collective discredit. That such events *are* common is clear from his description, especially of the extent to which bystanders are usually "uncharitably amused" by such intimations of discord (1964: 137).

With only minor variations, what I have said about Campbell's use of Greek in this passage applies to the whole book. More often than not his invocation of local phrases allows him, as with the phrase indexing "in-law trouble," to avoid an actual translation, but to give us instead a contextualized account of how a word or phrase is used and interpreted. He makes no self-authorizing claims about the untranslatability of terms but meticulously documents words and phrases that he sees as significant to local actors.

Honorable Intentions?

This is especially true in his discussion of terms he glosses as honor and shame. As a somewhat critical heir – trained by Campbell himself – to the "Mediterraneanist" tradition to which these values were central (see Peristiany 1965), I soon found that its generalizing translations obscured rather than illuminated what I encountered in fieldwork. There was in fact nothing in Campbell's book – although he had studied with Peristiany, and although honor was a key word in the title – that required conformity with this paradigm. Campbell's work contributed to the debate precisely because it showed that the components of the local morality were specific to a complex cosmology in which these rather dour and not terribly law-abiding shepherds managed to calibrate their view of their social world to the teachings of the Orthodox Church. In this regard his work more closely resembled that of E. E. Evans-Pritchard (1940, 1956) than it did that of Peristiany, with the added twist of a doctrinal tradition at odds with the social practices of his informants. Campbell thus pushed Evans-Pritchard's rehistoricizing of ethnography, with its rejection of Radcliffe-Brown's (1952: 1) insistence on achronic and "nomothetic" descriptions, to its logical conclusion. The Sarakatsani had no choice but to engage with the ecclesiastical as well as the temporal authorities. But they turned the doctrine of Original Sin to their own purposes, thereby giving a specifically theological as well as social depth to their morality. Recognizing this, Campbell did not so much "translate" the term *ipokhreosi* into the relatively colorless "obligation" as show how it served to link unstable vertical alliances with politicians to the internal theodicy of Sarakatsan society.

Campbell thus brought state and local society into a juxtaposition that is far more complex than simply treating the honor code, as some have done (but see Gilmore 1990: 25 for a more nuanced view), as a displacement of male humiliation. At no point in his ethnography does he argue that Sarakatsan values are typical of Greece, let alone the whole Mediterranean region. Rather, by extreme example, they illuminate the complex relations between state and ecclesiastic authorities and their ideologically loyal but pragmatically insubordinate followers in ways that help us to understand the dynamics of superficially less "exotic" segments of the overall population.

In some ways the notion of obligation is more central to the work than that of honor. Campbell does explore the notion of *timi* in some detail, suggesting that, while the substantive *filotimo*, "love of *timii* (honor)," rarely if ever appears in Sarakatsan speech, the adjectival term *filotimos* frequently is applied to specific individuals. The *filotimos* man is one who observes his obligations: his patron feels he can be trusted to vote in accordance with their pact. What is the extent of the shepherd's loyalty to his patron? I have heard villagers on Crete describe how they will try to engage the services of more than one political patron by splitting the household's several votes among competing candidates. But this apparent duplicity allows a maximization of both political *and* moral capital: the voter creates multiple strands of mutual obligation, does not actually lie to any one of his patrons, and is insured against excessive reliance on a single powerful figure. The sense of obligation here is tied to a very specific type of transaction and has nothing to do with a generic sense of honor in the abstract. It is very much a social arrangement. Even the relatively innocuous duplicity that it entails, an unfortunate necessity for poor shepherds forced to depend on rich and powerful outsiders, is justified in terms of the pervasive imperfection of human society and specifically of the *moral community* – a concept that Campbell takes from Evans-Pritchard – of the Sarakatsani and, more generically, of all Greeks.

We have moved here from the sense of honor as a simple gloss on a historically rich English word to Campbell's sophisticated reading of a term taken from formal Greek discourse and imbued with ideas that represent a local adaptation to ecumenical doctrine. This is made possible by the deep specificity of the ethnography itself: as Friedl (1976) remarked some years later, anthropologists were never much concerned with "typicality" in Greece.

But this ethnographic specificity carries its own traps. When Campbell talks about honor, he is describing a Sarakatsan value with a traceable "family likeness" – although one that admits of wide variation (Herzfeld 1980) – that it shares with similar values, often marked by roughly the same set of terms, found throughout Greece. When the term is lifted from his ethnography to bolster arguments about generalized Mediterranean culture, however, it ceases to be the value of the Sarakatsani and becomes reconfigured to fit the analyst's preconceptions.

Above all what is lost here is the sense of intentionality. When Sarakatsani or other Greeks gossip about the motives of some miscreant, they are not contradicting the widely held Greek view that it is impossible to gauge the intentions of another person. They are simply joining in a guessing game that is itself part of the process of making and breaking reputations. Greeks generally insist that one cannot read others' minds – but that premise is itself a part of the complex of ideas and practices through which Greeks talk about each other. We do not even know whether they believe that it is possible to know another person's mind; we do know that they frequently make claims about having done so. In similar vein, they predicate future actions on an attributed sense of obligation. Generalized talk of "honor" obscures this dimension and leaves the field open to relatively mechanistic applications of game theory (e.g. Gambetta 1988; Paine 1989) – interesting exercises in their own right, but lacking that sense of tension between the socially observable and the personally ineffable that we find so richly present in Campbell's distinctly Evans-Pritchardian evocation of the "moral community" – a place of paradox and ambiguity, but also a place that we recognize: a place where the performance of intention, political commitment (Loizos 1975: 301, n. 2), and the ability to fulfill one's obligations reveals the impossibility of securely knowing about others' individual morality even while we depend on being able to act as though we could do exactly that.

Economic Facts and Fictions

Ernestine Friedl's ethnography (1962) presents relatively few terms in Greek. One element that her work nevertheless shares with Campbell's is the illustrative use of clichés for recurrent situations, such as the reiterated assurance in respect of unpleasantness that "what is past is forgotten" (*perazmena, ksehazmena*) (p. 76); the hurt "how was I to know?" when it turns out the speaker did not have the right equipment to do a particular job (p. 87) – implying, although Friedl does not mention this, the excuse that those in authority never educate "us" properly; or the response to inquiries about work (*palevoume,* "we are wrestling") that mark a conventional parallel between one's social relations in an agonistic society and those into which one enters with a harsh and capricious natural environment (Friedl 1962: 75). Friedl also supplies Greek terms and translations for social categories (such as ritual kin), spaces that mark important social boundaries (for example, the living room of a house and the market area of the village), and social institutions and socially validated objects (such as the elements of dowry and trousseau). Because the portrait she paints of a proclivity to use clichés frequently rings true for anyone who has spent time in Greece, the further impression is created that the referentiality of the socially salient terms is unproblematic.

Despite the brevity of her book, however, Friedl is also a meticulous context-ualizer. If certain phrases seem to be repetitious, she implies, this is because their constant reiteration provides a means for the villagers to affirm their worldview – a worldview as opaque to individual differences as the villagers are secretive about aspects of themselves.

Her choice of a phonemic transliteration places the community squarely in present time. Unlike Campbell, for whose Sarakatsani the relatively recent history of the Greek War of Independence (1821–27) is a living entity, and for whom the historical origins of the Sarakatsani themselves shed an interesting light on the Balkan politics of national identity, Friedl – whose explicit goal is to turn the anthropological focus on a contemporary Western society – is here interested in the past only inasmuch as she notes the villagers' highly generalized awareness of classical antiquity through, as she shows, a highly sanitized official rendition. Doubtless her choice of a very ordinary village made such a generalized sense of the past almost inevitable, notwithstanding her aversion – which I share – to making claims about typicality. But it is interesting nevertheless to note how this 'flat" temporality meshes with the effects of a purely phonemic transliteration system and the array of entirely conventional phrases that adorns the text.

Classicists dislike such transliterations, precisely because they conceal potent-ially interesting etymologies. Indeed, I have myself been taken to task for not using an Erasmean method of transliterating Greek, on precisely these grounds (Pinsent 1986). But these transliterations have the advantage of not begging any questions about possible links with antiquity, so that when Friedl (1962: 106) tells us how the villagers invoke *Ksenios Zefs* and then has to explain that this is "Zeus, the patron of strangers," we are all the more forcibly reminded that this is an erudite conceit, incorporated into village consciousness through processes that have also fashioned our own uncritical assumptions about cultural continuity.

Although it rests on a matter of fine detail, the impact of choice in transliteration is vitally important because it may determine a whole range of associations and, in consequence, the significance readers will attribute to particular utterances and the larger values and events they metonymically represent. Thus, the use of a classical and Erasmean transliteration will produce *proika* for the term usually glossed as "dowry," thereby suggesting to the philologically informed the etymologically correct derivation from ancient Greek *proix* (stem *proik-*). This in turn may lead to some curious assumptions about continuity between ancient and modern social institutions. While scholars who had a genuine acquaintance with rural practice managed quite explicitly to avoid these assumptions (Levy 1956), for some conservative local actors the classical association legitimated the status quo. By contrast, a phonemic transliteration captures the dialect pun conjoining *prika* (dowry) with its homonym *prika,* "bitterness" (cf. standard – and ancient – *pikra*), recalling the truly embittering pressure that the dowry system – formally abolished only in 1984 – placed on fathers and daughters.

Thus it is significant and salutary that an anthropologist with distinguished access to classical idioms chose instead to adopt a resolutely modernist trans-literation. Indeed, while Friedl did not discuss this kind of linguistic elaboration (but see Herzfeld 1980), she was one of the first contributors to our awareness of the burdens of the dowry system (see also Skouteri-Didaskalou 1991). As a result, she is able to acknowledges the Greeks' acquired pride in the classical past without participating in its nationalistic implications.

On the other hand, the conventionality of both the everyday phrases and these invocations of a rather newly acquired historicity mask any degree of individual critique or reaction. Yet we know that Greek villagers do not all act alike, or evaluate each others' actions in wholly consistent terms. Campbell – despite more numerous generalized descriptions of what people do at marriage, in a fight or feud, and so on – offers numerous highly individualized vignettes consistent with a society in which eccentricity exists even if it is not always approved: John Charisis who in tearing his shirt to shreds at weddings illustrates the idiosyncrasy known as *khouï* (Campbell 1964: 45–46), the man who discreetly throws a stone to warn a man beating his daughter that this excessive behavior has gone too far (1964: 190), the father who harangues a scholastically inept daughter without criticizing his wife for comforting her (1964: 157). Such incidents provide agency-sensitive specificity for terms and concepts, rendering purely referential translations increasingly redundant and indeed inadequate. Friedl offers much less of this specificity. Her villagers are by no means flat, lifeless figures; they are simply not so dramatically present.

This is in part the result of a difference between the two settings: the Sarakatsani, even if not always fully tolerant of the eccentricity that leads to excess (for which Campbell invoked the term *khouï*), live in a world of performances both dramatic and aggressive, while Vasilika is a settled agricultural community where calm is highly valued. But in part, too, it reflects the cultural bias of the tradition within which Friedl was writing – a search for configurations (Benedict 1934), or an eidos (Bateson 1958: 220) – that corresponds in its synchronicity to the social structure identified, despite his more processual orientation, by Campbell. Both the choice of what to render in Greek and then to translate, and that of what transliteration or other representation to us, are directly tied to the dominant concern in the anthropology of the 1950s and 1960s, in both Britain and the United States despite the much-touted distinction between social and cultural anthropology, to describe *entities* and to avoid the methodological individualism suggested by such terms as *experience*. This was healthy inasmuch as it avoided begging questions about intentionality at the level of the description of everyday norms and characteristic events. But it did of course sidestep a difficult question: Meaning is the result of the agency, not of words, but of the people who speak them; and, if we cannot read their thoughts, how can we actually talk about meaning?

Inclusive Pragmatics

Here the growing influence of ordinary language philosophy on both sides of the Atlantic was crucial on both sides of the Atlantic. In Britain, Needham (1972) ridiculed the very idea of describing psychological inner states, rather than observing a negotiation of the collective representation of these states. In the United States the rise of sociolinguistics, notably the work of Bauman (1977), Gumperz and Hymes (1964), and Labov (1972), raised new possibilities, including that of rescuing language from its social isolation and bringing its demonstrable performativity to bear on explanations of social and cultural change. Despite now obvious criticisms, all these approaches together created new possibilities for social analysis – especially, perhaps, in those cultures (and I would argue that Greece is one such) in which talk and even linguistic form are subjects of everyday speculation. Perhaps in part because of the centrality of linguistic continuity to the ideological sustenance of their national identity, even relatively ill-educated Greeks often evince a fascination with etymology (especially of toponyms) and the play of neoclassical, demotic, and dialect idioms in the negotiation of social authority and political clout. Such linguistic reflexivity poses especially interesting questions for our discussion of translation, because it indicates, however opaquely, a degree of intentionality that makes the referential illusion that words rather than people "mean" increasingly unsustainable.

One criticism of these approaches is nevertheless that they reduce everything to language, text, and performance. I have addressed some of those objections elsewhere (Herzfeld 1997a). Here, let me note that many of the so-called linguistic models (e.g. diglossia, poetics) are in my view wrongly restricted to language (and therefore wrongly considered to be linguistic models) because they reflect patterns observable in a much wider range of semiotic systems, including the entire gamut of social interaction. I should also add that if we can find evidence for semantic inventiveness in seemingly "inert" verbal texts – bits of museologically preserved folklore such as teasing songs that have been snatched from their social contexts and set down in the frozen written form beloved of traditional philologists – then, *a fortiori,* we should be able to identify in a whole range of activities the *effects* of agency even if we cannot, in functionalist fashion, divine either the *motives* or the *purposes* that may have generated these effects. In this sense, I suggest, we are not translating at all – but we must still try to translate the verbal elements that constantly recur, because these provide us with a pragmatic link between the ineffable elements of social intention and the rhetoric of referentiality that all social science discourse shares with all other forms of social action. Translation is a necessarily provisional device, as Vellacott recognized: it is the first toehold up the slope, but it is emphatically not a substitute for contextual description. It plays a part in ethnographic description – a pragmatic part – but ethnographic description cannot be reduced to it.

Even the analysis of folklore texts, properly contextualized, can provide some sense of this. When I was still a student I tried to translate a set of *mandinddhes* (Cretan rhyming or assonant verse couplets) into English, matching rhyme scheme for rhyme scheme: "I went and found a lonely church and prayed on bended knee,! and I beheld the Mother of God as she shed tears for me" (*pigha ke proskinisa s' ena erimoklisi, k' idha ti Mana tou Khristou ya mena na dhakrizi*). I took these to a well-known poet and translator of modern Greek literature, who offered blunt advice: these were doggerel, the Greek originals were not, and perhaps I could overcome the difficulty by rendering the English in dialect? Discouraged, I took my leave, and – perhaps fortunately – never tried to inflict them on anyone else.

In reflecting on this incident now, I am struck by the thought that the advice was in itself an interesting commentary. Most scholars would generally, I suspect, experience less acute social discomfort with using relatively low-status dialects of foreign languages that they already know well in standard or official form than with speaking similarly low-status dialects of their own mother tongues – an act that could all too easily be construed as condescending. At the time I wrote these translations I was beginning to acquire a slight grasp of Cretan, but certainly had no ability to speak any dialect of English other than my own "received" version. Yet what we both shared was a view that these Greek verses were far from trite. Was the solution to the apparent triteness of any rhymed rendition in English through the internal exoticization of dialect? Perhaps my interlocutor was right.

The alternative was to avoid rhyme altogether. Yet for me the rhyme scheme was crucial – and it became all the more so when, graduating beyond the analysis of texts for which the social context largely had to be intuited from the internal evidence of the texts themselves, I found myself working with a community of shepherding families in west-central Crete whose members had very decided ideas of their own about the production of meaning – that notion of *simasia* that I was to be chastised for recognizing as a theory and for "failing" to see that its social import was separate from its semantics. For these people, context was everything, because one could perceive the effects of a particular set of *mandinadhes* without assuming anything about either intentions or referential meanings – two aspects about which, anthropologically sensitive to a fault, they expressed pervasive skepticism. A rhyme served to give iconic palpability to the sense of "capping" that was considered the main achievement of competitive versifiers – that, and other poetic devices all consistent with a Jakobsonian vision of poetry, but with the added specificity that the "diagrams" these versifiers were producing were iconic of social relations. In particular, rhyme served as a convention for encapsulating antithesis, paralleling (for example) the way in which, at weddings, pairs of men compete in turn to toast the newly-weds and to insult each other in a genial fashion, expressing thereby the tension of a community in which solidarity is predicated on the recognition of mutual aggression and potential hostility.

Now it is also true that these verses were couched in a dialect that differed in certain key respects from the national standard language. That language is so hegemonic that the Greek-born copy editor of my ethnography of the village tried to change all my Cretan texts to standard Greek on the grounds that I apparently did not know Greek well enough! So would not a translation into a dialect of English – say, Geordie – not have similarly marginalized my verse translations? Moreover, dialect speakers have their own quiet – or not so quiet – forms of revenge against the domination of standard forms. These devices included, in the Cretan village, expressive liberties taken with grammatical rules, many of them explained in my text (see also Herzfeld 1985b, and doubtless the major source of the copy editor's linguistic disgust. In the end it seemed advisable to include both highly literal translations and the phonemically translated "originals," along with as much context as possible. And in providing that context my informants were assiduous, realizing even more viscerally than anthropologists (for these texts were drawn from their own life experiences, after all) that without context there could be no meaning.

(It is true that in my first book I rendered a pompous poem by a nationalistic folklorist in archaic English in order to convey something of the flavor – to use the conventional metaphor – of the *katharevousa* original [Herzfeld 1982: 82]. But here I was moving between two academic universes that were closely linked by historical ties and continuing interaction, so that the Greek – which was partly written in imitation of Western models in any case, syntax and all – was relatively accessible to the devices of translation.)

Since the *mandinadhes* reproduced the forms of social relations, moreover, and since they were also used to negotiate the practical consequences of those relations, they came to play a central part in my ethnography. I was not interested in focusing *only* on language, as a "linguistic anthropologist" might have done. But I did want to highlight the constitutive role of language in the ongoing relationships among the villagers, and above all the capacity of villagers to enunciate, to acknowledge, and above all to *use* analogies between the aesthetic economy of speech and the moral economies of other domains such as raiding, sex, and politics. For the absence of much discussion of these issues in most ethnographies was as much of a distortion of Greek social worlds as perhaps my heavy emphasis on them was seen to be. It seemed worth the risk of new distortions – and what description is not skewed? – in order to refocus analysis and rectify the earlier omissions.

Such a move, however, moves the problems of translation into an altogether more central place. Translation is no longer just a metaphor for ethnographic labor, to be adopted or rejected according to one's convictions, but a necessary part of the enterprise. Even if Campbell and Friedl, in their very different ways, had been able to offer and then contextualize glosses on key terms and expressions, their principal contributions lay much more in the description of the contexts than in their actual translations.

Yet I would argue that in my greater focus on language issues I have adopted essentially the same tactic as that used, especially, by Campbell, albeit on a much more massive scale. Like him I provide glosses on all Greek terms, then attempt to suggest a sense of the range of contexts in which those glosses would not outrageously violate the villagers' own understanding of the originals. Since I also believe that the villagers contributed significantly to my theoretical equipment, not solely to the collection of data, I am able to use their exegetical commentaries on the meaning of verbal texts and other social actions alike – indeed, from an Austinian perspective that very distinction looks as absurd as it apparently did to the villagers – as a means of moving my own readers from the role of passive consumers of translation to that of actively engaged interpreters. They may not be ready yet to throw the book into the fire – at least, not on these grounds – but they should already have a vision of village life that is not dependent on my providing them with a purely referential list of characteristics: this is a dowry, this is their creed, and so on. Readers are invited to see the villagers' *use,* not only of terms and categories, but also of the entire range of their symbolic universe.

The Writing Effect

The question of intentionality became more prominent again for me when I recently turned my hand to writing an "ethnographic biography" (Herzfeld 1997b). Here I was concerned to use the life and writings of a novelist and occasional historian – Andreas Nenedakis – who had lived and worked in many of the sites of my own ethnographic work, in order to explore the relationship between novels and ethnographies through a comparison of our respective idioms of representation.

A significant component of that project was the exploration of the role played by representations of psychological inner states in anthropological analysis and discourse. Following on the suggestive writings of Cohen (1994: 180–191) about the relevance of novels – and aware, too, of Benedict Anderson's (1983: 32–40) musings on the interrelations among novels, language standardization, and the ostensible routinization of sentiment in nation-states – I worked from the likelihood that novelists' willingness to portray motives and emotions provided a space for contesting and affirming currently prevailing collective representations of such states of mind. In the reactions of critics and the general public as well as in arguments about genre (fiction vs. history, etc.), one might arrive at a more pluralistic rendition of "culture" than the ordinary ethnographic mode of description usually permits.

Hybrid genres encourage hybrid tactics. On the one hand, I found myself translating large segments of Nenedakis's novels in a manner designed, I hope, to convey accurately my understanding of the original without necessarily being literal to the point of ugliness. On the other hand, in passages where I was discussing Nenedakis's use of words and ideas, I resorted to a classic ethnographic ploy: implying, in effect, that certain terms simply did not yield to direct translation (a classic translators' conceit), I expounded at great length on the meaning of such terms as *kaïmos,* which is usually glossed as "grief."

Now an ethnopsychological classification, given the ultimate irreducibility of terms denoting psychological inner states, must – at least implicitly – be a classification of *overt responses and the circumstances to which they are appropriate.*

If – this is an old chestnut in Greek folklore studies – we can clearly distinguish between performance genres such as "lament/dirge" and "song" (with a sub-category of marriage song), we are making a distinction based on the appropriate idioms for expressing emotion, not on the emotions themselves. We may then perceive a degree of similarity between the formal classification of genres and that of emotions (see Herzfeld 1981). But even this does not mean that we have arrived at an understanding of how speakers of the language actually experience emotions (although, as Leavitt [1996] notes, we may have a pretty good sense of real empathy with them at moments of great crisis or joy). It means that they recognize a homology between presumed emotional states and the genres locally said to be the most appropriate for expressing them.

So when Nenedakis describes an emotion, and attributes it to one of his characters, we may feel – particularly if we know the cultural background well – that he probably knows whereof he speaks. When, for example, in his novel about a struggling young art student from the provinces whose lover's parents humiliate her because she will not bring a dowry into the family (or even a marriage, for that matter), his descriptions of her frantic, jumbled, often agonized frustration are deeply moving (Nenedakis 1976). But since this is a fictional character, the only standard of verisimilitude he must satisfy is a *cultural* standard of verisimilitude. (Think again of Austin's [1971] treatment of excuses, which only had to be cult-urally and socially plausible but not necessarily factually persuasive.) As long as he stayed within that idiom, no one would challenge him on the grounds that "young women do not think that way" – because many of his Greek readers will have heard young women *speaking* that way (although perhaps too secretly to have made it into the writings of anthropologists thus far!).

The student's voice is also convincing because what it says is not the only kind of self-pity we meet in Greece. It belongs to a whole range of exasperated – and to some extent competitive – victimology (see Dubisch 1995: 212–217). Indeed, it is clear that Nenedakis has often been concerned to explore the feelings of underdogs of all categories, so that the hapless art student serves also as an allegory of the persecuted political Left and of the working class. The *idiom* of victimization should be rather transparent to any Greek, even a male generally unsympathetic to the social plight of ambitious young women from the countryside – especially as a hitherto dominant strain in the cultural life of the country has been the image of the generic Greek as "underdog," and as "competitive suffering" is a well-estab-lished mode of social interaction (Diamandouros 1994; Dubisch 1995: 214). How can we show that the whining tone of self-pity is both normative and, in its deep cultural resonances, actually interesting? Because he can transcend both his own interests and those he attributes to the rather complaining, dirt-poor student, Nenedakis can project a powerful sense of the idiom that his readers are assuredly able to recognize and appreciate.

When Nenedakis writes about emotion, novelist that he is, he usually employs both direct description and the sheer suggestiveness of his prose. For example, the crushing boredom of life on a prison island, interspersed by moments of extraordinary cruelty, is conveyed poetically and iconically by the dull thud of repetitive, leaden phrases dramatically interrupted by painful flashes of vivid memory. When Andreas wants us to understand *kaïmos,* he does so by invoking Theodorakis's haunting song of that name, a setting of a poem about the endless misery of life in an island prison camp, to conjure up that extraordinary moment when oppressed Greeks began to realize that the military dictatorship could be resisted and began to sing this song *sotto voce*; and it is I who must by turns invoke its salience ethnographically by describing my own reactions to hearing that song under related circumstances and then spell out the ethnosemantic dimensions of a word that can mean both consuming grief (in part through a folk etymology linking it to "burning") and the longing excitement of the dedicated enthusiast.

It is thus in the construction of the ethnographic biography that I eventually faced the problem of translation as a rendition of intentionality – of meaning as intention. In this deliberately hybrid genre, I could afford to bring the speculation about inner states that is appropriate to fiction into direct juxtaposition with the ethnographic commitment to recording only observable representations. What is more, I could do so without having to pretend that novels and ethnographies were the same thing and perform the same labor. To the contrary, I could exploit the limitations of each mode in order to highlight the advantages of the other for any attempt to understand the complex, constantly shifting worlds that, for want of a better device, we freeze-frame as reified images of "culture."

As for the translations used by ethnographers, they are – like all translations – necessarily imperfect, if only because we cannot know exactly what meanings were intended by the original actors. That is why we provide anecdotal examples; these suggest many possibilities, but foreclose none. Our translations are thus also, in a field where descriptions make some claims to verisimilitude, necessarily provisional. Ethnographers' constant reminders that the terms they translate are always ultimately untranslatable presuppose that provisionality: where the trans- lator of fiction may insert unobtrusive aids to understanding, the ethnographer's aids *must* obtrude, *must* serve as constant reminders that the job is never done even as they seek to achieve that impossible closure. Failure to do so is a failure, intriguingly, in the mutually opposed terms of two supposedly irreconcilable epistemological camps. For the positivist, it removes the possibility of falsifiability (Popper 1968: 40). For the deconstructionist, it imposes a textual closure that denies the possibility of infinite alternative interpretations. It is the act of trans- lation, then, not in spite but *because* of its precarious provisionality, that holds ethnographic description to an honest awareness of its own limitations. For trans- lation, like the social life we study, is often risk-fraught in the extreme: the higher the risks taken, perhaps, the truer to life?

The question of what it means to view psychological inner states as culturally defined refocuses attention on the agency entailed in all forms of representation. If we can consequently build into the writing of ethnography this sense of the provisionality of its embedded translations, we will also have surrendered some of that privileged incommensurability of which Asad (1993) justly complains. For while he is right to interrogate translation as a metaphor *of* ethnography, the presence of some form of translation *in* ethnography is a precondition for its existence. If we embrace the risks that it entails, however, we potentially – in the vastly interconnected world we now inhabit – render ourselves more accountable, not only to our colleagues, but to those we study and who can comment knowledgeably, and with reciprocal accountability, on our competence as revealed in the act of translation.

References

Anderson, Benedict R. O'G. *Imagined Communities: Reflections on the Origin and Spread of Nationalism.* London: Verso, 1983.

Asad, Talal. *Genealogies of Religion. Discipline and Reasons of Power in Christianity and Islam.* Baltimore: Johns Hopkins University Press, 1993.

Austin, J. L. "A Plea for Excuses." In *Philosophy and Linguistics.* Cohn Lyas (ed.). Pp. 79–101. London: Macmillan, 1971.

Bateson, Gregory. *Naven: The Culture of the Iatmul People of New Guinea as Revealed through a Study of the "Na yen" Ceremonial.* 2d ed. Stanford: Stanford University Press, 1958.

Bauman, Richard. *Verbal Art as Performance.* Rowley, MA: Newbury House, 1977.

Beidelman, Thomas O. (ed.). *The Translation of Culture: Essays Presented to E. E. Evans-Pritchard.* London: Tavistock, 1971.

Benedict, Ruth. *Patterns of Culture.* Boston: Houghton Mifflin, 1934.

Brown, Roger and Albert Gilman. "The Pronouns of Power and Solidarity." In *Style in Language.* Thomas A. Sebeok (ed.). Pp. 253–276. Cambridge, MA: MIT Press, 1960.

Campbell, J. K. *Honour, Family, and Patronage: A Study of Institutions and Moral Values in a Greek Mountain Community.* Oxford: Clarendon, 1964.

Cohen, Anthony P. *Self Consciousness: An Alternative Anthropology of Identity.* London: Routledge, 1994.

Crick, Malcolm. *Explorations in Language and Meaning: Towards a Semantic Anthropology.* New York: John Wiley/Halsted, 1976.

Diamandouros, P. Nikiforos. *Cultural Dualism and Political Change in Post-authoritarian Greece.* Madrid: Centro Juan Mach de Estudios Avanzados en Ciencias Sociales, Estudio no. 50, 1994.

Drummond, Lee. "The Serpent's Children: Semiotics of Cultural Genesis in Arawak and Trobriand Myth." *American Ethnologist* 8, 1981, pp. 633–660.

Dubisch, Jill. *In a Different Place: Pilgrimage, Gender, and Politics at a Greek Island Shrine.* Princeton: Princeton University Press, 1995.

Evans-Pritchard, E. E. *The Nuer: A Description of the Modes of Livelihood and Political Institutions of a Nilotic People.* Oxford: Clarendon, 1940.

—— *Nuer Religion.* Oxford: Clarendon, 1956.

—— *Essays in Social Anthropology.* London: Faber & Faber, 1962.

Fabian, Johannes. *Time and the Other: How Anthropology Makes its Object.* New York: Columbia University Press, 1983.

Ferguson, Charles. "Diglossia." *Word*, 1959, pp. 325–340.

Friedl, Ernestine. *Vasilika: A Village in Modern Greece.* New York: Holt, Rinehart, and Winston, 1962.

——. [Remarks]. In *Regional Variation in Modern Greece and Cyprus: Toward a Perspective on the Ethnography of Greece.* Muriel Dinien and Ernestine Friedl (eds.). Pp. 286–288 (= *Annals of the New York Academy of Sciences* 268. pp. 1–465). 1976.

Geertz, Clifford. *The Translation of Cultures.* New York: Basic, 1973.

Gambetta, Diego (ed.). *Trust: Making and Breaking Cooperative Relations.* Oxford: Blackwell, 1988.

Gilmore, David D. *Manhood in the Making: Cultural Concepts of Masculinity.* New Haven: Yale University Press, 1990.

Gumperz, John J. and Dell Hymes (eds.). *The Ethnography of Communication.* Washington, D.C.: American Anthropological Association, 1964.

Heelas, Paul, and Andrew Lock (eds.). *Indigenous Psychologies: The Anthropology of the Self.* London: Academic Press, 1981.

Herzfeld, Michael. "The Dowry in Greece: Terminological Usage and Historical Reconstruction." *Ethnohistory* 27, 1980, pp. 225–241.

—— "Performative Categories and Symbols of Passage in Rural Greece." *Journal of American Folklore* 94, 1981, pp. 44–57.

—— *Ours Once More: Folklore, Ideology, and the Making of Modern Greece.* Austin: University of Texas Press, 1982.

—— *The Poetics of Manhood: Contest and identity in a Cretan Mountain Village.* Princeton: Princeton University Press, 1985a.

—— "Gender Pragmatics: Agency, Speech, and Bride-Theft in a Cretan Mountain Village." *Anthropology* 9, 1985b, pp. 25–44.

—— *Anthropology through the Looking-Glass: Critical Ethnography in the Margins of Europe.* Cambridge: Cambridge University Press, 1987.

——. *Cultural Intimacy: Social Poetics in the Nation-State.* New York: Routledge, 1997a.

——. *Portrait of a Greek Imagination: An Ethnographic Biography of Andreas Nenedakis.* Chicago: University of Chicago Press, 1997b.

Jackson, Michael. "Introduction." In *Things As They Are: New Directions in Phenomenological Anthropology.* Michael Jackson (ed.). Bloomington: Indiana University Press, 1996, pp. 1–50.

Just, Roger. Review of Herzfeld. *Canberra Anthropology* 10, 1987, pp. 126–128.

Karakasidou, Anastasia. *Fields of Wheat, Hills of Blood: Passages to Nationhood in Greek Macedonia, 1870–1990.* Chicago: University of Chicago Press, 1997.

Karp, Ivan. "New Guinea Models in the African Savannah." *Africa* 48, 1978, pp. 1–16.

Labov, William. *Language in the Inner City: Studies in the Black English Vernacular.* Philadelphia: University of Pennsylvania Press, 1972.

Leach, Edmund R. "Lévi-Strauss in the Garden of Eden: An Examination of Some Recent Developments in the Analysis of Myth." *Transactions of the New York Academy of Sciences,* ser. 11, vol. 23, 1961, pp. 386–396.

Leavitt, John. "Meaning and Feeling in the Anthropology of Emotions." *American Ethnologist* 23(5), 1996, pp. 14–539.

Levy, Harry. "Property Distribution by Lot in Present Day Greece." *Transactions of the American Philological Association* 87, 1956, pp. 42–46.

Loizos, Peter. *The Greek Gift: Politics in a Cypriot Village.* Oxford: Basil Blackwell, 1975.

Lutz, Catherine A. and Lila Abu-Lughod (eds.). *Language and the Politics of Emotion.* Cambridge: Cambridge University Press, 1990.

Needham, Rodney. *Belief, Language, and Experience.* Oxford: Basil Blackwell, 1972.

Nenedakis, Andreas. *To khiróghrafo tis Skholis Kalón Tekhnón.* Athens, n.p. 1976.

Paine, Robert. "High-Wire Culture: Comparing Two Agonistic Systems of Self-Esteem." *Man* (n.s.) 24, 1989, pp. 657–672.

Peristiany, J. G. (ed.). *Honour and Shame: The Values of Mediterranean Society.* London: Weidenfeld & Nicolson, 1965.

Pinsent, L. Review of Herzfeld 1985a. *Liverpool Classical Monthly,* March, 1986, pp. [2–3].

Popper, Karl. *The Logic of Scientjfic Discovery.* 2d ed. New York: Harper and Row, 1968.

Radcliffe-Brown, A. R. *Structure and Function in Primitive Society.* London: Cohen and West, 1952.

Rosaldo, Renato. "From the Door of His tent: The Fieldworker and the Inquisitor." In *Writing Culture: The Poetics and Politics of Ethnography* Janes Clifford and George B. Marcus (eds.). Berkeley: University of California Press, 1986, pp. 77–97.

Rosen, Lawrence (ed.). *Other Intentions: Cultural Contexts and the Attribution of Inner States*. Santa Fe: School of American Research Press, 1995.

Skouteri-Didaskalou, Nora. *Anthropoloyiká ya to Yinekio Zitima*. 2d ed. Athens: 0 Politis, 1991.

Steedly, Mary. *Hanging Without a Rope: Narrative Experience in Colonial and Postcolonial Karoland*. Princeton: Princeton University Press, 1993.

Vellacott, Philip. "Introduction." *The Bacchae, and Other Plays*. Harmonds-worth:Penguin, 1954.

–5–

Translating Folk Theories of Translation
Deborah Kapchan

The event of a translation, the performance of all translations, is not that they succeed. A translation never succeeds in the pure and absolute sense of the term. Rather, a translation succeeds in promising success, in promising reconciliation. There are translations that don't even manage to promise, but a good translation is one that enacts the performative called a promise with the result that through the translation one sees the coming shape of a possible reconciliation among languages. (Derrida 1985a: 123)

In the history of anthropology, Western theoretical perspectives have consistently been privileged over vernacular or folk theories. Although the latter are often objects of interest, they are deemed to possess little explanatory potential, usually because they assume ways of knowing and being incompatible with those of the analyst (Gellner 1970; cf. Asad 1993). What happens when this hierarchy is challenged and folk theories share the status of Western theory? What does an analysis of folk theories of translation, for example, contribute to the anthropologist's translation of cultural poetics? In order to answer these questions, this chapter examines the folk theory of one Moroccan verbal artist, a storyteller who translates literary texts written in classical Arabic (fusHa, or CA) into oral renditions performed in Moroccan dialectal Arabic (darija, or MA). Through his metanarratives, we are able to ascertain an emergent theory of local translation between languages (CA and MA) and modalities (oral performance and written text) that reveals important junctures in cultural attitudes toward language, aesthetics and the performance of modernity.

The Storyteller in the Age of Information Translating the Written Text in Oral Performance

Storytellers carry us from one realm to another, from the mundane and material to the imaginal and ethereal. Storytellers are translators by definition insofar as the verb "translate" means to "transport" or to make to pass over.[1] Traveling from one imaginary world to another, their power lies in their ability to traverse these worlds, somewhat like a shaman, bringing the listener with them. Contemporary Moroccan storytellers apprentice themselves not to the masters of epic memory and meter as in preceding generations, however (cf. Reynolds 1995; Slyomovics 1987), but to *books* wherein these hybrid tales of diverse and oral provenance have been transcribed and codified into classical Arabic texts. Like public writers, Moroccan storytellers have functioned as brokers of literary culture, acting as bridges between the world of written tales and those of aural imagination. In the diglossic context of Moroccan verbal art this has entailed translating epics from classical Arabic back into oral colloquial Arabic for speakers of Moroccan dialect. Yet the verbal art tradition in Morocco has changed radically in the space of several generations. Whereas the old remember the epic storyteller in the marketplace as a respected and central figure in social life – someone responsible for recounting legends, stories and history to an illiterate audience – the young know these narratives, if they know them at all, through television reenactments and only rarely through books. This is due to the fact that the marketplace as a site of public performance has diminished in importance, replaced by television and other forms of media. It is also attributable to rising literacy rates which render the storyteller's function as translator less essential. Although the storyteller can still be found in the open air marketplace (particularly in the halqa, the performance space of the market), he has now become something of an anomaly, frequented by the old and the unemployed, an object of nostalgia, appropriated as an icon of Moroccan "folklore" in local and international venues.[2]

In Morocco there are several languages spoken by overlapping communities: three different dialects of Berber, some French and Spanish, as well as Moroccan Arabic. The latter, a grammatically simplified form of classical Arabic with syntactical borrowings from Berber and vocabulary from both Spanish and French, is one of the dialects most impervious to comprehension by speakers of other Arabic dialects due to the isolation of North Africa, the shortening of its vowel system (vis-à-vis Middle Eastern dialects) and its eventual convergences with other languages (see Heath 1989). Its status as the mother tongue for the majority of Moroccans is unquestionable. Moroccan Arabic is a purely oral communication, a sound system without a written representation.[3] It is the language of intimacy, of anger and desire. In the diglossic context of Moroccan verbal art the storyteller translates epics from classical Arabic into oral colloquial Arabic for speakers of Moroccan dialect. The storyteller's translation of these epics makes these stories local; it is a means of appropriation, in the Ricoeurian sense (1976), whereby a written text discloses itself to another world – in this case a world of orality and affective meaning – thereby creating a third domain, a new world of in-between.

The epic stories told in the marketplace in Morocco have long histories in oral tradition. *A Thousand and One Nights*, the epic of Ben Hillal (*al-Hillaliyya*) and the story of 'Antar (*al-'Antariyya*) were all originally oral texts, spoken in different languages and dialects, before being written down and codified in classical Arabic.

Unlike the storytellers of even a generation or two ago, however, contemporary storytellers in Morocco do not go through an apprenticeship with a master, nor do they learn their oeuvres through audition and committing formulae and form to memory. Rather, these storytellers buy books, most of them published in Beirut, read them carefully and then translate them to less-literate audiences with different degrees of fidelity.

In the following story about storytelling, the raconteur's explanation of this process reveals much about the importance of style in rendering the affective qualities of language. In the longer narrative he recounts how he learned his craft. It is not through verbal formulae, rhyme or memorization. In fact, it is the inverse of oral formulaic theory proposed by Lord (1960) wherein a poet memorizes a metric and sonic scheme and infuses it with content; here a literate man *reads* texts in classical Arabic in order to *translate* them into dialect for his less literate audience. It is a story that involves the translation (of desire, of meaning, of affect) from the written medium to the verbal one, from the high literary language to the maternal language of 'home' and from the visual (the text) to the auditory and performative.

Speaking of his trade, Moulay 'Omarr notes:

#1
The storytellers go out   1
m-malin l-qisas kay-khurju

between afternoon and sunset prayer
f-nus 'assr l-skhar qrabat l-maghreb.

They go out when it gets cool.
kay-khurju f-brudet l-hal

so people will stay
bash bnadem y-g'ud . . .

People have to stay   5
khassu bnadem y-g'ud

and for this the earth needs to be cool for them
u 'la had khas l-'ard tebred li-hum.

The epic teller in Marrakech
u mul s-sira lli f-marraksh

is behind the Koutoubia [mosque]
kayn ura l-kutubiya

– 137 –

behind the House of Baroud
ura dar l-barud,

on the side of the cemetery   10
f-janb r-ruda.

He, too, recounts from the book.
walakin kay-'awd ta huwa men l-ktab.

He reads from the book.
kay-qra men l-ktab.

In classical Arabic, not in dialect.
b-l-fuha mashi b-d-darija.

He reads.
kay-qra.

He doesn't know how to interpret.   15
ma y-'arf-sh ma y-'arf-sh y-shrah.

He doesn't interpret.
sh-harh ma 'andu-sh.

He reads from the book.
kay-qra men l-ktab.

Like now, he holds the book
bhal daba kay-shad l-ktab

He starts: "Antara Son of Shadded said . . ."
y-bda: "qala 'antara ibnu shaddad . . ."

and this and that   20
kada 'ila 'akhirih.

Those people are used to his telling style
dak bnadem daba mddiyn 'la t-t'awid dyal-u.

They are taken with what he says.
mddiyn 'la dak sh-shi lli tay-gul.

Like those here now [in this town] –
bahal hadi daba lli hnaya –

could the audience of Moulay Ahmed come to me?
wesh y-qadru shab mulay hmid y-jiu l-'and-i l-hnaya?

No, Moulay Ahmed's audience doesn't come to me.   25
la shab mulay hmid ma kay-jiu-sh 'and-i ana.

Because they've taken to his style.
li-'anna dau 'la t'awid-u.

They have been with him for a long time.
haduk m'a-h qdam.

You just find old people with him now.
daba kat-lqay 'and-u huwa ghir sh-shiyab.

Moulay Ahmed tells in his style.
mulay h kay-'awed dak t'awid dyal-u.

Those old people are taken with his style.   30
ddau duk sh-shiyab 'la t-'awid-u.

In classical Arabic, he tells them just from the book.
b-l-fusha ta huwa kay-'awed ghir men l-ktab.

Now with epics I'm going to . . . I can't add anything that's not . . .
daba s-sira ghadiya . . . ma n-qdar-sh n-dakhel fi-ha shi haja lli . . .

because if you add something
li'anna huwa daba ila dakhelt-i shi haja

there are people sitting there
kaynin n-nas lli ga'din m'a-k

they've heard it before.   35
faytin sam'in u faytin kada.

If you start saying something [different],
ila jit-i t . . . ila jit-i t-gul li-hum ye'ni wahed l-haja lli kada,

they're going to tell you, "stop sir,
ghadi y-gulu l-ak "wa hda flan,

"where the hell did you get that from?"
"wayli mnin jibt-i hada?"

Now they don't remember the whole epic
daba huma ma 'aqlu-sh 'la s-sira kamla

but when you start talking   40
walakin melli kat-bda nta kat-hdar

you start making their memories come alive
kat-bda thya li-hum dik th-thakira

old memories.
th-thakira l-qdima.

You can't leave what's written in the book
l-ktab ma t-qdar-sh t-khruj 'l-ih

unless you add something funny
llah-huma 'ila zedt-i shi haja dyal d-dhak

and simple.   45
u bast.

They say, "perfume it with a little laughter"
tay-gul l-ak "wa 'allil-hu bi-shay'in mina l-mazhi" [CA]

"If you give it humor
"fa 'itha 'a'tayta-hu l-mizha

Then give it just as much as you put salt in food."
"fa 'a'tihi qadra ma tu't-i t-ta'ama mina l-malh."

That is, just a little laughter,
ye'ni wahed sh-shwiya dyal l-mzah,

just a little,   50
u wahed sh-shwiyya kada

and you keep talking.
u kat-zid tani f-l-hadra.

don't [laugh] a lot, don't . . .,
ma t-qawwi, ma t- . . .,

just like food with its salt.
bhal 'ila t-t'am m'a l-malh.

– 140 –

If you add too much, you're stuck,
'ila katart-i l-ih wahla,

if you don't put enough, it's tasteless.   55
'ila qallat-ti l-ih, y-ji basel.

Because you have to translate what is there
li-'annahu khass-ek t-tarjem dak sh-shi lli kayn.

You translate it in *darija*
kat-ttarjm-u b-d-darija

and transform it into dialect.
u trud-u dariji.

You talk with people as if you're talking with [them] ordinarily.
t-kallem m'a l-'insan bhal 'ila kat-t-kallem m'ah 'adi.

Now, me, if I talk epics with people up there [in the marketplace]   60
daba ana bnadem 'ila kan t-kallem m'a-hum tema l-fuq f-s-sira

it's like people see it right next to them.
bhal 'ila kay-shuf-u f-bnadem f-l-fas qudam-hum

In the narrative above, Moulay 'Omarr talks about two kinds of storyteller – those in Marrakech who read from the book in classical Arabic, and those, like himself, who base their stories on the book but who translate and perform the words in dialect. Classical Arabic, though closest to the mother tongue, is referred to as *al-lugha* in the dialect; it is "the language," the proper name, the code against which others are marked. This language, according to Moulay 'Omarr, is not interpretable – the storyteller simply reads it. Here, Moulay 'Omarr makes the distinction between representation and performance, between imitation and mimesis; although reading the text in classical Arabic involves the translation of the written word to spoken utterance, he does not consider it interpretation; it is recounting, relating, representation, but it is not invested with the more personal and performative elements of the improvisation that, he goes on to say, take place in the mother tongue of Moroccan Arabic. Of his rival storyteller in the marketplace who reads the classical Arabic word for word he says, *sh-harh ma 'andu-sh*, literally, his colleague doesn't "have" (or possess) the art of interpretation. Moulay 'Omarr's distinction recalls the Greek meaning of interpretation, which included a performative, as well as an intellective process, here denied to the simple "reading" of texts, despite their being made audible.[4] The "style" that Moulay 'Omarr refers to is the

Arabic word, *t'awid*, literally, an oral rendering, a customary repetition, a habitual way of doing things.

Although the classical Arabic telling qualifies as a style among others, it is not "seasoned"; rather, Moulay 'Omarr qualifies it as "tasteless" (*basel*). Where Moulay Ahmed reads the classical text, Moulay 'Omarr leaves the classical text to enter an imaginative world, embellishing and appropriating the plot. For Moulay 'Omarr, translation is of several orders – not simply conveying the literal meaning, but performing the taste of his own translated words. Synaesthesia – here the blending of words and taste – becomes the criterion for a good interpretation. The translation of one sense into another bespeaks an enfoldment, a depth – for food is ingested, penetrating the depths of the body, giving pleasure and nourishment as it does so. For a man who trades in words, the tastiness of his product is of great import. What's more, the affect that resides in the mother tongue is not only tasty, but profitable. Whereas Moulay 'Omarr characterizes the audience for classical Arabic as "old" (which is why they are taken with this style, as it corresponds to old memories), *his* audience, he says, is comprised of a younger generation : *bezzaf dyal d-drari*, a lot of kids. Furthermore, his performative style – in Moroccan Arabic – is more vivid; he says that people are "grabbed by it [his story]," *kay t-khtaf b-had sh-shi hada*. They inhabit the narrative event fully because of his performance style. He thus has a much larger audience than his colleague Moulay Ahmed.

Moulay 'Omarr's decision to interpret and perform the text in the mother tongue intead of rendering it word for word is a conscious choice. He is able to read the classical Arabic, but subtly maligns classical Arabic style (and his competitor in the marketplace) by himself citing a proverb in classical Arabic (lines 46–48).

They say, "perfume it with a little laughter"
tay-gul l-ak "wa 'allil-hu bi-shay'in mina l-mazhi" [CA]

Here Moulay 'Omarr makes plain the intimacy of the two forms of Arabic (see Herzfeld 1997; and Chapter 4 of this volume);[5] classical Arabic is not a foreign language, but simpy a higher register. As the language of the Qur'an, it is comprehensible to most Moroccans with even a minimum of religious education in Qur'anic schools (before the French protectorate, a few years of Qur'anic education was the means to acquiring literacy in Moroccan society; see Eickelman 1992; Wagner 1993). Moulay 'Omarr's choice of when he will cite classical Arabic and when he will "translate" into Moroccan dialect are motivated, however, related to memory and fidelity; the memories that live in the body must be respected and reactivated. Just as the physical comfort of the audience aids in their attention ("the ground must be cool for them"), so the revivifying of their recollections must run true to past course. "When you start talking," he says, "you start making their memories come alive; old memories." Time depth is here expressed. Moulay 'Omarr uses the word <u>mddiyn</u>, "taken with," (rather than the more common <u>m'uluf</u>, "used to") to express the relation between audience and style – the audience is "taken with" the style, they have been transported by the translation. On the other hand, classical style without laughter and improvisation is tasteless. Although talking about classical Arabic, a written more than a spoken language, Moulay 'Omarr is specifically referring to its oral rendition. It is the performative aspect of Moroccan Arabic that the audience is taken with. And Moulay 'Omarr exemplifies this, citing the reported speech of his colleague:

> He [Moulay Ahmed] starts: "Antara Son of Shadded said . . ."
> *y-bda: "qala 'antara ibnu shaddad . . ."*
> and this and that
> *kada 'ila 'akhirih.*

The double-embedding of citation brings Moulay 'Omarr's attitude toward classical Arabic to the fore. He is imitating and thereby mocking the seriousness of his colleague who reads in classical Arabic. The quotation marks that he places around his colleague's words transform the act of mere repetition into one of performance and interpretation. In parodying the style of his colleague, Moulay 'Omarr performs his own theory – the high seriousness of classical Arabic must be brought down, reframed with quotation marks, and "perfumed" with laughter. Given thus taste and smell, the spoken text ceases being a mere repetition and is transformed into a successful translation.

Citation practices are common in classical Arabic, where genealogical delineations of reported speech – who said what to whom – are a common rhetorical strategy used to create textual authority by invoking other texts (cf. Briggs and Bauman 1992; Kapchan 1996). Here, however, Moulay 'Omarr verges on hyperbole. By mimicking the classical Arabic style, he challenges its authority (it doesn't make people laugh). "Because if you don't tell it in dialect (<u>darija</u>), there are people who won't undertand. Take Moulay Ahmed now; he starts working and he begins, that is, and TAN! He starts talking classical Arabic. There aren't many who will understand." Despite his critique, however, outside the frame of the quote in classical Arabic Moulay 'Omarr continues to use what in this region would be considered a *classicalized* Arabic: <u>kada 'ila 'akhirih</u>, "and this and that." In other words, his critique of classical style is made by appropriating the style and register itself. He thus demonstrates his own competence in the two registers of Arabic and well as their interpermeability.

Moulay 'Omarr clearly recognizes the necessity of faithfulness to the text ("You can't leave what's written in the book"), for extant memories are recalled and revivified in their evocation. Nonetheless, on being asked whether he memorized all the epics that he recounts, Moulay 'Omarr answers,

#2
There's no one who can remember 82 books.   1
ma kayn-sh l'insan y-qdar y'aqal 'la tnin u tmanin ktab.

It's among the impossible.
min l-mustahil

Even if he has an electronic mind he's not going to remember 82 books.
wakha y-kun 'and-u dmagh iliktrunik ma ghadi-sh y-'aqal 'la tnin u tmanin ktab.

Like now, the first [book] I can recall completely;
bhal daba, l-uwal n-qdar n-'awd-u kamal;

but after that, you go here   5
walakin min ba'd twelli t-amshi huk

you go there
u t-mshi huk

and you leave the epic here
u t-khalli s-sira hna

and you go over there
u t-amshi l-had j-jih

and turn it this way and only then
u dawer-ha l-had j-jih u 'ada

come back to those first words.   10
t-ji tani l-dak l-klam l-uwal.

Now take my case
daba ana had qadiya lli 'and-i

When I read the book for the first time
melli kan-kun kan-qra f-l-ktab l-marra l-uwla

I begin to read and I mark the important parts –
kan-bda n-qra u kan-ershum l-muhim –

the important parts that need to be told of the epic
l-muhim lli khasu y-t'awed f-s-sira,

that [part] which takes the epic straight ahead.   15
dak l-muhim kay-ddi s-sira nishan.

[Concerning] a description of a palace or something
bhal dak sh-shi dyal l-wasf dyal had ksar u kada u kada

we have no use for that stuff.
hadak sh-shi ma-'and-na ma-n-diru b-ih.

When you get to the part about the palace, *I'LL* describe it myself.
mahma kat-usel l-wahed l-qsar kan-wasf-u RASS-*i.*

I just mark that which is important.
kan-bda n-'allem ghir dak sh-shi lli huwa muhim.

Like this tower, it's called the Tower of Shitban,   20
bhal had l-qal'a 'asmit-ha qal'at sh-shitban,

you mark it;
kat-'alem 'li-ha.

you get to know it as the Tower of Shitban.
kat-bqa t-'raf-ha 'la 'anna-ha qal'at sh-shitban.

From the Tower of Shitban, they went and got another one –
men qal'at sh-shitban zadu talbin l-qal'a dyalt kada –

the Tower of Constantine.
qal'at qustantiniya.

You mark "Constantine."   25
kat-sharet 'l "qustantiniya."

Moulay 'Omarr marks the surface structure, the epidermis, so to speak, placing a cross, an x, by the places where he needs to come out of his affective depths and be attentive to the text, to the outer form, to the second language, and to naming as a self-conscious enactment. He reads – already an act of translation; and then he marks. He uses two words to describe this: ershim [root: ra-sha-ma], to mark, to designate (line 13), and 'allem [root: 'la ma], to physically inscribe, to mark with a cross (line 19). Lines that advance the literary plot are marked for their referential meaning (denken) – the kind that, like philosophy, lends itself to translation because the text as text is effaced. The poetry (dichten), in the form of descriptions, remains unmarked; that is, the storyteller takes responsibility for it himself, in the mother tongue. So whereas it remains unmarked in the written text, it becomes marked in the oral rendition – his responsibility, authored and performed by the storyteller himself, expressive of another world.[6]

The places that Moulay 'Omarr marks are proper names, names of places. The limits of translatability, they become the pillars of the story, landmarks upon which he constructs his performance. Descriptions, however, are places of liberty. Here he moves into his own interpretations, into poetry and gesture.

In Moulay 'Omarr's metanarrative it is not only the proper name, as such, but classical Arabic – al-lugha, "the Language" – that becomes marked, and, in Derrida's formulation, "synonymous with [the] confusion"[7] that so often characterizes relations of intimacy, for in challenging the boundaries between languages, between sign systems and genres of affect (as Moulay 'Omarr does above) the translator moves in a reversible world, swinging between surface and depth.[8] These different languages represent two different emotional worlds that together inhabit the narrative event that Moulay 'Omarr and other verbal artists in the Moroccan public domain narrate for their audiences: one, official, authoritative, transcendent, citational; the other playful, ironic, time-bound and "salty." These two repertoires find recognition in most all male Moroccans old enough to have spent their youth among storytellers in the marketplace, and are called to life again from the depths of experience for strategic and context-dependent reasons. It is not gratuitous that Moulay 'Omarr makes such careful note of where the storytellers in Marrakech hold forth ("behind the Koutoubia [mosque], behind the House of Baroud, on the side of the cemetery"). Placenames are also proper names, impermeable to translation, grounding the interlocutor firmly in time and space. This location, along with its temperate climate, functions to "emplace" the audience, to give them an affective home, a place to be "in."

If the epic, like the myth, is often associated with the transcendent quality of "time immemorial," this metanarrative about the epic expresses a certain anxiety about the telectronic age, wherein memory is conferred to computers. Note that the word for "electronic" is a direct borrowing from the French *électronique*:

Even if he has an electronic mind he's not going to remember 82 books.
wakha y-kun 'and-u dmagh iliktrunik ma ghadi-sh y-'aqal 'la tnin u tmanin ktab.

Although modernization in the form of television viewing has diminished his audience and thus radically affected his profession, Moulay 'Omarr seems not to be intimidated by the change in paradigm. Indeed he began his career going to the cinema at night to watch Indian films, the next day recounting the stories he saw there, substituting Moroccan names and places. In this process of "intersemiotic translation,' or translation between two different sign systems (Jakobson 1960), he implicitly employed the same processes of translation that he employs today, only instead of reading classical texts, he translated visual plots, rendering it in dialect and making it local. When speaking of his performances in the marketplace today, he compares them to the evening news – "If you do that 'news short', people gather and sit still and stay." Moulay 'Omarr's performances are self-consciously episodic and visual – you see the stories next to you. Perhaps it is not so much that "the storyteller in his living immediacy is by no means a present force" in contemporary society as Benjamin asserted (1969: 83), as that the genres that the storyteller lives and narrates are changing, along with their affective "sense."

Conclusion

The verbal artist discussed in this chapter is engaged in translation – from one language to another, from one modality (written/oral) to another (oral/written). For him the promise of the reconciliation of languages – the hope and promise that translation is realizable – is an important one. He does not celebrate its failures; to the contrary, he imagines its possibility and embodies his vision. In this, he shares much in common with Moroccan essayist and novelist Khatibi whose oeuvre theorizes and poeticizes the predicament of the bilingual (see *Amour Bi-lingue*, *Maghreb Pluriel*, *La Blessure du Nom Propre*). Khatibi is inhabited by the desire to translate the limits of the untranslatable, to delineate them and make them recognizable. Speaking of the second language as a lover, or the foreign lover as language, he says (1990: 20),

> There was no exact symmetry between them, no encounter both vertical and parallel; rather there was a kind of inversion, the permutation of an untranslatable love, that had to be translated without respite.

There is no question here of fidelity to the text in terms of literal translation. Duplication is not possible. It is the process of translation that holds promise, and not its product.

From Moulay 'Omarr's metanarrative we learn the following about his implicit theory of translation: 1) in the diglossic context of Morocco, the mother tongue of Moroccan Arabic is preferred as the more performative and affectively powerful medium of expression; 2) although the promise of translation is operative, the storyteller is not preoccupied with fidelity; to the contrary, he takes great license with the *form* of the narrative, all the while respecting its storyline, which he takes from the untranslatable elements of the story – namely, the proper names, places, events; 3) fidelity leads to boredom, while innovation responds to the marketplace. The storyteller has no anxiety about changing tradition. To the contrary, he models his performances on those of the mass media – news shorts; 4) the power of a performance come from its performative depth – that is, its ability to move all the senses and between all the senses (synaestheia).

For the storyteller Moulay 'Omarr, the mother tongue is the language of poetic elaboration and description. Further, it is a language that allows him to reach a larger and younger audience, one whose memories are not as conditioned by past literary renderings of epic stories. It represents a deeper engagement with his body and a more superficial engagement with the body of the text, that he nonetheless always holds in his hands. In analysing Moulay 'Omarr's metanarrative we learn that his criteria for a successful translation are intimately related to synaesthesia, to the ability of the translator to make words both tasty and odiferous. For him, a translation is not purely textual, but it must be performative. Classical Arabic texts are part of this performance – the script, so to speak; however, a successful translation makes the images come alive – visually, aurally, olfactorily and gustatorily. These senses blend together in the body of the performance as they do in the body of the performer. In the folk theory of Moulay 'Omarr, orality and literacy, low and high registers of Arabic, representation and performance, are all dyads that don't match, but that are locked in a relation of permeable and often painful intimacy, "the permutation of an untranslatable love, that [must be] translated without respite" – the promise of translation.

Notes

1. *faire passer* in French.
2. During 1999, the "Year of Morocco" in France, a series of performances in Paris celebrated Moroccan culture. Among these events was a reenactment of performances that take place regularly in Jma' al-Fna square in Marrakech, including herbalists hawking their goods, musicians, and storytellers.
3. Once a pupil attends kindergarten he or she begins learning the literary language – classical Arabic – the language of the Qur'an, and of all "official" and written texts. In fourth grade the pupil begins learning French, the most recent colonialist language, and in sixth grade English, the imperialist one.
4. "Everyone knows that the term 'hermeneutic' has had different connotations throughout its long history. As Jean Pépin has pointed out ('L'Herméneutique ancienne,' *Poétique* 23), in Greek thought the term hermeneia signified not so much the return, by way of exegesis, to a kernal of hidden meaning within a shell, but more the act of extroversion by the voice, the natural instrument of the soul. It is an active and prophetic productivity which is not connoted by the

Latin term *interpretatio*. For the Greeks, the poetic performance of rhapsodes was a 'hermeneutic' performance." Eugene Vance quoted in Derrida, 1985: 136.

5. Such interdependency between languages characterizes the Moroccan novel as well. Samia Mehrez remarks (1992: 122) that "By drawing on more than one culture, more than one language, more than one world experience, within the confines of the same text, postcolonial anglophone and francophone literature very often defies our notions of an 'original' work and its translation. Hence, in many ways these postcolonial plurilingual texts in their own right resist and ultimately exclude the monolingual demand of their readers to be like themselves: 'in between,' at once capable of reading and translating, where translation becomes an integral part of the reading experience. In effect, this literary production is in and of itself plurilingual and in many instances places us, as Khatibi has suggested, at the 'threshold of the untranslatable.'"

6. Commenting on Heidegger's remark that to make poetry is to think (*dichten ist denken*) Derrida remarks (1985a: 130): "On the subject of '*Dichten–Denken*,' Heidegger of course associates them, as you have said. But there are also texts where he says very precisely that, while 'Dichten–Denken' go together and form a pair, they are *parallels* that never meet. They run parallel one beside the other. They are really other and can never be confused or translated one into the other. Yet, as parallel paths, '*dichten*' and '*denken*' nevertheless have a relation to each other which is such that at places they cut across each other. They are parallels that intersect, as paradoxical as that may seem. By cutting across each other, they leave a mark, they cut out a notch. And this language of the cut or break is marked in the text of Heidegger's I'm thinking of: *Unterwegs zur Sprache* [*The Way to Language*]. They do not wound each other, but each cuts across the other, each leaves its mark in the other even though they are absolutely other, one beside the other, parallel. There is also, therefore, a trend in Heidegger emphasizing the irreducibility of '*Dichten–Denken*' and thus their nonpermutability."

7. "The proper name is a mark: something like confusion can occur at any time because the proper name bears confusion within itself. The most secret proper name is, up to a certain point, synonymous with confusion. To the extent which it can immediately become common and drift off course towards a system of relations where it functions as a common name or mark, it can send the address off course. The address is always delivered over to a kind of chance, and thus I cannot be assured that an appeal or an address is addressed to whom it is addressed." (Derrida 1985a: 107–08)

8. A similar reversibility (this time between French and Arabic) is noted by Moroccan writer Khatibi, in his work *Love in Two Languages*: "Permanent permutation. He understood this better thanks to a brief sense of disorientation he had experienced one day at Orly, waiting for a boarding call; he found

himself unable to read the word South, seen backward, through a window. Turning it around, he realized he had read it from right to left, as if it were written in Arabic characters – his first written form. He could place the word only by going by way of his mother tongue."

References

Asad, Talal. *Genealogies of Religion: Discipline and Reasons of Power in Christianity and Islam.* Baltimore and London: John Hopkins University Press, 1993.

Benjamin, Walter. "The Task of the Translator: An Introduction to the Translation of Baudelaire's Tableaux parisiens." In *Illuminations.* Hannah Arendt (ed.), trans. Harry Zohn, pp. 69–82. New York: Schocken, 1969.

Briggs, Charles. L. and Richard Bauman. "Genre, Intertextuality, and Social Power." *Journal of Linguistic Anthropology* 2(2), 1992, pp. 131–172.

Derrida, Jacques. "Des Tours de Babel." In *Difference in Translation.* Graham, Joseph (ed.) Ithaca: Cornell University Press, 1985a.

—— *The Ear of the Other: Otobiography, Transference, Translation.* English edn Christie V. McDonald (ed.), trans. Peggy Kamuf. New York: Schocken, 1985b. (The section of this book entitled "Otobiographies: The Teaching of Nietzsche and the Politics of the Proper Name" is translated by Avital Ronell.)

Eickelman, Dale. "Mass Higher Education and the Religious Imagination in Contemporary Arab Societies." *American Ethnologist* 19(4), 1992, pp. 643–655.

Gellner, Ernest. "Concepts and Society." In *Rationality.* B. R. Wilson (ed.). Oxford: Basil Blackwell, 1970.

Heath, Jeffrey. *From Code-Switching to Borrowing: Foreign and Diglossic Mixing in Moroccan Arabic.* London: Kegan Paul, 1989.

Herzfeld, Michael. *Cultural Intimacy: Social Poetics in the Nation-State.* New York: Routledge, 1997.

Hymes, Dell. "Breakthrough into Performance." *Folklore: Performance and Communication*, pp. 11–74.The Hague: Mouton, 1975.

Jakobson, Roman. Concluding Statement: "Linguistics and Poetics." In *Style in Language.* Thomas Sebeok (ed.), Cambridge, MA: MIT Press, 1960.

Kapchan, Deborah. *Gender on the Market: Moroccan Women and the Revoicing of Tradition.* Philadelphia: University of Pennsylvania Press, 1996.

Khatibi, Abdelkebir. *Love in Two Languages.* Trans. Richard Howard. Minneapolis: University of Minneapolis Press, 1990.

—— *Amour Bilingue.* Paris: Fata Morgana, 1983.

Lord, Albert Bates. *The Singer of Tales.* Cambridge, MA: Harvard University Press. 1960.

Mehrez, Samia. "Translation and the Postcolonial Experience: The Francophone North African Text". In *Rethinking Translation: Discourse, Subjectivity, Ideology.* Lawrence Venuti (ed.). pp. 120–138. New York and London: Routledge, 1992.

Reynolds, Dwight Fletcher. *Heroic Poets, Poetic Heroes: The Ethnography of Performance in an Arabic Oral Epic Tradition.* Ithaca: Cornell University Press, 1995.

Ricoeur, Paul. *Interpretation Theory : Discourse and the Surplus of Meaning.* Fort Worth: Texas Christian University Press, 1976.

Slyomovics, Susan. *The Merchant of Art: An Egyptian Hilali Oral Epic Poet in Performance.* Berkeley: University of California Press, 1987.

Wagner, Daniel A. *Literacy, Culture and Development: Becoming Literate in Morocco.* Cambridge and New York: Cambridge University Press, 1993.

– 6 –

Second Language, National Language, Modern Language, and Post-Colonial Voice: On Indonesian

Webb Keane

The Otherness of One's Own Best Language

In August 1998, an interviewer for the Indonesian news weekly *Tempo* asked Amien Rais, a major figure in national Islamic politics and founder of the National Mandate Party (*Partai Amanat Nasional*), why he had altered the name of the party from the originally proposed *Partai Amanat Bangsa*. He replied "We chose Partai Amanat Nasional because it would be better translated into English as *National Mandate Party*, not *People's Mandate Party*. Because the word *people* in English has leftist connotations" (Amien 1998; English words italicized in the original, translation mine). Of course Amien Rais was making a shrewd political calculation in this bid for international support, but what is striking is how unapologetically he expresses the decision with reference to translation. He seems to find it a perfectly ordinary matter to encounter Indonesian as doubly foreign. Having been a child-hood speaker of Javanese, he already comes to it as a second language. In addition, he readily imagines it from the perspective of English. Moreover, he has already, and one assumes unself-consciously, incorporated a so-called "loan-word," *nasional*, into the Indonesian, as if in anticipation of this future translation.

Readers of Indonesian print media will be familiar with this pattern of glossing backwards that, as it were, views the language from the position of a hypothetical English speaker – or of an Indonesian unsure of his or her words. What does a national language like Indonesian offer, that so easily invites its speakers to take a view from afar? Certainly not the possibly untranslatable values of local partic-ularity and rich aesthetic heritage. Shared with Malaysia, Singapore, and Brunei, the language is rarely portrayed as the bearer of primordial identities, much less a closely guarded cultural property.[1] In this respect it is, perhaps, similar to Swahili or Filipino. Nor has any of this seemed to trouble either its promoters or most ordinary speakers, for whom its "modern" and relatively cosmopolitan character – its inherent translatability – are unquestionable, if not always unproblematic.

The self-conscious modernity and even cosmopolitan claims of Indonesian as a national standard have been inseparable from a certain projection of "otherness." This otherness is related to, but ideologically distinct from the forms of linguistic difference characteristic, for example, of lingua francas, honorific registers, taboo vocabularies, scriptural and high literary languages, or commonplace plurilingualism. Like them, it draws on semiotic features immanent in language *per se*, which underlie its potential for producing both intersubjectivity and objectification, for being disembedded from and reinserted into particular contexts, for providing speakers with a range of distinctive social "voices," and for mediating their reflexivity. It does so, however, in order to underwrite Indonesian's apparent potential as a superordinate and cosmopolitan language of purportedly "anti-feudal," in some sense, decentered social and political identities. This promise is inseparable for the imaginability of the nation as a project of modernity – and it is this promise to which Amien Rais seems to be responding.

Indonesian is a language whose ideological value has from its early days derived in part from being portrayed to its speakers as a markedly second and subsequent language. If it can seem, in some ways, to demand the sacrifice of one's first language, or at least its relegation to the past, the private, the local, or the subjective, this potential loss often seems to provoke remarkably little mourning: ethnic-language politics or revitalization movements have been surprisingly rare in the archipelago. If the national language does not inspire love in all who claim it, this is largely for *other* reasons, having to do with general paradoxes of national subjecthood, and the specific violence and tedium of an authoritarian state. Moreover, for all the peculiarities of Indonesian colonial and postcolonial history, the rise of the national language and its attendant ideologies also reflect pervasive problems in the semiotic mediation of translocal identities and large-scale publics – in the unstable articulation of ideologies with semiotic practices.

As scholars such as James Siegel (1986, 1997) and Joseph Errington (1998) have pointed out, the perceived "otherness" of Indonesian has at least two aspects. One is biographical: for most of its speakers Indonesian was acquired as a second language in marked contrast to languages denoted as "local" (*bahasa daerah*; see Keane 1997a). The second is cognitive. In contrast to the first language children learn at home, and even to such second languages as are picked up, say, in playgrounds, plantations, or marketplaces, Indonesian is encountered as relatively objectified, something one learns by way of explicit rules. Unlike that first language, it is commonly spoken of as needing to be "developed," "modernized," and made into a cosmopolitan literary vehicle. It is the object of purposeful manipulation in a way one's mother tongue is not.

In being portrayed as a language that, in some sense, belongs to no one in particular, it would seem to be readily learnable and translatable – open to anyone. In this respect, the dominant language ideologies of Indonesian run counter to the

Herderian tradition that seeks in language the deep spiritual or cultural roots of an organic people that preexists the nation. The rise of Indonesian has been associated with a rather cheerful view of the claim that nationalist aspirations are founded on universal categories. And, no doubt, this involves other paradoxes. According to Benedict Anderson (1996), the Indonesian language seemed for many early nationalists to lend itself to openness to ideas, signified by European words for categories – politician, striker, citizen – into which anyone, in principle, might enter. But this is more than a matter of introducing new words and ideas. It involves self-conscious efforts to take advantage of language's general pragmatic capacities for abstraction and decontextualization in order to make possible new and expansive modes of circulation. Indeed, when those nationalists imagined liberation, from colonialism to be sure, but also from kinship, villages, and what (under this new universalism) came to be thought of as "feudal" (*feodal*) traditions, they envisioned a language purposefully stripped of social indexes and cultural particularities. Thus it would seem to be this very otherness, and the sense of openness and even historical agency it evokes, which makes it peculiarly suitable as the language of the nation as a project of modernity. But as the failure of Indonesian (so far) entirely to fulfill these visions suggests, such projects do not come into being – or fail – as thought-worlds or representations alone. They require both practical embodiment in concrete semiotic forms, and the conceptual specificity by which those forms are interpreted within political contexts – the forms and their interpretations, however, existing in unstable and even contradictory relations with one another.

In terms of linguistic ideology (Kroskrity 2000), Indonesian makes two claims to universality that reflect those of modernist nationalisms more broadly, since it is in principle available to anyone, and is supposed to be transparent to other languages, unhampered by untranslatable opacities or untransferable indexes of context. It should therefore be a suitable medium for the projection and fostering of a certain kind of persona, one that speaks in public and is potentially identified with the nation. And it should allow its speakers to take a recognizable place in the cosmopolitan plane of *other* languages understood to be modern in character and global in scope. Indonesian may turn out to be only an extreme instance of a common circumstance in the semiotics and linguistics of nations and their potential publics. The language that carries the greatest political and cultural weight may involve a willful sort of self-displacement, as speakers in important respects understand themselves as giving up, or at least subordinating, a local language, retrospectively construed as their "mother tongue," in favor of one deemed to transcend the local in both space and historical time. Indeed, this process, in one form or another, is widespread as linguistic standardization is recasting normal plurilingualism into a hierarchy of localities encompassed within larger linguistic spheres that explicitly aspire to hegemony (Silverstein 1998: 410).

Yet we should not assume we know in advance just what speakers see themselves as giving up. The history of Indonesian suggests that the perceived value
of that "mother tongue" does *not* necessarily lie in its ties to local group identity.
(Indeed, its "value" may well be produced only in retrospect [Keane 1997b].)
These are questions of language ideology, but not all possible claims about language are equally plausible. Ideologies of national and postcolonial languages, draw
on the historically specific interpretations and the exploitation of universal, but
underdeterminant, semiotic features. Indonesian has been a central part of a self-
consciously "modern" project of national self-creation. It is tied to ubiquitous
concepts of modernity that orient both high-level policies and everyday activities.
Of particular relevance here are popular ideas about historical rupture with "tradition" and its implications for the capacities of humans to be the agents of their
own transformation (Berman 1998; Taylor 1989). For such ideas to be inhabitable
requires concrete forms of semiotic mediation, among which the sheer pervas-
iveness of linguistic habitus gives it a privileged role. But this habitus is never
sufficient unto itself, and inevitably involves the meta-linguistic and, by extension,
meta-cultural (Urban 2001) interpretations offered by linguistic ideologies. And
these come to the fore especially to the extent that a heightened sense of agency,
for instance in the guise of instrumentalist policies of language reform, makes them
the special focus of attention. As the example of Indonesian suggests, an account
of the historical particularities of languages and the power relations they involve
cannot overlook the endemic problems posed by the semiotics of language, and
their implications for the identification of speakers with "their" language – and
their potential alienation from it.

Babel as the Semiotic Condition

National languages have usually been posed, in part, as solutions to the problem
of divisiveness figured by the Tower of Babel. Babel is an account of social
difference that focuses on the material forms of lexical signifiers. In his classic
discussion, George Steiner (1975: 58), portrays the story of Babel as the loss of
a world in which Adam's act of naming brings things into being. We may see this
as implying two kinds of separations. One is a rupture between two linguistic
functions, reference and denotation on the one hand, and performativity, with all
the active and interactive features of speech, on the other. Thus, the story would go,
once upon a time to name was already to act; subsequently, in our postlapsarian
world, naming has become distinct from action proper, or at most merely a certain,
highly attenuated kind of act, the (mere) saying of words. The other separation
follows on the first: if naming is only a linguistic act (and if denoting is the only
linguistic act), then there exists a rupture between what exists in the world and the

names for what exists. This is the foundation for the arbitrariness of the sign, the semiotic condition of possibility for linguistic diversity. Only, according to this narrative, it is the rupture in language which brings about the subsequent social diversity. By combining two kinds of distinction (between linguistic functions, and between signifier and signified), the story implicates the loss of socio-linguistic *unity* with the loss of the full *power* of words. The question of unity among the speakers of now disparate languages merely compounds the quandaries of identity of speakers' relationships to their "own" words that are *already* found in language's basic characteristics.

How can a view of language that is so general shed light on the more particular questions of national identity and its specific language ideologies? Certain semiotic properties come to be topics of interest or sources of concern only under certain circumstances. Not everyone at every historical moment, for instance, has taken the existence of the sound/sense distinction to be troubling. That the mediation of language itself must necessarily involve some sort of alienation or violence is a common theme in some religious contexts, notably in times of reformism. For example, reformers have tended to see the distinction between sound and sense in hierarchical and often historicizing terms. If sense should be dominant, sound perpetually threatens to disrupt it. Thus, for instance, Protestantism saw Catholic uses of language as insincere and even idolatrous – marks of their supposedly archaic character (Keane 1997b). By using prayer books, worshipers took their words not from the heart but from external sources. Since prayer books emphasize the iterability of texts across contexts, they seem to privilege material form over immaterial content and thus, in this view, tempt the worshiper to fetishize ritual rather than the true spirit of faith. Conversely, orthodox Muslims respond to the same semiotic problem by asserting that the Qur'an can exist only in the original divine Arabic words, to which translation would do ontological violence.

In less religious terms, the hierarchical and anxious aspect of this critique was expressed early on by Wilhelm von Humboldt (Steiner 1975: 82), who portrayed language as external to humans and thus doing violence to them. What Humboldt shared with Protestantism is a devaluing of the materiality of the word relative to the human spirit and the autonomy of the human subject. Playing up the post-Adamic separation of words from the world, this view sees language as standing between us and the things themselves, a view whose implications persist in one of the dominant linguistic postulates of the early twentieth century, Saussure's (1986 [1915]) doctrine of the arbitrariness of the signifier/signified relation. These worries about the form–sense distinction produce a variety of alternative scenarios. In utopian or messianic thought the notion is that if humans can get beyond differences of form, they might find translation's underlying enabling condition, namely, a deeper universality. And this recurrent theme animates an important strand in ideas of "modernity."

The arbitrariness that lies at the heart of the linguistic sign in most academic theories at least since John Locke (Bauman and Briggs 2000) can be a source of ambivalence for modernizing projects. Potentially a source of alienation, it also allows one to see language as the object of human actions. Language may be manipulated, improved, developed, perhaps even created anew. That which renders language a possible object of suspicion at the same time makes it available for a certain optimism about what language engineering can achieve. Therein has often been seen to lie some of the promise of the national language. It should share certain properties of divine language (transcending existing disunities), but also remain human (it communicates). It should translate in both a vertical sense – elevating speakers out of the social and even semantic confines of their local languages – and a horizontal sense – situating them on a plane that will permit them to circulate among other languages of the world. This potential for publicness and circulation are functions, in part, of the suppression of those indexical links to particular contexts – to social interactions, parochial memories, traditional hierarchies, obscure places – that are part of what make "local" languages supposedly unfit for the nation.

These fundamental semiotic issues bear specific historical entailments. Whether people take the decentering that language entails to be of interest and whether negative or positive, and how they respond in practice, are historically variable questions. This decentering also raises questions about the political status of languages. If national language takes the decentering inherent in language and carries it to a higher degree, making it an objectified focus of ideological concern, then what does it mean to say it "belongs" to the people of the nation?

Babel and Domination in Postcolonial Critique

The story of Babel asks us to wonder why there should be differences when once there was unity – and, it would seem, expresses a yearning for that lost universality. This question, most puzzling when language is taken primarily to be a vehicle for the making of (potentially) true statements, becomes less mysterious when the social and political pragmatics of language are taken into view. Sociolinguistics has long recognized, for instance, that distinctions of language construct social boundaries and constitute hierarchies. The need for translation, in this light, is not simply an unfortunate, even contingent, by-product of our fallen state, but displays speakers' and listeners' political *insistence* on their distinctiveness from others. As Judith Irvine and Susan Gal (2000) have argued, boundaries between languages do not simply reflect differences of social or political identity, nor is the very existence of such boundaries merely a "linguistic" fact. Rather, the constituting of identities involves ideologies about language differences, including shifting perceptions about the very existence of boundaries. Moreover, it is clear that boundaries do not simply separate but also hierarchize. Linguistic differences are rarely if ever neutral, but typically involve both ideological and practical relations of encompassment, subordination and dominance (Silverstein 1998).

In the postcolonial context, these basic semiotic problems underlie arguments about efforts to reclaim local linguistic identity and discursive powers from the effects of colonial domination. On the one hand, a modernist and development-oriented position tends to stress the view that a standardized national language is a vehicle of the movement toward universality, bringing peoples together in a global ecumene. Indeed, a supposedly "richer" language should provide resources for the improvement of one that is more "impoverished." To some extent, the Nigerian writer Chinua Achebe (1994 [1975]) draws on both views in his argument that African writers should use English because it allows them to communicate across Africa and with the world at large.

An opposed position stresses the ways in which translation offends against the self-possession of the speaker. More specifically, translation requires some sort of explication or contextualization that is not necessary in the original, and so offends against the shared tacit knowledge that defines intimates. Explication performs an act of interpretation on words that had been left to the recipient to interpret and can thus appear as a form of aggressiveness. In colonial situations, the Western claims to understand and master indigenous others that are enacted through translation may be crucial to the everyday workings of power. Here the claims of universality mask and legitimate a historically specific set of political relations. Thus the reinstatement of opacity between languages becomes a means of resisting domination and fostering autonomous agency.

The Kenyan writer Ngugi wa Thiong'o wrote that when he was a child, he spoke Gikuyu, "the language of our evening teach-ins, and the language of our immediate and wider community, and the language of our work in the fields were one" (1994 [1986]: 438). This harmony was broken when he went to the colonial school, introducing a rupture between the language of education and that of home. Moreover, those who spoke their mother tongue were punished, and "English became more than a language: it was *the* language, and all the others had to bow before it in deference" (1994 [1986]: 438; italics in the original).

Invoking this experience to attack Achebe's modernist optimism, Ngugi treats language as the property of its speakers; it has owners (1994 [1986]: 436). Thus colonial education is a form of violent expropriation – it takes away the language one truly possesses – and alienation – it forces one to use a language that belongs to others, the colonizers and the indigenous "petty bourgeoisie." Ngugi links this property model of alienation to another, a rupture within experience, between spoken and written language, between the language that is the "carrier" of one's culture (1994 [1986]: 439) and that which is only a means of communication with outsiders. He thus seems to conflate two kinds of "violence," that which transpires in the power relations of colonialism and a more general schism that lies between authentic speech (that of the mother, the hearth, of "real-life struggles" 1994 [1986]: 437) and the general semiotic properties that decenter language – its learnability, what Derrida (1982 [1971]) calls its iterability, and the decontext-ualizing effects of writing. But by conflating these semiotic properties, which are inescapable characteristics of language, with colonial relations, which are historic-ally specific forms of power, he risks making any challenge to actual relations of domination unthinkable or at least unspeakable.

Achebe and Ngugi represent two versions of high modernism, cosmopolitan and identitarian, which flourished in the early postcolonial world. Since that time, complexities and contradictions have become increasingly evident. Cosmopol-itanism draws indigenous elites into foreign allegiances which may exclude people at home for whom the requisite education and mobility are not available. The essentializing claims common to national historiography and identity politics are marked by their colonial genealogies (Chakrabarty 1992). The respective language ideologies of the cosmopolitan and the nationalist are equally suspect since the poststructuralist turn in postcolonial studies. The presumption of universal trans-parency that allows Achebe to assume that the African writer could enter freely into English literature has been thrown into doubt; so too Ngugi's romantic assimilation of ethnic group to language, and both to an originary self-presence. If the colonial translator worked under assumptions of universality, and thus transparency among languages, postcolonial critics commonly insist on particularity or heterogeneity, and thus the resistance to translation among languages, as crucial to larger projects of historical agency (Jacquemond 1992, Mahrez 1992, Niranjana 1992; cf. Liu 1995, Spivak 1992).

One Language, One People: From Malay to Indonesian

The modernizing projects that have been so central to nationalist movements and postcolonial states therefore reflect certain older anxieties that respond to persistent semiotic features of language. One of these is the notion that language, consisting of forms external to, and not fully in possession of or under the control of the indiv-idual speaker, is a form of violence to human self-presence. Thus, for example, Ngugi sees the move between languages to involve not merely political domination whose medium includes language, but an assault on the intimacy of one's relation to one's words in a violence both parallel to and serving the violence of colonial-ism. But what if one's own most politically vital identity is constituted through a language whose greatest strengths lie in its supposed *distance* from the intimacies of the mother tongue? What if that identity even seems to demand a certain willing *sacrifice*, a letting-go, of one's first language (cf. Kulick 1992)? The Indonesian case raises questions about what it means to "possess" a language, and thus, to translate between that and other languages also felt to be "one's own" or "others'."

Indonesian, the official language of nationhood, government, education, formal and most mass-mediated informal communication, is a variant of Malay. The transformation of Malay into the increasingly standardized language of, by turns, a colonial administration, a nationalist movement, and a state apparatus and a national culture was, if nothing else, an effective response to an extreme linguistic situation. Even now some 500 languages are spoken in Indonesia, 14 of them by over a million speakers each (Steinhauer 1994). But the choice of Malay for national language was not obvious. It was the native language of a small minority, in contrast to numerically dominant groups such as the Javanese, Sundanese, and Madurese. For the first half of the twentieth century, the educated elite was far more comfortable in Dutch, and many agreed with their Dutch teachers in considered Malay – "that preposterous language" (Sutherland 1968: 124) – to be crude and ill-suited for serious undertakings. Yet compared to, say, the more contested position of Hindi in India – Indonesian is remarkable for its apparent "success." Due in part to the absence of any of the ethnic or political resistance encountered by many postcolonial national languages, being identified directly with neither the colonizer nor any single privileged ethnic group, knowledge and use of Indonesian has spread rapidly in the last fifty years.[2]

Malay originated along the Straits of Malacca between Sumatra and the Malay peninsula, but by the time Europeans arrived in the area in the fifteenth century it had become a well-established lingua franca from the Moluccas to the Indian Ocean.[3] Dutch colonial policies and practices further reinforced its position across the Indies. Unlike the British in India and French in Africa, the Dutch never seriously attempted to inculcate their own language as the medium of rule and, until the twentieth century, often tried to prevent even indigenous elites from speaking it (Groeneboer 1998). Instead, missionaries and local officials tended to rely on some form of Malay. By the end of the nineteenth century, scholars were attempting to produce a standardized "high" variety of the language for administration. The nationalist standardizing project during and after the colonial era continued along similar lines, enforcing grammatical and phonological norms – and introducing vocabulary – that were quite distinct even from the existing practices of most Malay speakers.

The birth of "Indonesian" under that name is conventionally dated to the Youth Oath of 1928. From that point, Dutch and Javanese rapidly ceased to be serious contenders as languages of the nationalist movement. The oath committed the movement to one land, one people, one language, and "bahasa Indonesia" was increasingly viewed not just as a useful medium for communication but as an emblem of nationhood. Propagation was largely a top-down process, and it is perhaps a fitting irony that one of the most effective forces for its dissemination was the Japanese occupation during the Second World War. Under the Japanese, use of Dutch was prohibited and Indonesian promoted as the chief medium of schooling and propaganda – even the talking bird in the Batavia zoo was retrained to greet ladies in Indonesian instead of Dutch (Wertheim 1964).

From the 1920s there also began a growth in self-conscious efforts to produce an Indonesian literature in publishing ventures marked by strenuous efforts at standardizing, "improving," and "modernizing" the language. The major landmarks in the subsequent rise of Indonesian, such as the 1945 Constitution and later Language Conferences (Halim 1984 [1976]), were highly self-conscious acts of elites attempting to make language the object of their deliberate actions. The rapid increase in centralizing and developmental efforts under Suharto's New Order regime (1966–1998) greatly expanded the infrastructure for controlling and disseminating the standard through vast expansions of the school system, publishing ventures, and television. In this light, Indonesian is modern in the very processes by which it has come into being.

Many non-standard varieties of spoken Malay flourish across the archipelago (Collins 1980). But these variants are often so distinct from Indonesian, both linguistically and ideologically, that to switch between them is a highly marked discursive move; indeed, some speakers of one may not even fully command the other. In certain ways, therefore, Malay speakers' relationship to Indonesian differs from that of speakers of other local languages only in degree. For the switch from a "local" language into Indonesian is, in metalinguistic and ideological terms, distinct from other kinds of "code switching." This may be a function of a common productive aspect of linguistic ideology, what Judith Irvine and Susan Gal (2000) have described as "fractal recursivity," the projection of ideological oppositions from one level to another. By this logic, the distinction between Low Malay and Indonesian can be identified with that between the "local" and the national, along with the private and the public, interpreting and reinforcing at the plane of ideology Malay speakers' experiences of *both* Indonesian *and*, by projection, "the local language" at the level of practice (see Keane 1997a). In this way Indonesian's authority and alterity may impose themselves over even "native" speakers of closely related variants of Malay (see Kumanireng 1982).

Official Cosmopolitanism

According to the scholar Ariel Heryanto (1995), it is the Indonesian language more than anything else that gives substance to the idea of there being a national culture at all. Yet by the 1990s, Indonesian had come by many of its speakers to be identified with an oppressive state apparatus, its ideologies, and its heavy-handed models of development, and for some is felt to lack subtlety, beauty, or depth (e.g. Anwar 1980: 1). These two perspectives, I want to suggest, are two faces of the same thing, the peculiarly "modern" character of Indonesian in its ideological attributes and practical functions. It is the perceived otherness of Indonesian that makes it particularly well-suited as a language for national and personal development, an emblem of modernity and cosmopolitanism, a vehicle for translation among local, national, and international planes. What for the romantic nationalist may seem to be liabilities, such as the lack of deep historical roots in a core population group, have for most of the history of Indonesian nationalism been virtues. The question remains open whether Indonesian can be detached from the hegemony of school and officialdom or whether its promised virtues are inseparable from the sense of flatness and alienation so often imputed to it.

For the vast majority of the population at the beginning of the twenty-first century, Indonesian remains a clearly defined second language, acquired after a "local language." Even when linguistically close to that first language, it bears a distinct social, political, and cognitive status. The uses of Indonesian tend to follow the patterns of register or code-switching familiar from other high, official, and national languages. It is the language most appropriate for public, official, national, educated, and technological settings and topics, of mass media and the economically higher-order marketplaces, a mark of sophistication, and a medium for speaking across social distance.[4] These contexts and associations may not, however, all function in the same way or open up the same sets of possibilities. Schools, speeches, and official documents attempt quite explicitly to authorize the standard's claims. These are contexts in which the capacity of the language to index *other* contexts, apart from abstractions like statehood and rationality, is suppressed. As such they are meant to impose ordering effects on uses of the language in other situations. But there is no reason to assume that the centralizing project of the state has been fully effective. It is too soon to predict how this standardizing project will fare in post-New Order Indonesia. If anything has become clear since the fall of Suharto, however, it is that we should be wary of taking the attempt for the result.

Hierarchy and Internal Translation

The modernity of Indonesian does not lie in the mere fact of being a marked linguistic alternative to some "prior" language, nor even in being an object of metalinguistic awareness and ideology. After all, plurilingual societies have always involved movement among linguistic varieties. This movement can be habitual and unconscious but also subject to highly self-aware actions and forms of linguistic self-objectification (Voloshinov 1973 [1930], see Lucy 1993). The ubiquity of taboo and avoidance vocabularies, respect registers, ritual speech forms, secretive jargons and so forth shows the ubiquity of a capacity to step into a language perceived as markedly apart from ordinary speech. Marked linguistic varieties can be highly productive, drawing on speakers' metalinguistic awareness to create new forms, commonly by putting the materiality of signifiers in the foreground, as in punning, acronyms, and so forth.

Crossroads like the Indonesian archipelago have long been swept by linguistic currents and even the relatively hegemonic monologism of precolonial central Java was permeated with words and phrases of Arabic, remnants of scriptural Sanskrit, Malay, and perhaps bits of Hokkien. With these resources to draw on, the region is well known for certain highly elaborated register differences. "Internal translation" (Zurbuchen 1989) is the hallmark of traditional Javanese and Balinese performance, in which archaic languages steeped in Sanskritic vocabulary alternate with commentaries in contemporary idioms that permit audiences to follow the action. Central Java is especially famous for its elaborate register differences by which minute distinctions of social hierarchy are marked by lexical choices among the vocabulary sets of "high," "middle" and "low" Javanese. One register forms the unmarked category, often conceptualized as the speech of casual relations and intimacy figured as that between mother and child (Siegel 1986). Against it, the marked category is the speech of seriousness, formality, adulthood and, often, maleness. It is this analogy of Indonesian to other such forms of register-shifting, especially in Javanese, that has stimulated some of the most insightful contemporary interpretations of the national language. Benedict Anderson (1990a [1966]; see Hooker 1993) pointed out that within a generation of independence, formal Indonesian had appropriated so much foreign and archaistic vocabulary that it was growing increasingly incomprehensible to all but the elite, and taking on many of the social functions of "high" Javanese. Errington (2000) has argued that this is part of an alternative kind of linguistic authority to that of the rationalist modernist standard, a persistence of the authority of "exemplary centers" characteristic of much older Javanese and other Southeast Asian forms of hierarchy. These functions, however, may go beyond the strategic play of status and exclusion. Thus, James Siegel (1986, 1997) has argued that Indonesian is functionally similar to "high" Javanese in that children learn to replace what they would have said in their original language with words imposed from without. To speak the high language is thus to display the suppression of the low (as retrospectively construed), with profoundly decentering implications for the speaker's sense of having an "own" language.

But if taboo and slang languages aim to create barriers within relatively more open language varieties, by contrast Indonesian is ideologically supposed to open outward. Indonesian thus differs from earlier forms of "internal translation" in its links to the modernist and cosmopolitan aspirations that underwrote its emergence, its vision of referential transparency, and the fact that it presents itself as an alternative to hierarchical registers. Despite its deep roots in Old Malay, Indonesian has not generally called on primordialist ideologies for its legitimacy. Rather, it has always been portrayed as modern, and as a vehicle for the modernization of Indonesian subjects and society. This is more than a matter of explicit claims on its behalf. As I have noted, the very practices through which Indonesian emerged bear the marks of language ideologies that are linked to ideas of modernity, treating language as a set of arbitrary signs that are subject to self-liberating forms of human agency.

Free, Egalitarian and Vulgar

In the early decades of the twentieth century, the elites typically considered Malay a vulgar language. But both the apparent crudity and the foreignness of Malay were also sources of its appeal. Indonesian even today is widely perceived to lack two things that other languages are supposed to have (but in this respect, it perhaps only displays openly what is ideologically obscured for other languages). It is not commonly perceived to possess either a clear social-geographical "center" or exemplary "best" speakers (Goenawan 1982: 321; cf Silverstein 1996). But in the heyday of modernist nationalism, the lack of centers was taken to be an advantage. Thus the common assertion that Indonesian – like Swahili (Fabian 1986) and Hindi (Cohn 1996 [1985]) – is an "easy" language (Anwar 1989, Moeliono 1994) expresses a degree of ambivalence: its supposed lack of subtlety and depth is inseparable from its accessibility.

Spatially and socially demarcated linguistic centers enable speakers to measure their linguistic correctness – or failings. Lacking a presumed "center," Indonesian by contrast is supposed to be open to all. As a late colonial-era Javanese guide to etiquette advised, "If you are asked a question by someone, what language should your answer be in? Use the language of the questioner. But if you cannot speak that language, use Malay" (quoted in Errington 1985: 59). Unlike a Herderian language of the "people," it does not, in principle, exclude any potential speakers.

The value of Indonesian was not a mere matter of conveying denotations across linguistic boundaries, but its promise of escape from register systems altogether. This was one source of the perception that Indonesian was vulgar, since it failed to provide speakers with clear positions of hierarchy relative to one another. Nobles in early twentieth-century Sumba, for instance, avoided Malay as being a demeaning "language of merchants" (Wielenga 1913: 144). The very lack of status markers that they avoided was something that others sought. As one Javanese man recalled of the late colonial era, although Malay "lacked intimacy," it was a good way to speak with a friend, not too distant, too close, or too condescending (Errington 1985: 60). At least in the early years, the use of Indonesian seems to reach for this neutrality and freedom from hierarchy. The modernity and rationality imputed to Indonesian produced its supposed egalitarianism, which was seen as a function of its apparent "ease." For young Javanese, at least, this "ease" is reportedly less a matter of linguistic code than of interaction; the risks concern the projected self and its presupposed others. What is remarkable is that this ease is granted not by the speaker's intuitive and habitual mastery of a first language, but by the conscious control associated with the second.

Even if Indonesian failed to sustain this egalitarian promise through the New Order period (1965–1998), the sense of otherness remains a component of its modernity. The formal learning process and the association with writing encourage a sense that one ought to have an active, self-conscious, and rational control over this language, in contrast to the relatively unself-conscious mastery of one's mother tongue (Kumanireng 1982). This sets up Indonesian as peculiarly the object of metalinguistic discourses and fosters the notion that it can be subject to purposeful manipulation. Unlike one's mother tongue, Indonesian is commonly portrayed as incomplete, its speakers feeling their command to be imperfect. Both language and speaker would thus need improvement. To these ends, the state since its inception has been actively working to foster "good and true" (*baik dan benar*) Indonesian. But this effort is not restricted to the state. From the beginning (Adam 1995), Indonesian usage and vocabulary has been the subject of advice columns, pamphlets, and letters to editors. Not surprisingly, the plethora of public criticism seems to have produced insecurity, a combination of personal and national anxiety captured in the book title *Have You Sufficiently Cultivated Our Language of Unity?* (Tjokronegoro 1968).

The ordinary experience of learning Indonesian and the critical discourses surrounding it reproduce one of the central features of its supposed modernity, the privileged role of rational human agency. In 1948, Sutan Takdir Alisjahbana, a crucial figure in forging language policy, attacked nationalist primordialism by asserting that Indonesia is a creation of the twentieth century (Takdir Alisjahbana 1977 [1948]: 14–15). Writing in an Indonesian sprinkled with Dutch words, he said that the task of the young Indonesian is "culture creation (Dutch *cultuurscheppen*), erecting a new culture in accordance with the passion of the spirit and age" (1977 [1948]: 16). To the extent that it is seen to be non-natural and "external" to the actor, language is also, in principle, available as an object of manipulation. Indeed, in view of the notion, which I have taken to be central to ideologies of modernity, that humans can and *must* take their destiny in their own hands, one's language *should* be improved.

Writing for the World

In the egalitarian aspirations of early Indonesian nationalists and many speakers today as well, the move into Indonesian is meant to avoid the overt display of status differences. In practice, this means a language supposedly abstractable from interactive contexts and the cultural presuppositions they invoke. Such abstraction, in effect, denies the indexical, performative, and poetic dimensions of language in favor of reference and semantics – an emphasis that seems to be endemic to ideologies of the public sphere (Warner 2002: 83). This is evident even in simple lexical innovation. For example, Indonesian takes advantage of the alternatives afforded by preexisting register differences. According to Minister of Education and Culture Daoed Joesoef (1983), one might replace the everyday form *sakit* (ill) with high Javanese *gering*, or *makan* (to eat) with *dahar* to indicate respect without necessarily implying adherence to the entire register system of Javanese. In effect, this aims to remove words from the cultural context that made them indexical of status differences or other aspects of interaction and locality. Linguistic innovation thereby is supposed to fulfill the early nationalist project of eliminating the more "feudal" elements of local culture. It does so by seeking a language *beyond* any particular culture. Thus the transparency and translatability of Indonesian, as a modern language, should work in collaboration with its egalitarian promise: both presume an ability to transcend the limits of interactive contexts.

A language removed from the supposed restrictions and hierarchies of localized cultural contexts should, it would seem, be free to become cosmopolitan and egalitarian (see Gal and Woolard 1995). There should, for instance, be no puns, significant rhymes, difficulties of phrasing due to syntactic peculiarities, proper nouns in which semantic sense clashes with sense-less reference, deictics with specific topographical anchors, pronouns indexical of interaction-relative status, phrases with magical powers, expressions presupposing local knowledge, and so forth. In contrast to the workings of, say, taboo languages or underworld slangs, a modern national standard, in this view, should seek to render its denotative functions transparent and work against the materiality of signifiers. It should aspire (however impossibly) to eliminate those aspects of meaning that might be altered when repeated in different contexts, or that might be lost in translation. In common with some religious utopias, this aspect of idea of modernity might even, at the extreme, imply an urge to escape from semiotic mediation itself (Keane 2001).

Pragmatic Paradoxes of the Public

This story contains many ironies. Here's one: Indonesian was supposed to replace the social hierarchies built into local languages with a modern egalitarianism. As in other language-reform movements, such as the Quaker refusal to say *you* in seventeenth-century England, the most direct attack seemed to be to eliminate the most obvious – that is, lexicalized – indexes of status.[5] To that end, there have been many experiments in replacing those most fraught elements, first and second person pronouns. For second person, for instance, one occasionally encounters people who use the English *you*, and the supposedly neutral *anda* coined in the 1950s has found its true home as the term for the universal addressee of advertising and public announcements. The fact that *anda* has met very limited acceptance in spoken interaction suggests how difficult it is to inhabit so abstract a social position.

Among the attempted reforms, the once-intimate word *aku* was promoted as the preferred first person singular of literary writing. According to Goenawan Mohamad (1995), when the poet Chairil Anwar used it in the 1940s, it seemed a heroic challenge to hierarchy. By the 1990s, however, it had come to sound arrogant and egotistical. Goenawan says this is because the authoritarian climate of the Suharto regime made individualism seem dangerous. This is surely true, but it does not explain why the supposedly neutral and egalitarian *aku* should have those particular connotations. I want to suggest this may be due, at least in part, to its associations with certain aspects of the modernist project. The conscious choice of this word seeks not only to dislodge the speaker from existing social relations, the world of his or her birth, but also asserts a modernist claim to personal autonomy. This autonomy is manifested in the speaker's agency relative to language itself, in the choice to step out of – even to sacrifice – one language and not only to speak another one (this, after all, has always been an option in multilingual situations) but to improve it, and in the process, to claim a public persona markedly apart from some presupposed prior self and its social relations. One may hear echoes of a common theme in early Indonesian literature (as in much nationalist and early postcolonial writing), the clash between modern urban freedom and the constraints of village, kinship, and tradition, resulting in ambivalences and anxieties that are far from resolved (see Siegel 1997).

By the time of the New Order regime, the cosmopolitan aspirations of Indonesian faced a conjoined set of paradoxes. In political terms, a medium whose most powerful claims on its speakers included the promise of liberation, had become deeply associated with the centralizing project of the authoritarian state. Indeed, in some respects the paradox may be implicit in some modernist visions of freedom to the extent that they couple enhanced agency with increased control over an object world. And, second, in semiotic terms, what had begun as a rationalist effort to escape the indexical links to interaction and localized contexts had itself become a meta-discursive index in its own right. The elites of the New Order increasingly laid exclusive claims over the language through the proliferation of Javanisms, Anglicisms, Sanskritisms, and an ever-growing number of opaque acronyms. As critics of such usages made apparent, the weight this put on the sheer materiality of signifiers as well as their capacity to index access to restricted sources of knowledge was a direct threat to the cosmopolitan openness of a transparent language that had been sought by high modernists. Overall, the effort to create a national public through language reform either failed (by producing an exclusive and controlling "high" language of the state) or succeeded only ambiguously (by offering speakers only the most notional public identities and constrained rhetorical possibilities). Yet wordplay, subversive slangs, new vernaculars, and even growing Islamicist uses of Arabic, continue to emerge outside the officially constituted "public" (e.g. Chambert-Loir 1984; Widodo 1997; Zimmer 1998). They commonly focus on the materiality of linguistic form, as if to deny the modernists' claims for transparency. Perhaps we can see in these hints of alternatives to engineered standardization that may yet emerge.

To the extent that the project of asserting historical agency retains its genealogical ties to ideologies of the modern, however covertly, it seems to exist in a paradoxical relation to the claims of national cultural identity in two respects. First, the process of associating language with projects of development and especially with literary culture entails not just an obvious elitism, but a certain disembedding of what a national "culture" could mean. As a modernist project, national identity commonly seeks culture in language that one can stand outside of, finding there not something that escapes translation – something one could call uniquely one's "own" – but that which is most translatable, most open to being understood from within other languages, least confined to particular geographical, historical, or interactive contexts. Such openness to other languages through translation would seem to render problematic the nationalist claim to "possess" that language for oneself (while avoiding the potentially dangerous politics of language and ethnicity that "possession" can invite). Recall the anecdote with which this essay began: Amien Rais at his most authoritatively public, founding a national party in a moment of historical crisis, seems to aspire to a cosmopolitan transparency. To do so requires that he – like, notably, Sukarno himself (Leclerc 1994) – imagine and take on the perspective of his most distant potential interlocutors. Seeking their recognition begins by his own effort to recognize who they might be (say, American political observers), and entails a degree of risk – that, failing to translate his words correctly, they may not recognize him for who he would be for them.

Second, to the extent that it aspires to the most textual and most translatable pole of language, the standard language as an emblem of national culture and political identity seems to depend on an ability to take the materiality of semiotic form to be plastic matter, subordinate to immaterial denotations and the intentions of those who could somehow stand apart from it. So functionally reductive and objectified a view of language would seem to presuppose and promote the self-possession of subjects for whom nothing important eludes translation and everything can be made explicit. As a dominant language ideology, this vision of Indonesian, however betrayed and disappointed, thus retains a certain modernist austerity and even heroism. By the same token, it ties the project of asserting historical agency to a more problematic one of mastery over language itself – a tie that, as it unravels, may yet unleash new possibilities.

Notes

1. *Bahasa Indonesia*, literally "the language of Indonesia," is a variant of Malay; whether the linguistic distinctions between them matter ideologically is highly context-dependent.
2. In 1928, about 4.9 percent of the population of the Indies spoke Malay as their native language, compared to 47.8 percent speaking Javanese and 14.5 per cent Sundanese (Moeliono 1994: 378). Post-independence censuses show those claiming Indonesian as their first language as 12 percent in 1980 and 15.5 percent in 1990 (compared to 38.8 percent Javanese and 15.6 percent Sundanese [Hooker 1993: 273; Mühlhäusler 1996: 205; Steinhauer 1994]).
3. For the history of Indonesian see Anwar 1980, Hoffman 1979, Maier 1993, 1997, Pramoedya 1963, Takdir 1957, 1977, Teeuw 1973.
4. See the sociolinguistic accounts in Errington 1998, Kumanireng 1982, Moeliono 1994, Oetomo 1987, 1989, Wolff and Poedjosoedarmo 1982.
5. By reducing the options among even those pronouns available in Malay (Errington 1998), standard Indonesian has sought to deny their social implications. In the process, they were subsumed within an objectivistic ideology by which language was seen to function primarily to refer to and denote an external world. On the problem of pronouns and Indonesian national identity see Benedict Anderson (1990a) and James Siegel (1997). For a succinct statement linking proper choice of first person pronoun and the "anti-feudal principle of democracy" see Ali 2000: 153–6.

Acknowledgments

Earlier versions of this chapter were presented at a Wenner-Gren Conference on Translation and Anthropology, the Association for Asian Studies annual meeting, and at the Universities of Chicago, Columbia, Cornell, and Michigan, and owe something to less formal conversations in the Michicagoan Linguistic Anthropology Faculty Workshop. Thanks to Pete Becker, Joe Errington, Nancy Florida, Sue Gal, Goenawan Mohamad, Ariel Heryanto, Mellie Ivy, Henk Maier, Rudolph Mrázek, John Pemberton, Beth Povinelli, Yopie Prins, Vince Rafael, Lee Schlesinger, Henk Schulte Nordholt, and Amrih Widodo, for their comments. I am grateful for support from the Institute for Advanced Study, Princeton, NJ, and the University of Michigan Humanities Institute.

References

Achebe, Chinua. "The African Writer and the English Language." In *Colonial Discourse and Post-colonial Theory: A Reader.* Patrick Williams and Laura

Chrisman (eds.), pp. 428–434. New York: Columbia University Press, 1994 [1975].

Adam, Ahmat B. *The Vernacular Press and the Emergence of Modern Indonesian Consciousness (1855–1913)*. Ithaca: Southeast Asia Program, Cornell University, Studies in Southeast Asia No. 17, 1995 .

Ali, Lukman. *Lengser Kaprabon: Kumpulan Kolom tentang Pemakaian Bahasa Indonesia* Jakarta: Pustaka Firdaus, 2000.

Amien Rais Wawancara Amien Rais: "Saya memilih sebagai tokoh bangsa daripada tokoh umat." *Tempo Interaktif* Edisi 25/03–22 Agustus 1998 (http://www.tempo.co.id /min/25/nas2.htm), 1998.

Anderson, Benedict R. O'G. "The Languages of Indonesian Politics. In *Language and Power: Exploring Political Cultures in Indonesia*. pp. 123–151. Ithaca: Cornell University Press, 1990a [1966].

—— "Language, Fantasy, Revolution: Java 1900–1950." In *Making Indonesia: Essays on Modern Indonesia in Honor of George McT. Kahin*. Daniel S. Lev and Ruth McVey (eds.), pp. 26–40. Ithaca: Cornell University Southeast Asia Program, 1996.

Anwar, Khaidir *Indonesian: The Development and Use of a National Language* Yogyakarta: Gadjah Mada University Press, 1980.

—— "Bahasa, feodalisme dan egaliterisme." *Prisma* 18, 1989, pp. 54–60.

Bauman, Richard, and Charles L. Briggs. "Language Philosophy as Language Ideology: John Locke and Johann Gottfried Herder." In *Regimes of Language: Ideologies, Polities, and Identities*. Paul V. Kroskrity (ed.). Pp. 139–204. Santa Fe: School of American Research, 2000.

Berman, Marshall. *All that is Solid Melts into Air: The Experience of Modernity*. 2d ed.) New York and Harmondsworth: Penguin, 1998.

Chakrabarty, Dipesh. "Post-coloniality and the Artifice of History: Who Speaks for 'Indian' Pasts?" *Representations* 37, 1992, pp. 1–26.

Chambert-Loir, Michel. "Those who Speak *prokem*." Trans. James T. Collins. *Indonesia* 37 (April), 1984, pp. 105–117.

Cohn, Bernard S. "The Command of Language and the Language of Command." In *Colonialism and its Forms of Knowledge: The British in India*. pp. 16–56. Princeton: Princeton University Press, 1996 [1985].

Collins, James T. *Ambonese Malay and Creolization Theory*. Kuala Lumpur: Dewan Bahasa dan Pustaka, 1980.

Daoed, Joeseof. "Bahasa akademik, bahasa asing, bahasa Indonesia." *Sinar Harapan*, 28 October 1983, pp. 6, 7.

Derrida, Jacques. "Signature Event Context." In *Margins of Philosophy*. Trans. Alan Bass. Chicago: University of Chicago Press, 1982 [1971].

Errington, J. Joseph. *Language and Social Change in Java: Linguisic Reflexes of Modernization in a Traditional Royal Polity*. Athens OH: Ohio University Monographs in International Studies, Southeast Asia Series, No 65, 1985.

―― *Shifting Languages: Interaction and Identity in Javanese Indonesia.* Cambridge: Cambridge University Press, 1998.

―― "Indonesian('s) authority." In *Regimes of Language: Ideologies, Polities, and Identities.* Paul V. Kroskrity (ed.), pp. 205–257. Santa Fe: School of American Research Press, 2000.

Fabian, Johannes. *Language and Colonial Power: The Appropriation of Swahili in the Former Belgian Congo 1880–1938.* Berkeley: University of California Press, 1986.

Gal, Susan and Kathryn A. Woolard. "Constructing Languages and Publics: Authority and Representation." *Pragmatics* 5(2), 1995, pp. 29–138.

Goenawan Mohamad. "Bahasa." In *Catatan Pinggir (1)*, Jakarta: Grafiti, 1982, pp. 321–322.

―― "Aku." *Catatan Pinggir (4)* Jakarta: Grafiti, 1995, pp. 298–99.

Groeneboer, Kees. *Gateway to the West: The Dutch Language in Colonial Indonesia, A History of Language Policy.* Trans. Myra Scholz. Amsterdam: Amsterdam University Press, 1998.

Halim, Amran. "Fungsi Politik Bahasa Nasional." In *Politik Bahasa Nasional (1)*. Halim, (ed.). (Pusat Pembinaan dan Pengembangan Bahasa, Departmen Pendidikan dan Kebudayaan). Jakarta: Balai Pustaka, 1984 [1976], pp. 13–25.

Heryanto, Ariel. *Language of Development and Development of Language: The Case of Indonesia* Pacific Linguistics Series D – 86. Canberra: Australian National University, Dept of Linguistics, Research School of Pacific and Asian Studies, 1995.

Hoffman, John. "A Foreign Investment: Indies Malay to 1901." *Indonesia* 27, 1979, pp. 65–92.

Hooker, Virginia Matheson. "New Order Language in Context." In *Culture and Society in New Order Indonesia.* Hooker (ed.). Kuala Lumpur: Oxford University Press, 1993.

Irvine, Judith T. and Susan Gal. "Language Ideology and Linguistic Differentiation." In *Regimes of Language: Ideologies, Polities, and Identities.* Paul V. Kroskrity (ed.). Santa Fe: School of American Research Press, 2000, pp. 35–83.

Jacquemond, Richard. "Translation and Cultural Hegemony: The Case of French-Arabic Translation." In *Rethinking Translation: Discourse, Subjectivity, Ideology.* Lawrence Venuti (ed.). London and New York: Routledge, 1992, pp. 139–158.

Keane, Webb. "Knowing One's Place: National Language and the Idea of the Local in Eastern Indonesia." *Cultural Anthropology* 12(1), 1997a, pp. 37–63.

―― "From Fetishism to Sincerity: On Agency, the Speaking Subject, and Their Historicity in the Context of Religious Conversion." *Comparative Studies in Society and History* 39(4), 1997b, pp. 674–693.

―― "Sincerity, 'Modernity,' and the Protestants." *Cultural Anthropology* 17(1), 2001, pp. 65–92.

Kroskrity, Paul V. (ed.). *Regimes of Language: Ideologies, Polities, and Identities*. Santa Fe: School of American Research Press, 2000.

Kulick, Don. *Language Shift and Cultural Reproduction: Socialization, Self, and Syncretism in a Papua New Guinean Village*. Cambridge: Cambridge University Press, 1992.

Kumanireng, Threes Y. "Diglossia in Larantuka, Flores: A Study about Language Use and Language Switching among the Larantuka Community. In *Papers from the Third International Conference on Austronesian Linguistics*. Vol. 3: *Accent on Variety*. Amran Halim, Lois Carrington, S.A. Wurm (eds.). Pacific Linguistics, C-76, 1982, pp. 131–136.

Leclerc, Jacques. "Le dernier 17 Août de Sukarno Président." In *Texts from the Islands: Oral and Written Traditions of Indonesia and the Malay World*. Wolfgang Marschall (ed.). Berne: University of Berne Institute of Ethnology, 1994, pp. 311–316.

Lee, Benjamin, and Edward LiPuma. "Cultures of Circulation: The Imaginations of Modernity." *Public Culture* 14(1), 2002, pp. 191–213.

Liu, Lydia H. *Translingual Practice: Literature, National Culture, and Translated Modernity – China, 1900–1937*. Stanford: Stanford University Press, 1995.

Lucy, John A. (ed.). *Reflexive Language: Reported Speech and Metapragmatics*. Cambridge: Cambridge University Press, 1993.

Mahrez, Samia. "Translation and the Post-colonial Experience: The Francophone North African Text." In *Rethinking Translation: Discourse, Subjectivity, Ideology*. Lawrence Venuti (ed.). London and New York: Routledge, 1992, pp. 120–138.

Maier, Hendrik M. J. "From Heteroglossia to Polyglossia: The Creation of Malay and Dutch in the Indies." *Indonesia* 56, October, 1993, pp. 37–65.

—— "'We are Playing Relatives': Riau, the Cradle of Reality and Hybridity." *Bijdragen tot de Taal-, Land- en Volkenkunde* 153(4), 1997, pp. 672–698.

Moeliono, Anton M. "Contact-induced Language Change in Present-day Indonesian." In *Language Contact and Change in the Austronesian World*. Tom Dutton & Darrell T. Tryon (eds.). Trends in Linguistics: Studies and Monographs 77. Berlin and New York: Mouton de Gruyter, 1994, pp. 377–388.

Mühlhäusler, Peter. *Linguistic Ecology: Language Change and Linguistic Imperialism in the Pacific Region*. London and New York: Routledge, 1996.

Ngugi wa Thiong'o. "The Language of African Literature. In *Colonial Discourse and Post-colonial Theory: A Reader*. Patrick Williams and Laura Chrisman (eds.). New York: Columbia, 1994 [1986], pp. 435–455.

Niranjana, Tejaswini. *Siting Translation: History, Post-colonialism, and the Colonial Context*. Berkeley: University of California Press, 1992.

Oetomo, Dédé. *The Chinese of Pasuruan: Their Language and Identity*. Pacific Linguistics Series D–No. 63, Canberra: Research School of Pacific Studies, 1987.

—— "Bahasa Indonesia dan kelas menengah Indonesia." *Prisma* 18, 1989, pp. 17–60.

Pramoedya Ananta Toer. "Basa Indonesia sebagai basa revolusi Indonesia." *Bintang Timor.* 22 September et seq. 1963.

Saussure, Ferdinand de. *Course in General Linguistics.* Charles Bally and Albert Sechehaye (eds.). Trans. Roy Harris. La Salle, IL: Open Court, 1986 [1915].

Siegel, James T. *Solo in the New Order: Language and Hierarchy in an Indonesian City.* Princeton: Princeton University Press, 1986.

—— *Fetish, Recognition, Revolution.* Princeton: Princeton University Press, 1997.

Silverstein, Michael. "Monoglot 'Standard' in America: Standardization and Metaphors of Linguistic Hegemony." In *The Matrix of Language: Contemporary Linguistic Anthropology.* Donald Brenneis and Ronald K. S. Macaulay (eds.). Boulder, CO: Westview, 1996, pp. 284–306.

—— "Contemporary Transformations of Local Linguistic Communities. *Annual Review of Anthropology* 27, 1998, pp. 401–26.

Spivak, Gayatri Chakravorty. "The Politics of Translation." In *Destabilizing Theory: Contemporary Feminist Debates.* Michèle Barrett and Anne Phillips (eds.). Cambridge: Polity, 1992, pp. 177–200.

Steiner, George. *After Babel: Aspects of Language and Translation* London, Oxford, and New York: Oxford University Press, 1975.

Steinhauer, Hein. "The Indonesian Language Situation and Linguistics." *Bijdragen tot de Taal-, Land- en Volkenkunde* 150(4), 1994, pp. 755–784.

Sutherland, Heather. "Pudjangga Baru: Aspects of Indonesian Intellectual Life in the 1930s." *Indonesia* 6 October, 1968, pp. 106–127.

Takdir Alisjahbana, Sutan. *Dari Perdjuangan dan Pertumbuhan Bahasa Indonesia.* Djakarta: Pustaka Rakyat, 1957.

—— *Language Planning for Modernization: The Case of Indonesian and Malaysian.* The Hague: Mouton, 1976.

—— "Menuju masyarakat dan kebudayaan baru Indonesia – Prae-Indonesia." In *Polemik Kebudayaan: Pokok Pikiran.* **Achdiat K.** Mihardja (ed.). Jakarta: Pustaka Jaya, 1977 [1948].

Taylor, Charles. *Sources of the Self: The Making of the Modern Identity.* Cambridge, MA: Harvard University Press, 1989.

Teeuw, A. *Pegawai Bahasa dan Ilmu Bahasa.* Trans. J. B. A. F. Mayor Polak. Jakarta: Bhratara, 1973 [1971].

Tjokronegoro, Sutomo. *Tjukupkah Saudara Membina Bahasa Kesatuan Kita?* Djakarta, Bandung: Eresc, 1968.

Urban, Greg. *Metaculture: How Culture Moves through the World.* Minneapolis: University of Minnesota Press, 2001.

Voloshinov, V.N. *Marxism and the Philosophy of Language.* Trans. Ladislav Matejka and I. R. Titunik. New York: Seminar Press, 1973 [1930].

Warner, Michael. "Publics and Counterpublics." *Public Culture* 14(1), 2002, pp. 49–90.

Wertheim, W. F. *Indonesian Society in Transition: A Study of Social Change.* 2d ed. The Hague: W. van Hoeve, 1964.

Widodo, Amrih. "Samin and the New Order: The Politics of Encounter and Isolation." In *Imagining Indonesia: Cultural Politics and Political Culture.* Jim Schiller and Barbara Martin-Schiller (eds.). Athens, OH: Ohio University Center for International Studies, 1997, pp. 261–287.

Wielenga, D. K. "Zending en taalstudie." *De Macedoniër* 17, 1913, pp. 138–150.

Wolff, John U. and Soepomo Poedjosoedarmo. *Communicative Codes in Central Java.* Linguistic Series viii, Cornell Southeast Asia Program, Data Paper no 116; Ithaca: Cornell University Press, 1982.

Zimmer, Benjamin G. "The new dis-order: Parodic *plésétan* and the 'Slipping' of the Soeharto Regime." *Antara Kita* 54, 1998, pp. 4–9.

Zurbuchen, Mary S. "Internal Translation in Balinese Poetry. In *Writing on the Tongue*, A.L. Becker (ed.). Ann Arbor: Michigan Papers on South and Southeast Asia, University of Michigan, 1989, pp. 215–279.

Notes on Transliteration
Brinkley Messick

"Transcription always raises questions about translation."

James Clifford (1990: 58)

I

Included in the front matter of *Seven Pillars of Wisdom* (1935), in a Preface prepared by the author's brother A. W., is a quoted remark by T. E. Lawrence about his spelling of the many Arabic names that appear in his book:

> Arabic names won't go into English, exactly, for their consonants are not the same as ours, and their vowels, like ours, vary from district to district. There are some "scientific systems" of transliteration, helpful to people who know enough Arabic not to need helping, but a wash-out for the world. I spell my names anyhow, to show what rot the systems are. (p. 21)

In the back matter of the book, in Appendix II (p. 664), which gives the dates of his movements in Arabia in 1917–18, he adds, "Arabic names are spelt anyhow, to prevent my appearing an adherent of one of the existing 'systems of transliteration'."

Before quoting his brother in the Preface, A. W. Lawrence (p. 20) had calmly explained that only three vowels are recognized in Arabic, and that some of the consonants have no equivalents in English. The general practice of orientalists in recent years has been to adopt one of the various sets of conventional signs for the letters and vowel marks of the Arabic alphabet, transliterating Mohamed as Muhammad, muezzin as mu'edhdhin, and Koran as Qur'an or Kur'an. A. W. then anticipates his brother's remark as he goes on to say that,

> This method is useful to those who know what it means, but this book follows the old fashion of writing the best phonetic approximations according to ordinary English spelling. The same place-name will be found spelt in different ways, not only because the sound of many Arabic words can legitimately be represented in English in a variety

of ways, but also because the natives of a district often differ as to the pronunciation of any place-name which has not already become famous or fixed by literary usage.

Also quoted in the brother's Preface are some samples of behind-the-scenes exchanges between the publisher and the author in connection with the production of an abbreviated version of the book (known as *Revolt in the Desert,* 1927). The publisher gives a list of queries raised in reading the proofs which, although otherwise "very clean," are found "full of inconsistencies in the spelling of proper names." The publisher: "Jeddah and Jidda used impartially throughout. Intentional?" Lawrence: "Rather!" The publisher: "Nuri, Emir of the Ruwalla, belongs to the 'chief family of the Rualla'. On Slip 23, 'Rualla horse', and Slip 38, 'killed one Rueli'. In all later slips 'Rualla'." Lawrence replies, "Should have also used Ruwala and Ruala." To "The Bisaita is also spelt Biseita," Lawrence says, "Good;" to "Jedha, the she-camel, was Jedhad on Slip 40," the reply is, "She was a splendid beast;" and to "Sherif Abd el Mayin of Slip 68 becomes el Main, el Mayein, el Muein, el Mayin, and el Muyein," the author counters, "Good egg. I call this really ingenious."

Later, I shall return to examine some disciplinary versions of such remarks, which take the published form of the "note on transliteration."

II

Translations from Arabic to English are a routine aspect of my work on the various textual genres of Islamic law. When focused primarily on doctrinal texts (e.g. Messick 1993), my translations could in some instances draw on prior Orientalist efforts that date to the nineteenth century and earlier. The pattern of target texts for these earlier translations of Islamic legal manuals generally followed the interests of the Orientalists' respective colonial regimes. Thus French scholars mainly concentrated on texts from the Maliki school of law predominant in North Africa; English scholars on the Hanafi school adhered to by Indian Muslims; and Dutch scholars on the Shafi`i school followed by Muslims in Java and elsewhere in Southeast Asia. The main genre translated was the authoritative basic instructional manual of each of the law schools, texts which typically are very brief, often stripped-down in expression, and sometimes even rhymed to facilitate memorization. The much longer but also conventional prose commentary works have not been translated. In my research on highland Yemen, which historically has followed two different schools of law, I could refer to the Dutch translations (into French) for my work on basic Shafi`i texts, but there was no equivalent translation for the authoritative text of the indigenous school of law, which flourished only in uncolonized highland Yemen.

Over about a century and a half, cutting across this colonial patterning in the incidence of translations, there was a sense of scientific progress in Orientalist translations. Roughly characterized, the movement was from early renderings marked by loose paraphrase to a form of rigor that required that a single word must be the consistent translation of a given Arabic term and that any additional words or phrases necessitated in the Western language (to make regular sense of the extremely concise Islamic manuals) would now be set off in parentheses. A persistent problem in such translations was the unquestioned use of Western legal terms as the translations of Islamic ones, and in my own work the explication of such Islamic concepts has been a central activity.

I also work at a very different generic level of the law, that of the judgments issued in shari`a court cases. Few of these have been translated in any region of the Muslim world. The Yemeni texts are in handwritten Arabic on vertical paper rolls. In examining such features as the structure of competing legal narratives, the detailed devices for the quotation or indirect reporting of evidential testimony and the textual markers of an authoritative legal record, I translate large segments of the judgment texts. When doing so, I employ a series of seemingly mechanical presentation devices which also may be understood as deeply transformative in their own right (see Chartier 1992). These begin with such spatial interventions as the creation of sentences, and punctuated pauses within sentences, where neither capital letters nor periods or other such punctuation exists in the Arabic text. Unlike the modern Arabic of the printed newspaper or book, in which punctuation is standard, my judgment texts are continuous in the original. Similar issues are raised by my occasionally creating paragraphs. Also, I not only create a print version of a handwritten original but my English translations make implicitly vowelled "readings" of the unvowelled (and sometimes also unpointed) Arabic original. These already weighty issues taken into consideration, I then might reflect on whether, and for which reasons, my English versions are relatively faithful, or not. As I translate, I am constantly aware of two mundane pulls: between accuracy in rendering this distinctive legal Arabic and accessibility for the reader of English.

III

In part because I do not produce integral translations of texts, and in part because I find a direct assault on the phenomenon of translation daunting, I will address what may be considered the comparatively minor practice, the mere technique, of rendering single foreign-language words or phrases in an English language text. This practice takes two very distinct forms, known by the related terms transcription and transliteration. Both are techniques of the "trans," of the relations and movements between languages, and it is my ultimate hope that in this chapter an understanding of their restricted work across languages may shed some light on that of their more formidable relative-by-prefix, translation. These techniques would seem to raise none of the thorny "meaning" issues of translation: they do not dramatically carry meaning "across," at least not in the complex manner of translation, and in their mechanical faithfulness they also seem to avoid the dangerous *traditore* in *traduttore*.

Received into an adapted English letter system, and thus partially domesticated, the foreign fragment nevertheless retains its identity as a fragment of another language. While translation tends to leave the other language behind, seemingly eradicating its physical traces, transcription and transliteration actively preserve such traces and, in the process, construct a bridge between two languages, between two worlds, their geographies, temporalities and metaphysics.

As part of his "translinguistics," Bakhtin (1986) has discussed the analytic relations surrounding intertextual movements, specifically, in what is termed "reported speech," the relations between reported texts and reporting texts. The trajectory of such movements commences with the excerpting of the text to be reported, a line to be quoted, for example, from its original source or context. It concludes with its insertion in a new textual location in the reporting text. In the process, arriving in its new location, the reported text both retains certain connecting filaments and resonances with its original textual site and also assumes new attachments and significances in the reporting text. In this sense, even simple quotation within the same language begins to have some of the character of translation between languages.

If, however, in the analogous realm of interlanguage movements, one considers the relation between a reported language and a reporting language, then a distinctive difference is clear between translation and its relatives, transcription and transliteration. In translation, the relations between the reported and reporting languages are obscured, whereas in transcription and transliteration these relations are revealed and even foregrounded. Compared with the total transformation wrought by translation across languages, the movements carried out by transcription and transliteration appear stalled or interrupted. The resulting fragments are left betwixt and between, in a halfway stage of language, having neither completely departed from the reported language nor completely arrived in the reporting language. The foreign word or phrase has been excerpted and inserted but, by design, remains not fully transformed, or translated, into the language of the reporting text. In this sense, transcriptions and transliterations might be thought of analytically as the scaffolding for translation, which must drop away or be hidden in the finished product.

The transcribed or transliterated text remains suspended between languages and belonging properly to neither; or rather, it belongs to a special intermediate language of its own. This special language never exists as such, at least independently, but is only given rise to in the interstices of two languages. It is rare to see a transcribed or transliterated text stand on its own two feet. One exception, however, is a book of foreign-language texts in which the medium of conveyance or instruction is the system, or language, of transcription or transliteration. Other instances arise when anthropologists develop special languages with their informants, but such texts characteristically remain in the background of research. I taught Moroccan Berbers to read Berber folktales published in transcription; Fabian (1992: 86–88) describes the reoralization of a deficiently transliterated Shaba Swahili text as a step prior to translation.

This special language or system is marked, identified and specified by its characteristic meta-site, the textual locale where it is spoken of, which typically takes the form of a brief "note" in the front-matter of a book. Such "notes" have their own (admittedly minor) generic history and they might be compared with those that pertain to statements about translations found in approximately the same locale, and the same lower-case Roman numerals. In a scholarly article, by contrast, the text already has to have passed into the system used by the journal in question, and in publication this adoption is implicit. Both "notes" on transcription or transliteration and those on translation partake, of course, of the enigmatic problematic of the "preface," or "pretext," as exposed, for example, by Derrida (1974) and his translator, Spivak. "Notes" on transcription and transliteration characterize the about-to-be-introduced, special in-between language or system which is to represent a particular foreign language as it appears from time to time within the standard language of the work in question. When this formal system is characterized by a scholar, we usually also get a view of the author's sub-disciplinary identity. Additionally, such notes sometimes permit authors to speak directly to us or, as in the case of Lawrence and some others to be sampled below, they reveal an irreverent personality, occasionally including some irascibility or wittiness. How much more interesting such notes can be than that other minor passage of the "pretext," the comparatively staid and predictable "Acknowledgments."

IV

Transcribe: trans + scribere (write)
Transliterate: trans + litera (letter)

I have referred thus far to the two techniques, transcription and transliteration, as examples of the same phenomenon. Some dictionaries (e.g. *Webster's Third International*) have them as synonyms. Are they the same? One distinction may be suggested by their respective Latin etymologies. Where transcription is a practice of written entities, that is, of full passages and their dynamics, transliteration is one of pieces or parts, of individual letters, with little attention to interrelations.

In the usage of anthropologists, transcription is the original technique (see Clifford 1983: 135–42; 1986: 116–7; 1990: 51, 57–9). It was elaborated in the early professional method of "text-taking," by Franz Boas and others.[1] It is the name also for the characteristic method subsequently employed by linguistic anthropologists for recording an oral text from an unwritten language. As such, it is an activity of trained hearing, on the part of the anthropologist, and then of writing. Transliteration, by contrast, is a relatively new technique for anthropologists, and its technical lineage is traced not to linguistics but to the orientalists, the specialists in non-Western written texts. Transliteration techniques were developed by these textual specialists to represent the written texts of another language. In their practice, it was an activity of reading, then of writing.

Both techniques have "scientific" roots, but their genealogies go back to different sciences. Transcription's pedigree leads to the universalizing aims of linguistics, to such tools as the International Phonetic Alphabet, and the aim of accurate renderings of "any" sequence of speech. Transliteration pertains to the philological sciences and involves not a universal system but a series of particular (even idiosyncratic) ones, designed to represent particular languages. In both genealogies there are histories of competing systems and, over time, a sense of scientific refinement and advance.

What are the designs of such usages? To what ends are the techniques employed? This depends on the particular authority claimed by a given reporting text, which, in turn, involves the author's sub-disciplinary (scientific) identity. At issue is the need to produce a final product with legitimating or confirming "evidence" in the form of a reported passage from the other language in question. Like many other devices, including the presentation of photos, transcription and transliteration figure as elements in historically specific forms of "ethnographic authority," as linguistic traces of "being there."

Parallel to these histories, of course, are the general and specific histories of the scientific refinement of scholarly translation, and also the histories of such detailed related techniques as date conversion (e.g. from the Muslim lunar calendar, originally to AD and now to CE years). Together with such discipline-marking techniques as systems of citation and referencing, which also have their own histories (e.g. the footnote, Grafton 1997), transcription and transliteration are elements in what was known as a book's "scholarly apparatus."

In scholarly writing, the two techniques of transcription and transliteration often are closely associated with translations. For Boas, transcriptions were stepping-stones to translations. There were both the rough, crossed-out, "heard" transcriptions of the fieldnote stage and the polished, rewritten ones that were published on pages facing translations of different types, interlinear and standard English. In the orientalist tradition, transliterated words or phrases usually appear following their English translation, or gloss. When longer texts – normally poetry in my field of research on the Middle East – are transliterated, these and their accompanying translations usually are placed in an appendix. Where publishers will happily print translations they tend to resist publishing extended transcribed or transliterated texts.

Revealing now my own sub-disciplinary lineage, I turn from attempting a history of transcription, which I do not know first hand, to a closer focus on transliteration, with which I have some experience. The rise of sophisticated transliteration among anthropologists interests me as an indicator of interdisciplinary movements toward the study of written texts. This has occurred partly in connection with the discipline's historical and linguistic turns. New disciplinary engagements with societies with writing have led to new methods and new requirements concerning the reporting of written texts, and these have drawn critically on the long-established techniques of the orientalists and their successors in the fields of area studies.

V

There are three major systems of transliterating Arabic, those of the Library of Congress, the *Encyclopedia of Islam* (Leiden: E. J. Brill) and IJMES, the *International Journal of Middle East Studies* (Cambridge), with the last now the standard in most quarters. The Library of Congress system is on the march, however, especially with the streamlining of its transliteration that has occurred with the computerization of its catalogue entries. One recalls, however, Nicholson Baker's "Discards" article (*The New Yorker,* April 4, 1994, pp. 64–86) and the potential he identifies of unexpected losses as the older work, especially the hand annotations of generations of specialist librarians, is lost in the scientific advance of digitalization. Increasingly, the Library of Congress is carrying out the transliteration of foreign titles, work that had been central to the job descriptions of specialist librarians.

The *Encyclopedia of Islam* system is the most venerable and also the quirkiest, and it is now rarely adopted as such. At the same time, its system cannot be forgotten by experts, for every one of the authoritative articles in nine massive volumes (and counting) of the second edition has a title that is a transliteration of an Arabic, or Persian or Turkish word. To consult the article on "mosque," for example, you have to know to turn to "masdjid." The "dj" here for the Arabic letter jim is an example of a transliteration found only in this encyclopedia; in most other systems it is now simply represented by a "j," giving masjid.

In notes on transliteration it is common to find statements concerning certain words from the other language that have crossed over into full reception in English. Typically such receptions are explicitly authorized by reference to entries in dictionaries. They also usually occur in a formation of letters that is correct neither in transcription nor in transliteration. While the vowels are "incorrect" in such system terms they tend to make fuller use of the vowel structure of English. Thus we find Mecca preferred by scholars over the technically correct Makka. Sometimes there is something of a specialist crusade in support of correctness: Muslim now has made solid inroads against Moslem, and Quran (or Qur'an), likewise, versus Koran. Beijing supplanting Peking is probably the same phenomenon in the reporting of Chinese.

In specialist texts, reported foreign words are often underlined and fully marked with diacritics, that is, formally transliterated, only when they first appear in the text. After this they appear unmarked, without either italics or diacritics, as if received in the English of the book in question. Such editorial conventions adopted by scholars and academic presses also involve a history that, in the case of Arabic, may be linked to the reproduction of Arabic script in Western academic works, and, further back in time, to the printing of Arabic texts in the West and, later, the history of the advent of print in the Middle East (cf. Messick 1993, ch. 6; 1997).

At about the middle of the twentieth century and for a couple of decades thereafter, anthropological field workers in the Middle East and North Africa exclusively used colloquial languages. This was the era of the disciplinary distinction between spoken "field" languages and written "research" languages. For anthropologists, Arabic had the status of a "field" language, as opposed to French, for example, in the case of North Africa and it was historians and literature specialists who worked with written Arabic. In the post-Boasian, scientific-modern tradition of Margaret Mead (see the 1939–1940 exchange between Lowie and Mead in the *American Anthropologist*), the anthropologist learned the spoken language during the first few months in the "field." With such understandings, the disciplinary identities of historian and anthropologist could be retrospectively glossed by statements such as, "the historian is given a text and the anthropologist has to construct one" (Asad 1986: 144), or "the ethnographer does not . . . translate texts the way the translator does. He must first produce them" (Crapanzano 1986: 57).

Mid-century anthropology was a discipline devoted, if no longer exclusively to peoples without writing, then at least to spoken forms of culture within literate civilizations. As a "field" language, colloquial Arabic posed some particular problems, the first among them the fact that Arabic was the original example language in the study of diglossia (Ferguson 1959). The two basic features of the various spoken Arabic dialects were their variable distances from written forms (of several levels and types) and from each other. It often is difficult to ascertain the register of Arabic being dealt with, and no regular conventions exist for representing spoken forms of Arabic in written Arabic itself. At first, anthropologists used transcriptions adapted from colloquial language dictionaries written by linguists. Rapidly, however, transcription was replaced by early attempts to employ systems of transliteration, and the use of transcription thereafter mainly was reserved for, and marked, a specifically linguistic type of inquiry. No transliteration system existed for any form of spoken Arabic, however, and when anthropologists made a shift to the systems of the written language specialists, their mistakes often betrayed their ignorance of those systems, and also of written Arabic itself. The skill and precision with which a given system is used may be an index of knowledge of the foreign language, which is a basic ingredient in judging scholarly achievement. A contemporary irony is that as the discipline becomes ever more demanding in terms of required language skills, native speakers and writers of Arabic who are becoming anthropologists also must learn proper transliteration lest their work be judged deficient in language terms.

VI

Has the spirit of T. E. Lawrence's resistance to expert standardization been extinguished by the normalizing procedures of science? Yes and no. In contemporary books, most authors deploy their "note" mainly to report on the system adopted. But there remain significant traces of anxieties and frustrations, together with glimpses of distressed authorial personalities, including those of major disciplinary figures such as Evans-Pritchard, Gellner, and Geertz.

I begin with the mid-century remarks of Carlton S. Coon, ethnographer, physical anthropologist and generalist author of the classic introduction, *Caravan: The Story of the Middle East.* Coon begins, "No man could hope to draw together the various fields from which the materials of this book are derived if he were a scholar in any one of them." (1951: v). He continues,

> No one could feel less scholarly than I do. This becomes particularly evident when the subject of Arabic transliteration arises, as it always does in forewords to books on the Middle East. I have before me the handiwork of Hitti, Gibb, and Calverly, three men whose erudition and integrity are of the highest order, and yet I cannot find complete agreement among them. Take the word for judge. Hitti spells it q_di, Gibb $k\_d\_$, and Calverly $q\_d\_$. At this point the lay reader may exclaim, "So what?" – but the lay reader does not review these books. To the myopic dotter of i's and crosser of t's, a dot under a consonant or a macron over a vowel are matters of utmost importance. The presence or absence of a dot under the k will distinguish between the word for "heart" and that for "dog." Only a heartless dog would countenance such confusion.

More in Lawrence's vein, in his famous non-academic travel account *Arabian Sands* Wilfred Thesiger writes, "Any transliteration of Arabic words leads to dispute. I have tried to simplify as much as possible and have consequently left out the letter ʿAin, usually represented by ʿ. In any case, few Englishmen can pronounce this letter correctly; to the majority of readers the frequent recurrence of this unintelligible ` would be both confusing and irritating. For the difficult letter, Ghain, I have used the conventional 'gh'. Experts say that this soft ghuttural sound is pronounced like the Parisian 'r'. (1959: xv).

Within the discipline, consider the explicit reference by social anthropologist and non-Arabist William Lancaster in *The Rwala Bedouin Today,* in his "Note on Transliteration" (1997, [1981]: xiii). It may be recalled that his group's tribal name had been rendered by T. E. Lawrence as Ruwalla and Rualla, and that Lawrence also mischievously wished he had used Ruwala and Ruala as well. Lancaster sticks to Rwala, but he states, "As names are variously pronounced and spelt in different dialects and areas, I have relied on commonsense. I agree with T. E. Lawrence that the official system only helps those who know enough Arabic to need no help." Lancaster goes on to detail the extent to which he intends to override the relevant distinctions: "I have made no distinction between light and heavy consonants nor between long and short vowels." Likewise, two Arabic letters are collapsed into one mark: "The apostrophe (') is either a glottal stop or the Arabic `ain, a sort of silent growl: the 'gh' is the Arabic ghain, a not-so-silent growl. In common place names, like Amman, I have stuck to the conventional spelling." He concludes, "I hope that experts will forgive me."

A more recent reference to Lawrence and to explicit dangers right and left is found in Patrick D. Gaffney, *The Prophet's Pulpit* (1994: 10): "Finally, with regard to transliteration and related conventions, I have attempted to steer a middle course between a pedantic obsession with consistency and a defiant abandonment to arbitrary phonetic approximations of the sort that T. E. Lawrence justifies in the barbed and witty 'Preface' to *Seven Pillars of Wisdom.*" Like many others of his generation, Gaffney adopts the IJMES system with some qualifications. He adds, however, adds an issue rarely remarked upon by other authors: "In the case of personal names I recognize the right to orthographic self-presentation, as confusing as it may appear. Here I follow the lead of Richard Mitchaell who, in his peerless study *The Society of the Muslim Brothers*, gives the surname of two brothers within the space of three lines, one as Najib, the other as Neguib. This is a difference of three characters in the transcription of a word that only has four letters in the original Arabic."

For their part, some Arabists have another anxiety which occasionally is made explicit. Roy P. Mottahedeh (1980: x), for example, writes, "I apologize for cluttering the text with transliterated Arabic words."

In the Preface to his classic ethnography (and innovative anthropological history), *The Sanusi of Cyrenaica* (1949: iv), E. E. Evans-Pritchard distinguishes between his own work and that of the Arabist: "I have transliterated Arabic words in the simplest way. The Arabist will know, or can easily discover, how they are written in Arabic, and those who do not know the language would be little the wiser had I transliterated them differently." In a following list Evans-Pritchard begins by identifying a spoken-language phenomenon found among groups of Arabic speakers from Morocco to Iraq: "For the uninitiated it need only be said that the letter 'q', which stands for the Arabic letter qaf, has in Cyrenaica the value of a hard 'g' as in the English word 'goat,' that 'gh', which stands for the Arabic letter ghain, has the value the Parisian gives to the 'r' in 'Paris', and that `, which stands for the Arabic `ain, is a guttural sound peculiar to Arabic."

Equally classic is Ernest Gellner's *Saints of the Atlas* (1969). Unusual in its placement in the book's back matter, Gellner's "Note on Transliteration" (pp. 305–6) describes two basic intentions: to insure the proper identification of places, groups, etc., and to give an "impression" of the "actual sound" of words and names. Gellner writes, "It is not always possible to satisfy both these principles at once, and I have given the first principle priority, partly because I am ill-equipped to satisfy the second, possessing a bad ear and no linguistic training." Unlike the other cases thus far mentioned, the language in question for Gellner is Berber, an unwritten language usually rendered either in French or Arabic. "I respect ordinary French transliterations," he says, "but only within reason." But, he adds, "It is not only French which has a privileged position in the transcription of Moroccan Berber words. In the eyes of both Muslims and Orientalists, Arabic has a privileged position. But the historical accident, so to speak, of a shared life and religion, implies nothing, one way or another, about the phonetic affinity of Berber sounds and Arabic letters, and I have not attempted to use this method." He thus declines to use the conventional Arabic transliteration systems. Something of the hard-headed spirit of Lawrence is found in social scientist Gellner as well:

> With respect to words heard locally and not occurring significantly in previous records, I have preferred to rely on my untrained and insensitive ear, rather than to allow myself to be persuaded retrospectively that I *must* have heard something other than what I remember having heard or recorded in my notes. Thus, for instance, there is a local name . . . which I write as 'Sidi Moa'. Some linguistically trained scholars assure me that "Moa" is a phonetic impossibility. I am partly reassured by the fact that some French administrators also, and of course independently, transcribed the name in the same way, though others write it 'Sidi Moh'. Anyway, phonetically impossible or not, Sidi Moa is what I hear.

Gellner concludes, "I take responsibility for the social and semantic information contained in this study. In view of my incompetence in this field, the *phonetic* information has in any case been reduced to the minimum . . . But anyone who wished to use this residual phonetic information for serious scholarly purposes would, I fear, be misguided."

An example of a once important system no longer adopted, and also of non-attention to the requirements of colloquial expression, is found in anthropologist Abdalla S. Bujra's *The Politics of Stratification* (1971), in the Preface of which he states that "All Arabic words in this book have been transliterated in accordance with the system used by the new edition (1960) of the *Encyclopedia of Islam*."

A decade later, Americans had begun to figure prominently in the anthropology of the Middle East and North Africa. In the "Transcription note" of their *Meaning and Order in a Moroccan Society*, Geertz et al. (1979) state that "The problem of transcribing Arabic remains a vexed one" (pp. xi–xii). These anthropologists now find themselves in an awkward position located between the dictates of colloquial versus those of written Arabic and also between the schemes of competing academic disciplines. "The orthographies that exist are designed for classical Arabic, which, for the most part, exists only in literary form. One is caught between what one hears said and what one sees written, and thus, – a worse fate yet – between the passions of linguists and those of philologists." It was considered equally important to avoid burdening the text and aggravating the reader, and a simple procedure had by this point become standard: "In order not to clutter the text with italics and diacritics, Arabic words are strictly transcribed in each essay only the first time they appear, except when their appearances are widely separated . . . [T]his system should make it possible for the Arabist to determine what the word in fact 'really' is, while leaving the non-Arabist free from distracting technicalities." Anthropologists had not yet become Arabists in their own right, and this distinction is marked in this "Note:" "We are indebted to a number of our Arabist colleagues for generous help in these matters, but leave them unnamed for fear of implicating them in the errors that remain." In the Preface to his 1984 *Bargaining for Reality*, Lawrence Rosen identifies the two envisioned poles of his readership. "By this system," he writes, "it is hoped that Arabic scholars will have no difficulty identifying words and comparing them to entries in the Wehr dictionary, *The Encyclopedia of Islam* or other standard reference works, while the ordinary reader will not be distracted from the central issues with which we will be concerned" (p. xii).

Dale F. Eickleman also worked in Morocco in the same period, but he was one of the first anthropologists also trained in written Arabic. Concerned about similar issues of readability, Eickleman also privileges the spoken forms. In "Note on Transliteration" in his *Moroccan Islam* (1976: xi–xii), he writes, "Most Arabic words, even those which occur in written, classical Arabic, are transliterated as they are pronounced in the spoken Arabic of the region in which I worked. The text would have been unnecessarily complicated had I followed separate conventions for the spoken and written variants . . . In any case, specialists will easily be able to reconstitute the classical forms." He selects a linguist's system: "I have preferred Richard S. Harrell's system for transliterating Moroccan Arabic vowels (Harrell 1966: xiii–xix) for two reasons. First, it is more accurate than the system of the International Congress of Orientalsts (ICO), designed primarily for classical Arabic. Second, Harrell's system contains the publishing advantage of eliminating the macron for long vowels." A decade later, in his *Knowledge and Power in Morocco*, Eickelman reaffirms his commitment to the spoken: "Any analysis that draws upon extensive interviews as well as written sources must necessarily cross the line between colloquial and written usage. I have usually given preference to the colloquial form of terms and phrases" (1985: xviii).

A slightly different intellectual genealogy, and a non-North African field location are involved in the work of Paul K. Dresch, an anthropologist with Arabic training and historical as well as ethnographic interests. In "Transliteration" in his *Tribes, Government, and History in Yemen* (1989), Dresch offers lengthy passages of transliterated and translated tribal poetry in appendices, and there are translations from written Arabic histories scattered throughout the book. Dresch begins with modesty:

> I cannot claim to be an Arabist. Those who are Arabists will soon spot that my knowledge of the language is essentially practical; although I was taught when I started what a diptote is, for instance, I would not always recognize one now (but then neither would tribesmen). However, anthropologists who do not know Arabic should be aware that the language is remarkably regular and its different varieties are often closely connected – with the result that an Arabist can, in practice, often play Mauss to the anthropologist's Malinowski and spot, without ever going there, that one has misunderstood what one heard. (xxviii–xxix)

As a potential "Malinowski" figure, Gellner would continue to differ and hold to his impossible Sidi Moa. In a remark reminiscent of Gellner, Dresch admits, "I do not have a trained ear." Unlike ethnographers such as Eickleman, who privilege spoken forms, Dresch says that "when in doubt" he has "reverted to classical voweling." But he maintains that "my simplified and classicizing versions probably do not obscure all that much." Like Gellner, however, he adds that "one should certainly not use them for any fine-grained linguistic purposes." His overall system choice is to follow a simplified version of the transliteration used in the modern standard Arabic dictionary by the German scholar Hans Wehr, *A Dictionary of Modern Written Arabic*, (1976). Unlike the common earlier practice of leaving as is transliterations that appear in material quoted from other Western scholars, Dresch imposes his own system on these reported texts as well: "Where I quote from other people's translations I have modified their transliteration to conform with the scheme used here."

Dresch's students are also trained in written Arabic. Walter Armbrust's "Note on Transliteration" in *Mass Culture and Modernism in Egypt* (1996: xi), on the complex genre of film screenplays among other texts, follows the IJMES system for literary Arabic and *A Dictionary of Egyptian Arabic* (1986) for the colloquial, with some modifications: "consonants that conform to literary pronunciation are rendered according to IJMES guidelines; long vowels in colloquial texts are marked with a macron as in IJMES rather than the doubled letter used in Badawi and Hinds." Andrew Shryock's *Nationalism and the Genealogical Imagination* (1997), is on oral Bedouin histories and poems and their conversion into written history. His Appendix A, "Transliterations of `Abbadi and `Adwani Poems" (329–339), presents "English transliterations of the Arabic originals." Shyrock uses the standard IJMES system, but as in many other locales, here again "the reader is warned that the Balga Bedouin pronounce *q* as *g*, . . . ; and so on." In an unusual step, he also refers readers to "A Note on Transcription" in Lila Abu-Lughod, *Veiled Sentiments* (1986: xv–xix).

Martha Mundy is another Arabist-anthropologist who, like Dresch, works on tribal Yemen. In her *Domestic Government*, in a "Note on Anthropological Terms and Arabic Transliteration," she adopts the IJMES system. Mundy comments, however, that

> in the case of vernacular poetry, I have adopted transliteration similar to that current for classical Arabic, without attempting a phonetic transcription. Likewise, when citing from unpublished manuscripts, local documents or vernacular poetry, I have not corrected the occasional departure from standard grammar but have transcribed the text verbatim. (1995: xii)

Mundy's procedures are to be distinguished from those of scholars who once controlled the analyses of written Arabic texts. A certain delight in discoveries of "mistakes" and the associated task of correcting extant manuscript versions with the aim of producing a newly authoritative text were hallmarks of Orientalist philology. In an appendix, Mundy takes a significant step beyond transliteration by including a printed Arabic text. This innovation (in anthropological monographs) and others likely to come are facilitated by the availability of foreign-language word-processing programs. It will be complained by language specialists, however, that in printing an Arabic text in this manner she skirts the scholarly task of "voweling" the Arabic, that is, of giving it a "reading."

The combination of classical Arabic texts and phonetic representation is now found in the work of (non-anthropological) Arabists. Baber Johansen's historical study of early legal texts, *The Islamic Law on Land Tax and Rent* (1988), provides an interesting example. In what he calls "Notes on Transcription" (x), Johansen first introduces his list of letter equivalents: "The following signs are used in the transliteration of Arabic letters: . . .". He then explains his different uses for transliteration and transcription, for fragments versus phonetic wholes: "Book titles, single words and half sentences are simply transliterated, i.e. the transliteration reproduces the Arabic letters and not their phonetic value. Whole sentences are transcribed. And the transcription, in their case, reproduces the phonetic changes that occur when sentences are spoken." Here, the linguistic technique for the reporting of spoken texts becomes the chosen technique for the vocalization of written texts, which are treated as if spoken. Johansen concludes, "Arabic words that have a common English form (e.g. Medina, mufti, Iraq) are neither transliterated nor transcribed."

In her *Gender on the Market*, Deborah Kapchan's note also concerns "Transcription and Transliteration" (1996: xi–xii). Like many others now, she must contend with both "CA" (Classical Arabic) and a colloquial language, here "MA" (Moroccan Arabic). In her extensive reporting of spoken texts Kapchan explains, "my ear is tuned to the dialects of Beni Mellal and Marrakech and my transliterations reflect this." She refers to dialectical language studies by Harrell (1962) and now Heath (1987), and also provides a Glossary, a back-matter item that also has become *de rigueur*.

Susan Slymovics' *The Object of Memory* (1998) also uses both terms. In an unusual location in the back matter, her Appendix 1, "Notes on Transliteration and Transcription" (211–13) treats both Hebrew and Arabic. For Modern Standard Arabic, she follows a different system from those discussed, the American Library Association–Library of Congress System. For "colloquial Palestinian Arabic dialect," by contrast, she follows the specialist system of *Zeitschrift fur arabische Linguistik.*

Although, as just seen, the two terms sometimes may be used interchangeably, a strict sense use of transcription is retained among some linguistic anthropologists together with a set of conventional signs used by them alone. Arabist Johansen's previously mentioned "transcriptions" of whole written texts, by contrast, use the conventional signs of transliteration. In "Notes on Transcription" in Niloofar Haeri's *The Sociolinguistic Market of Cairo* (1996: vi) we find an example of an anthropological linguist who studies language variation. Such scholars use a system of formal transcription. Haeri states, "Most transcriptions in this study are attempts at phonemic representation, and exceptions are provided within the usual phonetic brackets." The chart she provides "is adapted from Broselow (1976) *The Phonology of Egyptian Arabic.*" Using technical terms only one or two of which ever appear among anthropological transliterators, Haeri places "Labial, Dental, Palatal, Velar, Uvular, Pharyngeal and Glottal" along one axis and "Stop, Spirant, Nasal, Lateral, Flap, and Glide" along the other. In the resulting transcription system, the Arabic consonant commonly transliterated as "sh" is rendered as "š" with an inverted circumflex, "kh" as "x," "gh" as , and the letter ʿayn by the sign instead of the transliterator's raised "c" or the " ` " of my keyboard. Also in this system, for the emphatic consonants, capital letters replace the dots under letters used in transliteration systems.

Even the sub-disciplinary linguistic folks segment into subgroups whose identities are marked by their adopted systems. A very different variety of linguistic anthropology is exemplified by work on vernacular Yemeni poetry by Arabist-anthropologist Steven Caton, whose *"Peaks of Yemen I Summon"* contains "A Note on Transcription" (1990: xv). His use of the term "transcription" is appropriate for a linguistic inquiry, but in contrast to the sort of work represented by Haeri, the system actually intended is one of transliteration. Thus Caton writes, "The transcription system of the *International Journal of Middle East Studies* is used here. However, because this is a study of an Arabic dialect and not the literary language, I have had to introduce certain changes." He also provides a "detailed description of Yemeni Arabic (specifically tribal) phonology" in his Appendix A.

Michael Meeker's "Note on Transliteration and Translation" in his *Literature and Violence in North Arabia* (1979: xiv) is a special case. This is an anthropology of colloquial poetry – once again involving the Arabian tribe known as the Rwala (Ruwalla, Rualla, Ruwala, Ruala) – but it is based on the historical corpus of research by Alois Musil (1928). "Musil devised a system of recording Rwala dialect which he hoped would accurately indicate its sound values in a Western script. There is a debate about the degree to which he was successful." Meeker has "changed and simplified Musil's script so that the reader with some knowledge of Arabic might easily recognize Rwala cognates," but "Musil's vowelizations of the Rwala dialect have been preserved since he is virtually the sole authority on this matter." Unlike the practice adopted by later Arabist-anthropologists, Meeker states that "quotes from authors other than Musil have often retained their methods of transliterating Arabic."

Stefania Pandolfo's "Note on Transcription" in her *Impasse of the Angels* (1997: ix–xi) deals with the special case of a "multilingual environment" of Berber and Arabic. Mainly, however, her text reports spoken Arabic. "In the transcription of speech I have tried to follow as much as possible the actual pronunciation of words, attempting to convey the diversity and distinctive character of the vernacular idioms, while keeping the grammar visible and the syntax understandable. The outcome is necessarily a compromise. For the sake of readability I have chosen not to use a phonetic transcription, but one based on the regular English alphabet." In an argument also found in the work of Timothy Mitchell (1988: 19), she points out (illustrating her version transliteration in the process) that "Written Arabic does not have vowels but only harakat, "movements.""

VII

My "notes" here – I hope they compensate for the absence of one in my 1993 book (with some interesting company) – have explored transliteration and transcription, minor dimensions or intermediate systems of the larger "trans" relation between languages. The cases examined involve the representation of Arabic in English, mainly within a single discipline, together with some examples from Arabists and travelers. The usages in question are of two basic types, either stand-alone proper names or terms, or words and phrases accompanied by a translation or gloss. They occur in passages involving a surrounding discussion in English, in passages in English which translate Arabic, or as separate texts located in an appendix. Directly or indirectly, transliterations and transcriptions interact with translations, providing indices not only of disciplinary identities but also of the detailed bases of interpretations. Transliterations or transcriptions usually concern key concepts, incisive formulations or significant statements which, in citation, figure centrally in the making of an account. Differing registers of Arabic complexly relate to social relations and, for renderings in English, represent a special challenge involving a range of technical options. The choices made and the skills demonstrated bear on our assessments of the subtlety and accuracy of the anthropological inquiry in question.

As forbearance is sought from readers, and especially from the "experts," many "notes" make reference to debates and disputes about transliteration. Quibbles or full-blown criticisms of an author's transliterations are not uncommon in professional reviews, in journals such as *IJMES*, but I will not detain you with pedantic examples. The "Preface" to *Seven Pillars of Wisdom*, by contrast, provides us an unusual glimpse into the behind-the-scenes of publishing, the back-and-forth between the publisher and the author concerning "transliterations." Figuring among the unrecorded "pretexts" of a published book, expert readers' comments conveyed to the author by the publisher could leave scars apparent in the vexed tone of the published "note." With their bursts of spleen, admissions of weakness, false pleas for forgiveness, etc., some "notes" may be read as the records of a prior ordeal.

Or at least that is the way it was. The voice of the "note" seems quieter now, the witticisms and the anxieties alike mostly replaced by the advance of the professional apparatus. The earlier sensitivity of this pretextual site may itself have been linked to a transitional moment in the field, when anthropologists, in the case of Middle East studies, first were coming to terms with the complexities of Arabic as both a spoken and a written language. In the early days, before the outing of the "self" and the associated venting in the discipline's "reflexive" turn, the personality of the anthropologist found few textual channels for expression, other than in such "notes." Now, however, the florid and revealing "Note on Transliteration" seems to have gone the way of the old-fashioned polemical footnote.

Note

1. Malinowski (1961[1922]: 23–4) set the pattern for the British school of social anthropology. In a famous methodological introduction he describes his advance from the ethnographers of the former Cambridge school, who "tried to quote

verbatim statements of crucial importance" and who also reported the *"termini technici"* of native usage, to his own method which was based on far more extensive competence in the native language. He reports that his initial efforts to translate into English gave way to his writing directly in Kiriwinian: "at last," he states, "I found myself writing exclusively in that language." Over time this led to the production of what he called a *"corpus inscriptionum Kiriwiniensium."*

References

Abu-Lughod, Lila. *Veiled Sentiments*. Berkeley: University of California Press, 1986.

A Dictionary of Egyptian Arabic. Cairo: Badawi and Hinds, 1986.

Armburst, Walter. *Mass Culture and Modernism in Egypt*. Cambridge: Cambridge University Press, 1996.

Asad, Talal. "The Concept of Cultural Translation in British Social Anthropology." In *Writing Culture*. J. Clifford and G, Marcus (eds.), pp. 141–64. Berkeley: University of California Press, 1986.

Bakhtin, M. M. *Speech Genres & Other Essays*. Austin: University of Texas Press, 1986.

Burja, Abdalla S. *The Politics of Stratification*. Oxford: Oxford University Press, 1971.

Caton, Steven. *Peaks of Yemen I Summon*. Berkeley: University of California Press, 1990.

Chartier, Roger. *The Order of Texts*. Stanford: Stanford University Press, 1992.

Clifford, James. "On Ethnographic Authority." *Representations* 1(2), 1983, pp. 118–4.

—— "On Ethnographic Allegory." In *Writing Culture*. J. Clifford and G. Marcus, (eds.), pp. 98–121. Berkeley: University of California Press, 1986.

—— "Notes on (Field)notes." In *Fieldnotes*. R. Sanjek (ed.), Ithaca: Cornell University Press, 1990, pp. 47–70.

Coon, Carlton S. *Caravan, The Stort of the Middle East*. New York: Henry Holt, 1951.

Crapanzano, Vincent. "Hermes' Dilemma: The Masking of Subversion in Ethnographic Description." In *Writing Culture*. J. Clifford and G. Marcus (eds.), pp. 51–76. Berkeley: University of California Press, 1986.

Derrida, Jacques. *Of Grammatology*. Trans. G. C. Spivak. Baltimore: Johns Hopkins University Press, 1974.

Dresch, Paul K. *Tribes, Government, and History in Yemen*. Oxford: Oxford University Press, 1989.

Eickleman, Dale F. *Moroccan Islam*. Austin: University of Texas Press, 1976.

—— *Knowledge and Power in Morocco*. Princeton: Princeton University Press, 1985.

Evans-Pritchard, E. E. *The Sanusi of Cyrenaica*. Oxford: Oxford University Press, 1949.

Fabian, Johannes. "Keep Listening: Ethnography and Reading." In *The Ethnography of Reading*. J. Boyarin (ed.), pp. 80–97. Berkeley: University of California Press, 1992.

Ferguson, Charles. "Diglossia." *Word* 15, 1959, pp. 325–40.

Gaffney, Patrick D. *The Prophet's Pulpit*. Berkeley: University of California Press, 1994.

Geertz, C., Geertz, H. and L. Rosen. *Meaning and Order in a Moroccan Society*. Cambridge: Cambridge University Press, 1979.

Gellner, Ernest. *Saints of the Atlas*. Chicago: University of Chicago Press, 1969.

Grafton, Anthony. *The Footnote: A Curious History*. Cambridge, MA: Harvard University Press, 1997.

Haeri, Niloofar. *The Sociolinguistic Market of Cairo*. London: Kegan Paul, 1996.

Harrall, Richard, S. *A Short Reference Grammar of Moroccan Arabic*. Washington, D.C.: Georgetown University Press, 1962.

Heath, Jeffery. *Ablaut and Ambiguity: Phonology of a Moroccan Arabic Dialect*. Albany: State University of New York Press, 1987.

Johansen, Baber. *The Islamic Law on Land Tax and Rent*. London: Croom Helm, 1988.

Kapchan, Deborah. *Gender on the Market: Moroccan Women and the Revoicing of Tradition*. Philadelphia: University of Pennsylvania Press, 1996.

Lancaster, William. "Note on Transliteration". In *The Rwala Bedouin Today*. Prospect Heights, IL: Waveland, 1997 [1981].

Lawrence, T. E. *Seven Pillars of Wisdom*. New York: Anchor, 1935.

Malinowski, Bronislaw. *Argonauts of the Western Pacific*. New York: E. P. Dutton, 1961 [1922].

Meeker, Michael. *Literature and Violence in North Arabia*. Cambridge: Cambridge University Press, 1979.

Messick, Brinkley. *The Calligraphic State*. Berkeley: University of California Press. 1993.

——. "On the Question of Lithography." *Culture and History* 16 (Copenhagen), 1997, pp. 158–176.

Mitchell, Timothy. *Colonizing Egypt*. Cambridge: Cambridge University Press, 1988.

Mottahedeh, Roy, P. *Loyalty and Leadership in an Early Islamic Society*. Princeton: Princeton University Press, 1980.

Mundy, Martha. *Domestic Government*. London: I. B. Tauris, 1995.

Musil, Alois. *The Manners and Customs of the Rwala Bedouin*. New York: Crane, 1928.

Pandolfo, Stefania. *Impasse of the Angels*. Chicago: University of Chicago Press, 1997.

Rosen, Lawrence. *Bargaining for Reality*. Chicago: University of Chicago Press, 1984.

Shryock, Andrew. *Nationalism and the Genealogical Imagination*. Berkeley: University of California Press, 1997.

Slymovics, Susan. *The Object of Memory*. Philadelphia: University of Pennsylvania Press, 1998.

Thesiger, Wilfred. *Arabian Sands*. New York: Dutton, 1959.

Wehr, Hans. *A Dictionary of Modern Written Arabic*. 3d ed. Ithaca: Spoken Language Services, 1976.

–8–

The Ethnographer as Pontifex
Benson Saler

Incident at Cajamarca

Some of the difficulties attendant on understanding and then translating religious concepts are illustrated by an incident that occurred during the Spanish conquest of the Inka Empire. The first verbal exchanges between the Spaniards and the Inka ruler Atahuallpa were mediated by an interpreter named Felipe. According to the chronicler, Garcilaso de la Vega, nicknamed "El Inka," Felipe was

> a native of the island of Puna, a man of very plebeian origin, young – for he was scarcely twenty-two – and as little versed in the general language of the Incas as in Spanish. He had in fact learned the language of the Incas, not in Cuzco, but in Túmbez, from Indians who speak barbarously and corruptly as foreigners; we have already explained that to all the Indians but the natives of Cuzco this is a foreign language. He had also learnt Spanish without a teacher, but merely by hearing the Spaniards speak, and the words he heard most often were those used by the ordinary soldiers . . . Though baptized, he had received no instruction in the Christian religion and knew nothing about Christ our Lord, and was totally ignorant of the Apostles' creed. (Vega 1966: 682)

As might be expected, Felipe translated poorly from one language to the other. Thus when Fray Vicente de Valverde addressed a long and uncompromising speech to Atahuallpa in which he outlined the Christian faith and demanded the Inka's submission to the Pope and to the Emperor, Felipe mangled the translation. He did so not out of malice, the chronicler tells us, "but because he did not understand what he was interpreting, and spoke it like a parrot" (Vega 1966: 682). Among other things, "Instead of God three in one, he said God three and one make four, adding the numbers in order to make himself understood. This is shown by the tradition of the *quipus*, or annual records in knots, kept at Cajamarca, where the event occurred" (Vega 1966: 682).[1]

Garcilaso, while clearly no admirer of Felipe, does not blame him entirely for mistranslating Fray Vicente's speech. Felipe, he claims,

> could not express it [the doctrine of the Trinity] in any other way; for there are no words or phrases in the Peruvian language for many of the concepts of the Christian religion,

such as Trinity, Holy Spirit, faith, grace, Church, sacraments, and similar words. These are totally unknown to the gentiles, and the words have never existed, and still do not exist [twenty-nine years later], in their language. For this reason, when the Spanish interpreters of these times wish to express these ideas adequately, they have to seek new words or phrases, or use with great care suitably dignified expressions in the old language or else lay hands on the many words the cultured and scholarly Indians have taken from Spanish and introduced into their own languages, adapting them to their own ways of speech. The Indians of today do this with great elegance, thus helping the Spaniards to find the words that are lacking, so that they can say what they want and the Indians can understand the sermons that are preached to them. (1966: 682)

I return eventually to Garcilaso's remarks about how the doctrines of Christianity may be "adequately" conveyed to Peruvian Indians. Here, however, I want to consider one particular doctrine, that of the Trinity.

Felipe added three Gods and one God and came up with four, at least partly, it seems, out of profound ignorance. But even well-schooled and greatly respected Christian theologians have confessed to difficulties in understanding the doctrine of the Trinity. They nevertheless proclaim it to be central to their faith and of crucial significance for their salvation. The doctrine of the Trinity, moreover, has proven difficult to translate from one language to another, beginning with efforts to render Greek formulations of it into Latin.

Difficulties in understanding and conveying the doctrine of the Trinity are traceable in part to a major factor affecting the comprehension and translation of many religious ideas: the matter of their partial counter-intuitivity. I explore that point by first describing certain problems posed by theologians respecting the doctrine of the Trinity. I go on from there to consider some recent theoretical claims about the counter-intuitive aspects of religious ideas, and certain of the implications of such claims for translation.

The Doctrine of the Trinity

Despite a fair amount of heterogeneity in opinion among Christian theologians, they commonly recognize certain constraints on their theologies. Two are especially relevant here.

The first we may term anthropocentric pragmatism. That is, thoughtful theologians generally evaluate their theological options in light of this consideration: what may be the likely consequences – indeed, the potential harm – of any doctrine for the possibilities of human salvation? (Placher 1983: 69)

The second, adapting and amending a theoretical construct advanced by Brian K. Smith (1987), can be called the principle of "canonical reflexivity." Smith maintains that a religion is to be identified by the repeated references or returns, if only formulaic, that its adherents make to some canon, whether written or oral. The canon is invested with authority, and the positive references that people make to it are definitive of their faith or perspective, even if they do not explicitly discuss its substance. (Many Hindus, for example, are ignorant of what is contained in the Vedas, but their regard for the chanting of those works in Sanskrit is important to their identity as Hindus.) By resting religion on this one criterion, Smith is forced to identify "Marxism" and "Freudianism" as religions. I criticize him elsewhere for doing so (Saler 2000 [1993]). And while I do not hold that canonical reflexivity is either necessary or sufficient for identifying religion, I acknowledge that it is often important in religions.

These two principles relate to the development of the doctrine of the Trinity. The New Testament depicts Jesus Christ as more than a man. At the same time, however, he is canonically distinguished from the Heavenly Father (e.g. "the Father is greater than I" [*John* 14:28]). What, then, is Jesus? And how is he related to the Father? And if human salvation comes through Jesus Christ, what other considerations might that implicate? Thus, for instance, if Jesus were a creature, as Arius claimed, he would have come into existence at some time, and doing so betokens change. If he had changed once, from nothing to something, might he not change again? And dare we entrust human salvation to a creature capable of change (Placher 1983)?

These and other considerations entered into the development of the doctrine of the Triune God. Much of the early argument in the developing Church focused on the relationship of the Second Person of the Trinity (the Son) to the First (God the Father). While the Third Person (The Holy Spirit) was discussed, it received less polemical attention in the first few centuries – albeit argument over whether the Spirit "proceeds" *both* from the Father "and from the Son" ("*filioque*"), as Augustine of Hippo and the Western Church proclaimed, or only from the Father, as the Eastern Church maintained, proved to be of major divisive significance within Christendom.

The Council of Nicaea (AD 325) was called by the Emperor Constantine largely to settle the issue of whether the Son is co-eternal with the Father or whether, like a creature, he had come into existence at some time. The Council concluded that the Son is co-eternal with the Father and that he is "begotten not made," his begetting, by eventual consensus, being an eternal begetting, for unlike creatures he was not begotten at some point in time. Further, the Council, in proclaiming the Son to be "true God from true God," also declared him to be "of the same substance (*homoousios*) as the Father."

This matter of being *homoousios* proved to be theologically problematic. While the translation of this Greek term – *homo*, 'same' + *ousios*, 'substance' – by Latin-speaking churchmen was generally in harmony with the literal meaning assigned to it by their Greek-speaking colleagues, there were divisions among both Greek and Latin speakers as to the theological interpretation of the term. Some church-men at the Council apparently understood "the same substance" to mean of the same divine stuff, which would be somewhat like saying that two pieces of oak furniture are of the same substance because they are both made of oak wood. But Athanasius, a leading fourth-century theologian, insisted that the term means the very same substance, which would be analogous to saying that our two pieces of oak furniture are cut from the very same oak tree (adapted from Placher 1983). Some of the theologians who supported the idea of the same divine stuff (oak in general) rather than the very same stuff (the same oak tree) eventually endorsed the claim that the Son is *homoiousios* with the Father, of a "similar substance" rather than of the same substance.

Arius held that "There was a time when the Son was not." The debate at Nicaea between those who inclined to his opinion and Athanasius and his supporters was influenced significantly by Greek philosophy. Indeed, Alan Kolp (1975: 101) suggests that "Without noting it the Arian controversy is a struggle over the correct use of Platonic philosophical categories." The Athanasian *homoousios* theology was eventually strengthened by the Cappadocian Fathers, Basil the Great, Gregory of Nyssa, and Gregory of Nazianzus, who creatively reformulated certain Greek metaphysical categories. They maintained that the Father, Son, and Holy Spirit are all of one *ousia*, one "substance", but they are three *hypostaseis* ("individuals," "persons").

This terminology immediately raised problems in Greek, where the terms *ousia* and *hypostasis* were sometimes employed as synonyms for "substance," as in some of the writings of Athanasius (Placher 1983: 78). And it raised problems for translation into Latin, for, as Placher (1983: 78–79) points out,

> Since the time of Tertullian, Latin-speaking Christians had made a parallel distinction between three *personae* . . . and one *substantia*. Unfortunately, *substantia* is the literal Latin translation of *hypostasis* (both words mean "that which stands under"), so horrified Latin-speaking Christians read Greek references to "three *hypostaseis*" as meaning "three *substantiae*."

Eventually, however, things were more or less sorted out by those who took the trouble to acquaint themselves with the peculiarities of usage in Cappadocian theo-logical Greek and the problems encountered in translating from that discourse to Latin. The Cappadocian Fathers assisted in clarifying understandings by extended explications. They declared, for instance, that while the Three Persons are each distinct, they always act in perfect harmony and concert, unlike any other three persons. Further, the Three Persons of the same divine *ousia* are the only form that *ousia* has ever taken or could ever take (Placher 1983: 78). And, of course, and in case anyone was not aware of it, they called attention to the fact that they were using the terms *ousia* and *hypostasis* in special, non-synonymous senses.

Difficulties in Comprehending the Doctrine of the Trinity

Despite the attempts at clarification described above, and others as well, many theologians (to say nothing of ordinary Christians) deem the doctrine of the Trinity exceedingly difficult to understand. Some, indeed, declare it to be beyond the powers of human comprehension, at least in this life. Thomas Aquinas takes that position.

In the first of his two *summas*, the *Summa contra gentiles* (Bk. IV, Chapt. 1), Thomas writes that there are three ways for humans to obtain a knowledge of things divine. The first is by the unaided exercise of human reason and the third is by the post-mortem attainment of the Beatific Vision, wherein the human mind will be elevated to more powerful understandings. The second, which is the one that most directly concerns us here, is by revelation from God. Thomas declares, however, that revealed truths – he supplies two examples, the Incarnation and the Trinity – are given to us "not, however, as something made clear to be seen, but as something spoken in words to be believed" (SCG IV, 1:5). The truths of the Incarnation and Trinity, the "angelic doctor" teaches, are not merely difficult to understand; they are, in a profound sense, impossible to understand, at least in this life. Yet they are fundamental facts of reality and of crucial importance for the possibility of human salvation. In short, one of the greatest theologians in Christendom maintains that his religion turns on certain truths that the faithful must accept but cannot fully fathom.

A more contemporary consideration of the difficulty of understanding the doctrine of the Trinity (and thus, by implication, the difficulty of translating it) is given by John Henry Newman in his *An Essay in Aid of a Grammar of Assent* (1985 [1889, 1870]). Newman's Grammar is a major nineteenth-century work dealing with the epistemology of belief.

Newman is concerned with what is involved in apprehending, inferring, and assenting to propositions. He characterizes apprehension as the mind's imposition of sense on the predicate of a proposition. Inference is the relating of a proposition to others as a conclusion. And assent is the mind's acceptance of the truth of a proposition.

While John Locke (1959 [1689]) holds that assent is conditional, that it can be proportional to evidence, Newman denies it. He allows that inference may be conditional, but not assent. Assent, he says, does not admit of degrees (1985: 32).

"The terms of a proposition," Newman writes,

> do or do not stand for things. If they do, then they are singular terms, for all things that are, are units. But if they do not stand for things they must stand for notions, and are common terms. Singular nouns come from experience, common from abstraction. The apprehension of the former I call real, and of the latter notional. (1985: 22)

In the case of real propositions, that is, "the terms stand for things external to us" (1985: 13) insofar as there are impressions of those things in the imagination. In the case of notional propositions, in contrast, the mind is directed to its own creations rather than to "things." The apprehension of a proposition, moreover, varies in strength because, according to Newman, "what is concrete exerts a force and makes an impression on the mind which nothing abstract can rival. That is, . . . because the object is more powerful, therefore so is the apprehension of it" (1985: 31).

Newman's distinction between "real" and "notional" beliefs resembles to some extent distinctions that certain contemporary philosophers draw between "*de re*" and "*de dicto*" beliefs (see for example Woodfield 1982: v–xi). Rather than digress to sketch the similarities (and differences), however, I focus instead on the applications that Newman makes of his own distinction to what his Church teaches about the Trinity.

The dogma of the Trinity, Newman says, consists of nine propositions. Each of the nine, taken separately, can be the object of real assent, for the devout can image each by a lively act of the imagination. But if the nine propositions are taken together as a "systematized whole," that combination "is the object of notional assent" (1985: 91). The nine propositions, in Newman's words, are these:

> 1. There are Three who give testimony in heaven, the Father, The Word or Son, and the Holy Spirit. 2. From the Father is, and ever has been, the Son. 3. From the Father and Son is, and ever has been, the Spirit. 4. The Father is the One Eternal Personal God. 5. The Son is the One Eternal Personal God. 6. The Spirit is the One Eternal Personal God. 7. The Father is not the Son. 8. The Son is not the Holy Ghost. 9. The Holy Ghost is not the Father. (1985: 91)

Combining the nine into a whole, says Newman, produces a theological mystery – that is, an affirmation that is beyond our full comprehension and that is to be accepted on faith. Newman remarks that the Holy Trinity in Unity "is never spoken of as a Mystery in the sacred book, which is addressed far more to the imagination and affection than to the intellect" (1985: 90). Nor is it termed a mystery in the Apostles', Nicaean, and Athanasian Creeds, "which have a place in the Ritual" and are "devotional acts . . . of the nature of prayers, addressed to God; and in such addresses, to speak of intellectual difficulties would be out of place" (1985: 90). Further, it is not called a mystery in "Confession after confession, canon after canon," though Popes and Councils "have found it their duty to insist afresh upon the dogma" (1985: 91). But the "custom is otherwise," Newman informs us, "as regards catechisms and theological treatises. These belong to particular ages and places, and are addressed to the intellect." And in them, he relates, "the mysteriousness of the doctrine is almost uniformly insisted on" (1985: 91).

The Counter-intuitive

While numbers of Christians maintain that the Trinity is a divine mystery revealed to finite human minds by God, and that the theologians whose doctrines about it became mainstream were guided by the Holy Spirit, a secular intellectual history of the doctrine takes a different tack. A major impetus to that development, as suggested earlier, was a certain tension or paradox in the canonical texts, which presented Jesus as more than a man yet as distinct from God the Father. The unfolding doctrine of the Trinity, in secular perspective, was in large measure the unfolding of efforts to resolve that tension or paradox. Numbers of theologians, moreover, attempted to do so in ways that would not challenge scriptural authority or jeopardize the possibility of human salvation, given the fan of understandings and hopes that motivated and constrained those efforts.

A major problem is reconciling the Three with the One and the One with the Three. Conventional Christian theological applications of those numbers to the Godhead contravene present-day, ordinary uses of numbers in the West and associated intuitions about numeration in our society. Newman, cognizant of that circumstance, opines that in speculating about "the Supreme Being, . . . it may be unmeaning, not only to number with other beings, but to subject to number in regard to His own intrinsic characteristics. That is, to apply arithmetical notions to Him may be as unphilosophical as it is profane" (1985: 39).

Closely related to that problem is the problem of reconciling the individuation of the Three Persons of the Trinity with their eternal and perfect unity in thought and action. The explications that Christian theologians furnish respecting the individuation of the three Persons, for example, do not fully jibe with the understandings that many contemporary Westerners entertain about the nature of individualism. Nor, I think, are they entirely harmonious with the somewhat different understandings of Westerners of yesteryear. In both cases, experience and folk belief-desire psychology testify that individuals often disagree in significant ways and pursue different ends. Thus even when the believer accepts it on authority that three individual divine Persons always act in complete agreement and concert, how might he or she explain it meaningfully to others – to Atahuallpa, say, who had difficulties with his brother, or, for that matter, to those of us non-believers who have logged many hours in attendance at department meetings?

In addition to the above problems, there are others, such as the problem of understanding (let alone translating) the concept of "eternal begetting." In short, the doctrine of the Trinity – the doctrine that the one true living God who created all else consists of three eternal Persons of the same substance who always act in perfect concert – is difficult to comprehend because it violates several of our work-a-day intuitions and expectations about numbers, identity, personhood, and procreation – and, more broadly, it violates our intuitions about living things.

The Persons of the Trinity, the "living God" of mainstream Christianity, are not merely different sorts of "person." They violate a constellation of ontological assumptions – a constellation of assumptions in Western societies and, according to Pascal Boyer (1994), a constellation of assumptions likely to be found, more or less, among people in other societies – about persons and, more broadly, about living things, that structures expectations. Persons, as exemplars of living things, are physical objects and therefore visible. Their identity, sentience, and intentionality are individuated. Predicates that might well apply to individual persons (e.g. "is lustful," "is contentious," "is malleable") are doctrinally declared to be inapplicable to the Persons of the Trinity. And some of the predicate terms that are applied to the Persons of the Trinity (e.g. "perfect in knowledge," "unchangeable," "one in understanding and purpose") are not usually applied to human persons, either individually or collectively. Further, and especially among those who champion "negative theology," it is sometimes claimed that predicate terms applied to divinity do not mean the same things that they mean when applied to human persons: that, for instance, God is "wise" not in the same way that Allen Greenspan is "wise," but in a special way applicable only to God.

Now, the counter-intuitive plays important roles in human life. It is, for example, associated with modern science, especially insofar as modern science transcends and subverts naive realism. And it is often invoked to good effect in science fiction (Disch 1998). But it may well be so salient and consistent in the configuration and transmission of religious ideas as to mark them off from other ideas. Such, at any rate, is one of the arguments of Pascal Boyer in his complex book, *The Naturalness of Religious Ideas: A Cognitive Theory of Religion*, where he observes that

> Religious representations typically comprise claims or statements that violate people's ideas of what commonly takes place in their environment. For instance, some entities are described as invisible, yet located in space, intangible yet capable of mechanical action on physical objects; things fly in the air instead of falling to the ground, aging and death do not affect certain beings, and so on. (1994: 35)

Indeed, not only do religious representations violate intuitive expectations, but, according to Boyer, "Religious notions would not be interesting, would not be attention demanding, if they complied with intuitions about ordinary events and states" (1994: 48). This, however, does not mean that there is nothing intuitive or ordinary about religious ideas.

As Boyer sees it, the sorts of religious ideas that will be transmitted from one generation to the next – the religious ideas that will prove successful in the competition, so to speak, among ideas for places in human memory – are those that strike an optimal cognitive balance between the intuitive and the counter-intuitive (1994: 121). Their intuitiveness, their harmony with expectations supported by ordinary ontological assumptions and commitments, invests them with plausibility and renders them learnable. But their violation of such expectations, their seeming intuitive unnaturalness "to the subjects who hold them" (1994: 3), makes them interesting and "attention demanding." If the mix is right, they are more likely to be remembered and more likely to be transmitted to the next generation than ideas that are either unexceptional or entirely counter-intuitive.

In addition to attempting to account for the transmission of religious ideas, Boyer also attempts to account for "important recurrent features in the religious representations that can be found in very different cultural environments" (1994: vii–viii). He takes pains to point out, however, that he is not postulating substantive universals in religious ideas (1994: 5). Rather, beyond our minimal recognition that in many human groups there are ideas "concerning non-observable, extra-natural agencies and processes[,] . . . the similarities between religious ideas are a matter of family resemblance rather than universal features" (1994: 5). I fully agree with that position, and I would add that since we deal cross-culturally with *resemblances* rather than *identities* (Saler 1993, 2000), the problem of translating is all the more difficult. While ideas, say, about witches in two societies may show appreciable conceptual overlap, there are also likely to be significant differences, and a scrupulous translator will have to take pains to avoid obscuring important differences in relevant contexts.

Boyer links his consideration of transmission processes with his appreciation of family resemblances among religious representations in different cultural settings. He aspires to explain both by working toward a complex theory of the cognitive foundations of religious ideas. Suffice it for present purposes to foreground only certain features of his theorizing.

Boyer argues that there are universal features (following Needham 1972, I prefer to say natural resemblances) in human cognition. People throughout the world, for instance, tend to distinguish between living things and artifacts and they develop similar general understandings of what is normal for each. These and other widely distributed cognitive resemblances both motivate and constrain the transmission of religious ideas. Among other things, we humans develop rich, domain-specific ontologies, both explicit and tacit, in our attentions to the world, and those ontologies provide us with a host of expectations and intuitions in all walks of life, including the religious. The "intuitive assumptions that are used in all religious representations," Boyer (1994: 121) writes, "provide the main substance of all inferences and conjectures." But they also constrain the acceptability of counter-intuitive claims. Further, Boyer argues, while religious ideas are subject to selective pressures in the transmission process, their contents are likely to be underdetermined by that process.

The processes that we call socialization and enculturation do not account for the richness of many religious ideas. Individuals enhance their religious claims by making inferences from their established ontological assumptions and expect-ations. The richness of religious ideas, Boyer argues, therefore need not depend on exhaustive cultural transmissions. On the basis, moreover, of cross-cultural ethno-graphic data, experimental studies of concept development in children, and certain arguments advanced by evolutionary biologists and evolutionary psychologists, Boyer suggests that on the level of such macro-categories as person, plant, animal, and artifact, people throughout the world have similar ontological assumptions and expectations, and so can be expected to make similar inferences, and to respond in similarly orderly ways to the inferences of their fellows. This would account for the recurrence of certain religious ideas in diverse cultural settings. And, I would add, it enhances the prospects for warrantable explications of religious ideas across populations.

Boyer claims, in general argument and with the support of some ethnographic examples, that religious believers themselves often sense something "unnatural" or counter-intuitive in their beliefs – that, in fact, an apprehension of the unnatural or counter-intuitive, however inchoate, sparks the imagination and in that wise renders the beliefs attractive. Believers may not render their sense of the "unnat-ural" immediately explicit, but it can be fathomed, in my experience, on asking them to explicate and extend their assertions.

I agree with Boyer's general argument about the counter-intuitive, and I recom-mend that we attempt to capture and convey some appreciation of our informants' sense of it – and of the intuitive structures that render it both possible and signif-icant – in our ethnographies.

Some anthropologists (e.g. Leach 1967), however, perhaps because of their commitments in the "rationality" debate that has occupied the attentions of many of us, describe and analyze beliefs in ways that mask, minimize, or explain away violations of the intuitive, thus seeming to render those beliefs less troublesome for their readers to apprehend and in some sense accept. That, of course, in a crude, uninformed, but not apparently ideological fashion, is what Felipe of Puna did in mistranslating Fray Vicente's profession of the doctrine of the Trinity: he added the numbers, Garcilaso tells us, "*in order to make himself understood*" (1966: 682, emphasis added). But intelligibility purchased at the cost of fidelity is not worth much.

My suggestion that our ethnographies of religious ideas include explicit consid-erations of the counter-intuitive – and its dependence on the intuitive – is a facet of a more inclusive suggestion: that we strive for fidelity in a "global" sense. I have in mind "translation" – good translation – very broadly conceived. Perhaps I can make my widened understanding of translation clearer by briefly comparing it to translation in a narrower, more conventional sense.

Garcilaso's Solution and Explication

The chronicler Garcilaso de la Vega, it may be recalled, was concerned with how Christian ideas might be "adequately" expressed to Peruvian Indians. Garcilaso had an interest in good translation. Translation is always motivated. In Garcilaso's case, there was not only the hope of benefiting the souls of the Indians, but also concern for minimizing stresses stemming from the incorporation of the conquered into a new order. Garcilaso himself traced roots to both the Indians and the Spaniards. His father was a *conquistador*, and his mother was an Inka noble, a second cousin to Atahuallpa.

When Spanish interpreters of "these times," Garcilaso wrote, wish to express Christian ideas adequately, "they have to seek new words or phrases, or use with great care suitably dignified expressions in the old language or else lay hands on the many words the cultured and scholarly Indians have taken from Spanish and introduced into their own languages, adapting them to their own ways of speech" (1988: 682).

Garcilaso's solution is to coin new terms and expressions, to use with great care possible correspondences (glosses) across languages, and to adapt loan words. These are conventional instruments of translation in a narrow sense, and they can be productive where the translator is sensitive and skilled.

Although the solution endorsed by Garcilaso may serve for purposes of religious conversion (or, at any rate, the appearance of religious conversion), it is inadequate for anthropological purposes. If by "translation" we mean translation in the narrow sense sketched above, then the anthropologist, I think, should subsume translation in explication. Indeed, in my opinion the task of the ethnographer is *explication* rather than "translation" in the narrow sense of glossing expressions in one language with terms from another or with freshly minted neologisms. Such explication involves the examination of contexts in which targeted expressions occur and the analysis of any encountered polysemy. Our intellectual grasp and appreciation of key terms will be enhanced by an understanding of the domains with which they are associated in native usages.

A well-known example of explication is found in Evans-Pritchard's (1956) discussion of the Nuer term *kwoth*. I am aware that some anthropologists suggest that Evans-Pritchard's explication of that term is biased by his personal religious proclivities. I do not know enough about the case, however, to evaluate that claim. Regardless of possible inaccuracies or other deficiencies in the contents of what he writes, however, the form of his explication deserves admiration on two counts. First, Evans-Pritchard examines how the term is used in different contexts, and even though his examination may not be exhaustive, he demonstrates the polysemy of *kwoth*, and he makes efforts to deal with it in ways that we, his readers, may comprehend. Second, his explication is alive to the significance of tropes; and although his fame in that regard largely rests on his analysis of the "twins are birds" metaphor, he alerts us generally to how a sensitivity to tropes might expand our understandings of religious terms and expressions, and so enlarge and potentially improve the translation task.

Efforts to achieve "global" fidelity in the ethnography of religious ideas are efforts at explication that include discussion of the environments and likely polysemy of important religious terms, the determination and exploration of relevant and revealing tropes, and systematic efforts to make explicit what is significantly implicit, both with respect to the intuitive structures and understandings that support the plausibility of religious ideas and the counter-intuitive features of those ideas that render them memorable. Yet more, I think, is required. Serious efforts should also be made to learn who professes or endorses the reported ideas, for not everyone in a given population may do so. Attempts, moreover, should be made to assess the relative strength of professions of belief, which may well vary from hedged or weak affirmations to those that seem vigorous and confident. These efforts will collectively support and make more convincing the anthropologist's theorizing about the functions of religious ideas in discrete populations and in human history.

Efforts at global fidelity are not solely focused on the human population under study. They are also inevitably motivated, weighted, and constrained by considerations relating to the eventual target audience of the ethnographic monograph.

The ethnographer has the difficult task of conveying, as accurately and as cogently as possible, what he or she has come to understand about religious ideas studied in the field to an audience (often largely of other anthropologists though sometimes a wider audience) that lacks comparable knowledge and experience of the field situation. Explication of categories and ideas encountered in the field, moreover, is attempted in the language of the eventual target audience, the readership of the ethnographic monograph. In addition to using that audience's "ordinary language," explication is also likely to involve the so-called professional analytical categories of anthropologists. And these, in the overwhelming majority of cases, are specially refined and often contested versions of Western folk categories (see Saler 2000 [1993] for "religion"). In short, conveyance depends on the artful and problem-plagued application and adjustment of categories from different sources, sources that themselves answer to different interests. Such conveyance, in any case, constitutes "translation" in that term's fundamental etymological senses: "transfer" and "transformation". It amounts to a task of mediation or bridge-building between disparate but not entirely incompatible clusters of understandings. It is, indeed, something of a secular analog to what some religious communities expect of their priests.

The Ethnographer as Pontifex

Dictionaries and other sources in English generally state that the "literal" meaning of *pontifex* is "bridge-builder," from the Latin *pons*, bridge + *facio*, to do or to make.

Emile Benveniste (1971 [1966]: 255–256) relates the Latin *pons* and the Greek *pontos*, "sea," to the Sanskrit *pánthah*, one of several terms in Vedic texts for "road." That particular Sanskrit term for "road," he writes, "implies difficulty, uncertainty, and danger, it has unforeseen detours, it can vary depending on who is traversing it . . . It is indeed . . . a 'crossing' attempted over an unknown and often hostile region . . ." Its sense of crossing rather than road, Benveniste opines, "explains the diversity of the documented variants."

Although we may start with the sense of "road" as crossing associated with the Sanskrit term *pánthah*, Benveniste writes, "this sense is no more 'primordial' than the others; it is only one of the realizations of the general signification defined here." Thus in a Latin approximation to the realization of such a general signification, "*pons* will designate the 'crossing' of a stream of water or a dip in the ground, hence a 'bridge'." A bridge crosses something, and it may facilitate our crossing.

In ancient Rome the term *pontifex* (pl., *pontifices*) was applied to the members of a college of priests, the leader of whom was called *pontifex maximus*. There were probably three members in the days of the monarchy, and they advised the king on religious matters. By the time of the late Republic they numbered sixteen, and they administered the *ius divinum*, the laws governing the state cult, which included the regulation of the official calendar. They were termed "bridge-builders," some classicists speculate, because they may have had charge of the Pons Sublicius, a bridge over the Tiber River that was invested with a sacred significance (Bailey 1932: 162).

In the early Christian church a bishop was termed pontifex, but that term was eventually reserved for the Bishop of Rome, the Pope. In contemporary Roman Catholic sources the symbolism of bridge-building, of bridging two domains, the divine and the human, is often made explicit, and I use the term pontifex analogously here.

The ethnographer is, metaphorically, a "bridge-builder," one charged with the task of facilitating a "crossing" into the sensibilities and sensitivities of others. The major purpose of ethnographic bridges, of ethnographic monographs, is to allow the reading public to cross over to new understandings, new understandings of others and perhaps of themselves. And among the building materials utilized to construct such bridges, creatively figured analogies and glosses are salient.

An analogy is a way of establishing resemblances between things that otherwise differ. Ethnographers not only depend on analogies in their descriptions, but they

are beholden to them in recognizing problems and interests. Numbers of populations, for example, have no term or category for what we call "religion," but the
ethnographer recognizes "religion" in their societies by observing local assertions
and other behaviors reminiscent of what he or she deems to be religious behaviors
elsewhere. Religion, that is, is established by analogy. And that, of course, suggests
an important question: analogy to what?

Ironically enough, I think that some students of religion have done a better job
of exploring the religious categories of other peoples than have those of the
populations for which they write, with the consequence that their analogies might
not be as detailed nor as cogent as they could be. As I put it elsewhere,

> If we suppose that there is warrant to construct bridges of some sort to span the semantic
> chasms that separate us from others, we would do well to remember that bridges
> normally have two anchoring foundations, one on either side of what they span. Much
> mischief, I think, has accrued from our failures to prepare the ground profoundly enough
> on *our* side of the divide. (Saler 1993: 124–125).

Glosses can be viewed as lexical analogies, and they can be problematic in ways
that are similar to those of other forms of analogy. Take a case put to me by the
editors: Malinowski's use (in *Argonauts of the Western Pacific*, 1922) of the gloss
'flying witches' for the Kiriwinian term *mulukwausi*. Has Malinowski, I am asked,
"actually captured the meaning" of the Trobriand concept to which his gloss
refers? I think that he has, but not because of the gloss itself, although it is plausible
both analytically and holistically.

The gloss is plausible in these ways: First, when broken down into its components, those resonate with our understandings. We identify flying as a mode of
locomotion. And we identify witches as malevolent beings who utilize magical
means to harm others (although I suspect that the term was somewhat less ambiguous in Malinowski's day, since in our time Wicca, *The Wizard of Oz*, and certain
television serials and cartoons support the understanding that not all witches are
bad). Second, the expression is holistically meaningful, for the idea of flying
witches is well established among us, and it is an idea that occurs in many other
societies. That is, there are family resemblances among the flying-witch representations in numbers of cultural settings (our witches, for example, typically fly
on broomsticks, whereas those of the Fang of Cameroon typically fly on banana
leaves [Boyer 1994]).

Still and all, Malinowski's gloss 'flying witches' is inadequate by itself, despite
its overlap with our ideas. Fortunately, however, Malinowski supplies more than a
gloss. He provides us with an explication of certain relevant Trobriand ideas, and
by so doing justifies his gloss.

Again, "translating" ("glossing") in a narrow sense is unlikely to suffice for anthropological purposes. More is required if we are to cross over to warrantable understandings. The "global fidelity" of which I have spoken is, of course, a desideratum and an ambition, unlikely ever to be achieved in full. But there are degrees of approximation, and we should aim for the maximum possible.

Some persons claim that adequate translation is impossible. They aver, indeed, that attempts at bridge-building or crossing-over are inevitably and fatally subverted by cultural barriers encoded in language. That, however, strikes me as too pessimistic a point of view. There are, of courses, difficulties in crossing over the barriers of language and culture. For the most part, however, those difficulties are extensions of the difficulties that we encounter in understanding others in our own society. As extensions, to be sure, they are rendered complex by the necessity of dealing with newly encountered lexicons and grammars. Yet, as Boyer's work suggests, there is reasonable hope that such barriers can be overcome, if not completely then sufficiently enough to satisfy most of our needs.

We would do well to remind ourselves that even where we suppose that we control the language and are familiar with the culture, we encounter difficulties in understanding. Indeed, we cannot honestly claim full comprehension of our spouses, children, parents, and colleagues, let alone the Three Persons of the Trinity, but we go on trying, sometimes with apparent if only limited – but nevertheless gratifying – success. And, lest we forget, we also experience genuine difficulty in understanding ourselves. Indeed, of all the commandments that humanity has saddled itself with, perhaps the most difficult to obey is the Delphic Imperative, "Know thyself!" Such difficulties in understanding may help explain why even persons accounted to be non-religious sometimes avail themselves of priests.

Note

1. The quipu was a mnemonic device consisting of knots of different kinds tied in various positions on strings. The types of knots, their locations, and their syntactic relations to other knots were assigned semantic values that stimulated and constrained the memories of specially trained personnel. A collection of quipus, as at Cajamarca, was in effect a sort of archive. By referring to these records, Garcilaso de la Vega does what good historians normally do: he supports his narrative by citing sources for it.

References

Aquinas, Thomas. *Summa contra gentiles*, Book IV, trans. Charles J. O'Neil. Notre Dame IN: University of Notre Dame Press, 1975.

Bailey, Cyril. *Phases in the Religion of Ancient Rome*. Berkeley: University of California Press, 1932.

Benveniste, Emile. *Problems in General Linguistics*, trans. Mary Elizabeth Meek. Coral Gables: University of Miami Press, 1971 [1966].

Boyer, Pascal. *The Naturalness of Religious Ideas. A Cognitive Theory of Religion*. Berkeley: The University of California Press, 1994.

Disch, Thomas M. *The Dreams Our Stuff Is Made Of: How Science Fiction Conquered the World*. New York: The Free Press, 1998.

Evans-Pritchard, Edward E. *Nuer Religion*. Oxford: Oxford University Press, 1956.

Kolp, Alan Lee. *Participation: A Unifying Concept in the Theology of Athanasius*. Unpublished Ph.D. dissertation, Harvard University, 1975.

Leach, Edmund. "Virgin Birth". *Proceedings of the Royal Anthropological Institute* 1966: 39–49, 1967.

Locke, John. *An Essay Concerning Human Understanding*. New York: Dover, 1959 [1689].

Malinowski, Bronislaw. *Argonauts of the Western Pacific*. New York: E. P. Dutton, 1961 [1922].

Needham, Rodney. *Belief, Language, and Experience*. Oxford: Basil Blackwell, 1972.

Newman, John Henry. *An Essay in Aid of a Grammar of Assent*. Oxford: Clarendon, 1985 [1889, 1870].

Placher, William C. *A History of Christian Theology: An Introduction*. Philadelphia: Westminster Press, 1983.

Saler, Benson. *Conceptualizing Religion: Immanent Anthropologists, Transcendent Natives, and Unbounded Categories*. Leiden: E. J. Brill. Paperback Edition with a new Preface, New York and Oxford: Berghahn Books, 2000 [1993].

Smith, Brian K. "Exorcising the Transcendent: Strategies for Defining Hinduism and Religion." *History of Religions* 27(1), 1987, pp. 32–55.

Vega, Garcilaso de la, El Inca. *Royal Commentaries of the Incas and General History of Peru*, Part Two, trans. Harold V. Livermore. Austin: University of Texas Press, 1966.

Woodfield, Andrew. "Foreword." In *Thought and Object: Essays on Intentionality*. Andrew Woodfield (ed.), pp. v–xi. Oxford: Clarendon, 1982.

–9–

Text Translation as a Prelude for
Soul Translation

Alan F. Segal

Bible Translation and Translation to Heaven

I will deliberately confuse two different uses of *translation* – (1) a meaning carried from one language to another with (2) a soul carried from earth to heaven. I intend to investigate some of the strangest literature of the ancient world, where the metaphor of translation to heaven also expresses a biblical concept of ecstasy. But the process of producing these mystic meanings is deeply involved in the translation of Biblical texts into new idioms and the hermeneutic process in general.

But let us start with its plain meaning before we get to its mystic meaning. Translation as a literary art is an ancient and complicated issue in biblical studies. Rabbi Simlai once quipped that translation is an impossible task: "He who translates is a heretic but he who refuses to translate is a blasphemer."

No book is more important to Western civilization than the Bible and no book has been more often or more self-consciously translated. In all its various editions and versions, it still outsells every other book. But the problems with understanding the Bible come from its very ubiquity. Everyone thinks that he or she understands it because powerful contemporary social institutions continually convince us of its relevance. Sermons in churches and synagogues are largely devoted to the argument that the Bible does and should apply directly to our lives. Editorials, literary works, advertisements and even cartoons remind us of the Bible's importance to our culture and society.

Yet the Bible is not really the book we think it is; it is, first of all, an anthology of little books (its name in Greek, *Ta Biblia*, literally means "the little books") stretching from approximately 1300 BCE (or BC) to the First Century of our era. If Genesis 12 be taken as the beginning of history in the Bible, then the book can be said to cover history from about the Eighteenth Century BCE. If the creation is taken as its starting point, then we go back a fictional 5759 years, more or less. In short, the Bible is a very strange and exotic book that does not share many of our moral and cultural assumptions directly. Scholarship has been able to isolate the time and reasons for some of the contents of the Bible, demonstrating that it was written over a much shorter period than it claims, though still a long time by historical reckoning.

To scholars, the Bible is hardly a unity in either composition or purpose. Rather, being an anthology, it has editors, who have made a selection about what the collection should contain and occasionally supplied hints about their varying and sometimes contradictory principles of composition and goals. So our notion that it applies to us and has a message for us is the result of a constant process of hermeneutics, meaning *interpretation* or figuratively, interpretative "retranslation." Without this constant process of translation and hermeneutics, the Bible would seem to us a very strange and unusual work, but this merely underlines the remarkable success of the process. Translation or the hermeneutic process generally gives us the impression of the Bible's timeliness, an illusion purchased at the expense of historical accuracy. But it is an illusion that has gone on since the Bible was assembled and it is an illusion that has a decent future in front of it.

Thus, the passage of time itself naturally raises the issue of translation and hermeneutics for any scriptural community. This process can be exemplified within the Bible itself as well as in all the important translations of the Bible's text throughout the ages. Just as with the passage of time itself, as the language of the dominant power changed, new translations of the Bible's text became necessary to allow the scriptural community access to it. The history of Bible translation itself shows us the constant need of translation. As history progressed, Israel fell under the domination of the Babylonians, the Persians, the Greeks, and the Romans. These empires ruled Palestine through Aramaic and then Greek mostly, leaving Latin only for later official correspondence. Translations of the Bible into Aramaic, called *Targums*, and a definitive translation into Greek, called the *Septuagint* (from the word "70" in Latin, hence abbreviated LXX and really a series of different texts too) was used in the Jewish community by the Third Century BCE. The Vulgate, a Latin translation of the LXX, became the Scripture of Western European Christianity until the Reformation.

The purpose of these translations was to render clearly passages that seemed obscure to a community whose tongue had evolved – first to a new dialect, then to a new language and finally to a new language family, though in the land of Israel there is evidence that educated people spoke all three. Innovations too were often hidden in the translation, innovations sometimes great enough to call forth a new divine revelation for justification.

For instance, the Greek-speaking Jewish community of Alexandria in Hellenistic Egypt could not understand the Hebrew of the original document, so "septuagints" were in use there even before this famous story of its composition circulated: According to legend, Ptolemy Philadelphos, successor to the Pharaohs and descendant of Alexander the Great's general, wanted to know the seemingly secret truths of the Jews. He therefore commissioned a school of advanced studies on Pharos Island in the Nile delta, building 70 small offices to be filled with the most skilled translators. By a miracle they all came up with the same translation. For anyone who knows academia this miracle ranks with the creation of the world. It also justified the still suspect process of translation and, of course, the innovations in religious conceptions which were hidden inside the new document.[1]

Although contemporary biblical scholarship values the skill and consistency of the translations of the Targums and the LXXs as important witnesses to ancient understanding of the Bible's refractory text, the ancient translations are at best tricky tools. Neither the Septuagints nor the Targums are notably literal in their rendering of Hebrew syntax or concepts. The Targums could be quite literal, since Aramaic is grammatically and lexically close to Hebrew, often making simple word-for-word translation feasible. Even so, the *meturgemans* often produced rather long elaborations, presumably as the result of their sensitivity to something in the ancient text. Many targumic passages resemble *midrash* as much as translation; the *meturgemans* noticeably even introduced technical names for God's hypostases into the text to avoid saying anything which might seem primitive or uncomplimentary about God.

The Septuagint was in some ways a more controlled translation but in other ways it was equally a commentary. Philo Judaeus, a wealthy and important Alexandrian Jewish Bible commentator of the First Century, posited that in commenting one must guard against saying anything unworthy of God. He could certainly have derived that rule from studying the Septuagint, had he known enough Hebrew to compare the two. He also said that everything in the Bible could be understood allegorically but only some things could be understood literally – a rather modern hermeneutic strategy.

The writers of the LXX allowed themselves less freedom than Philo allotted to himself. But Philo's work shows us something else important – how the translation was accepted and used and with what freedom the translation could be taken. And there is no doubt that the LXX was also a profound reinterpretation of the meaning of the Hebrew text. Difficult or primitive notions, especially anthropomorphisms and anthropopathisms, were often rendered in more abstract form – though not entirely, preventing easy generalizations about the LXX's theory of translation. Various important ways of dealing with God's attributes or appearances or physical shape were developed. Orthographic conventions in some LXX versions seem to be based on the Palestinian custom of not pronouncing God's name.

Philo's allegorical theory remained the dominant method for interpreting scripture in the West and certainly helped explain how his, Maimonides', and even Aquinas' *summae* could be couched as biblical commentaries. With this flimsy justification, we can skip to the Reformation when a more literal school of biblical translation came into vogue. If Scripture were going to be the only authority and the believer the ultimate judge, then Scripture would have to be provided in a form that every believer could immediately apprehend. Of course, this process stimulated and then was furthered by the development of "scientific" or disinterested criticism of the Bible. Most contemporary Bible translations are as slavishly literal as the two languages will allow. For a while, especially in Departments of Near Eastern Studies around the world, comparative Semitics and intense word studies were considered the basic method for removing dogmatic, doctrinal, and denominational biases. In our postmodern world this seems naively optimistic.

It is in that context that I wish to bring you two different problems in translation – one quite short, the other very complex – in an attempt to point to some methodological issues. Of course, every aspect of Bible translation has been studied and reviewed thousands of times, so I will simplify wherever possible.

For instance, let us take the famous example of the Virgin Birth. This New Testament doctrine is proof-texted in Isaiah 7:14, as understood by the Vulgate, which translated the verse into Latin as: "A virgin shall conceive and bear a child . . ." (virgo concipiet et pariet filium).[2] But in Hebrew the "virgin" is merely a young woman (*'almah*), thus the Hebrew says only that a girl will conceive and bear a child. Although the Vulgate is clearly reflecting NT doctrine, it has some justification for its word choice because the *young woman* in Hebrew was already previously translated as *parthenos* in Greek, a word which usually but not always means *virgin* (like the Parthenon, the temple to the virgin Athena). Whether or not the virgin birth arose as a mistranslation, however, is a moot point. The translation of the Hebrew *'almah* by the LXX *parthenos* is not necessarily wrong; rather, the Greek translation provided the possibility for the development of a new meaning: The Greek translated *parthenos* for *'almah* and then the NT doctrine arose with the translation already in place, so it represents an opportunity for pinning on a new doctrine. Otherwise, the doctrine would have to be validated in other ways, for instance directly with a new prophetic revelation.

In going from the Jewish community to a gentile community (the vector being Hellenistic Judaism and then early Christian preaching), the meaning of the text changed radically to resonate in an environment where the sexual relations between gods and virgins signalled the birth of a hero. Indeed, in the Second Century, when the Christian community responded to the Jewish charge that the doctrine was based on a mistranslation, their focus was turned not to the translation itself but the force of the Hebrew. Why had the *Hebrew* text used *'almah*, a relatively rare term, in place of the ordinary *na'arah*, which clearly and unambiguously means young woman? Could it be that *'almah* meant virgin after all?[3]

That pattern is exemplary of many hermeneutical problems in scriptural religions: every significant translation problem also conceals an even more significant problem in changing cultural forms or religious ideas because so much can hinge on one verse of scripture. We shall return to this paradigm later.

Inspired Texts and Religiously Interpreted States of Consciousness, a Problem of Cultural Translation

The major problem which I want to bring up is how modern scholars and religious persons interpret and translate terms indicating religiously altered states of consciousness (RASC, for short) or religiously interpreted states of consciousness (RISC, for short).[4] The Bible often records that its texts were received by inspired prophecies of various kinds, including states of consciousness which are often suspiciously "abnormal" to moderns. Thus, RASC is often the description of the native actor, while RISC is a term which would satisfy any modern observer, whether granting the validity of the religious experience or not. Claims to religiously altered states of consciousness are an especially difficult question for modern religious exegetes who either want to show that their own religion is rational or, at least, want to explain religious phenomena in rational terms. In this respect many are miles behind the methodological sophistication achieved in Anthropology but, in fairness, textual scholars have more difficulty squeezing information out of refractory, haphazardly preserved, and often fragmentary ancient texts than field workers have squeezing out of unco-operative informants.

But I will try to show that RISC and RASC were not only very important in Hebrew thought but, like the legend of the LXX, they help us understand how change enters religious communities. For instance, it is impossible to understand how Christianity gained the authority to reevaluate scripture without beginning with the Christian notion of the presence of the Holy Spirit – the spirit of prophecy, if you will, but certainly often a RASC – within the early Christian community, justifying changes in translation and interpretation. Novel interpretations were legitimated by direct revelation, either from Jesus directly in the Gospels or from his disciples and apostles, often in RASC. Good examples would be Jesus' hard-line preaching about divorce (Mk 10:1–12, Matt 19:1–12, Jesus takes the authority to change the law himself) or Peter's vision that all food was suitable for Christian consumption (Acts 10:9–29, where Peter has an ecstatic vision).[5]

Any detailed notion of an afterlife had been banished for so long from biblical literature that when it appeared for the first time, in the prophecy of Daniel 12:2f, its belated presence required special revelatory authority:

> Many of those who sleep in the dust of the earth* shall awake, some to everlasting life, and some to shame and everlasting contempt. Those who are wise shall shine like the brightness of the sky,** and those who lead many to righteousness, like the stars forever and ever. (Daniel 12:2)

* or *the land of dust*
** or *dome*

This passage essentially outlines a novel idea, resurrection, which culminates in some of the leaders ("those who are wise") being transformed into angels, as the stars were conventionally understood as a kind of angel (See Judges 3:20 and Job 38:7). Resurrection and translation to heaven followed by astral immortality for some of the leaders entered Israelite thought together. Before this the dead were usually thought to go to *Sheol*, a place of darkness much like *Hades*. In fact, *Sheol* is very often parallel simply to "the grave" in Hebrew poetry.

Such a major change in a scripturally based religion takes a very special kind of justification. Daniel 7 represents the new dispensation as having arrived in revelatory dream visions, not the usual method for the literary prophets, but certainly well known as a medium for God's Word, since the story of Joseph. Daniel thus needs a new revelation to promulgate his new ideas: "In the first year of Belshaz'zar king of Babylon, Daniel had a dream and visions of his head as he lay in his bed. Then he wrote down the dream, and told the sum of the matter" (Daniel 7:1).

I take this to be an example of a religiously interpreted state of consciousness (RISC), as dreams are being used to justify the revelatory nature of the information gained. Like the ancient world, we certainly grant that ordinary people have dreams, though we would not usually grant them prophetic power. But the notion of resurrection needs an even greater justification. It is revealed not in a dream but in an ecstatic vision (hayyπι niRdam), a religiously altered state of consciousness (RASC):

> At that time I, Daniel, had been mourning for three weeks. I had eaten no rich food, no meat or wine had entered my mouth, and I had not anointed myself at all, for the full three weeks. On the twenty-fourth day of the first month, as I was standing on the bank of the great river (that is, the Tigris), I looked up and saw a man clothed in linen, with a belt of gold from Uphaz around his waist. His body was like beryl, his face like lightning, his eyes like flaming torches, his arms and legs like the gleam of burnished bronze, and the sound of his words like the roar of a multitude. I, Daniel, alone saw the vision; the people who were with me did not see the vision, though a great trembling fell upon them, and they fled and hid themselves. So I was left alone to see this great vision. My strength left me, and my complexion grew deathly pale, and I retained no strength. Then I heard the sound of his words; and when I heard the sound of his words, *I fell into a trance* [italics added], face to the ground. But then a hand touched me and roused me to my hands and knees. (Daniel 10:2–10)

This experience is like the previous dream in that it is being interpreted as a religious experience but it is clearly a higher and more potent form of religious experience in the opinion of the narrator. From my perspective then, the apocalyptic literature of the first centuries BCE and CE (or BC and AD) may credibly be understood as having developed out of real visions (RASCs) and dreams (RISCs), which provide the basic authority and justification for the innovation, even though some modern religious skeptics might doubt the reality of the experience and modern religionists might want to translate the religious experience into more rational terms that can be more readily accepted by a modern religious audience.

Although Daniel and most subsequent apocalypses describe a variety of revelatory experiences, I will show that some believing Jews and Christians and many modern scholars have remained skeptical about their revelatory content. For the faithful, apocalyptic truths can be doubted because many apocalyptic books are not part of the canon. Then too, since many Americans prefer their religion rational, Paul and the prophets are often more comfortably treated as social critics and theologians rather than as ecstatic preachers and visionaries. The biggest differences in American religions today are to be found between the liberal and mainline denominations on the one hand and the evangelicals, conservatives, and fundamentalists on the other, not between Protestants, Catholics, and Jews. Belief in a literal resurrection is one of the most obvious and clear indicators of that gulf: liberal and mainline denominations do not take the ancient ideas literally while the conservative, evangelical, and fundamentalist groups do. This applies equally to Protestants, Catholics, and Jews (Gallup and Proctor 1982; Gullup and Castelli 1989).

But scholars also have scholarly and well-documented reasons for their skepticism of these revelations. Like Daniel, the vast majority of the apocalyptic documents are pseudonymously attributed to patriarchal and antediluvian biblical heroes. Since we know that the attribution to Daniel, Adam, Abraham, Ezra and the rest must be spurious, it is natural to suspect that the experience narrated in them is equally spurious.[6] And certainly few modern scholars would admit that the seers actually took trips to heaven, as the texts maintain.

The History of the Study of Biblical RISC and "Jewish Mysticism"

Although Gershom Scholem, who virtually invented the field of Jewish mysticism as an object of study, certainly believed that there was a continuous tradition of RASC and RISC in Judaism, he never adequately described what he meant by "mysticism."[7] This left room for scholars of Judaism of a more rational persuasion to demur. For instance, Ephraim Urbach, in a famous article in the Scholem *Festschrift*, questioned whether the texts themselves claimed actual mystical experience (Urbach 1967). He suggested that especially the talmudic texts had no original mystical content and that the rabbis themselves practiced no more than "ascetic ecstasy" (whatever that may mean). Peter Schäfer, writing on the later *hekhaloth* ("Palaces") material in Jewish, Merkabah mysticism, suggested that the basic early mystical texts are considerably younger in their present form than Scholem thought and contain little visionary material. (Schäfer 1981, 1984, 1991).

David Halperin's *The Faces of the Chariot* (1988; see also his 1980) makes innumerable new and very fine points about the development of the tradition of the Merkabah (mrkbh), the throne chariot which Ezekiel saw (Ez 1) and which carried a figure which the text calls "the Glory of the Lord" (Ez 1:26). However, he remains unreceptive to the notion that there was any religious experience present in these texts. He begins by narrating a conversation between him and his teacher Isadore Rabinowitz, in which he decides to begin the project of the book by distinguishing between the "true" and "false" exegeses of Ezekiel 1.[8]

Every scholar right now must begin with a critique of Gershom Scholem, the one scholar who perspicaciously noticed a continuous mystical tradition in Judaism – all the more remarkable as modern Jews overwhelmingly wanted to present Judaism as a rational religion based on a revealed law, indeed *more* rational than Christianity. Halperin criticized Scholem for thinking that the texts could have any valid religious experience. They were a kind of faulty exegesis or even hallucination:

> Scholem's stress on the reality of the *Merkabah* mystics' ecstatic experiences can be misleading. He did not, of course, mean that they "really" ascended to heaven, but that they "really" believed that they had done so. But it is easy to slip from this into the illusion that we can explain the ascension materials in the apocalypses and the *Hekhalot* by pointing to the supposed reality of the experience underlying them; whereas, of course, this hallucinatory "experience" itself cries out for explanation. This fallacy seems to me to dog much of Scholem's presentation. (p. 7)

In spite of Halperin's many accomplishments in this book, on this fundamental issue Scholem's position is the more rational. The forced choice between *hallucination* and *exegesis* is fallacious. Events experienced as real do have real consequences for the people experiencing them, even if they are influenced by exegesis and even if they seem to us "hallucinations" because they recount events which we assume to be impossible or which take place only "internally."

Martha Himmelfarb's research is also characteristic of the reaction to Scholem's valorization of the ecstatic dimension of Jewish mysticism. In her relatively recent book, *Ascent to Heaven in Jewish and Christian Apocalypses* (1993), she follows David Halperin's and Peter Schäfer's skepticism of actual visionary experience in the hekhaloth texts. But she takes this scepticism about RASC backward in time to the Jewish and Christian apocalypses of the first few centuries. Though she admits the widespread presence and valorization of visionary experience in Hellenistic culture in general and in Philo Judaeus, she eliminates any of these texts from consideration because they are mystical texts or philosophical treatises and not Jewish or Christian *apocalypses*. She further restricts her purview only to those texts which explicitly discuss ascent, eliminating many apocalypses where ecstasy is claimed and the contents of the heavens or divine plans for history are discussed without an explicit ascent narrative. In the process she eliminates a good many valuable examples of RISC or RASC experience from consideration. She then maintains that wherever the texts say that the seer is having a religious experience, we should read the text as merely conforming to a literary convention. There is no religious experience in the texts at all:

> No need for the mystic to ascend, for telling the story is enough. The actual performance of the acts is attributed to a mystic past, the era of the great rabbis of the Mishnah; recitation itself has become the ritual.
>
> No such claim can be made for the ascent apocalypses [*I. e.* no claim for actual religious ritual or ascent]. Reading them was not a ritual act. Their stories performed no task, and they effected nothing outside the mind of the reader, which is where stories always perform their work. If I read them correctly, their most important accomplishment was to suggest an understanding of human possibility, of the status of the righteous in the universe, that goes beyond anything found in the Bible and was profoundly appealing to ancient Jews and Christians. In the midst of an often unsatisfactory daily life, they taught their readers to imagine themselves like Enoch, like the glorious ones, with no apparent difference. (p. 114)[9]

This position thoroughly confuses the experience of the creators of the text with that of the readers. For Himmelfarb, the early apocalypses were merely literary creations, the purpose of which was to give solace to a demoralized community. The readers of the texts did not even use them to ascend vicariously to the heavens through the process of reading. This hypothesis, for it is only an hypothesis, needs to be carefully considered and, I think, rejected soundly. Himmelfarb's position is not naive rationalism. Even the exceptionally well-reasoned book of Moshe Idel, *Kabbalah: New Perspectives* (1989) which forcefully demonstrates that meditative experiences were regularly sought by Jewish mystics, was unable to dissuade her.

In place of religious experience, Himmelfarb suggests we talk only about a *literary motif* of "rapture," which is a slippery category. She uses this term because she wishes to emphasize that the heavenly journey comes unbidden, not by mystical praxis, and is not in any way under the control of the mystagogue. But this term itself is confusing because "rapture" is the same term that especially Christian fundamentalists use to describe the salvation of the just at the apocalypse, based on 1 Thessalonians 4:13f and 2 Thessalonians 2. Her dismissal of ecstasy, based on the notion that the ascent can be explained in the apocalypses purely in a literary way, therefore as a totally literary motif and not mystical, is to my way of thinking incorrect in a number of ways, which I will try to correct as we go along. To begin with, her conception is rather similar to thinking that the Virgin Birth is purely a translation problem and reflects no social realities in Hellenistic Judaism and the early Church.

We must be clear about something very fundamental: we cannot ever know the experience of another directly. We live in a world where we cannot actually be sure that we all experience the color red in the same way. How much more so in the case of experience narrated in text. The question is not what the experience is in itself. The question is really that of what is being claimed for the experience and of how the claims are validated and competing claims adjudicated.

The question which Himmelfarb asks therefore boils down to one of religious authenticity: are they religious texts or are they frauds, historical novels pretending to be the actual religious experience of prophets in the way that Defoe's *Robinson Crusoe* pretends to be the journal entries of a shipwrecked sailor? Is there any religious experience behind the texts or are they merely novels, fraudulently purporting to be from the ancient personages to whom they are ascribed? Can the scholar imagine that these experiences were legitimate and authentic, even if they presuppose journeys which are literally impossible?

At first, the whole question seems inappropriate. All we have are the texts. We cannot automatically move from written word to the narrator's state of mind. The sincerity of any historical writer is extremely hard if not impossible to evaluate without more extra-literary evidence. We can sense irony, for example, in a novel or poem, but without knowing some things about the writer it is often very hard to specify what kind of irony it is. Authenticity is very similar. Nor can we question an actual adept as we might in contemporary fieldwork. Yet, one cannot merely doubt the religious value of a text because of modern skepticism about the possibility of ascending to heaven as is so often reported in ancient Jewish texts. To do so we must equally doubt all ancient texts, even the ones which Himmelfarb accepts as revelatory.

Pseudonymity and Fraud in RISC

We must, first of all, develop a little more sophistication in dealing with the question of pseudonymity and authenticity. Categories of authenticity are seldom simple. Pseudonymous authorship does not automatically disqualify the work from being religious or accurate or real experience and certainly does not render a text useless. Because of Scholem, we know that the *Zohar* was written in Spain in the Thirteenth Century by Moses of León and his circle, not in Palestine in the Second Century by Rabbi Simon bar Yohai and *his* circle. That does not mean that it is not important for understanding the religiosity of the Thirteenth Century. It does not immediately relegate the writing to fraud and fiction – even in the way that, say, Carlos Castaneda's books are now regarded.[10]

Lévi-Strauss, in his famous seminal essay "the Sorcerer and his Magic" (1983), narrated the case of a sorcerer who candidly admitted to tricking the audience. Yet, even in this case, the sorcerer felt that the tricks improved the effectiveness of the cure because some patients were healed. In other words, the perpetrator of a fraud can still think that his healings or visions are valid. Furthermore, there is a clear process of socialization where the practitioner comes to learn what is expected of him or her by the guild and the populace. (Ripinsky-Naxon 1993). During the process, the practitioner can have a wide variety of cognitions, both consonant and dissonant, about the relationship between technique, sincerity, and effectiveness. But usually the practitioner in the end learns to think of his or her contribution as sincere if the role played is highly regarded in the society.

On the other hand, anthropological literature is full of examples of the ways cultures can distinguish between effectiveness and sincerity of ecstatics and healers. People in many traditional societies are quite sophisticated in discovering feigned possession and insanity. The rules and clues within the society differ, depending on whether possession or trance is expected of revelations and, alternatively, the decisions may be entirely due to social processes. In other words, most often these judgments are due to the social position of the actors in the situation; they are perspectival within the society.[11] All of these issues seem to say that religious experiences can be faked easily and frequently by people wishing to claim the charismatic authority that comes from revelation. On the other hand, it also suggests that the qualifications for real vision do not entirely depend on what the subject intends at the time. People learn what is expected of certain roles, and also people do have unbidden RASCs not under their conscious control, especially in societies and cultures where such events are expected.

RISC in Ancient Hebrew Culture

Neither ecstasy nor possession nor the techniques to achieve it were foreign to Israel, although there were some strict conventions about conceptualizing them. But since RASC has been disputed in Israelite culture, a brief history is in order. RASC and RISC were regular features of pre-literary Israelite prophetic culture. God's Word could come to prophets through a variety of paranormal means – mostly through dreams and auditions, but also in waking visions. The earliest prophets in Israelite history, the pre-literary prophets, of which Nathan, Elijah, and Elisha are merely the most famous, could receive messages from God by paranormal means. In 1 Kings 22 Micaiah ben Imlah, a lesser-known but very important prophet, describes a complete scene in the heavenly throne room which he saw through prophetic vision. The conclusion of the deliberation is that God appoints a spirit to mislead all his legitimate prophets so as to ensnare Ahab into attacking Ramoth Gilead, where he will die (1 Kings 22:19–23).[12] In this narrative RASC is described among the bands of prophets who were Micaiah's rivals as well, and we see an explosively subversive notion that God can deliberately mislead some of His prophets to effect His own designs.

Ecstatic behavior was also sometimes criticized, at least for potential rulers. Saul and David were both criticized for dancing amid the prophets. So notions of role differentiation were evolving even in the earliest period of Israelite culture. And these defined roles were by no means unique among Ancient Near Eastern cultures. There are ample precedents for the role of these religiously altered states of consciousness in the neighboring cultures of the ancient Near East. Indeed, Israelite culture was parochial and rural by comparison to the civilized conventions in the great river valleys.[13]

Bible scholars sharply diverge on the role of RISC in the formation of literary prophecy (those prophets who left us books). It is not known whether or how these related experiences correspond to the literary prophetic books in the canon, because they are universally admired as great literary creations and it is hard to know how trance, ecstasy, and literary creation went together for Israelite prophets. We cannot even be sure that they all used the same techniques. The evidence, in fact, suggests a variety of different techniques. Though we know that dancing and wild antics were sometimes reported of prophetic guild members, we cannot be sure precisely whether trance and possession was characteristic of all the prophets and, if so, what kinds of trance and possession were found among them, since there are equally a wide variety of behaviors and consciousnesses describable by trance or ecstasy. The only thing we can say for sure is that the Spirit of the Lord continues to possess the literary prophets and gives them legitimacy. Indeed, if anything, our knowledge of the vocabulary of RISC is greatly aided by the literary prophets. I think it would be unwise merely to dismiss this evidence as a mere idiom.

Daniel and Apocalyptic Writings

Apocalypticism is a literary form in which the writer *reveals* (the Greek verb *apokalypto* means "I uncover") heavenly secrets, usually concerning the operation of the universe and final disposition of the righteous and sinners and the end of time. It seems to start as prophecy is waning and continues the literary traditions which are found in prophecy. For instance, both terms, *appearance* and *image*, are technical terms expressing human resemblance to God and God's ability to appear as a human, but they also function as indicators of RASC in prophecy. We see the same conventions three centuries later in the book of Daniel, the most obvious apocalyptic book in the Bible. In Daniel 7, we remember that we are explicitly being told about a RISC. The scene is a dream vision (Dan. 7:2) and the preposition "*k*" ("like" or "as") makes clear that the experience is understood to be unusual and paranormal. The scene is actually God's heavenly throne-room with two manlike figures, one an "Ancient of Days" and the second a "son of man" (*bar enash*, in biblical Aramaic and in the post-biblical dialect *barnasha*). *Son of man* is not a title and can only mean the divine figure has a human form because the phrase "son of man" usually means simply *a human being* in most Semitic languages. The exact phrase in Daniel is "one *like* a son of man" (*kbar 'enash*), signifying that the next figure in the vision was shaped *like* a man and reminding us that this is not Daniel's usual consciousness.

The best guess as to the identity of the figure shaped like a man is that he is simply the Glory of the Lord, the *Kavod YHWH,* the principal human manifestation of God – an angel if you will, in whose form God deigns to appear, for some angels were envisioned in human form. At his second appearance, Gabriel is described as "the man Gabriel whom I had seen in the vision at first" (9:21). In Daniel 10:5 "a man clothed in linen," probably an angel, is described in a way reminiscent of Ezekiel's description of God's glory. Again in Daniel 10:16, Daniel sees a human figure, probably as before, an angel "shaped in the likeness of a man" (*kdemuth bnei adam*).

All this would be conventional except for one thing: there are two different manifestations of God, one old ("The Ancient of Days") and the other young ("the son of man"). God appearing in two different forms at once is very puzzling and it clearly innovates in a very daring way on the notion that God can appear as human or not, since it suggests that there may be more than one divinity. Behind this passage is originally a Canaanite mythologem describing El's enthronement of his son Ba'al but no one knows how it has become a "kosher" vision.[14] It is hard to imagine that anything other than a "prophetic dream" would have made this heretical scene possible!

The Daniel passage is based upon the Ezekiel passage but no one would say that it is simple exegesis. No exegete would have spelled out such a heretical implication. The prophet stays on earth in his bed but at the same time he is translated to heaven at the same time as he translates the Ezekiel passage into more personal experience. Somehow the experience of the later prophet, writing under the pseudonym of Daniel, is being translated and conditioned by the writings of Ezekiel. At the same time the prophet incorporates all kinds of new experience including the Canaanite mythological image into his scene. If this is not a vision then it ought to be. It cannot be merely exegesis of the Ezekiel passage because there is so much manifestly new material in it, quite unique in the biblical canon in fact. In fact, in such a traditional culture no one could make up such a heretical scene as two divinities who are one without relying on some divine sanction. Novelistic imagination could not have done the trick for the ancients. So a reflection of real experience is quite obvious. The big question is: "What kind of experience is it?"

Well, it's a dream vision; the text tells us that. The hypothesis that we have a transcript of the dream-vision – with the attendant *caveat* that all discursive language implies some interpretation – is the best explanation for the event. We have no way of knowing how many changes may have entered the text before it is witnessed in the archeological record. But from early texts that we do have, we know that biblical text thought to contain the Word of God was transcribed very conservatively.

Christopher Rowland (1982: 217f.) describes the way in which apocalyptic material relates to its biblical past. He notes, for instance in 4 Ezra 12:11, that the man (*vir perfectus*) who rises from the sea is an allusion to Daniel 7 and, most especially, verse 13, which describes the "son of man," who comes with the clouds of heaven. However, allusions to figures rising from the sea come from earlier in the chapter, where the beasts are said to arise from the sea. This kind of mélange of images is not the result of exegesis, indeed it is totally anathema to any educated Hebrew exegesis, but actually the result of meditation on the whole chapter, reorganized through RISC: "It is most unlikely that a careful interpreter of Daniel 7 would have linked the divine envoy with the home of the beasts and thereby deliberately linked the divine with the demonic in the way in which we find it in this chapter" (p. 218). Now, the specific details of the vision in 4 Ezra are brought about, according to the text, not just by dream visions but induced by fasting and mourning. But the characteristics of the text remain the same. They do not comment on the text and produce a commentary. They seemingly combine the images at will and come up with a detailed new narrative which uses the fragmentary images of the Bible to forge a new story of consolation, one that is beholden to RASC.

Even more obvious is the relationship between the various ascent texts in Enoch and their biblical forebears. Many of the traditions found in the Enoch cycle are excellent examples. The ascent texts appear to flesh out various biblical texts into a vision of heavenly reward and punishment. Thus, we are constantly given the details of Daniel 12 spelled out in many ways. The good are rewarded and the evil punished. We see the leaders rewarded with heavenly immortality as stars and the very worst of the sinners punished for having persecuted the righteous. A very interesting relationship between biblical texts and those found in Enoch is formed by the elements from chapter 1 of Ezekiel and Isaiah 6. The theophany in 1 Enoch 14:8ff is clearly related to the theophany in Ezekiel, but there are very few precise contacts. Apart from the reference to the throne which is just as much influenced by Isaiah 6:1 (see 1 Enoch 14:18, "a lofty throne") the frequent mention of fire and certain key words like "lightning" and "crystal," as well as the reference to the wheels of the merkabah (14:18), there are very few actual contacts. But the chapters from Ezekiel and Isaiah are clearly informing the Enoch texts. Of course, we must not completely deny the idea that somewhere along the line, a literary copyist glossed some of the biblical material. But the most obvious way to describe the relationships between the two sets of texts is that the biblical quotations were read and understood by people who studied them carefully and then they became parts of the dreams and visions which they experienced. The reading is the process by which the seer assimilates details of the text into memory, which makes them available later as the bits of experience out of which the ascensions are formulated.

So I am saying that Jews of the First Centuries BCE and CE, like in all preceding and succeeding centuries, took RASC very seriously.[15] They also certainly valued ecstasy or trance as a medium for revelation and developed techniques for signaling that ecstasy or trance was occurring. (see Saake 1973; Benz 1952). Strangely enough, the same language also seemed to the ancients to suggest something very deep and mystical about the way in which humans resembled God and conversely how God could be figured in human form. These beliefs pervaded Jewish culture as well and enriched Jewish spirituality. As we have seen, in the Hellenistic period, these terms rightly became associated with the language of translation in two senses – in the translation of the texts and also in the sense of ascent, ascension, or theurgy, the magic use of shamanic techniques to stimulate these "out-of-body" experiences. This vocabulary in Greek was known to Paul and became a central aspect of Paul's explanation of the Christian message (Kim 1984: 214).

Jewish Mysticism as Continuous with Prophecy and Apocalypticism

In Jewish mysticism, the so-called *Shiur Koma Literature* (vy[wr qwmh, "Measure of the Stature," meaning speculation on the measurements of the divine stature of God) gives the exact measurements of each organ and appendage of God's angelic human manifestation, in mantra-like phrases which are evidently meant to promote contemplation and trance – like the songs, spells, and charms of the *hekhaloth* ("Palaces") literature.

One stated purpose of Merkabah mysticism, as it is outlined in the hekhaloth texts, is to "see the King in His beauty" (Grünwald 1980: 156, 193 n. 4). In the Ninth Century, Hai Gaon recounts that the journey to view this divine figure was undertaken by mystics who put their heads between their knees (the posture Elijah assumed when praying for rain in 1 Kings 18:42),[16] while reciting repetitious psalms, glossolalic incantations, and mantralike prayers, which are recorded in abundance in the hekhaloth literature:

> When one seeks to behold the Merkabah and the palaces of the angels on high, one must follow a certain procedure. One must fast a number of days and place one's head between one's knees and whisper many hymns and songs whose texts are known from tradition. Then one perceives the chambers as if one saw the seven palaces with his own eyes, and it is as though one entered one palace after another and saw what is there. And there are two *mishnayoth* which the tannaim taught regarding this topic, called *Hekhaloth Rabbati* and *Hekhaloth Zutreti*.

Luckily, texts called *Hekhaloth Rabbati* and *Hekhaloth Zutreti* have survived. Even if they now contain some further additions, they also contain instructions on how to perform the ritual that Hai Gaon relates. Clearly, these are RASC techniques and are recognized by the Gaon to be such. We know that the adept is on earth but that he travels through the heavenly palace – as it turns out, to visit God's Vice-regent, the human figure on the throne, who partakes of the divine name YHWH in a mystical way, details which we learn from the texts themselves. The "palaces" appear to be alternative names for the heavenly spheres (Morray-Jones 2002, *contra* Scholem). The Gaon is aware of the mystical techniques for heavenly ascent and describes them as "out-of-body" experiences where the adept ascends to heaven while his body stays on earth. This does not happen without some form of RASC. But note that even at this late date the language which conveys the RASC is the description of the ascent itself.

The question which most intrigues me is how to judge the issue of consciousness in the ancient texts of the Hellenistic world. By the Second Temple period, historical prophecy was in the eyes of the central authorities either a phenomenon of the distant past or the eschatological future (see Aune 1983: 81–152). But that is precisely what makes it so important to the understanding of the sect that produced Daniel or the early Christians. They felt that the end of time was upon them and therefore it was expected that prophets would again speak. Such an important doctrine as life after death for the righteous (and especially the martyrs), in the form of resurrection and translation to the heavenly realm where angelic transformation was effected, was not merely discussed as a philosophical option. Nothing in Hebrew thought could be exegeted to find such a doctrine. It was a ferocious revelation of vengeance against the enemies of God and eternal happiness for the martyred saints, a revelation which arrived through the media of dreams and visions to a nameless seer whom we know only as Daniel in approximately 165 BCE. Ecstatic experience was present in biblical prophecy; it was present in the Hellenistic world; and, as we have just seen, it was sought with consciously articulated techniques in Jewish mysticism thereafter as late as the Ninth Century. The easiest hypothesis is that it was present in the Jewish and Christian apocalypses as well.

Elliot R. Wolfson's (1994) recent and quite sensitive book, on the Merkabah mysticism flatly rejects the excessive reductionism or a literary fiction. It takes issue with Halperin, Himmelfarb, and Schäfer on the issue of the reality of the experience:

Bearing the inherently symbolic nature of the visionary experience in mind, we can now set out to answer another question that has been posed by scholars with regard to the visionary component of this literature. Did the Merkabah mystics actually ascend to the celestial realm and did they see something "out there," or should these visions be read as psychological accounts of what may be considered in Freudian language a type of self-hypnosis? Or, to suggest yet a third alternative, would it perhaps be most accurate to describe the heavenly journey in Jungian terms, as a descent into and discovery of the archetypal self?

From a straightforward reading of the extant sources it would appear that some texts assume a bodily ascent, a translation into the heavenly realm of the whole person with all the sensory faculties intact, whereas others assume an ascent of the soul or mind separated from the body as the result of a paranormal experience such as a trance-induced state. But even in the case of the latter explanation, typified most strikingly in *Hekhalot Rabbati* in the story concerning the recall of R. Nehuniah ben Ha-Qanah from his ecstatic trance, it is evident that the physical states are experienced in terms of tactile and kinesthetic gestures and functions appropriate to the body, such as the fiery gyrations of the eyeballs, ascending and descending, entering and exiting, standing and sitting, singing and uttering hymns, looking and hearing (p. 108–109).

Wolfson must be correct in thinking that the experience has some salutary component for the mystic or it would not have been recounted and retold. He expresses this importance with Jungian terms, which I would not want to defend for long. Jung suggests that these images are in various ways part of the fundamental psychological processes of human beings and aid in our ability to successfully individuate and mature. I would certainly agree that they are normal occurences and can be significant, meaningful, and salutary to human life in cultures that value them, as we shall see below.

In fact, the apostle Paul gives us sure and certain evidence that First Century Jews were receiving revelation through RASC. Paul here tells us that he knows someone who has had both revelations (*apokalypseis*) and visions (*optasiai*): the problem for Paul is not to decide whether this heavenly journey was sane but rather whether it took place inside or outside of the body:

> I must boast; there is nothing to be gained by it, but I will go on to visions and revelations of the Lord. I know a man in Christ who fourteen years ago was caught up to the third heaven – whether in the body or out of the body I do not know, God knows; and I know that this man was caught up into Paradise – whether in the body or out of the body I do not know, God knows – and he heard things that cannot be told, which man may not utter. (2 Corinthinians 12:1–4)

Whether Paul is describing his own or someone else's experience, we know that someone in the First Century is having this experience. The vast majority of scholarship thinks that Paul is describing himself.[17] What is more important is that Paul is flatly stumped by the mechanism. He will not risk a guess as to whether this ascent was "in the body" or "out of the body." Second Corinthians therefore suggests – at the very least – that Paul has not entirely adopted the Platonic notion of the immortal soul – *psyche*. Had he done so, he could not have allowed the possibility that a body could ascend to heaven and he would have had soul flight as a ready-made for the mechanism of the journey.

Soul flight is the explanation of the aforementioned description of Rabbi Hai Gaon, especially when supplemented by the famous passage in *Hekhaloth Rabbati* where a rabbinic adept, Nehuniah ben Hakkanah, is described as sitting on a pure marble slab traveling in heaven explicitly in a RASC while describing the sights to an assembled group of rabbis sitting on earth and listening in ordinary consciousness. It is reminiscent of taking testimony in a courtroom. Nehuniah is recalled for further questioning when he says something puzzling and then is sent back into his trance to finish his journey. So the trance and the trip to heaven are entirely parallel. When they wish to recall him they touch him in a such a way as to give him the slightest bit of cultic impurity. But it is clear from the context that his body is on earth, so the language of ascent is functioning to express the RASC. No doubt this is a fictionalized account but exactly how much of it is augmented by literary imagination cannot be discussed here.[18]

Thus, the issue of consciousness and the evaluation of various mental states is an iceberg underlying both the ancient texts and much of the scholarly discussion as well.[19] Implicit within the judgments of the modern scholars are a number of assumptions about what kinds of consciousness are appropriate or sane. Because modern commentaries are suffused with the scholar's own interpretation of the value or possibility of these experiences, it is very difficult to reach some scholarly disinterestedness about what is happening in these heavenly translations. Suffice it to say, following most modern anthropologists and social scientists, it is important to realize that all these terms are being mediated by modern social norms as well as ancient ones.

Brain Functioning, Normality, and RISCs

In his recent book on zen and brain functioning, James H. Austin relates various zen states to perfectly normal or trainable aspects of brain activity. In one interesting place, he narrates a vision which came to him in Zen meditation and which deeply impressed him in clarity and lucidity. As a neurologist and experimental physician, he can suggest how his experiences relate to various functions in the brain, miraculous as it appeared to him; on the other hand, to his immense disappointment, his visions were denigrated by his Zen Roshi as undesirable snares to his further enlightenment. One can easily see that in other mystical traditions and societies these visions would have been one of the highest goals of consciousness (Austin 1998: 469–80).

Indeed, there has been a great deal of research of late on the various neurological bases of religious and other anomalous experiences (Persinger 1987; Cardeña et al. 2000; Newberg et al. 2001). These books demonstrate that perfectly normally functioning brains can spontaneously or by various techniques be stimulated to have anomalous and other religious experiences. These experiences are quite different from the hallucinations that produce permanent mental illness, derangement, and random acts of violence, although they are alike in that they all have an etiology in unusual functioning of our brain. For instance, all the scientists report that religious feelings of leaving the body and being at one with the universe correlate quite fully with quieting the proprioceptive processing areas in the parietal lobes of our brain. This center controls our feelings of where we are in space, and when that center is quiet subjects report that they no longer perceive their bodily location. Some people seem to be able to do this spontaneously; others achieve the state in meditation; others report the state after disease or trauma or under the effects of various drugs. Depending on the cultural context in which they live, this can be understood as being a heavenly journey, being at one with the universe, being one with Brahma perceiving the state of no duality. Obviously, the intellectual scheme used for expressing this state will depend on the cultural assumptions of the subject. In the 1970s and 1980s Huston Smith discussed the prospect that notions of the afterlife and the soul's immortality were developed out of these feelings which he experienced experimentally with LSD and psylocybin.[20] He quotes Mary Bernard, who asks: "Which was more likely to happen first: the spontaneously generated idea of an afterlife in which the disembodied soul, liberated from the restrictions of time and space, experiences eternal bliss, or the accidental discovery of hallucinogenic plants that give a sense of euphoria, dislocate the center of consciousness, and distort time and space making them balloon outward in greatly expanded vistas?" (p. 47 note). If we make allowances for the fact that a variety of different stimuli can produce similar effects in ways we are just beginning to understand, then we have not so much a justification for the afterlife as an explanation for why the afterlife was located at the end of a heavenly journey. The physical experience and the culture cooperate to produce various experiences which we find impossible to verify from the perspective of our cultural norms. Nevertheless, they were real and important and quite normal for those who experienced them. Heavenly journey has a correlative in the functioning of the brain. *Translation* is the process of finding words for the experience in the brain in the language which the culture provided. It takes translation to produce a translation. Exaltation in the mind produces the myth of exaltation.

The Heavenly Journey

Mary Dean-Otting, in her 1984 book *Heavenly Journeys*, displays in convenient form many of the motifs which appear in the heavenly journeys. Dean-Otting shows that the night vision motif is present in 1 Enoch 14, the Testament of Levi, 3 Baruch, the Apocalypse of Abraham, and 4 Ezra. One could easily add several other visions to the list. The notion that God communicates through dreams is part of the epic tradition in Israelite thought, being a special characteristic of the E source in the Pentateuch. Furthermore, the Book of Daniel is probably the source for the notion that revelation could be sought by incubating dreams. Dean-Otting herself does not shy from the conclusion that these are characteristics of mystical ascent in Hebrew thought.

Now, of course, dreams are a special case in human experience. We all have them, several times a night, but without special training we only remember a very few; indeed, the physiology of dreams suggests that they are not designed to be remembered, as the chemicals which the brain uses in the storing of memories are usually noticeably absent at dreamtime. We can stimulate that remembrance either directly by waking up during the dream and reciting or writing it down or by consciously or unconsciously making conditions which disturb sleep indirectly – such as by eating too much or little or by praying or otherwise predisposing the dream to be seen in a particular light. We can train ourselves to remember dreams, as well as direct them. Dreams are very much related to daily experience, both in content and emotional tone. Anyone who spent his or her time in careful exegesis of the texts which describe the heavens, the divine throneroom, and the journey there would likely dream about the same details. Lastly, oral reporting, correction and literary processes are always available after the fact to censor the dream, or to subject the dream experience to correction when it goes far from the expected details, in much the same way that people ordinarily re-edit their conversion experiences over time to bring them closer to expected norms within their community (see Segal 1988: App. 1, pp. 285–301).

A person who seeks out a dream and treats it as a revelation is relying on an ordinary reflex of human experience but is choosing to treat the experience as a non-normal state of consciousness and a divine message, in short, as a RISC. And since we cannot privilege any sort of experience in our modern world, that is all that we mean when we say that someone is receiving a dream vision (Proudfoot 1985). Usually in cultures that posit a non-normal state of consciousness for prophecy, dreams are also specially marked as having a divine origin (Miller 1994, esp. 3–123).

Furthermore, in 4 Ezra there are three famous other techniques – fasting, eating herbs of the field, and drinking a fiery liquid.[21] Fasting is clearly a well-understood technique for achieving RASC; in some sense it doesn't matter whether the culture chooses to mark the activity as directly related to the vision or merely as one of the preparations, like obtaining ritual purity. As a physical stimulus, fasting, like its opposite over-eating, which is specifically mentioned at the beginning of the *Poimandres*, can bring on vivid dreams and – in people with susceptible dispositions or training – trance and psychagogic states. While we do not know whether the plants eaten had any psychotropic or psychedelic properties, the description of the special diet may imply a specific agent and is, at the very least, a significant part of the fasting regime. It may be even more, since poppies, marijuana, and jimson weed, as well as other psychoactive plants and mushrooms, grow wild everywhere around the Mediterranean.

Let us see how the ascent theme works out in Hebrew culture and make some observations about this special kind of "shamanism." As early as Daniel, the theme of night visions becomes important. Daniel 7 announces itself as both a dream and a vision. This compares with the dream of Nebuchadnezzar in Daniel 2:1, 4:6–7 and the subsequent revelations which are called *visions* (*Hazon* 8:1, *ma'reh*, 10:1). Both are technical terms for RASC in prophetic literature. Also we can note that Daniel receives visions of his head on his bed, which he writes down. This seems like a definite technique of RASC together with the details for recording it, *pace* Himmelfarb. Indeed, it is precisely the kind of formulation one finds in the early parts of 1 Enoch:

> This is the book of the words or righteousness and the chastisement of the eternal watchers, in accordance with how the Holy and Great One had commanded in this vision. *I saw in my sleep what I now speak with my tongue of flesh* [italics added] and the breath of the mouth which the Great One has given to man (so that) he (man) may speak with it – and (so that) he may have understanding with his heart as he (the Great One) has created and given it to man. (1 Enoch 14:2–3)

This passage shows that Enoch too receives his ascent vision in his sleep and then communicates it afterward. In the Testament of Levi, the first vision is accomplished with a spirit of understanding. Later, sleep falls upon the seer, perhaps as in Genesis 28:12, and experiences a translation or ascent. In 3 Enoch, the seer begins in a scene of great mourning for the destruction of the temple. In the Apocalypse of Abraham, Genesis 15 provides the structure of the story, where "a deep sleep" falls upon Abraham. The apocalyptic narrator interprets this "deep sleep" as a waking vision:

> And it came to pass when I heard the voice pronouncing such words to me that I looked this way and that. And behold there was no breath of man. And my spirit was amazed, and my soul fled from me. And I became like a stone, and fell face down upon the earth, for there was no longer strength in me to stand upon the earth. And while I was still face down on the ground, I heard the voice speaking . . . (Apocalypse of Abraham 10).

Here, the apocalypticist has interpreted the Hebrew word *tardemah* in Genesis 15, usually translated as *deep sleep*, as purely a daytime trance.[22] His body is completely incapacitated but he sees the arrival of the angel and then uses the sacrificed birds to ascend. The implicit theory is not so much "rapture" as explicitly RASC or "ecstasy" in its technical sense (extasia = *ek* + *stasis* = "standing outside," or more colloquially, soul flight), as the narrator states that his soul "fled." He means this flight to signify a RASC, and he further characterizes the physical trauma with a description of a seizure, as in the *Arda Viraf Nameh*. It makes sense to think that terminology of ecstasy, dream vision, spirit possession, and soul flight are used interchangeably here to indicate that the experience was a RASC. This may be loosely called "shamanism" (Davila 1994, 2001), although it is not at all clear what this experience has in common with Central Asian shamanism, or how it could have traveled from its original home.[23]

Differences between RISC and Exegesis as discoverable in Texts

But, the point must be exceedingly clear by now: bidden or unbidden, ecstatic states of this type – RASCs – are common in biblical tradition. The lack of a specific description of a preparatory inducement, which was so strongly cited by Himmelfarb as an argument against its presence, is neither a fair reading of the evidence nor a bar to the presence of RASC: indeed, the lengthy keening or lamenting which precedes the vision in 4 Ezra may have already become the physical stimulus for inducing RASC, as it surely is in the later Jewish mysticism. None of these techniques invariably leads to RASC; but it may – under the proper circumstances, attitude, and context – especially when the state is fervently sought. Of course, in this context, the social interpretation of the experience is by far the most important indicator, not the physical stimulus.

Hymn singing should also be mentioned here as a technique for achieving RASC because hymns are frequently inserted into these narratives, either described as sung upon ascent, or given with the direction to be sung in mystical texts. In fact, repetitious hymn singing is the most important means of achieving the ascent in the merkabah texts. But the merkabah texts explicitly start the ascent by saying that a certain psalm, which is printed in full – is to be recited by the adept 112 times exactly. This corresponds to the experience which Hai Gaon narrates in the medieval period.

Himmelfarb accepts the burden of proof for comparison when she compares the visions of the First Century with an important Jewish mystic of the Seventeenth Century, Hayyim Vital (1542–1620). Vital is visited with a prophetic dream late one Sabbath eve, after weeping over his personal problems. Weeping and keening and mourning are quite well understood techniques for inducing RISC in Jewish mysticism. In the dream, Vital sees the throne of the Ancient of Days, which is just what his tradition has taught him to expect and just what the apocalypticists of the First Century expected to see. Indeed, it is a striking coincidence, as he might have seen any of a number of other things but, in fact, he sees a scene from precisely the

throne tradition which we have been studying. He suffers the conventional emotional responses of fright and trembling. He falls on his face until God raises him,
just as the angel raises Enoch.

According to Himmelfarb, what sets this vision off as a real experience and
shows that the older texts are not is precisely what happens next. Vital receives
reassurance that his *personal* troubles are over and that he has been elected for
divine leadership in place of his rival, Josef Karo. Since Vital's dream has these
"intensely personal aspects," Himmelfarb assumes that the personal detail serves
as an indicator that real experience is present.

Of course, what she suggests is possible but it is not the only or even the most
logical explanation for a difference between two reports in the same tradition
separated by 1500 years. Historical circumstances themselves, the passage of time,
and indeed the rise of specific modern concepts of personality intervene as well,
to say nothing of the specific history and situation of Seventeenth-Century Safed.

Himmelfarb suggests there are no such personal experiences in the apocalypses.
What she appears to mean in my estimation is that we have at this moment no way
of knowing what kind of personal experience is narrated in them. We simply do not
know whether there are any personal elements in 1 Enoch or 4 Ezra because we
have no idea who wrote them and only our own deductions as to why they were
written. But, many scholars have independently pointed out a distinctly personal
voice in the narration of 4 Ezra which appears to learn developmentally (see for
example Stone 1990: 30–33, 119–125). But even more important is to realize that
"solution to personal problems" is a quite modern category that may play no role
in the definition of RASC/RISC in the ancient world. The issue in the ancient world
was both personal and social – it was the problem of how God was going to make
his justice known when so many evil enemies of God's people seemed to be in
charge.

What is conventional in the first few centuries seems to me to be something
entirely different. When people deal with texts exegetically in the first few centuries,
they normally produce *midrash* or commentary. The apocalyptic and pseudepi-
graphical literature is something entirely different. They are not exegeses in any of
the well-known canons of the first *century – midrash, pesher*, allegory, typology,
etc. Instead, they are vivid, internalized descriptions of heaven and of God and His
court, figured as a contemporary record of a vision, just as is the material in Vital's
dream. We may doubt that the narrative is a coterminous transcription of the event
but the same is obviously true in the Seventeenth-Century case. Comparison is a
knife that cuts both ways here. Analysis of text seems to demonstrate that certain
kinds of narration are produced by RISC, not by exegesis of previous texts alone.

Three short scenes from the famous "Parables of Enoch," an early text, illustrate
the point. In 1 Enoch 46, we have the description of the divine throneroom, which
is first described in Daniel 7:

This is the Son of Man, to whom belongs righteousness, and with whom righteousness dwells. And he will open all the hidden storerooms; for the Lord of the Spirits has chosen him, and he is destined to be victorious before the Lord of the Spirits in eternal uprightness. (1 Enoch 46:3)

This passage (and the next too) is manifestly a paraphrase of Daniel 7:13. But it is not an exegesis of Daniel 7. Enoch uses not only different terms but also new conceptions to describe the scene. Now we have hidden storerooms and a "Lord of Spirits." Since these are all conventional items from other texts, there is no way to tell whether they appear here because they were personally experienced by the adept. But, shortly after this scene there is a quite interesting expansion on Daniel 12:

In those days, Sheol will return all the deposits which she had received and hell will give back all that which it owes. And he shall choose the righteous and the holy ones from among (the risen dead), for the day when they shall be selected and saved has arrived. (1 Enoch 51:1–3)

In this case, we are not merely given a paraphrase of Daniel but a fairly large expansion including an experience of salvation, experienced proleptically. It is not the same as saying the text reflects a RASC. But it is important to note that the passage is not just a commentary on it. Would it be too much to suggest that the exegete's own experience in visions or dreams has mediated the previous text and filled in some details? Given the inherent conservatism of exegetical arts, I think it is the most obvious explanation. It makes no difference whether the intervening experience is a waking vision, a dream, a psychagogic state, or even a daydream. What matters is that the imaginative act is interpreted religiously. The proleptic presence of the eschaton, which is also a feature of Christian documents, can be easily explained as being a product of a prophetic RASC in which the anticipated millennium is experienced as already happening in the vision.

In the last example, we have yet a greater change from the passage in Daniel 7. This is the very famous passage in which Enoch ascends to the throne of the Son of Man and is transformed into him:

(Thus) it happened after this that my spirit passed out of sight and ascended into the heavens. And I saw the sons of the holy angels walking upon the flame of fire; their garments were white – and their overcoats – and the light of their faces was like snow. Also I saw two rivers of fire, the light of which fire was shining like hyacinth. Then I fell upon my face before the Lord of the Spirits. And the angel Michael, one of the archangels, seizing me by my right hand and lifting me up, led me out into all the secrets of mercy; and he showed me all the secrets of righteousness. He also showed me all the secrets of the extreme ends of heaven and all the reservoirs of the stars and the luminaries

– from where they came out (to shine) before the faces of the holy ones. He carried off my spirit, and I Enoch, was built in the heaven of heavens . . . And I saw countless angels – a hundred thousand times a hundred thousand, ten million times ten million – encircling that house. Michael, Raphael, Gabriel, Phanuel, and numerous (other) holy angels that are in heaven above, go in and out of that house – Michael, Raphael, Gabriel, Phanuel, and numerous (other) holy angels that are countless. With them is the Antecedent of Time: His head is white and pure like wool and his garment is indescribable. I fell on my face, my whole body mollified and my spirit transformed. (1 Enoch 71:1–5, 8–11)

Here is the same kind of expansion of Daniel which we have just noticed in the earlier passages in the Parables. But there is an even more interesting part of the expansion. A whole new character is introduced, Enoch. He now goes to the heavenly throneroom which is described in Daniel 7:13 and testifies that the prophecy of Daniel 12 is starting to happen. No place in scripture is this made clear; rather it is the result of a new prophetic insight about the events of the eschaton. And it is impossible to derive without adding a new character into the scene. Of course, he is the same Enoch who is mentioned in Genesis 5, so he is yet another pseudonymous character, albeit an antideluvian hero, who is serving as the mouthpiece for the innovation, and most obviously for the adept experiencing RASC. He narrates the scene and discusses his personal feelings in ways which are totally new and foreign to the original Daniel passage. To me, there is no question but that the text is reproducing the experience of someone who is hiding behind the conceit of Enoch. This does not prove that the expansion was taken during RASC. But what could prove it? Even if we had the adept here for an EEG, the evidence would be ambiguous as there are no single indicators of RASC. But it is at least a personal, first-person narration, which Himmelfarb said was absent in this literature. And, of course, it is presented as a RASC.

And what he narrates is exceptionally important. He narrates the confessional experience of being transformed into an angel. We have seen that this is the very prophecy predicted by Daniel 12. Thus, we have a clear example of a future prophecy experienced confessionally as a RASC with the many novelties in the translation, especially the personage of Enoch, showing us that personal experience is present. I see no reason to disbelieve that RASC is part of the religious tradition.[24]

The conventions of the First Century are very different from those of the Seventeenth. Although issues of authority dominate earlier texts as well, as they dominate all religious writing, they are phrased as the personal problems of the narrator, the supposed author, not of any historical character. Instead they appear to be issues of the nature of the saved group and their hopes for the redress over the seeming lack of justice in the world. The purpose of the text is theodicy because the expected end will right the wrongs of the present situation. The one universal in all these texts seems to me to be that every one eventually addresses the issues of theodicy by turning his or her attention to the eschaton or "millennium." Revealing the contents of heaven, with the righteousness of the martyrs rewarded and the sinfulness of the persecutors punished, is an answer to the question of why the righteous cult members are persecuted. All the texts function in other ways too, but they never seem to neglect this issue.

Obviously, historical circumstances and individual consciousness, whether ecstatic or not, may conflict in any religious text. This is the religious concomitant to Harold Bloom's notion of the anxiety of influence, except in scriptural religious terms the anxiety seems to be mostly on the other side – not anxiety in admitting influence but anxiety in admitting novelty. People try to demonstrate that they are not innovating, often by adopting the persona of ancient heroes, even when they manifestly are. Instead they claim that God has delivered a new insight about His approaching plan of vengeance for the wicked. As Himmelfarb has helped illustrate for us, one characteristic of claiming a special revelation, which makes it subversive to received authority, whether it be Josef Karo or the Second Temple administration or stimulated by the shock of the Roman victory over the Jews and their destruction of the Herodian Temple, is precisely that it does invoke other, more charismatic sources of religious authority than the literary and exegetical skills which trained religious exegetes claim (Lewis 1971).

The experiences of Enoch in 1 Enoch and the mystical ascenders in the merkabah documents are based on the writings of Daniel and Ezekiel especially, but on a great many theophany texts as well. They present a further development of the tradition; and that development, in turn, is not easily explainable by exegesis alone. Another imagination is filtering it and changing it in significant ways; the rules for changing it are not exegetical rules, for the expansions go wildly beyond exegesis.

In those documents, a major theme is the ascent of the adept where he is transformed into the gigantic angelic figure who embodies the name of God. This is probably the confessional experience of becoming a star, as narrated in Daniel 12:2, which we saw earlier. It probably also explains Paul's use of the language, "in Christ" as Christ functions as the human representative of God, just as in Jewish mysticism. The large difference between Paul and the Merkabah mystics is that Paul uniquely identifies the angelic figure with the messiah (Christ, *Christos*, cristo~).[25]

Paul reveals much about personal mystical experiences in the First Century in his own confessional accounts. Often Paul talks about transforming the believers into the image of God's son in various ways (Romans 8:29, 2 Corinthians 3:18–4:6, 1 Corinthians 15:49; also see Colossians 3:9):

> And we all, with unveiled face, beholding the glory of the Lord, are being changed into his likeness from one degree of glory to another; for this comes from the Lord who is

the Spirit . . . In their case the god of this world has blinded the minds of the unbelievers, to keep them from seeing the light of the gospel of the glory of Christ, who is the likeness of God . . . For it is the God who said, "Let light shine out of darkness," who has shone in our hearts to give the light of the knowledge of the glory of God in the face of Christ. (2 Corinthians 3: 18–4:6)

that I may know him and the power of his resurrection, and may share his sufferings, becoming like him in his death, that if possible I may attain the resurrection from the dead. (Philippians 3: 10-11)

But our commonwealth is in heaven, and from it we await a Savior, the Lord Jesus Christ, who will change our lowly body to be like his glorious body, by the power which enables him even to subject all things to himself. (Philippians 3:20–21)

My little children, with whom I am again in travail until Christ be formed in you! (Galatians 4: 19)

Do not be conformed to this world but be transformed by the renewal of your mind, that you may prove what is the will of God, what is good and acceptable and perfect. (Romans 12:2)

Paul says that all believers are being changed into the likeness of the Glory of the Lord. He uses the Greek words for transformation, principally *symmmorphosis,* a word which connotes a *metamorphosis* into the same person, though he also uses *metamorphosize* and *metaschematize* to describe the event. This is to be contrasted in Romans 12:2 with *syschematize,* to conform or fit in. He sees the process as having begun with the resurrection of Christ and as ending with the eschaton, soon to arrive. Baptism and enduring sufferings are what bond the believer to Christ, through His sufferings and death. But, at the eschaton, they will all be transformed into angels as they are translated to a better existence.

Conclusion

This is not a mere novelistic consolation, it is a very potent religious and mystical testimony, which can console but can also propel cult members to action. This confessional experience is a kind of breakthrough of the end-time experience into ordinary life. Paul, like the other mystics, knows that God will continue to justify the righteous because he has already personally felt the beginning of the long-prophesied transformation of the righteous leaders (*hamaskilim* of Daniel 12, those who are wise) to angelic substance. The seer, whether known to us or not, acts as a prophet consoling the embittered and small minority, trying to show them why they must hold to their faith in spite of disconfirmation. He foretells that the righteous were supposed eschatologically to be promised unification and trans-formation into immortal creatures. These texts are surely more than imaginative renderings to remedy unsatisfactory daily life. They are not merely literary appraisals but were meant to be appropriated on a religious level. Some of the texts imply that they are imparting great secrets. The ascents all say that they reveal the secret, not evident structure of the cosmos. They offer religious consolation for a world in which the righteous do not seem to win and they promise far more than the thrill of ascent.

There are three stages in this little history of RASC in apocalypticism. The first stage is represented by key prophetic texts like Daniel and Ezekiel, in which God appears in a human form. In the second stage, the apocalyptic texts, famous heroes from the biblical past are pictured as uncovering in revelation (*apocalypsis*) more secrets about these prophetic writings, secrets which include the proleptic trans-formation of believers into the divine or angelic body sitting on the throne. Paul shows us that apocalypse and mysticism go hand in hand; he is the only named Jewish mystic to give us his confessional and personal experience in about 1500 years. In the later texts we get the confessional experience of the adepts as they develop specific ways to provoke and stimulate these experiences. The stages are not strictly chronological and they overlap a great deal; there are even many apocalypses in the later mystical literature. But it is clear that this history gives us a translation process in two respects. First it records the heavenly translation of the saints to receive their transformative reward in heaven. It also illustrates the way in which textual study is translated into confessional mystical experience in a Scriptural community, especially one which feels itself poised before the eschaton. For us to understand these seemingly impossible experiences we need to translate them from their language of vision, not to the language of fiction and hallucination, but to the language of the neurological basis of our experiences and a historically developing set of cultural explanations about what these refractory experiences mean.

Now obviously this was intended to be a discussion on translation; after outlin-ing some methodological issues in word translation, I have taken up an inordinate amount of time describing mystical translation. I am suggesting that there are many ways of translating, one important way being by confessionally reexperiencing the previous prophetic texts. Translation from one conceptual universe to another is a much more metaphoric use of the term than the simple act of translating the word young woman in Hebrew to virgin in Greek and is even more fraught with mis-prisions. But calling attention to the relationship between the scholarly interpretive act and the simpler act of finding a good equivalent word in another language does underline that we need to be responsible for understanding the nature of the ancients' experience, even if we believe what they tell us is literally impossible. I am only saying that they may have been mistaken in their physics from our point of view, but it seems clear that they were not lying about the nature of their experiences.

I have also spent some time castigating scholars whose *interpretation*, not translation *per se* seems to me to be faulty. All the modern scholars would translate *dream* and *vision* by their proper names, even when they believe them to be feigning or fictionalizing these experiences. Yet, in their commentaries, they freely reinterpret the terms as signifying novelistic license, tropes of a literary genre, or even symptoms of insanity. And if they were still following the conventions of the translation in the LXX or the Targums, they would have placed their reductionistic interpretations right into the translation itself.

This is a much more complicated case than the Virgin Birth but it is similar methodologically in that relatively innocuous changes in wording – like the difference between vision and hallucination – signal enormous changes in our understanding of the nature of consciousness, in the nature of the experience being described in the words from a previous time. In this case, it is easy to miss the real experience of religiously altered states of consciousness in the texts or to denigrate them because we cannot duplicate the experience. But in observation of the centuries after Paul it becomes clear that translation to heaven itself serves as the basic language to describe and indicator of the RASC, as the two phenomena are highly correlated and the mystics begin to agree on the vehicle of the travel, the soul itself.

Not only does translation to heaven serve as a metaphor for ecstasy, it also illustrates what lies behind the process of biblical language translation. In a Scriptural tradition like the Bible, all translation is a kind of hermeneutics, the reconceptualizing of prior ideas to renew them for new times. So Paul and the prophets become theologians and social reformers to fit our world. In some sense, Himmelfarb has gotten the problem exactly wrong. It is not that these religious texts are actually novels, it is rather that we turn them from religious texts to novels to fit our world. The process of translation from language to language actually turns out to be a less intense way of doing what the mystics were doing – moving the meaning of texts from one cultural context to another. They did it by reexperiencing the prophecies in a RASC. We do it by reading them and commenting on them – different hermeneutics for different people and different times.

The past is a foreign land and, our biblical demogogues aside, the Bible is not self-evidently speaking to us. It is proper to admit that the adepts of the apocalyptic and mystical literature, those people who formulated these texts, are not like us. Some were mystical voyagers, psychic astronauts, heavenly translators who expected to be translated and transformed into angelic creatures in order better to do God's work in the coming apocalypse. Having those expectations, that is just how they experienced their RISCs. The Bible does not have to be talking about us and our lives. Aware of these massive differences between us and them, we ought to be able to do our relatively modest jobs of translating and commenting on their work with a bit more respect for the high purpose that they set for themselves, even if we cannot have their experiences and do not wish to emulate them.

Notes

1. Translation is inherently a dangerous process and official Islam avoids the question by eschewing translation entirely. All translations of the Qur'an are called merely commentaries.
2. A proof-text is a Bible citation used to demonstrate the truth of a doctrine and is used especially when scholars want to point out that some new doctrine is opportunistically justified by rereading or reinterpreting a biblical text which originally had nothing to do with it.
3. See Kamesar (1990). The material is from his Oxford D. Phil. thesis, which subsequently was published as well.
4. Of course, this distinction is somewhat arbitrary because RASC trances and altered states are complex and socially determined states. There may not be any difference between the two phenomena; indeed, all RASC is in a sense RISC because all states of consciousness are coded and interpreted by the culture. It is, however, helpful to distinguish between the two in the case in the period we are discussing because we feel that dreams are ordinary experience but can be interpreted as religious (therefore RISC) while we normally feel that visions are altered states of consciousness and therefore RASC. From the point of view of brain functioning they may all be simply religiously interpreted states of consciousness.
5. Notice that Peter falls into a trance in Acts 10:10. And he became hungry and desired something to eat; but while they were preparing it, he fell into a trance (*ektasis*).
6. Indeed, we should probably suspect a great deal of the Bible, since most of the canon is pseudonymous as well.
7. In Scholem 1956, the first chapter deals with the phenomenon of mysticism in Judaism but it does not address the issues that are central to this discussion. Instead it outlines a theory of Jewish mysticism which does not include and in fact is hostile to *unio mystica*. This now appears to be an overstated conclusion.
8. I can understand that scholars of religion once thought that some exegeses were "true" and others "false" in that they conformed to the simplest meanings of the text. But in a post-modern world, I would be hard-pressed to discover any disinterested notions of truth and falsity in a tradition exegesis. I would prefer

to merely to point out which exegeses had societal approval and which lacked it.

9. Himmelfarb is also making an interesting and justifiable claim against other scholars who claim that merely reading the texts was a ritual event in that the texts were performative utterances which brought about ascent in the mind. Of course they were but they may not have been ritual events. Himmelfarb's good point, as I will show, is taken to absurd lengths.

10. Even assuming that someone called Don Juan actually existed, it is clear that it could not be used to represent the experiences with a typical *Yacqui*. On the other hand, I am not saying that Castaneda's work is totally worthless. Though everyone thinks that much of it was fictionalized, it certainly remains useful to describe the counter-cultural religiosity of the 1960's and 1970's. And, of course, it is important to note that Castaneda steadfastly maintained that it was all true.

11. For a demonstration of these issues with regard to magic, see Segal 1987; see also Lewis 1986.

12. And Micaiah said, "Therefore hear the word of the LORD: I saw the LORD sitting on his throne, and all the host of heaven standing beside him on his right hand and on his left; and the LORD said, 'Who will entice Ahab, that he may go up and fall at Ramoth-gilead?' And one said one thing, and another said another. Then a spirit came forward and stood before the LORD, saying, 'I will entice him.' And the LORD said to him, 'By what means?' And he said, 'I will go forth, and will be a lying spirit in the mouth of all his prophets.' And he said, 'You are to entice him, and you shall succeed; go forth and do so.' Now therefore behold, the LORD has put a lying spirit in the mouth of all these your prophets; the LORD has spoken evil concerning you" (1 Kings 22:19–23).

13. Robert Wilson (1980) brings up the comparative material but is skeptical of its direct application to Israelite prophecy. Instead he tries to develop criteria showing where the evidence may be selectively and carefully appropriated to Israelite cases.

14. See for example, the summary discussion in Collins 1977.

15. See Kilborne; and also Hanson where he shows that such Hellenistic conventions surely influenced Luke's descriptions in Acts, especially 16:6–12. For a discussion of the shamanic techniques in healing, see esp. Culianu 1983; for dreams, see Kilborne and esp. Miller 1994.

16. The term often used to describe merkabah mystics, "the descenders into the chariot" (*yordei merkabah* ywrdy mrkbh), seems to me best understood as referring to this position, (*Pace* Grünwald).

17. To be conservative, we cannot actually tell whether Paul is suggesting that the actual adept cannot tell about the mechanism or whether he is just unsure of

the report he is narrating. If I had to wager, I would suggest that Paul is saying that he has experienced the ascent and he does not know whether he journeyed in the body or not. This certainly fits the apocalyptic and mystical evidence in early Christianity and Judaism where some ascents seem to be soul flights whereas others seem to be bodily journeys. Suffice it to say that these seemingly parenthetical remarks are quite an impressive and unusual pieces of evidence for a particular theoretical moment in Late Antiquity ascent texts.

18. It is also reminiscent of the famous Zoroastrian ascension text, the *Arda Viraf Nameh* where the hero takes a potion such as Haoma which results in a long seizure. When he recovers, he relates a heavenly journey.

19. I cite the "cult" classic: Julian Jaynes (1977) not to agree with his major points but only to suggest various possibilities in the development of consciousness and especially in the imposition of RASC within it. See more recent studies of consciousness for more plausible explanations: Chalmers, 1996; Dowling, 1998; Dennett, 1991, 1996; Searle et al. 1997; Noerretranders, 1998 [1991]; Tart, 1969.

20. See the reprints of these articles in Smith 2001.

21. The last report, however, should probably be excluded as an actual technique, because it is not suggested as a waking technique for achieving RASC. Rather, it occurs within the vision as a magic potion for the purposes of remembering scripture. None of the seers themselves are directed to do this before the vision starts. so it should probably be seen as a specific characteristic of that particular vision. It would be interesting speculate about any relationship between this report and Zoroastrian Haoma rituals.

22. It is from the same root as that of the word used for trance is Daniel 10. Indeed, modern Hebrew uses the word to express a drug "high," stupor, and anesthesia.

23. Michael Ripinsky-Naxon (1993) adopts a very broad phenomenology as a strategy to define Shamanism. If so, then the hekhalot material is clearly shamanism too. But it is still important to note that the issue of healing is almost entirely missing in the Jewish material. In its place is the virtually unique benefit of the "Sar Torah," the angel who visits the mystic and teaches him magically to remember vast amounts of Talmud.

24. With more time, I could show that this is exactly the experience behind the early Christian Church's experience of being in Christ, which Paul describes in some detail.

25. In some real sense we can say that the New Testament was written to prove that the man Jesus has been translated to heaven to become the second, young manifestation in the vision and is hence now part of God, but that is a story for another day.

References

Aune, David. *Prophecy in Early Christianity and the Ancient Mediterranean World.* Grand Rapids: Eerdmans, 1983.

Austin, James H. *Zen and the Brain: Toward an Understanding of Meditation and Consciousness.* Cambridge MA: MIT Press, 1998.

Benz, Ernst. *Paulus als Visionär.* Akademie der Wissenschaften und der Leteratur. Wiesbaden: Steiner, 1952.

Cardeña, Etzel, Lynn, Steven Jay and Krippner, Standley. *Varieties of Anomalous Experience: Examining the Scientific Evidence.* Washington, D.C.: American Psychological Association, 2000.

Chalmers, David J. *The Conscious Mind: In Search of a Fundamental Theory.* Oxford and New York: Oxford University Press, 1966.

Collins, John J. *The Apocalyptic Vision of the Book of Daniel.* Harvard Semitic Monographs 16. Missoula, MT: Scholars Press, 1977.

Culianu, Iaon P. *Psychanodia I.* Leiden: Brill, 1983.

Davila, James R. "The Hekhalot Literature and Shamanism." *Society of Biblical Literature 1994 Seminar Papers.* Atlantic GA: Scholars Press, 1994, pp. 767–789.

—— *Descenders to the Chariot: The People Behind the Hekhalot Literature.* Leiden: Brill, 2001.

Dean-Otting, Mary. *Heavenly Journeys: A Study of the Motif in Hellenistic Jewish Literature.* New York: Verlag Peter Lang, 1984.

Dennett, Daniel C. *Consciousness Explained.* Boston: Little Brown, 1991.

—— *Kinds of Minds: Toward an Understanding of Consciousness.* New York: Basic, 1996.

Dowling, John E. *Creating Mind.* New York: Norton, 1998.

Gallup, George Jr. and Castelli, Jim. *The People's Religion: American Faith in the 90s.* New York: Macmillan, 1989.

Gallup, George Jr. with Proctor, William. *Adventures in Immortality.* New York: McGraw-Hill, 1982.

Grünwald, L. *Apocalyptic and Merkabah Mysticism.* AGAJV. Leiden: Brill, 1980.

Halperin, David J. *The Merkabah in Rabbinic Literature.* AOS 62. New Haven: American Oriental Society, 1980.

—— *The Faces of the Chariot: Early Jewish Responses to Ezekiel's Vision.* Tübingen: JCB Mohr (Paul Siebeck), 1988.

Hanson, John S. "Dreams and Visions in the Graeco-Roman World and Early Christianity." *ANRW* II 23:2, pp. 1395–1427.

Himmelfarb, Martha. *Ascent to Heaven in Jewish and Christian Apocalypses.* New York: Oxford University Press, 1993.

Idel, Moshe. *Kabbalah: New Perspectives.* New Haven: Yale University Press, 1989.

Jaynes, Julian. *The Origin of Consciousness in the Breakdown of the Bicameral Mind.* Boston: Houghton Mifflin, 1977.

Kamesar, Adam. "The Virgin of Isaiah 7:14: The Philological Argument from the Second to the Fifth Century." *Journal of Theological Studies* ns 41, 1990, pp. 51–75.

Kilborne, Benjamin. "Dreams." *Encyclopedia of Religion.*

Kim, *The Origin of Paul's Gospel.* Tübingen: JCB Mohr (Paul Siebeck), 1984.

Lévi Strauss, Claude. "The Sorcerer and His Magic." *Structural Anthropology.* Trans. Monique Layton. Chicago: University of Chicago Press, 1983.

Lewis, Ioan M. *Ecstatic Religion: An Anthropological Study of Spirit Possession and Shamanism.* Baltimore: Penguin, 1971.

—— *Religion in Context: Cults and Charisma.* Cambridge and New York: Cambridge University Press, 1986.

Miller, Patricia Cox. *Dreams in Late Antiquity: Studies in the Imagination of a Culture.* Princeton: Princeton University Press, 1984.

Morray-Jones, Christopher. "A Transparent Illusion: The Dangerous Vision of Water". In *Hekhalot Mysticism: a Source-Critical and Tradition-Historical Inquiry.* Leiden: Brill, 2002.

Newberg, Andrew, D'Aquili, Eugene and Rause, Vince. *Why God Won't Go Away: Brain Science and the Biology of Belief.* New York: Ballantine, 2001.

Noerretranders, Tor. *The User Illusion: Cutting Consciousness Down to Size.* trans. J. Sydenham. New York: Viking, 1998 (orig. pub. as *Maerk verden.* Gyldendalske Bokhandel, 1991). *Otsar Ha-Geonim* ed. Lewin *Hagigah.* Jerusalem, 1932. *Teshuroth,* pp. 14–15.

Persinger, Michael A. *Neuropsychological Bases of God Beliefs.* Westport CN: Praeger, 1987.

Proudfoot, Wayne. *Religious Experience.* Berkeley: University of California Press, 1985.

Ripinsky-Naxon, Michael. *The Nature of Shamanism: Substance and Function of a Religious Metaphor.* Albany: SUNY Press, 1993.

Rowland, Christopher. "Towards an Understanding of the Origins of Apocalyptic." In *The Open Heaven: A Study of Apocalyptic in Early Judaism and Christianity.* Rowland. New York: Crossroads, 1982.

Saake, Helmut. "Paulus als Ekstatiker: pneumatologische Beobachtung zu 2 Cor. xii 1–10, *NovT* 15:2, 1973, pp. 153–160.

Schäfer, Peter. *Synopse Zur Hekhalot-Literatur.* Tübingen: JCB Mohr (Paul Siebeck), 1981.

—— *Geniza-Fragmente Zur Hekhalot-Literatur.* Tübingen: JCB Mohr (Paul Siebeck), 1984.

—— *Der verborgene und offenbare Gott: Hauptthemen der frühen jüdischen Mystik.* Tübingen: JCB Mohr (Paul Siebeck), 1991.

Scholem, Gershom Gerhard. *Major Trends in Jewish Mysticism*. New York: Schocken, 1956.

—— *Jewish Gnosticism, Merkabah Mysticism, and Talmudic Tradition*. New York: Jewish Theological Seminary of America, 1960.

Searle, John R. *The Mystery of Consciousness*. Exchanges with David Chalmers and Daniel C. Dennett. New York: New York Review Press, 1997.

Segal, Alan F. "Hellenistic Magic: Some Questions of Definition." In *Other Judaisms of Late Antiquity*. Brown Judaic Series 127. Atlanta GA: Scholars Press, 1987.

—— "Paul's Conversion, Psychological Studys." In *Paul the Convert*. New Haven: Yale University Press, 1988.

Smith, Huston. *Cleansing the Doors of Perception: The Religious Significance of Entheogenic Plants and Chemicals*. New York: Penguin Putnam, 2001.

Stone, Michael Edward. *Fourth Ezra*. Minneapolis: Fortress, 1990.

Tart, Charles T. (ed.). *Altered States of Consciousness: A Book of Readings*. New York: Wiley, 1969.

Urbach, Ephraim E. "The Traditions about Merkabah Mysticism in the Tannaitic Period". In Hebrew in the Hebrew section of *Studies in Mysticism and Religion Presented to Gershom G. Scholem*. Jerusalem: Magnes, 1967.

Wilson, Robert. *Prophecy and Society in Ancient Israel*. Philadelphia: Fortress, 1980.

Wolfsen, Elliot R. *Through a Speculum that Shines: Vision and Imagination in Medieval Jewish Mysticism*. Princeton: Princeton University Press, 1994.

Structural Impediments to Translation in Art
Wyatt MacGaffey

As Europe extended its reach around the world from the fifteenth century onward, it recorded its relations with exotic regions in the form of collections of "curiosities." From the sixteenth to the twentieth centuries, the categories in which these objects were framed, and the commentaries that elaborated the frames, changed to match changes in international relations. In parallel with this evolution, and closely related to it, social sciences developed from their original roots in theology and philosophy. By the mid-nineteenth century, commentary on exotic objects, housed in the new ethnographic museums, was being provided mainly by the new discipline of anthropology.

In Europe, over the same period, the idea of art acquired its modern sense, beginning in the mid-seventeenth century with the founding of the Royal Academy in Paris in 1648 and the professionalization of fine art (as opposed to the work of artisans) under the control of the state. Art was expected to uphold public morality by depicting edifying moments from history and mythology. The "theory" of this art, the classical ideal, was developed during the eighteenth century by such figures as Vico, Burke, Lessing and Kant, all of whom were preoccupied with the relations among art, morality and right thinking. Their discussions were prompted in part by increasing popular interest in reports from faraway places. The first visually pleasing or intriguing objects brought back from Africa,[1] the Americas and the Pacific in the sixteenth and seventeenth centuries were not yet "art" but curios without ascertainable meaning. The travelers' reports that accompanied them, and commentaries from Montaigne's essay *On Cannibals* to Shakespeare's *The Tempest*, mark the beginnings of anthropology.[2] Three centuries later, the reflexive turn in anthropology has led to controversial and still unsettled new perspectives on the means by which objects exhibited in the West were collected, and how they should be classified and viewed.

Civilization and the Idea of Art

Much of the talk about what art is and what it means uses the idea of art to campaign for particular definitions of what it is to be civilized. The idea of art, like that of the rational, has always been most clearly defined by what it is not or, more accurately, by whatever lack in other people explains the assumed absence of civilization among them. The classical norm in art, as Frances Connelly has shown, "cast the primitive as the dark image of itself" (Connelly 1995: 9). Primitives, motivated solely by impulse and emotion, were supposed incapable of abstraction and lacked any sense of history. Instead of art, they produced forms that were either grotesque (lacking discipline) or at best ornamental (lacking narrative). There was nothing there to translate, if by translation we mean to express in our own terms the significance of the objects to those who produced and used them. The type of the grotesque was the "fetish," especially as it was reported from Africa and Oceania; for Enlightenment thinkers from De Brosses to Hegel, "fetishism" was the antithesis of civilization; it was the product of merely random impulses and violated the elementary Cartesian distinction between animate and inanimate beings (Pietz 1985).

The nineteenth-century romantic reaction against the academy and the classical ideal brought about a reevaluation of emotion as against reason, and therefore of the primitive. Ornament became more respectable; the possibility that primitive arts were really art, or art of a sort, acquired plausibility.[3] The court arts of the Near and Far East and Peru that attracted attention by their aesthetic qualities were regarded as ornament rather than art because although their makers were credited with imagination they were assumed to be incapable of the kind of transcendent ideas that informed real art and endowed it with meaning.[4] Objects from Africa and Oceania still fell into the category of the grotesque; even Gauguin's "Tahitian" paintings were often based on Egyptian, Japanese or Javanese compositions, not on Polynesian art. Much has been made of the interest shown in African objects by Picasso, Modigliani and other artists in Paris a century ago, but it was the form rather than the "meaning" of the objects that intrigued them; *Les Demoiselles d'Avignon*, for example, makes use of African masks as "grotesques," and Picasso famously expressed his lack of interest in the meaning to Africans of their art by saying that the objects themselves told him all he needed to know.[5]

Objects brought back from colonial empires were housed in the new ethnographic museums, not as art (not even primitive art) but as demonstrations of the absence of civilization among those who produced them, illustrations for an evolutionary narrative.[6] Meaning was assigned to African and Oceanian works lodged in ethnographic collections in terms of the evolutionary assumptions they were called upon to illustrate. A notorious example was provided until recently by the Smithsonian's Museum of Natural History in Washington, D.C., where the African collection appeared in pseudochronological order after the neolithic exhibit.

The last quarter of the nineteenth century also discovered, or invented, folk art, to which most of the same ambiguities attach as to primitive art; in practice, it consisted of objects identified as art by members of the upper class.[7] Folk and primitive objects could suddenly be art, often considered morally preferable, somehow, to "academic art," but the idea of them remained negative, a "dark image." They were produced, supposedly, in response to collective tradition rather than individual genius, and they did not incorporate narratives of historical and moral importance. The history of these evaluations remains fossilized in the categories we find in dealers' catalogs and the art departments of museums, where, as at the Art Institute of Chicago, Africa and Oceania are lumped together only because, in the twentieth century, they were the last areas to be admitted as potential producers of art. The collectors and connoisseurs who constitute the primitive-art market codify tribal styles in order to control "authenticity" and therefore market value; they consider objects made by known and still living individual makers to be inauthentic (Steiner 1994).

These turns of thought and practice have generated the subdivisions of the general category, Art, that prevailed until recently and have yet to succumb entirely to scholarly challenges. The Fine Art of Others is limited, so far, to Oriental Art, now renamed "Asian," in recognition of the derogatory tenor of the original term. Primitive Art (sometimes now called "tribal" or "ethnic") is the Folk Art of Others who lack Fine Art. The constitutive variables of the set are "ours vs. theirs" and "higher vs. lower"; the significance of each category, and of "Art" as a whole, lies in the way it is contrasted with the others, rather than in the list of objects that may or may not be included. Folk art and primitive art have in common that they are supposed to be produced by ordinary persons whose names are not simply unknown but irrelevant; in both instances, the maker is unaware that his product is art, it is the privilege of the collector to discover it (Steiner 1994: 9, 44). The date of the work does not matter, except that it should be as old as possible, before the invasion of corrupting foreign or modern influences. Our folk, however, are superior to their folk in that their creativity represents the cultural heritage of a nation rather than the unthinking representational habits of the tribe (Ames 1977). Modern studies have shown the error of these assumptions; American folk art was often a popular hand-me-down from academic art, much of it not even American in inspiration (Janzen and Janzen 1991).

Whether these contrasts should be drawn, and where, are matters of ongoing debate, often attended by the acrimony appropriate to these and other essentially political matters, and energized by the desire to control (commercial) value. As Fred Myers observes, "the point of the struggle is almost entirely a question of how to represent others" (Myers 1995: 57). When acrylic paintings by Australian Aborigines appeared on the New York art market in 1989, dealers and their allies the critics debated the status to be accorded to them. Myers, finding himself unexpectedly in an ethnographic role, identified three critical positions: the romantic, in which the paintings, created in industrial media rather than with vegetable dyes on bark, failed as primitive art because they had been contaminated by Western influence; the modernist, in which they also failed as modern art, because by its standards they were no more than second-rate neo-Expressionism; and the self-described "postmodernist" perspective (incorporating some old-fashioned Marxist rhetoric), which denied that the works should be called art at all. "Such criticisms," Myers notes, "are part of the discursive practices that define 'high art'"; they are also about how we see "ourselves" in relation to "them" (Myers 1995: 81). The idea of art is still critically bound up with the idea we form of civilization; enduring myths, as Suzanne Blier calls them, constantly impede the task of translation. To convey "their" meanings, we must first become aware of our own, which are ethnographically interesting in their own right (Blier, 1996).

The constituent categories of the idea of art are found in our discursive categories but are also concretely institutionalized. Objects of each kind are normally housed in museums specializing in them and supported by the corresponding specialized journals and professional associations. The public, even though unable to define art, folk art or primitive art, knows what to expect in collections bearing these labels, and has been instructed at some level in the nature of the experience they should have when visiting one. In the Shelburne Museum, Shelburne, Vermont, an enormous and magnificent collection of weathervanes, quilts, seashell sculptures, trade signs, cigar-store Indians, hand-pumped fire-engines and craftsman's tools, housed in a collection of log cabins, barns, country stores and other antique buildings, announces the patronage that defines it. On a hill dominating the scene is a Greek Revival mansion specially constructed to house the New York City apartment of the wealthy collector and her husband, minus original utilities such as the bathroom. The living quarters are furnished with European paneling and paintings by Rembrandt, Degas, and Monet.

From Artifacts to Art

Among the commentaries on museum collections, including art, anthropology came late to the field, and has until recently restricted itself to primitive art. In the nineteenth century, the great age of imperial looting, anthropology still assumed that primitive cultures generated no ideas worth translating (Evans-Pritchard 1965: 105–108). Lewis Henry Morgan's opinion in 1877 is representative: "All primitive religions are grotesque and to some extent unintelligible"; in E. B. Tylor's more charitable view, our best guide to primitive thinking was the memory of our own childish days. Even Malinowski, for all his insistence on recording "the native's point of view," denied that native society could have its intelligent members from whom indigenous theories could be elicited. In the United States, students of Native America were much more sympathetic to indigenous thought, though Franz

Boas' pioneering *Primitive Art* (1927) was virtually restricted to formal analysis.[8] In African studies the first attempt to take seriously an indigenous system was Evans-Pritchard's *Witchcraft, Oracles and Magic among the Azande* (1937). In 1954, Daryll Forde's symposium on African cosmologies was still greeted with skepticism by British anthropologists; it was not until the 1960s that the work of Victor Turner, Luc de Heusch and Mary Douglas made the study of other people's "meanings" generally acceptable.

Bronzes looted from the Benin kingdom by the British in 1898 were the first African objects to be accorded the status of art, but it was generally assumed that they represented a Mediterranean intrusion into coastal West Africa. In the 1950s, as political developments in African colonies tended toward independence, pioneers such as William Fagg began the critical documentation of African art, but attention focused primarily on sculptural forms that corresponded well to the classical notion of representational art. During the 1960s, the study of art in Africa, much of it by anthropologists, became a growth industry, linked to rising interest in African objects on the part of art collectors. The founding of the journal *African Arts* in 1967 and the publication of the symposium *Tradition and Creativity in Tribal Art* (Biebuyck 1969) marked this new phase. A dramatic increase in prices encouraged the relabeling of more and more types of objects as "art."[9]

Besides reporting ethnographically on the arts of others and the contexts of their production, anthropologists engaged in a prolonged and only partly successful struggle against the invidious distinctions built into the idea of art. They insisted that the makers of primitive art were admired locally for their individual talent, that they were consciously creative and attentive to explicit aesthetic criteria, that their ateliers produced works commercially for distant markets, and that the works themselves embodied moral and historical themes. In short, anthropologists sought admission for primitive art into the exclusive precincts of fine art by arguing that it met the traditional requirements for European art. In the course of the struggle, they were aided by the twentieth-century movements known as anti-art, which challenged those same requirements from within and denied that art should be defined by the "hand" of the artist, the use of noble materials, or the exhibition of the works in bland and pillared spaces to be contemplated in the quasi-religious silence of "exalted looking" (MacGaffey 1998: 225–7).

On the other hand, anthropologists themselves still tend to reinforce the distorting effects of Western cosmographic assumptions. Anderson's characterization is explicitly residual: "We need the term 'primitive art' because nonprimitive societies typically have art based on complex technology; art training is institutionalized in schools; artists tend to be full time specialists; there is great diversity of art styles; art styles change rapidly over time" (Anderson 1979: 6). Primitive art, we are to believe, is essentially different from fine art because it is produced by people with simple technology, whose training is haphazard and who work part-time, endlessly reproducing the same things, expressing the eternal but inarticulate ethos of a particular tribe. More recently, in the second edition of his textbook, Layton restricts the anthropology of art to the products of small-scale societies, without explaining why (Layton 1991). In principle, rigorous theory should enable the anthropology of art to transcend its cultural commitments. In practice, art historians, including anthropologists, are resistant to theory, insisting that they should only gather facts; those that do venture into theory mostly borrow from other disciplines, such as linguistics, semiotics and philosophy (McNaughton 1993). In the anthropology of art, the only theoretical approach worthy of the name is the late Alfred Gell's *Art and Agency* (Gell 1998).

Traditional views are changing, as recent studies reveal the presence of art schools, individual masters, and training programs in the space once occupied by the blandly fallacious construction of the primitive, and as the rapidly growing field of museum studies reveals the tacit assumptions underlying choices about what to exhibit and how. Opposition continues between the curatorial approach, emphasizing an entirely visual experience of art, and the ethnographic approach, which seeks to translate the meaning of the objects by means of placards and increasingly weighty companion volumes. In every exhibition difficult decisions have to be made about the amount of ethnographic information to include. In his enormous "Primitivism" exhibition at the Museum of Modern Art in 1984, William Rubin set aside any evolutionary connotation of the word "primitive," but also declared that ethnographic information was irrelevant to the discovery of formal similarities between Western and other artworks (Rubin 1984). The result was denounced by critics as an imperialistic expropriation and an attempt to demonstrate the universal inevitability of the modern (Clifford 1988: ch. 9). Peter Schjeldahl recently reiterated the traditional curatorial view of the war between words and images: "Wall texts are a bane of late twentieth-century museology, turning art shows into walk-in brochures. We can't help but read them – I defy anyone to ignore writing on walls – and thus are jerked from silent reverie into nattering pedagogy. Art and education are terrible bedfellows" (Schjeldahl 1999: 83). Presumably, however, Schjeldahl hopes that museum-goers will read what he writes, even though they do not carry his graffiti about with them.

The debate about how much translation should be added to exhibited artworks is intimately related to class, as Bourdieu reported after an intensive investigation into the experiences of European museum-goers. Knowledge and taste arrange themselves in constellations linked to level of education; the classes best equipped with such aids as guidebooks and catalogs, and the knowledge of how to use them, are most likely to reject the services of professional guides and recorded commentaries (Bourdieu and Darbel 1990: 69). "To fear that written or spoken information about the works on display diverts visitors from the works themselves, by drawing their attention to extrinsic or anecdotal matters, is to be unaware that the ideal of contemplation without words or actions is only characteristic of those who possess the immediate familiarity acquired by the imperceptible training of prolonged exposure" (ibid.: 53).

The question of interpretation, or the translation of meaning and value, thus presents itself in different ways depending on the category of art in question and the social background of the audience. It is argued with respect to fine art, if I may use "translation" broadly to include information concerning the intent of the artist and the accepted evaluations of the work (that is, answers to the question "What does it mean?"). In much of twentieth-century art theory, art is said to be "about" nothing except itself. As Malevich put it in his "Suprematist" manifesto of 1913, "Art no longer cares to serve the state or religion; it no longer wishes to illustrate the history of manners, it wants nothing further to do with the object as such, and believes that it can exist in and for itself, without things." The idea of art as illusionistic representation of something other than itself is replaced by the idea that the experience of art should be a purely visual encounter between the work and the viewer. In practice, the eye is guided by the context of exhibition and by abundant verbiage available, at a price, in the museum's bookshop. "The colored daubs and streaks on the canvas become, in the proper context – that is, in the presence of the proper ventriloquist – statements about the nature of space, perception, and representation" (Mitchell 1986: 42). If, as it has been said, anthropology is defined by what anthropologists do, then art is whatever art critics write about. Conceptualists such as Joseph Kosuth discovered this, "the linguistic nature of art," in the 1960s, with apparent indignation; for them, being an artist came to mean "questioning the nature of art. If you make paintings you are already accepting (not questioning) the nature of art" (Prinz 1991: 47). They reappropriated art by making it, literally, out of words, and producing innumerable works which "challenged the viewer's assumptions" about the metapragmatics of the possibility of art, its implicit gendering, and the autonomy of the art work itself. Art came to be more and more an insider's game, to which the public responded often enough with bewilderment.

Reframing

Translating art begins with framing and reframing the physical experience of encountering art, which for most people takes place in a museum or gallery. The style of the museum's building and its announcements of the kind of art within go far toward shaping the visitor's self-definition and his or her sense of the experience to come. Erstwhile "primitive artifacts" are now increasingly being accorded the kind of architectural framing that announces their status as art. Leading American museums usually include a section of African arts, though

European museums are still segregated. The French government's recent rethinking of the place of primitive arts, amid intense argument, led to the massive and controversial exhibit "Magiciens de la Terre" at the Centre Pompidou in 1989; replacing the expression "arts primitifs" with "arts premiers" (whose implications are similar!); the introduction of a small section of "primal" masterpieces in the Louvre; and the planned construction of a grand new museum. Reframing extends to the way exhibits are mounted, and the commentaries attached to them. The great collection of art from northeastern Congo acquired by the American Museum of Natural History in 1915, which could not have been exhibited then as art, in 1990 could not have been exhibited as anything else, according to Enid Schildkrout, curator of "African Reflections" (Schildkrout and Keim 1990); resituating these objects in an alternative category means that visitors arrive with different expectations, that the objects are displayed and lit in a different way, appropriate to art, and that the accompanying narrative also changes.

Robert Farris Thompson, in his elaborate presentation of "African Art in Motion" at the National Gallery in Washington D.C. in 1974 (originally at the University of California, Los Angeles), insisted that African art could only be understood in relation to ritual, dance, and bodily gesture. He violated "fine art" conventions by complementing the objects with continuous audio-visual recordings, textiles and blown-up photographs. In a later exhibition in the same locale he was obliged to revert to a more restrained curatorial style and relegate his commentaries to an accompanying volume (Thompson and Cornet 1981). In a series of exhibitions at the Museum for African Art in New York, Susan Vogel experimented with different perspectives. "Art/artifact" (1988) discussed the careers followed by the objects on their way to becoming "art," and the effects of showing them in a variety of display styles. "Closeup" (1990) explored the tension between the simplifying, voyeuristic sense of African sculptures that the camera gives us, and the three-dimensional, performance-oriented nature of the pieces themselves.

Vogel's most ambitious venture, called "Africa Explores: Twentieth Century African Art" (1991) was intended to challenge the idea of art in Africa as tribal, static, and conventional, but radically different from and superior to whatever Africans have produced and are producing in colonial and postcolonial times. Besides showing examples of a wide variety of visually interesting objects, Vogel sought new lines of critical thinking about African artistic production. Though widely praised, the show was also condemned both for overturning traditional categories and perspectives, as it was meant to do, and for being conventionally ethnocentric. Critics asked whether there is a discrete unity, "Africa," the qualities of whose products could be independently discussed. African studio artists objected to being labeled as "African," aware that the term is close cousin to "primitive" and seems to exclude their work from the dignities of universal art. They objected to the display of cartoon-like popular painting and trade signs (not unlike those one can see at the Shelburne) as equally "African art" alongside the products of studio artists. And some denounced the ethnocentrism of the entire project, which they saw as raising traditionally Western issues and selecting its own answers. It is not clear, on the other hand, that African artists and critics would have any less difficulty than Aborigines do in translating their meanings across categories and preconceptions to a foreign audience. Fundamentally, the arguments are political, and it is not to be expected that any translation will earn consensus; argument itself, however, forces reconceptualization in the current political context.

Translating

The hefty volumes that accompany recent exhibits include essays which, besides challenging the enduring myths, complement the visual experience by ethnographically based interpretations of the works. Such commentary is traditionally "anthropological," although the contributors now often include specialists in history, literature, philosophy and other disciplines. Modern-art historians working in Africa usually engage in extended fieldwork in the anthropological manner; the disciplinary boundary is no longer clear. Translation in art resembles any other, but may be aided by the fact that the art works are there to "speak" for themselves.

Translations are always approximate, but good ones are best regarded as works of art in their own right. Even within one language, meanings vary in time and space. George Steiner begins his book on language and translation with critical interpretations of passages from Shakespeare, Jane Austen and Rossetti, showing how much interpretation is needed before the modern reader can come close to the resonances the texts may have had for their original audiences. He goes on to list the lexical aids available to the student of English literature, including for example the Admiralty's *Dictionary of Naval Equivalents*, which helps us to understand *The Wreck of the Deutschland* (no such sophisticated tools are available to most ethnographers). But, says Steiner, "these are externals. The complete penetrative grasp of a text, the complete discovery and recreative apprehension of its life-forms . . . is an act whose realization can be precisely felt but is nearly impossible to paraphrase or systematize" (Steiner 1975: 25). And, we should add, impossible to replicate, despite Steiner's confident use of the word "complete." The task of literary interpretation, as Steiner describes it, is closely similar to that of the ethnographer, although the latter's product will inevitably fall still further short of "completeness"; the comparison is explicit in Fernandez' approach to the Gabonese cult of Bwiti as an imaginative constellation of images comparable to Coleridge's poem, *Kubla Khan* (Fernandez 1982: 9–11).

Like other art, art in Africa is an experience of certain objects, not just the objects themselves. The answer to the question "What does this mean?" must begin with statements that – though the objects, like artworks elsewhere, are respected and visually powerful – the experience of the objects, in rituals and sumptuary displays, is likely to be very different from that of the museum or gallery. On the other hand, all countries in the world today incorporate a "modern" institutional sector whose buildings, practices and symbols resemble those of the corresponding institutions elsewhere, and probably includes museums and possibly art schools. This institutional plurality (in the United States or Canada, for example, the divide between Native America and the dominant sector), is traditionally the subject matter of anthropology. It creates translation problems of another order than those of the distance between Shakespeare's England and George Steiner's, or between Norwegian and Italian. Anthropologists, to their own considerable embarrassment, have not yet established a satisfactory vocabulary to designate such "otherness."

Seeing and Not Seeing

The concept of a "show" or exhibition creates the first problem. The dominant Western idea of knowledge since the Enlightenment is that it is a public good, to which everybody should have access. This idea is necessarily contradicted by others, such as that of privacy, and by the practical needs of government, business, the military and the judicial system; in Washington D.C., questions about who did or should have known what, and when, dominate discussion and political conflict. African ideas of knowledge are more realistic: knowledge that is free and open to everybody is not worth having; real knowledge is dangerous, and should be available only to specially qualified persons. In art, museums and galleries are ideally open to everyone; objects are displayed in them in ways favorable to exalted looking, from which it is believed that profound though unspecifiable benefit can be derived. African "art", on the other hand, draws attention to the necessary boundaries of knowledge by concealing as well as revealing, as Mary Nooter put it in the title of an exhibition and the accompanying book devoted to this topic: the visible functions to keep the invisible invisible (Nooter 1993). Whereas the classical function of art was to brag abut power, African art is more likely to hint at it.

In the book accompanying her most recent exhibition, devoted to Baule art from Côte d'Ivoire, Susan Vogel says that if she had written it earlier she would have used the language of art history to present the objects as Baule "art." But her many years of research have led her to the uncomfortable knowledge that Baule categories of objects and experience are so different from those of the culture to which the book is addressed that no direct translation is possible. "'Art' cannot be described from a Baule point of view at all, simply because their view does not include 'art' in the Western sense of the word." Vogel found that in order to understand Baule art she was obliged to explore lived facts of Baule existence, including many, such as "food and eyeglasses," that seem to have nothing to do with artworks but are just as relevant to them as Baule ontology and spiritual beliefs. The result of this exploration, she believes, parallels rather than substitutes for the appreciation of Baule work that can be developed from the perspective of Western museum culture; "neither approach is wrong, but neither is complete" (Vogel 1997: 17).

Baule may admit to having "seen" such sacred things as a men's mask, but nobody would "look at" one (Vogel 1997: 92). An African object that becomes art in a museum does not, when at home, stay put to be contemplated in silent reverie; it dances, amid noise and dust. It may rush past in deliberate obscurity, as does the Yoruba mask Eyánlá, the great mother, described by Henry Drewal: "Preliminary masqueraders prepare the entrance of Eyánlá, who comes in total darkness . . . for no one must gaze on the face of the mother." As she moves in a gentle, slow dance, matching her steps with the drum rhythms, the elders of the cult flock around her to limit the audience's view of the headdress, which is carried in an almost horizontal position and largely obscured by a long white cloth. When the carver has completed it, using a prescribed type of wood obtained from the forest in a pre-scribed fashion, the elders apply medicines to empower the mask, which otherwise is just a piece of wood; the medicines, which it is the function of the mask to hide, govern people's reactions as much as any visible motifs (Drewal 1977). What matters may not be what the thing looks like, but what it does, or even "who it is."

After creating the expected effect, an African art object may be returned to its special place, but many objects now collected as art would otherwise have been thrown away after use. Africans may conserve but do not "collect" their art and – so far from being trapped in tradition – make a point of freeing themselves from the dictates of the copy (Strother 1998: 31). When not in use, the Eyánlá mask is kept partially or completely concealed. Other artworks may be seen only by initiates, or only by men. The much-admired "caryatid" stools of the Luba in Congo are owned only by kings and spirit mediums; "swathed in white, and fastidiously preserved by an appointed official," such a stool, which is not a seat but a repository for the king's spirit, is only rarely brought out (Roberts and Roberts 1996: 154). "The more important a Baule sculpture is, the less it is displayed, just as in public debates the most senior and respected people speak the least" (Vogel 1997: 108).

What Are We Looking At?

The next problem is to label the object. The relationship between words and images is a vexed question with a long history in Western art. The tendency in twentieth-century art, as we have seen, is to insist that the visible object is sufficient unto itself, but in fact commentary has always been an essential adjunct of the artwork. W. J. T. Mitchell quotes Mark Twain on the power of the label, which makes all the difference between *Beatrice Cenci the Day Before her Execution* and the same painting if it had been entitled *Young Girl with Hay Fever* (Mitchell 1986: 40). Labels referring to fetishes, fertility cults or ancestor worship fit in with popular notions of the "spirituality" of "simple societies" but are often at best half-truths reiterating evolutionary assumptions in updated form; in fact, African cultures generally make no distinction between the natural and the supernatural, the physical and the spiritual (Wiredu 1992: 324–5). In the sixteenth and seventeenth centuries, Portuguese and Dutch sailors and merchants gradually adapted an ill-defined Portuguese term that became not only the word "fetish" but a whole theory of African culture, subsequently used by European philosophers such as Hegel to characterize their idea of the absence of civilization. As African art and religion came to be better known in the late twentieth century, art historians bothered by the derogatory connotation of "fetish" began to use the term "power-object" instead.

A translation is a metaphor, a structure of relations in the target language which is allegedly analogous to a structure in the original, but does not participate in it. Reacting against this estrangement, we may require our translation to include a certain number of terms regarded as essential to "meaning" but also as "untranslatable." At the National Museum of African Art in 1993, as curator of an exhibition of Kongo objects formerly known as fetishes, I decided to use the indigenous term for them throughout. The first thing visitors encountered was a photograph of Simon Kavuna and the translation of a text written by him in 1915 in his own language, KiKongo:

> In my country there is a *nkisi* called Na Kongo, a water *nkisi* with power to afflict and to heal; other *minkisi* have these powers also. They receive these powers by composition, conjuration and consecration. They are composed of earths, ashes, herbs and leaves, and of relics of the dead. They are composed in order to relieve and benefit people, and to make a profit. They are composed to visit consequences upon thieves, witches, those who steal by sorcery, and those who harbor witchcraft powers. Also to oppress people. These are the properties of *minkisi*, to cause sickness in a man, and also to remove it. To destroy, to kill, to benefit. To impose taboos on things and to remove them. To look after their owners and to visit retribution upon them. The way of every *nkisi* is this: when you have composed it, observe its rules lest it be annoyed and punish you. It knows no mercy.

This text shows clearly why *nkisi* has no verbal, conceptual or practical equivalent in English. The translation is mine, not Kavuna's own, and it includes disputable and perhaps tendentious glosses such as "taboo," itself a word with a certain imperial history. Reading the translation does not lead to an immediate and profound understanding of what *nkisi* means to KiKongo speakers, but it does prepare the reader to interpret further information more thoughtfully.[10] Since the exhibition, the KiKongo term has been widely adopted in other exhibitions and commentaries dealing with Kongo art. How many such terms (and their interrelations) are to be incorporated? Should I oblige my reader to get used to not only *nkisi* but also *nsiku, nganga, kindoki* and more? A fully metonymic "translation," continuous with the original, would necessarily be written in the original language and thus fail completely – except perhaps as an insider's joke, in the same way that a photograph of a famous photograph can be presented as a work of art in its own right.

Having identified the object, we will probably have to explain that the thing on view is only a reduced version of the original, that it was taken out of a more extensive material apparatus, much of which did not look like art to the collector or which did not lend itself to transportation; that it has suffered damage in the process of collection, transportation, and storage; that it perhaps was never sufficient unto itself but was something like a stage prop in a performance that the viewer will have to imagine. The performance itself had aspects of entertainment or commemoration, but may well have been expected primarily to make something happen; translation may have to explain that the forces to be manipulated have no direct equivalents in the viewer's experience or vocabulary.

The museum or curatorial approach characteristically focuses on the merit and authenticity of the portable and saleable object; contextual information such as the object's ritual use or the mythology associated with it may be considered but only as a supplement. Africans may well reverse the order of priority. An *nkisi*-object is only potent when the rules it imposes on those associated with it are being observed and while the expert for whom it was composed is still alive; if these conditions are not met, the object, even though it retains all of its necessary constituents and is therefore physically identical to the connoisseur's "African artwork," is "vain," "empty" (*mpamba*) and of no particular interest. A Kongo authority says of Kongo Ndunga masks that the carved wood part "is clearly incomplete and devoid of meaning unless we take account of many additional elements that specify and dictate, through a proverb, the role to be played by the wearer during a masquerade" (Mulinda 1995: 158). In her recent research on the makers of masks among the BaPende of Congo, Zoë Strother found that the making of a mask always begins with the idea for a dance, from which all else follows. Having worked out the steps, the originator seeks out competent drummers with whom to develop the rhythms; the masquerade performance centers on a dialogue between drummer and dancer. The last expert to be consulted is the sculptor who will make a mask consistent with the dance and the theme of the song that accompanies it. The wooden mask itself, as it may eventually be displayed on the wall of a museum, is only part of a costume intended, Strother says, to provide acoustic and visual enhancement of the dancing body (Strother 1998).

Representation

Classical European art, particularly after the discovery of vanishing-point perspective, took pride in its "realism." Much of the critique directed against primitive art held that it represented reality incompetently. Representation, however, can take many forms, and is always selective (Gell 1998: 25–26). A large rock in Lower Congo "is" (represents?) the late chief Me Mbuku Mbangala in his new role as a *simbi* spirit because it marks his presence at a particular place; it has not been collected as art because it is heavy and ordinary to look at, but its function is similar to that of an *nkisi* which might be so collected. An anthropomorphic *nkisi*, with threatening arm upraised and bristling with nails, is not a portrait of a punitive force but a visual statement of the relationship between that force and the unknown individual against whom it is to act; the details of which it is composed include a checklist of the restrictions and procedures to be observe when it is invoked (MacGaffey 2000: 113). The female figures in Luba stools, standing for a complex of ideas about kingship and its secrets, are those of ideally beautiful women, but they are not portraits of any particular woman. Eyánlá is a bold, simple shape, consisting of a head with a long, flat "beard." The relatively large size of the mask indicates its importance, the prominence of the forehead suggests that it is swollen with spiritual force, and the long white cloth symbolizes the unity and prosperity of the community. The "beard" is no ordinary beard; it indicates the ambiguous otherness of the mother, who "possesses two bodies"; that is, she embodies both genders, whose relations are at issue in the cult, and suggests by analogy that she mediates between this visible world and the more powerful world of spirits.

Though sculptors are perfectly capable of carving likenesses, with few (and debatable) exceptions they have avoided doing so until recent times. Pende sculptors made it clear to Strother that good sculpture abstracts from the physical appearance of real individuals to express deeper truths. They choose to emphasize the projecting ridge over the eyes in a male face, transforming it into a bulging protrusion visible from a distance. "The mouth of a man must be like an angry person . . . The upper lip is triangular, women have lowered lips" (Strother 1998: 133–35). These are brief quotations from elaborate Pende theories relating appearance to personality, which Strother compares at some length to Western physiognomies, finding that both kinds are "powerful systems for naturalizing social and cultural difference by making it seem natural and inevitable" (p. 106). In short, the viewer of objects now exhibited in a museum who seeks to understand them must be prepared to deal with complex codes relating to essence rather than appearance.

The object in its original context may have been "read" as much as it was "seen." In certain kinds of African art, the words that give meaning are "built in," quite apart from songs sung and stories told in accompaniment. Drewal says that the names of the empowering medicines applied to Eyánlá may have double meanings. *Kukubole*, "dust from the road," can also be translated "come down join us"; dust from the road induces target persons to go in a particular direction (Drewal 1977: 77). Many of the medicines in a Kongo *nkisi* are included on the same principle; not all of them would be visible, but those that were would have more than a visual impact on native speakers.

Conclusion

The work of translating art (endowing an object with an enabling narrative) takes place at several levels. Museum studies today pay much attention to the ways in which guiding narratives are implicit in the museum itself and the selection of the objects. For example, although the public may not have been aware of it, narratives about fine art have conveyed the message that great art is almost exclusively the work of men; recent books and exhibitions have been devoted to exposing and rewriting this story. It is still not fully resolved that "fine art" is not exclusively the product of Western or "modern" society. When the objects come from some other society altogether, the accompanying narrative is now likely to argue for their artistic value, whereas a century ago they would have been presented not as art at all but as evidence of the superiority of the society that had acquired it. The narrative is also likely to dwell on the history of the more or less violent ways in which many of them were acquired.

Impediments to translation in art include the art idea itself, which contains a set of invidious moral distinctions closely related to the ideological functions of art in modern society. Such distinctions are created, maintained, opposed and eventually changed by political action, including critical commentary, translation and retranslation. If elements of chauvinism, racism and condescension should be eliminated, translators still face the basic anthropological problem that societies (by definition) vary in their institutional structure – that is, the way they are organized to carry out basic social functions. In the present context, the principal relevant difference lies in the way objects destined to be set apart as sacred (because instrumental in maintaining social values both central and contested) are produced, experienced and conserved. Anthropologists, who know about this sort of thing, provide a relatively sympathetic and receptive audience for the translator, who may then be able to discuss with them his or her best understanding of the subtle congruences and noncongruences between Baule or Yoruba values and more familiar ones, but most people are not anthropologically trained.

Art attracts a wider public than most ethnography (the number of museumgoers rises by the millions every decade), and therefore presents anthropologists and other translators with a special opportunity to show that exotic arts are more than curiosities, and that little-known cultures are as full of interest as others. If the power of the artwork as presented sufficiently motivates the viewer to take time for words, commentary can explain what kind of object this is, how it was made and used, and whatever other aspects of the cultural context are relevant to reach some understanding of what it meant to those who produced it. I have given brief samples from a rich recent literature on African art, from works that are not, of course, definitive, nor meant to be, but which are helping to demolish earlier views of primitive art still entrenched in the minds of all too many people. They are helping to deconstruct the category itself, a stage in an ongoing ideological process.

Notes

1. Since I am by profession an anthropologist specializing in Central Africa, most of my examples in this chapter will refer to African objects and the ways in which they have been presented.
2. Human beings, alive and dead, were also imported as curios and exhibited in various entertainments and museums right through to the end of the twentieth century (Lindfors 1999). Herman Melville, in *Moby Dick*, mentions "'balmed New Zealand heads, great curios you know." Curios are now produced in large quantities for tourist and foreign markets and sold under such names as "international culture."
3. Museums devoted to ornament and design, such as the one that became the Victoria and Albert, were originally ridiculed.
4. Japanese artists, incredibly, were described in the late nineteenth century as childlike, close to nature, and incapable of abstraction (Connelly 1995: 15).
5. "Negro art" from Africa was valued by some in the 1920's because of the supposed limitations of "the Negro mind," which beyond a certain point rejected instruction, was inaccessible to scholarship, remained primitive and therefore retained basic ideas which were not frittered away by the invasion of the supplementary, superficial and extraneous (Robbins 1976: quoting a critic in the *New York Times*, 1923). This romantic view, still widely held, is believed by those who hold it to be generous, though in fact it is patronizing. The fifteenth edition of Gombrich's *The Story of Art* still tells us that tribesmen "sometimes live in a kind of dream-world in which they can be man and animal at the same time . . . It is very much as if children played at pirates or detectives till they no longer knew where play acting ended and reality began" (Gombrich 1995: 43).
6. The Ethnological Society of Paris was founded in 1839; 1866, the Peabody Museum, Harvard; 1868, Museum für Völkerkunde, Berlin; 1878, Trocadéro

Museum, Paris (now the Musée de l'Homme); 1898, the first version of the Congo Museum in Tervuren, Belgium.

7. The term "folklore" itself was coined in 1846; folklore societies were founded in Britain in 1878 and in America in 1888. Curry suggests that perhaps the best definition of "American folk art" is that it is stuff collected as such in the early twentieth century by people with certain attitudes (Curry 1987).

8. Boas distinguished art from decoration by the presence of meaning. A work with meaning was one that can be interpreted as representing some object or idea, realistically or symbolically.

9. Outstanding examples of Kongo "nail fetishes" (*nkisi nkondi*) now sell for upwards of one million dollars. The first picture of one in the journal *African Arts* appeared in a commercial advertisement in 1968; the first as an illustration to an article only in 1972.

10. Edwin Ardener called this approach in translation the method of language shadows. "The good ethnographer must . . . use categories and labels in an ambiguous manner . . . and hope that by applying enough of them, he will enable the reader to create from their elements new combinations that will be closer to the 'native experience' being recorded" (Ardener 1989: 94; MacGaffey 2000: 50). In this way the ethnographic text "at least provides in toto a chunk of something of a descriptive backing so the term can denote for the reader who makes it to the end" (Michael Silverstein, Chapter 3 in this volume).

References

Ames, K. "The Paradox of Folk Art." In *Beyond Necessity*. Winterthur Museum, 1977.

Anderson, R. L. *Art in Primitive Societies*. New York: Prentice-Hall, 1979.

Ardener, E. *The Voice of Prophecy and Other Essays*. New York: Basil Blackwell, 1989.

Biebuyck, D. (ed.). *Tradition and Creativity in Tribal Art*. Berkeley: University of California Press, 1969.

Blier, S. "Enduring Myths of African Art." In *Africa: Art of a Continent*. New York: Guggenheim Museum, 1996.

Boas, F. *Primitive Art*. New York: Dover, 1927.

Bourdieu, P. and A. Darbel. *The Love of Art: European Art Museums and their Public*. Stanford: Stanford University Press, 1990 [1969].

Clifford, J. *The Predicament of Culture*. Cambridge, MA: Harvard University Press, 1988.

Connelly, F. S. *The Sleep of Reason: Primitivism in Modern European Art and Aesthetics*. University Park: Pennsylvania State University Press, 1995.

Curry, D. P. "Rose-colored Glasses: Looking for 'Good Design' in American Folk Art." In *An American Sampler: Folk Art from the Shelburne Museum*. Washington, D.C.: National Gallery of Art, 1987.

Drewal, H. "Art and the Perception of Women." *Cahiers d'études africaines* 17(4), 1977, pp. 545–67.

Evans-Pritchard, E. E. *Witchcraft Oracles and Magic among the Azande*. London: Oxford University Press, 1937.

—— *Theories of Primitive Religion*. Oxford: Clarendon, 1965.

Fernandez, J. W. *Bwiti: An Ethnography of the Religious Imagination in Africa*. Princeton: Princeton University Press, 1982.

Gell, A. *Art and Agency: an Anthropological Theory*. Oxford: Clarendon, 1998.

Gombrich, E. H. *The Story of Art*. London: Phaidon, 1995.

Janzen, R. K. and J. M. Janzen. *Mennonite Furniture*. Intercourse, PA: Good Books, 1991.

Layton, R. *The Anthropology of Art*. New York: Columbia University Press, 1991.

Lindfors, B. (ed.). *Africans on Stage*. Bloomington: Indiana University Press, 1999.

MacGaffey, W. "'Magic or, as We Usually Say, Art': a Framework for Comparing African and European Art." In *The Scramble for Art in Central Africa*. E. Schildkrout and C. A. Keim (eds.). Cambridge: Cambridge University Press, 1998.

MacGaffey, W. *Kongo Political Culture: the Conceptual Challenge of the Particular*. Bloomington: Indiana University Press, 2000.

McNaughton, P. "Theoretical Angst and the Myth of Description." *African Arts* 26(4), 1993, pp. 14–23, 82–84.

Mitchell, W. J. T. *Iconology: Image, Text, Ideology*. Chicago: University of Chicago Press, 1986.

Mulinda, H. B. "Masks as Proverbial Language: Woyo, Zaire." In *Objects: Signs of Africa*. L. De Heusch (ed.), pp. 147–59. Tervuren: Musée Royal de l'Afrique Centrale, 1995.

Myers, F. R. "Representing Culture: the Production of Discourse(s) for Aboriginal Acrylic Paintings." In *The Traffic in Culture*. G. E. Marcus and F. R. Myers (eds.). Berkeley: University of California Press, 1995.

Nooter, M. H. *Secrecy; African Art that Conceals and Reveals*. New York: Museum for African Art, 1993.

Pietz, W. "The Problem of the Fetish, I." *RES* 5 (Spring 1985), 1985, pp. 5–17.

Prinz, J. *Art Discourse/Discourse in Art*. New Brunswick NJ: Rutgers University Press, 1991.

Robbins, D. "Folk Sculpture without Folk." In *Folk Sculpture USA*. H.W. Hemphill (ed.). New York: The Brooklyn Museum, 1976.

Roberts, M. N. and A. F. Roberts (eds.). *Memory: Luba Art and the Making of History*. New York: Museum for African Art, 1996.

Rubin, W. (ed.). *Primitivism in Twentieth Century Art*. New York: Museum of Modern Art, 1984.

Schildkrout, E. and C. Keim (eds.). *African Reflections: Art from Northeastern Zaire*. New York: American Museum of Natural History, 1990.

Schjeldahl, P. "Springtime for Kiefer." *The New Yorker*, January 18, 1999.

Steiner, C. B. *African Art in Transit*. New York: Cambridge University Press, 1994.

Steiner, G. *Beyond Babel*. New York: Oxford University Press, 1975.

Stocking, G. W. Jr. (ed.). *Objects and Others*. Madison: University of Wisconsin Press, 1985.

Strother, Z. S. *Inventing Masks*. Chicago: University of Chicago Press, 1998.

Thompson, R. F. and J. Cornet. *The Four Moments of the Sun*. Washington D.C.: National Gallery of Art, 1981.

Vogel, S. "Baule: African Art through Western Eyes." *African Arts* 30(4), 1997, pp. 64–77.

Wiredu, K. "Formulating Modern Thought in African Languages: Some Theoretical Considerations." In *The Surreptitious Speech*. V.Y. Mudimbe (ed.). Chicago: University of Chicago Press, 1992.

–11–

Are Kinship Terminologies and Kinship Concepts Translatable?

Abraham Rosman and *Paula G. Rubel*

The study of kinship systems has been central in the development of anthropological theory. Kinship terminology is a system of classification. The principles by which it is organized frame experience. The kinship terminology plays a crucial role in understanding how a kinship system is organized. Comparativists from Morgan to Murdock have used kinship terminologies which others collected without questioning their accuracy. Only Morgan and Malinowski, as we shall point out below, considered the quality of the translation of the terms from the original language into their English equivalents. Ethnographers, in their ethnographies, rarely discuss the degree of control that they have over the languages spoken in the area where they have done their field work, nor do they deal with the question of how they have handled translations. For example, some ethnographers, working in Papua New Guinea, did the bulk of their research in Pidgin English (Tok Pisin) rather than in the native language of the people with whom they worked.

Comparative studies of kinship by anthropologists in the nineteenth century assumed that kinship terminologies could be freely translated from one language to another. *Systems of Consanguinity and Affinity in the Human Family*, Lewis Henry Morgan's monumental study of kinship terminologies, was based upon schedules of kin terms, some of which he himself collected, while others were obtained by American missionaries and consular officials overseas. Initially Morgan praised the work of the missionaries because they resided for longer periods of time in distant places. However, in the section on Ganowanian kinship terminology, Morgan returned to the topic of missionaries working among Native Americans, and this time he was critical of them. Though they often resided for fifteen or twenty years among Indians and had extensive knowledge of the language, he noted they had difficulty in filling out the schedules. The problem, as Morgan saw it, was that missionaries did not know their own kinship systems and even after it was explained to them, the radical differences between our system and that of the Indians created additional difficulties (Morgan 1871: 133, 134). Morgan understood that if people recognize that in their own culture the kin terms that they use form a system, they are better able to recognize such systems in other cultures and they become aware of the fact that these systems differ from their own.

When Morgan collected information himself, he found that many Indians, particularly "half-bloods" (his term), some of whom had received some schooling, were able to provide him with precise information enabling him to trace out the system in minute detail. "Knowing their own method of classification perfectly, and much better than we do our own . . .," they were the most reliable translators (Morgan 1871: 134). However, such individuals can also have problems in translation because of their own situation and their particular relationship to their American Indian culture. He states, "It will thus be seen that to obtain their system of relationship it was far preferable to consult a native Indian, who spoke English even imperfectly, rather that a white interpreter well versed in the Indian language" (Morgan 1871: 135).

Though diplomats were able to procure information on the "Aryan" family for Morgan, when the differences of language were too great, such as in Africa, South America, Mexico and Central America, ". . . the failure was nearly complete" (1871: 6).

In his charts, Morgan arranges the two hundred odd kinship terms in vertical columns. Each column is headed by a kin term described descriptively, e.g. father's sister's son. Below the heading are the native terms for a series of different "tribes" or "nations" which Morgan, in his discussion, groups together into larger families. After the column for each native term there is a column labeled "translation" which contains the English translation, its equivalent in our kinship terminological system, e.g. cousin, son, father. This represents Morgan's attempt to map the native system on to our own system, in contrast to the use of a descriptive term. Using the descriptive term was the common "mistake" made in the diplomats' schedules. In that situation, the informant gives back the terms "father's sister's son" in the Crow or Choctaw language, instead of the Crow term for "father." In Crow kinship terminology, the same term, *ah-h.a*, is used for one's father and for one's father's sister's son.

The basic framework which organized the research described in *Systems of Consanguinity* was a linguistic one. Though the state of linguistic research on Native American languages was embryonic in Morgan's time, the philological work that had been done on these languages provided him with his table of organization. Morgan saw linguistic relationships as an indication of a historic relationship. For example, he presented a series of "propositions" which were said to characterize all of the "nations" in the Ganowanian family with the exceptions presented (Morgan 1871: 145ff). According to Morgan, his examination of what he called Ganowanian "structure" verified these propositions. Morgan recognized a number of deviations from these propositions including the absence of "aunt" and "uncle" terms among the Crow. It is interesting to note that when Morgan calls these deviations, he is implicitly assuming English kinship usage as the basis for his evaluation. However, he does not discuss the "deviation" in which father's sister's son is called father not only for the Crow but also for the southeastern tribes like the Creek and Cherokee. Though Crow and the Southeastern tribes had been placed in different branches or dialect groups, these two groups of tribes are next to one another in Morgan's chart, implying some kind of historic relationship. However, nowhere in the text is there any indication that Morgan recognized that these two groups of tribes had the same structure of kinship terminology, which we would today call "Crow", a structure different from that of the Dakota and Iroquois, which we now call Iroquois or Dravidian. The recognition that there is a structure or system, which is shared by several tribes, enables one to deal with translation in a more global fashion.

W. H. R. Rivers at the turn of the century made very significant contributions to the study of kinship. His article entitled, "The Genealogical Method of Anthropological Inquiry" presented a method of collecting kinship terminology which became the standard for future generations of field workers. Rivers, in the article, first described the way in which he collected the genealogy of an informant from Guadalcanal.[1] As Rivers noted, "The first point to be attended to is that, owing to the great difference between the systems of relationship of savage and civilized peoples, it is desirable to use as few terms denoting kinship as possible, and complete pedigrees can be obtained when the terms are limited to the following: father, mother, child, husband and wife" (Rivers 1968 [1910]: 97). The method which Rivers used to gain information on the kinship terminology was to ". . . ask my informant the terms which he would apply to the different members of his pedigree [genealogy], and reciprocally the terms which they would apply to him" (p. 100). As Rivers explains, this method ". . . was more particularly useful to those who, like myself, are only able to visit savage or barbarous peoples for comparatively short times, times wholly insufficient to acquire that degree of mastery over the native language to enable it to be used as the instrument of intercourse" (p. 107).

Though Rivers does not deal directly with the question of the translation of kinship terminology, there are several points implicit in his discussion. One is the assumption that the five minimal terms given above (Fa, Mo, Child, Hu, Wi) will be found in all societies. This presupposes that the child everywhere is born from two parents, that marriage is a cultural universal, that these five statuses or positions are recognized universally, and therefore there will be terms for them in every language. In the article, Rivers tells us that Arthur, his informant, had been in Queensland, probably as an indentured laborer. His knowledge of English enabled Rivers, using the five minimal terms, to elicit his genealogy or "pedigree," and then to obtain the Guadalcanal kinship terminology without Rivers knowing the language. As Morgan notes above, bilingual native speakers are the best sources of information about the kinship terminology.

Rivers was aware that the possessive in Melanesian languages takes two forms. The more general form is inalienable possession, used for parts of the body and for

"terms of relationship." The second form, alienable possession, is used for ownership and temporary possession (Rivers 1968 [1910]: 488). This information
regarding the way different forms of possessive pronouns are attached to kin terms
is important because it provides additional ethnographic information about the
meanings of the terms, and enables a more accurate translation.

In the first chapter of *Argonauts of the Western Pacific*, Malinowski presents
his discussion of "the methods used in the collection of ethnographic material",
and how he developed a procedure for translation. Regarding his own work in
Kiriwinian, he noted,

> I found still some difficulty in writing down the statement directly in translation which
> at first I used to do in the act of taking notes. The translation often robbed the text of all
> its significant characteristics – rubbed off all its points – so that gradually I was led to
> note down certain important phrases just as they were spoken in the native tongue. As
> my knowledge of the language progressed, I put down more and more in Kiriwinian, till
> at last I found myself writing exclusively in that language, rapidly taking notes, word for
> word, of each statement. No sooner had I arrived at this point, than I recognized that I
> was thus acquiring at the same time an abundant linguistic material and a series of
> ethnographic documents which ought to be reproduced as I had fixed them, besides
> being utilized in the writing up of my account. (Malinowski 1922: 24)

In his analysis of Trobriand horticulture, *Coral Gardens and Their Magic*,
Malinowski makes much greater use of ethnographic texts, word-for-word translation and free translation. This work also includes a more detailed discussion of
translation in general in a section, interestingly enough, entitled "The Translation
of Untranslatable Words." He begins with the "absolutely true proposition that the
words of one language are never translatable into another. This holds true of two
civilized languages as well as of a `native' and a `civilized' one, though the greater
the difference between two cultures the greater the difficulty of finding equivalents" (Malinowski 1965[1935]: 11). Since strict verbal equivalents are ". . . never
to be found. The translation must always be a re-creation of the original into
something profoundly different. On the other hand, it is never the substitution of
word for word, but invariably the translation of whole contexts" (pp. 11–12). Since
no simple equivalence of word for word is adequate, Malinowski's solution is to
see translation as a matter of representing the cultural reality of one society in the
language of another. Trobriand words are to be defined by being placed in the
cultural context in which they are used (like competitive kula, gardening, or love
magic), and then by having contrastive forms provided which are opposite in
meaning, and cognates of the word under discussion (p. 16). Malinowski also
cautions us about the need to keep "homonyms apart."

In Malinowski's "Supplement" to Ogden and Richards *The Meaning of Meaning*,
he again discusses this problem, noting,

> But the object of a scientific translation of a word is not to give its rough equivalent sufficient for practical purposes, but to state exactly whether a native word corresponds to an idea at least partially existing for English speakers, or whether it covers an entirely foreign conception. That such foreign conceptions do exist for native languages and in great number, is clear. All words which describe the native social order, all expressions relating to native beliefs, ceremonies, magical rites – all such words are obviously absent from English as from any European language. Such words can only be translated into English, not by giving their imaginary equivalent – a real one obviously cannot be found – but by explaining the meaning of each of them through an exact Ethnographic account of the sociology, culture and tradition of that native community. (1923: 300)

In the end, Malinowski notes that for "practical convenience", it is necessary to use the lexical equation of an English and a native word, though this is theoretically inadequate. This is to prevent the ethnography from becoming unreadable by overloading it with native terms. In Malinowski's eyes, language is an essential aspect of cultural reality and that cultural reality must be utilized in translations. The implication here is that the ethnographer must have a better than adequate knowledge of the field language in order to successfully convey the cultural reality of his or her informants.

Malinowski makes the point that one must also clearly understand the grammar and general structure of the language which one wishes to translate, for grammar compels a speaker to use one grammatical form, not another. In our discussions of Rivers, we saw that the organization of possessive pronouns was relevant to the consideration of kinship terminology. Malinowski, in his own analysis of kinship terminology, also recognizes their importance. He shows that there are two forms of possessive in the Kiriwinian language, as in other Melanesian languages – alienable possessive and inalienable possessive. As Rivers pointed out, kinship terms in Melanesian languages almost always take the inalienable form, and this indeed is the case in Trobriand kinship. The term (*gu*) – inalienable "my" – is provided as a suffix or an infix for almost all the kinship terms given in Malinowski's chart of the kinship terminology. However, a different prefix (*ulo*) is given for the terms for husband and wife. Though Malinowski does not specifically indicate that this is the alienable form, one suspects that it is, since this relationship can be ended through divorce. Although the father (*tama*) is considered an affine in Trobriand kinship, and not a true relative (*veyola*), the term *tama* takes the inalienable suffix *gu* like all the other kinship terms save husband and wife. This may be because the father relationship cannot be ended. This kind of analysis of pronoun use enables us to have a better understanding of Trobriand ideas about kinship. When translating alienable and inalienable pronouns into English, which has a single possessive form, the translation must indicate "my" – alienable or "my" – inalienable.

Nowhere does Malinowki describe the method he employed for gathering information on the Trobriand kinship terminology, which is discussed in *The*

Sexual Life of Savages. His field notes contain a whole series of genealogies. Did he use Rivers' genealogical method? Or did he gather the information about kinship terms in the form of a series of texts from which he extracted the terms and information regarding their use? His use of the kin terms and his translations in the text of *The Sexual Life of Savages* is not consistent.

Malinowski's position on meaning and its extension in the use of kinship terms is directly relevant to his approach to translation. He sees kinship terms from the point of view of the order in which a child learns terms. The primary meaning of a term refers to the first person for whom the child is taught to use the term. Its meaning is then extended to other persons up to the periphery of the vaguely defined boundary. When he cannot find a common denominator, Malinowski considers such terms anomalous. Some kinship usages he even considers to be homonyms. The alternative to Malinowski's approach is Leach's category approach to kinship terms. In Leach's approach, for example, "all dogs belong equally to the category, dogs," and all persons called *tama* in Kiriwinian are equally *tama*. Malinowski, in *The Sexual Life of Savages* talks about the "father" relationship. According to Malinowski, the term *tama*, in its primary meaning, is used for the individual who is recognized as the father of the child. The term is extended to a series of men. When the term *tama* is translated by Malinowski in the ethnography, these individuals are referred to as "fathers" by extension, in terms of the father relationship. The result for Malinowski, by doing this type of translation, is the anomaly of a father, *tama,* in ego's own generation.

Malinowski takes the position that the primary meanings of kinship terms are those within the family, and these are extended to members of other kinds of social groupings beyond the family. He notes, ". . . mother's sister, who, although she is called by the same term as the own mother, *inagu*, is very definitely distinguished from her. The word *inagu* extended to the mother's sister is, from the outset, given an entirely different meaning – something like 'second mother' or 'subsidiary mother' . . . there can be no doubt that the new use of the word remains always what it is, an extension and a metaphor" (1929: 442–443).

Similarly, in discussing the kinship term *tabu*, Malinowski argues that "The primary meaning of this word is 'father's sister'. It also embraces 'father's sister's daughter' or 'paternal cross-cousin,' or, by extension, 'all the women of the father's clan'; and, in its widest sense, 'all the women not of the same clan'" (1929: 423). In this sense, the term signifies "lawful woman" with whom both sexual intercourse and marriage are proper (see Malinowski 1929: 450–451). The term *tabugu* "also has the wider meaning of 'grandparent,' 'grandchild,' and wider yet, 'ancestor' and 'descendant'" (1929: 442). Malinowski does not recognize that there is a principle which places the two sets of kinship terms ("lawful woman" and "ancestor/descendant") in the same category. He treats them as homonyms, and he never considers their relation to the Trobriand word *tabu* meaning "forbidden act."

The use of the term *tama* (father) for patrilateral cross-cousin is one of the distinctive features which makes Trobriand kinship terminology a Crow terminology. In his "Table of Relationship Terms," Malinowski glosses *tama(gu)* as "Father, father's brother; father's clansman; father's sister's son," treating it like the term for a larger category, males of one's father's clan (1929: 434). However, later in the text he states, "The anomalous extension of the word for father (*tama*) to father's sister's son is important, for it demonstrates the influence which language has upon customs and ideas" (1929: 447). His argument is that, because the male cross-cousin calls his female cross-cousin (MoBrDa) "daughter," *latu*, and she calls him "father," *tama*, this inhibits their sexual feelings and prevents marriage. As they are here, rules about preferential or prohibited marriages must always be phrased in kinship terms in the native language. For example, if a Trobriand woman is called *latu* by a male ego, he may not marry her, since the primary meaning of *latu*, according to Malinowski, is "child."

What is the relationship between translation and this discussion of the way in which primary kin terms – that is, terms used within the nuclear family – are extended to kinsmen in other categories of relationship? In translating a term or word into another language, let's say English, as we noted earlier, Malinowski says that one looks for an English equivalent, in a word or phrase, or a page of description of "context." When confronted with the Trobriand kinship term *tama*, the translation applies "father" to "all males of father's sub-clan" including the father's heir (his sister's son), ignoring generational differences. Malinowski argues that Trobrianders can and do differentiate their real father from their father's sister's son, that the behavior toward the two is very different, and that the meanings of *tama* differs when applied to the two though they both are classified together in the single category, *tama*. In similar fashion, though we have a single category term uncle, we have no difficulty in distinguishing between our different kinds of "uncles" – maternal vs. paternal, consanguineal vs. affinal. When the anthropologist is confronted with the kin term for the first time and the need to translate it, how is he or she to know whether or not the term refers to someone within the nuclear family or to someone beyond it? It is the "context of cultural reality," the cultural context in which the terms are used, which provides a key to the meaning of the term – that is, as to whether the primary meaning or one of its extensions is intended. Malinowski never discusses the basis for his saying that the primary meaning of *tabu* is FaSi, not MoMo, implying that FaSi is closer than MoMo though the term for both is *tabu*. Nor does Malinowski inform us as to why one extension is "anomalous" and another not. In the translation of kin terms, when one attempts to map the meaning of terms in the "native language" onto a Western language the ethnographer's theory – such as Malinowki's regarding primary terms and their extensions – plays an important role. As we shall see below, Leach argues that kinship terms are category terms, quite a different theory from that of Malinowski.

Though Radcliffe-Brown used kinship terminologies in his comparative research, he assumed the accuracy of the data collected by other ethnographers and never discussed the accuracy of the translations. However, the dominant figures in British social anthropology after him ignored the topic. As Schneider notes, "Evans-Pritchard hardly touched it; Fortes paid only lip service to it; Firth thought it was . . . like ornaments" (1995: 131). Later, under the influence of Lévi-Strauss, both Needham and Leach return to a vigorous consideration of kinship terminologies. While Leach was very concerned with the translation and meanings of kin terms, as we shall see below, Needham used other people's translations of Purum, Lushai and Kuki terminologies in his analyses, without his shedding any light on the problems of translation.

Often knowledge of the structure of kinship relationships is of assistance in the translation of kinship terms. In Margaret Mead's collaboration with Reo Fortune during their Arapesh field work, it was Fortune who studied the Arapesh language and collected texts. Regarding Mead's knowledge of the Arapesh language, she notes, "I used pidgin English in talking to the men who had been away to work and Arapesh in talking to everyone else. The pidgin English conversations were, whenever necessary, supplemented with Arapesh special words" (1940: 337). Fortune's linguistic informant, who was fluent in pidgin English, taught Mead Arapesh. Since Mead published the data on kinship terminology, it can be concluded that she collected the data. She does not inform us whether she used Arapesh or pidgin English to collect the terminology. However, she does note that "the word for gens, *awhilap*, is hardly ever used; whether I should ever have found it without the help of the pidgin English 'pigeon', the word for clan or gens, derived from the Melanesian bird totemic practices, I do not know. When I made the census, however, as I recorded the names of adult males, I asked, 'What pigeon' and so received at once the local gens proper name" (Mead 1947: 181).

Mead "analyzed" Arapesh kinship and the kinship terminology without recognizing that it was an Omaha terminology and the implications of that. In her discussion of the Arapesh marriage rule, she did not phrase its limits in Arapesh kin terms. Instead, she stated the prohibitions on whom one may marry using English kinship terminology, in the following manner: "Formally, the children of parents who use brother and sister, cross-cousin, or two-generations-apart-child-of-cross-cousin terms to each other are not allowed to marry, nor may a man marry a woman whom he calls either aunt, daughter, or niece, nor may a woman marry a man whom she calls father, or mother's brother, or nephew" (Mead 1947: 199). But in an Omaha kinship system, there are no separate terms for what would be the equivalent of the English terms aunts, uncles, nieces and nephews, or cross-cousins. In the Arapesh system, one set of cross-cousins (MoBrChildren) are called by the same terms as MoBr and MoSi; the other set (FaSiChildren) are called by the terms for SiDa and SiSo.

Mead's chart of the kinship terminology includes two terms – *balahan*, glossed as "Mother's father's sister's son's son" and *balohan*, glossed as "Grandson; male children of all members of first descendent generation, as given above." Reworking her data on kinship terminology in terms of the structure of an Omaha terminology, it seemed that these two terms were, in reality, the same term and should have been spelled in the same way. Reo Fortune had done research on the language in the field and had collected texts in the Arapesh language. We consulted him in 1972 about this anomaly, and he informed us that there was only one term (*balohan*) and that the other was a misspelling. The kinship terminology was examined as it related to the marriage rule. When phrased in lineage terms it stipulates that ego cannot marry into the six lineages which have given or received women from his lineage in the three previous generations. The terms *balohan* (male) and *baloho'* (female) were used for FaFaSiSoSo and FaFaSiSoDa respectively, and for SoSo and SoDa, the former a collateral relative two degrees removed, and the latter a lineal relative two generations down from ego. In fact, Mead's definition for the term *balahan* (*balohan*), as MoFaSiSoSo, was also incorrect since that individual's lineage is neither a giver nor a receiver of women from ego's lineage.

The structural characteristics of the kinship terminology and the nature of the marriage rule have internal logics of their own, thereby providing important clues for the translation of these terms. Attempting to use English terms to characterize the marriage rule does not come close to providing an adequate translation of the meanings of the kin terms and the structure to which they are related.

Some time ago Lévi-Strauss made the point that the function of kin terms was to indicate which relatives ego, the speaker, could and could not marry. The marriage rule phrased in terms of the terminology provides a map which says that anyone called by this term is prohibited as a spouse; anyone called by that term is permitted. One might argue that Lévi-Strauss' dictum, which is unquestionably true, is far too narrow, and that kinship terminologies have other functions as well. If Malinowski, Radcliffe-Brown and Mead had paid attention to that observation, their analysis of the respective kinship terminologies they analyzed would have been strengthened. Thus, not only do kinship terms have meanings in that they designate a category of individuals, but in addition they contain meanings regarding marriageability. The translation of kinship terms must therefore pay attention to both of these aspects of meaning.

In 1945, just before Lévi-Strauss published *Elementary Structures of Kinship*, Leach published "Jinghpaw Kinship Terminology," in which he analyzed Kachin terms as category terms mapped onto to what Leach refers to as an "idealized form of the social order" (Leach 1945: 51). In this model, in accordance with matrilateral cross-cousin marriage, the marriage rule for the Jinghpaw, all other patrilineages were either wife-givers or wife-takers to ego's own lineage.

Early in this article, Leach stated that initially his approach to kinship owed much to the views of Malinowski, his teacher, but that he no longer accepted Malinowski's tenet of the "universality of the elementary family." He also rejected Malinowski's approach to the meaning of kin terms – that is, the primary meaning deriving from relations within the elementary family and the extensions outward to other more distant relationships. According to Leach, the problem was to discover the organization which makes Jinghpaw terminology 'logical' to a native (1945: 50). Jinghpaw terms fall into three distinct categories – *hpu-nau* (ElBr-YoBr), *mayu* (wife-givers), and *dama* (wife-takers) – and the relatives in each of these categories live in a different locality. Leach's approach to kinship terminology emphasizing categories, in contrast to Malinowski's approach, has clear implications for translation.

By the 1960s Leach had become the severest critic of Malinowski's approach to kinship and kinship terminology. According to Leach, it is a great error to translate Rivers' five basic terms from a native language (Crow, Trobriand or Jinghpaw) into "father, mother, brother, sister and child" (e.g. *tama* means father), as Malinowski does. In Leach's words, "This particular linguistic pitfall has in the past led to a vast amount of anthropological confusion; it still does. When you read anything that an anthropologist has written on the topic of kinship terminology be on your guard. The argument may not mean what you think; the author himself may not have understood what he is saying" (Leach 1982: 137–138). According to Leach, the problem lies in the fact that, ". . . while kinship words in most European languages are applied, with rare exceptions, only to relationships within the private domain and thus have quite specific meanings, the corresponding words in most other languages are highly polysemic" (pp. 138–139). The term "father" may have a single meaning in English, whereas in other languages it is applied to a large category of persons and has a wide range of meanings. Therefore in the translation of kin terms, it is not sufficient to merely use the primary term in English, but one must define who and what is included and who and what is not included in a category.

Leach returned to the Jinghpaw kinship terminology in 1967, this time drawing inspiration from Roman Jakobson, applying a more sophisticated linguistic approach to his reexamination of Jinghpaw kin terms. Leach begins his discussion by arguing that the Kachin view "relationships" in the same manner as a linguist does in phonological analysis – two male persons belonging to the same lineage have a kin relationship and are terminologically differentiated by the factor of age as younger brother and older brother. One brother must refer to the other brother as either older or younger. The Kachins say "they are *distinguishable* as brother and brother" (Leach 1967: 136).

Leach argues that the Kachin think of kin terms as 'category' terms. The concept of 'category' as found in Kachin must be a very fundamental one for Kachin speakers (Leach 1967: 136). And so it is. The term *myu* is the word for 'kind,' as in trees, fish, birds, etc. It is also the term for "lineage" – that is, humans are classified in lineages. One's *mayu ni*, mother's lineage, is the proto-type of 'different kind'. (*Mayu* and *myu* are related terms.) Leach disagrees with Malinowski's argument that the different meanings of a term such as the Trobriand term *tabu* represent homonyms. In Kachin, *nu* also means 'mother,' 'home,' 'original,' and 'the soft core of anything.' According to Leach, "Such uses are not 'metaphors', they are rather the application of the same idea to different situations. But I think that if we are to understand what the term *nu* 'really means' *when considered as a kinship term* we need to take these other uses into account" (Leach 1967: 138).

The meaning of the category *nu* (mother), as used for all mothers and people whom mother calls sister, includes the other meanings glossed above. The social structural category from which mother comes, the *mayu* lineage, epitomizes greed, constantly demanding gifts and tribute which the *dama* lineage must pay. Ego perceives his *dama* lineages as, ". . . those with whom we fight and those to whom we give women" (Leach 1967: 143). The mother's brother, who is in one's *mayu* lineage, can curse his sister's children. According to Leach, ". . . the metaphors which Kachins employ to represent social links are things which divide rather than things which tie together" (Leach 1967: 136). In the conclusion of the article, Leach maps the structure of kinship terminology onto other Kachin structures – that of the allocation of land–water, payment–debt and exchange, all of these structures consist of entities which are "divided" rather than "tied together" – thus demonstrating that they are "structural transformations" of one another. As a result of the analysis, the meanings of Kachin kin terms are greatly expanded, demonstrating that the domain of kinship does not exist in isolation.

The implications of Leach's theoretical approach for the translation of kin terms is considerable. He is arguing that the same principles of classification that unite and differentiate kinsmen into categories are also operative in other domains, and that the root meanings of kin terms are also in other Kachin words. Just as the English words "kin" and "kind" derive from an older common form, as do "time" and "tide," the various meanings of Kachin kin terms must all be considered together to arrive at the meaning of the category for which the kin term stands. Therefore the translation of kin terms, to Leach, must go beyond the category meanings of these terms. Through connections between these words and other structures, a whole range of other meanings of these terms is revealed. The translation of terms within a category will always depend on the cultural context of the particular usage.

David Schneider in *A Critique of Kinship* (1984) not only criticized the ways in which anthropologists had examined kinship terminology earlier, but also advocated what he saw as a new way of looking at kinship, which in turn had important implications for translation. He had promoted the idea that American kinship was a system of cultural symbols and should be examined in the same manner as other symbolic systems. In his analysis of American kinship, Schneider argues that in American kinship there is a basic distinction between affinal terms, which use the modifier "in-law", and consanguineal terms for "blood" relatives. "In-law" clearly has other meanings. The connection between the usages is that a relative-in-law has the connotation of a relationship constructed through legal means, as contrasted with a blood relative created by natural means. According to *Webster's Unabridged Dictionary*, the American modifier "step", used to refer to a relative created by the marriage of a parent, has no relationship to step, meaning step as in staircase, or the movement of the foot. They are homonyms. In Goodenough's research on American kinship, he found that informants saw "half-brother" as a kind of brother, but not "step-brother" (Goodenough 1965). The reasoning behind this is that a half-brother shares common blood, while step-brother is created through the marriage of a parent.

Schneider claims that anthropologists have always seen kinship as a "privileged system," in terms of "the way in which we define it and its functions" (Schneider 1984: 132). In Schneider's view, anthropologists "adhered to the traditional definition of kinship as the relations arising out of reproduction" (1984: 130). He then proceeds to call into question analyzing culture and dissecting it into separate "institutions" – kinship, economics, politics, religion, art, myth, etc. – which are alleged to carry out "functions". He argues that ideas about institutions like kinship are Western concepts which anthropologists impose on other societies. What we should be looking at, according to Schneider, are what Marcel Mauss referred to as "total social facts" (Schneider 1984: 197). The questions we should be asking are: ". . . of what blocks is *this* particular culture built? How do *these* people conceptualize their world?" (1984: 197).

Had Schneider attended more closely to what Levi-Strauss borrowed from linguistics and specifically from Boas, he might have looked at how systems of classifications in each language serve to organize semantic domains. These are the building blocks of which particular cultures are constructed, as Leach had pointed out earlier. A kinship terminology is one such system of classification. All societies have a category of persons which our culture classifies as "relatives". Within this domain, societies construct different categories. In fact, Schneider concurs, noting that, since every language has words for kinship categories, "it is a cultural construct or unit of some kind because there is a word for it, it has a name, the word has meaning . . ." (1980: 3). A set of kin terms, each of which is a native "cultural construct", together form a system or structure.

Schneider may be correct when he says the "domain" of kinship is vaguely defined in anthropology. In the minds of many anthropologists, such as Malinowski, the category of kinship seems to rest on assumptions about the biological nature of human reproduction. But, following Morgan, Boas, and Lévi-Strauss, one can begin with kinship terminology rather than kinship. Kinship terminology is not ambiguous or vaguely defined. It is a semantic category found in all languages, on the basis of which comparisons and typologies can be created.

Two problems present themselves with regard to the translation of kinship terms. The first is the problem that the field worker has in eliciting a kinship terminology from an informant. The knowledge that the field worker has of the language, and the presence or absence of bilingual informants, are important factors in this process. Rivers' genealogical method may be used to obtain a pre-liminary picture of the kinship terminology. One would then have recourse to what Malinowski called an examination of how kinship terms were used in a variety of cultural contexts. This would illuminate the categories or "spaces" of meaning encompassed by particular kin terms. The construction of each category would be revealed by specifying the cognates of the term and their various referents. The boundaries of such categories would be determined by specifying their "opposites" and what they contrast with.[2]

David Schneider's critique that the "building blocks" and units for each society should derive from the society itself echoes Boas' call that linguistic analysis should not proceed by imposing Latin grammatical categories onto native languages of the new world. The analytical categories must emerge from each language. It would appear that Schneider's dictum would lead to the conclusion that each culture had its own distinctive "cultural constructs", untranslatable into those of another culture. This leads to cultural relativism, the position of many postmodernists. But cultural relativism is not the answer. If one takes into account the cultural context of their use, kin terms and the systems which they comprise *are* translatable.

The constructs utilized in the analysis of kinship terminologies have been refined over the years. Cross-cultural comparisons have demonstrated that both terminologies and the kinship systems of which they are a part fall into a limited number of categories, fewer than the number of logically possible types. Cross-cultural comparison involves comparing and contrasting the structure of kinship systems in different societies. The semantic categories of a particular society's kinship terminology are mapped onto a map of genealogical spaces which have English labels. The typologies of kinship structures employed in anthropology are the products of such comparisons. A hundred years of ethnographic field work have demonstrated that there are a limited number of ways in which kinship terminology can be ordered.

Kinship terminologies echo an important point for translation. They are not collections of discreet lexical items; they are systems, like the phonological systems of a language. Each kinship terminology has an internal logic of its own; when one element of the system changes, the rest of the system will change accordingly. Other aspects of culture also have a systemic character, to a greater or lesser degree. For example, art and aesthetics, and religious beliefs have systems of their own. Terminologies carry out universal functions in all societies – to chart out, for the child, membership categories which serve as identities defining the self. "These are the members of the kinship group to which I belong. These are my relatives. Those others are not. They belong to other categories – those I may or may not marry, those who do or don't practice witchcraft towards me, those who may steal my cattle or suck my bones when I die." These groups and categories vary from one society to the next, but they can be specified on a universal genealogical grid. Kinship terms label these groups and categories. A single term in one kinship system may encompass a number of kin terms in a different kinship system.

Lastly, kinship terminologies fall into a limited number of types, and each of these types follows its own logic. The genealogical grid provides the basis for kinship terminologies, and the development of the analytical categories which allow cross-cultural comparison. Once this is realized, it can be of enormous help to the translator. He is no longer a lonely walker in space, in the dark.

Notes

1. Rivers notes that one of the difficulties in obtaining "pedigrees" or genealogies from informants is that there may be a taboo on the use of the names of individuals who are deceased.
2. The componential analysis of kinship terminology also deals with categories and the components which comprise their internal construction, and how a change in a component creates a different, contrastive category. However, componential analysis of kinship terminology in the hands of Lounsbury, for example, became an increasingly formal method of description, with no relationship to systems of marriage and descent or other cultural domains

References

Goodenough, Ward. "Yankee Kinship Terminology: a Problem in Componential Analysis" In *Formal Semantic Analysis*. E. A. Hammel (ed.). *American Anthropologist* (Special Publication) 67(5) pt. 2, 1965, pp. 259–87.

Leach, Edmund. "Jinghpaw Kinship Terminology – an Experiment in Ethnographic Algebra." *Journal of the Royal Anthropological Institute* 75, 1945, pp. 59–72.

—— "The Language of Kachin Kinship: Reflections on a Tikopia Model." In *Social Organization: Essays Presented to Raymond Firth*. M. Freedman (ed.), pp. 125–52. London: Cass, 1947.

—— *Social Anthropology.* Glasgow: Fontana, 1982.

Malinowski, Bronislaw. *Argonauts of the Western Pacific.* New York: E. P. Dutton, 1961 [1922].

—— "The Problem of Meaning in Primitive Languages" supplement to C. K. Ogden and I. A. Richards. *The Meaning of Meaning.* New York: Harcourt, Brace, 1923, pp. 296–336.

—— *The Sexual Life of Savages in North-Western Melanesia.* New York: Harcourt, 1929.

—— *Coral Gardens and their Magic.* 2 vols. Bloomington: Indiana University Press, 1965 [1935].

Mead, Margaret. *The Mountain Arapesh II. Supernaturalism.* Anthropological Papers of the American Museum of Natural History 37. pt. 3, pp. 317–451.

—— *The Mountain Arapesh III. Socioeconomic Life.* Anthropological Papers of the American Museum of Natural History 40. pt. 3, pp. 159–420.

Morgan, Lewis Henry. *Systems of Consanguinity and Affinity of the Human Family.* Smithsonian Contributions to Knowledge, No. 17. Washington, D.C.: Smithsonian Institution, 1871.

Radcliffe-Brown, A. R. "Introduction." *African Systems of Kinship and Marriage.* A. R. Radcliffe-Brown and C. D. Forde (eds.), pp 1–85. London: Oxford University Press, 1950.

Rivers, W. H. R. "The Genealogical Method in Anthropological Inquiry." In *Kinship and Social Organization.* Commentaries Raymond Firth and David Schneider, pp. 97–109. London: Athlone, 1968 [1910].

Schneider, David. *American Kinship: A Cultural Account.* 2nd ed. Chicago: University of Chicago Press, 1980.

—— *A Critique of the Study of Kinship.* Ann Arbor: University of Michigan Press, 1984.

—— *Schneider on Schneider: The Conversion of the Jews and Other Anthropological Stories.* As told to Richard Handler. Durham, NC: Duke University Press, 1995.

Index

Index

Index

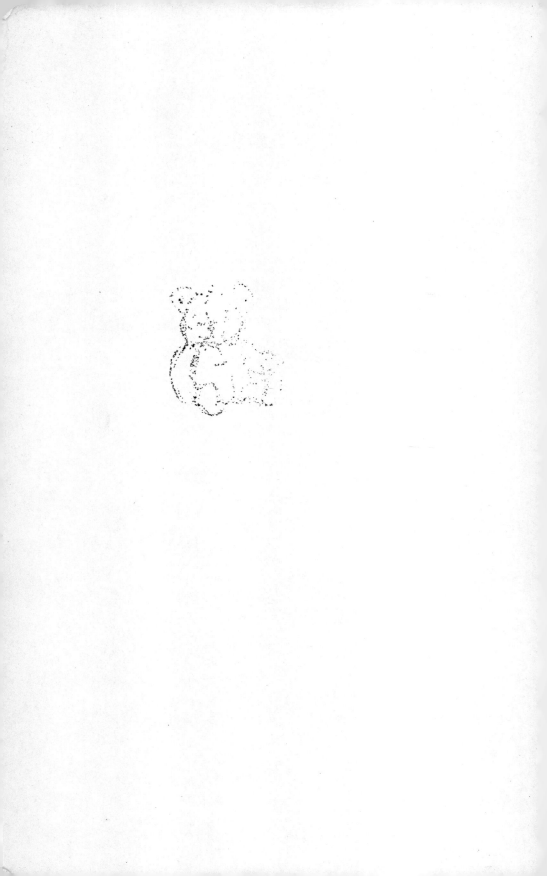